"Gary Tyra has set himself a daunting task, to develop a theology that is both missional and orthodox. On the whole, he makes an important contribution and enriches the discussion by bringing a Pentecostal perspective into it. He is an orthodox theologian who engages complementary traditions graciously and appreciatively and thus practices what some have called 'a more generous orthodoxy.'"

Darrell L. Guder, Princeton Theological Seminary

"A provocative effort to bridge the divide between the evangelical and emerging church worlds by drawing from a missional understanding of a missionary God who is active in the world. Tyra carefully grounds his proposal in a high Christology and then uses Borg and McLaren as conversation partners to work out a centered understanding of the Christian faith in relation to the classic systematic theological loci. The reader will appreciate this fresh approach to reengaging the riches of the Christian tradition."

Craig Van Gelder, Luther Seminary

"Good missional theology is essential to funding transformative missional movements over the long term. Given the strident voices to the left and the right, we could use more compassionately orthodox guides in the conversation. Gary's new book goes a long way to filling the need."

Alan Hirsch, author and founder of Forge Missional Training Network and Future Travelers, www.alanhirsch.org

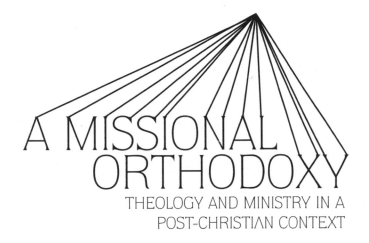

A MISSIONAL ORTHODOXY

THEOLOGY AND MINISTRY IN A POST-CHRISTIAN CONTEXT

GARY TYRA

IVP Academic

An imprint of InterVarsity Press
Downers Grove, Illinois

InterVarsity Press
P.O. Box 1400, Downers Grove, IL 60515-1426
World Wide Web: www.ivpress.com
Email: email@ivpress.com

InterVarsity Press® is the book-publishing division of InterVarsity Christian Fellowship/USA®, a movement of students and faculty active on campus at hundreds of universities, colleges and schools of nursing in the United States of America, and a member movement of the International Fellowship of Evangelical Students. For information about local and regional activities, write Public Relations Dept., InterVarsity Christian Fellowship/USA, 6400 Schroeder Rd., P.O. Box 7895, Madison, WI 53707-7895, or visit the IVCF website at www.intervarsity.org.

All Scripture quotations, unless otherwise indicated, are taken from THE HOLY BIBLE, NEW INTERNATIONAL VERSION®, NIV® Copyright © 1973, 1978, 1984, 2011 by Biblica, Inc.™ Used by permission. All rights reserved worldwide.

While all stories in this book are true, some names and identifying information in this book have been changed to protect the privacy of the individuals involved.

Cover design: David Fassett
Interior design: Beth Hagenberg
Image: © Marcus Lindström/iStockphoto

ISBN 978-0-8308-2821-0 (print)
ISBN 978-0-8308-6485-0 (digital)

Printed in the United States of America ∞

InterVarsity Press is committed to protecting the environment and to the responsible use of natural resources. As a member of Green Press Initiative we use recycled paper whenever possible. To learn more about the Green Press Initiative, visit www.greenpressinitiative.org.

Library of Congress Cataloging-in-Publication Data
A catalog record for this book is available from the Library of Congress.

P	21	20	19	18	17	16	15	14	13	12	11	10	9	8	7	6	5	4	3	2	1
Y	31	30	29	28	27	26	25	24	23	22	21	20	19	18	17	16	15	14	13		

This book is dedicated to the late Ray Anderson,
a professor and mentor who modeled for me a passionate,
thoughtful yet humble approach to doing
theology and ministry.

CONTENTS

ABBREVIATIONS

HC   Marcus Borg. *The Heart of Christianity: Rediscovering a Life of Faith*. San Francisco: HarperSanFrancisco, 2003.

SC   Marcus Borg. *Speaking Christian: Why Christian Words Have Lost their Meaning—and How They Can Be Restored*. New York: HarperOne, 2011.

MJ   Marcus Borg and N. T. Wright. *The Meaning of Jesus: Two Visions*. San Francisco: HarperSanFrancisco, 1999.

GWNK   Marcus Borg. *The God We Never Knew: Beyond Dogmatic Religion to a More Authentic Contemporary Faith*. New York: HarperOne, 1997.

MJA   Marcus Borg. *Meeting Jesus Again for the First Time: The Historical Jesus and the Heart of Contemporary Faith*. New York: HarperOne, 1994.

NKC   Brian McLaren. *A New Kind of Christianity: Ten Questions That Are Transforming the Faith*. New York: HarperOne, 2010.

GO   Brian McLaren. *A Generous Orthodoxy*. Grand Rapids: Zondervan, 2004.

RBA   Marcus Borg. *Reading the Bible Again for the First Time*. New York: Harper One, 2001.

PREFACE

What type of gospel presentation might succeed at encouraging the members of a post-Christian culture to take another look at Christ and his church? What theological moves might enable the members of the traditional evangelical, emerging and missional Christian communities to function as comrades rather than competitors in gospel ministry? These two crucial questions lie at the very heart of this work. To be more precise, this book is about doing theology and ministry in an increasingly post-Christian context in a way that is faithful to both the biblical text and the missional task. For centuries the Holy Spirit has used Jude 3 to provide the church with an ongoing sense of need to stay true to the apostolic understanding of the Christian faith.[1] Set within its context, this passage reads:

> Dear friends, although I was very eager to write to you about the salvation we share, *I felt compelled to write and urge you to contend for the faith that was once for all entrusted to God's holy people.* For certain individuals whose condemnation was written about long ago have secretly slipped in among you. They are ungodly people, who pervert the grace of our God into a license for immorality and deny Jesus Christ our only Sovereign and Lord. (Jude 3-4, emphasis added)

---

[1]New Testament scholar Michael Barram encourages missiological writers to exercise methodological rigor when using biblical texts ("The Bible, Mission, and Social Location: Toward a Missional Hermeneutic," *Interpretation* 61 [Jan 2007]: 51-52). With this in mind, and since Jude 3 is referenced several times in this work, I acknowledge that there are various ways in which the "faith" (Greek *pistis*) referred to by Jude might be conceived of (e.g., an attitude of confidence, a capacity for trust, a pattern of life, a set of core values or liturgical practices). However, careful consideration of the immediate literary and larger canonical context in which Jude 3 is located—i.e., the New Testament as a whole and 2 Peter 2 in particular—leads to the idea that there is some doctrinal content to the "faith" to which Jude refers.

At the same time, the same Spirit of mission[2] has spoken to the church through 1 Corinthians 9:20-22, encouraging Christ's followers to continually contextualize the Christian message for new people groups in culturally sensitive ways. In this influential passage the apostle Paul explains his ministry method. Within its immediate context, it reads:

> Though I am free and belong to no one, I have made myself a slave to everyone, to win as many as possible. To the Jews I became like a Jew, to win the Jews. To those under the law I became like one under the law (though I myself am not under the law), so as to win those under the law. To those not having the law I became like one not having the law (though I am not free from God's law but am under Christ's law), so as to win those not having the law. To the weak I became weak, to win the weak. *I have become all things to all people so that by all possible means I might save some.* I do all this for the sake of the gospel, that I may share in its blessings. (1 Cor 9:19-23, emphasis added)

The missional orthodoxy presented in this book is grounded on the presumption that the kind of missional faithfulness God desires and deserves requires that we do justice to both Jude 3 and 1 Corinthians 9:20-22.

Such a missional orthodoxy will benefit the Christian community in two important ways. The primary goal of this missional orthodoxy flows out of the conviction that the Spirit of mission is active in our world and in people's hearts and lives, readying each person for an encounter with a compelling presentation of the gospel. What would a presentation of the Christian gospel that is faithful to both the *text*—the biblical documents—and the *task*—the need to contextualize this message—look like? What would make such a presentation compelling? These are some of the crucial questions this book will address in its primary goal of providing the Christian community with a vision of the Christian faith that, precisely because it seeks to be faithful to both the text and task, can be

---

[2]Roland Allen surveys the work of the Holy Spirit in the book of Acts and comes to the following conclusion regarding the Spirit's identity: "These considerations are surely sufficient to convince us that the book of Acts is strictly a missionary book. But we have seen that it is the record of the acts of men moved by a Spirit given to them. The conclusion is irresistible, that the Spirit given was, in St Luke's view, a Spirit which impelled to missionary work, in fact a missionary Spirit." Roland Allen, *The Ministry of the Spirit* (Grand Rapids: Eerdmans, 1960), p. 17.

used by the Spirit of mission to enable a missional faithfulness and fruitfulness in our time and place.[3]

The secondary goal is to build bridges between the traditional evangelical, missional and emerging church movements.[4] Significant tension exists between some members of the traditional evangelical community (with its strong commitment to biblical authority) and some advocates of the emerging church movement (with their passionate concern regarding cultural relevance). It is my sense that many of these tensions center around varying understandings of the nature of the gospel and what constitutes an adequate and appropriate contextualization for an increasingly postmodern, post-Christian culture. Believing that it is possible to do justice to both Jude 3 and 1 Corinthians 9:20-22 at the same time, I believe that a benefit of this book is that the missional orthodoxy presented here identifies some common ground between many members of all three movements (traditional evangelical, missional and emerging), enabling us to do more than simply talk about being colleagues in ministry contextualization.

This book is constructed of two main parts. Part one lays the foundation for the missional orthodoxy that the rest of the book forges. Chapter one explains the concept of missional orthodoxy, arguing for its need at present and clarifying its nature. This chapter reveals the potentially provocative dialectical method by which this work will, ironically, strive toward a unifying orthodoxy that is faithful to both the text and the task.

In a nutshell, what is immediately dividing the rank and file of the

---

[3]Such a goal finds support in the work of theologian F. LeRon Shults, who speaks of the need for a "more subtle model of the relationality between theology and culture that captures their actual differentiation as well as their real coinherence" and that "would support a praxis of authentic response that neither dissolves nor dissects and that refuses to settle for mere conflation or conjunction." See F. LeRon Shults, *The Postfoundationalist Task of Theology: Wolfhart Pannenberg and the New Theological Rationality* (Grand Rapids: Eerdmans, 1999), pp. xiii-xiv.

[4]While completing the final draft of this book's manuscript I came across the newly published work *Missional God, Missional Church* by Ross Hastings, which addresses the tension between traditional evangelicals and proponents of the emerging church, seeking to provide a missional, middle way. Though our works differ in terms of purpose, style, structure and argument, there are enough similarities that our books might be viewed as companion volumes. See Ross Hastings, *Missional God, Missional Church: Hope for Re-Evangelizing the West* (Downers Grove, IL: IVP Academic, 2012).

traditional, missional and emerging evangelical communities is a slew
of false antitheses—antithetical, either-or doctrinal positions which
people are told they must choose between. The reality is that these bogus
dichotomies are produced not by Scripture or the nature of truth itself,[5]
but by an approach to ministry contextualization earmarked by an understandable but lamentable overreaction to Christian fundamentalism
and overcorrection to our current post-Christian ministry environment.
Unfortunately this unbalanced approach has failed to do justice to the
biblical text and missional task. This has, in turn, caused many mission-
minded followers of Christ to function as competitors rather than comrades in gospel ministry. I suggest that a missional orthodoxy that, while
faithful to Scripture, is modest rather than overreaching in its scope and
humble rather than arrogant and strident in its manner of presentation,
has what it takes to produce a greater sense of unity among traditional,
missional and emerging evangelicals, bringing glory to God (see Jn
17:20-23) in the process.[6]

Chapter two presents an argument-framing discussion of why, because of the balanced yet thoroughgoing method of gospel contextualization it espouses, a missional orthodoxy is the best of several possible
theological and ministerial responses to the cultural zeitgeist (spirit of
the age) currently prevailing in the developed countries of the West. Appended to this foundational chapter is an excursus that includes a provocative but necessary presentation of plausible reasons for the liberal/
emergent overcorrection to our post-Christian ministry situation—a

---

[5]F. LeRon Shults argues for an epistemological option between classical foundationalism, which
insists on the possibility of "absolute and certain knowledge," and nonfoundationalism, which
collapses into a "self-referentially incoherent relativism" (Shults, *Postfoundationalist Task*, p. 31).
This "middle way," which Shults and others refer to as "postfoundationalism," argues that "the
underlying problem is the way in which these two philosophical options have been cast as opposites. It aims to join nonfoundationalism in moving beyond foundationalism, but wants first
to challenge more deeply the *dichotomous assumptions* that have been uncritically accepted by
both sides. The dangers in each view are in the extremity of their claims, when they move beyond initially helpful intuitions to more exclusive and radical statements" (ibid., emphasis
added). This topic will be treated in more depth in chapter two.

[6]This work, for the sake of expediency and out of a sense of ecumenical optimism, refers to the
advocates of missional and emerging churches as evangelicals in the sense that they are, like
traditional evangelicals, committed to contextualizing the gospel *(evangel)* for our current ministry context. I understand the embrace of post-evangelicalism among some within the missional
and emerging movements and mean no offense by my collective use of the term *evangelical*.

dialogue which continues throughout the rest of the book. Also presented in this formal excursus is a discussion of the theological/philosophical perspective that makes possible an alternative to Christian fundamentalism and the liberal/emergent overreaction to it.

Building on the foundation provided in part one, the eight chapters that make up part two focus on the traditional theological loci. These chapters explain how embracing theological realism, acknowledging the missionary nature of God, and committing to the four christological verities that underwrite the Christian gospel, can help us respond to the false antitheses[7] that stand in the way of a missionally orthodox understanding of the Bible, God, Christ, the Holy Spirit, human beings, salvation, the church and the final things. It is by working our way through these false antitheses, striving, ironically, to learn from the mutually exclusive loyalties at work behind them, that an understanding of the Christian gospel can be forged that passes both the biblical and missional faithfulness tests. But make no mistake, what we are after is not an orthodoxy that identifies, but one that inspires. What is needed in our ministry location is a compelling vision of the Christian faith that, precisely because it strives to be faithful to both the biblical text and missional task, is something the Spirit of mission can use to entice our post-Christian peers to take another look at Christ and his church.

As for the style of this book, the reader should keep in mind: (1) I write as a biblical theologian, which means this work evidences a commitment to provide biblical support for the various theological positions discussed. (2) At the same time, the fact that the work endeavors to treat all the traditional theological loci will mean that it is impossible, due to space limitations, to provide a rigorous exegetical justification for

---

[7]At the heart of the argument for postfoundationalism, says Shults, is a discussion of how this middle way "overcomes and transcends" the several "false dichotomies" that together support the overarching "bogus [foundationalist/nonfoundationalist] dichotomy," which has shaped the philosophical discussion in the modern/postmodern era (see Shults, *Postfoundationalist Task,* pp. 11, 18, 20, 27, 49-50, 65, 67-68, 71, 77, 84, 90, 142, 146-47, 165, 240). Again, more will be said about the importance of a postfoundationalist epistemology to a missional orthodoxy in chapter two. Here I want to point out that since it is my contention that a series of false antitheses (or dichotomies) separate the traditional evangelical, missional and emerging church communities, a false-dichotomy-overcoming methodological approach similar to the one employed by Shults is also at work in this book.

each Scripture reference cited. (3) Given the book's target audience (evangelical students and church members preparing for ministry), the themes of the book are presented in an essentially introductory manner so as to make the material as accessible as possible. (4) Nevertheless, I have provided in the footnotes numerous references to ideas and resources that promote and assist further reflection. (5) Some footnotes contain rather long lists of biblical references that are intended to function not as strings of prooftexts but as opportunities for readers to engage in prayerful, thoughtful discernment of what the New Testament has to say about some important theological matters. (6) Because my thesis is that the rough contours of a missional orthodoxy can be arrived at by careful, irenic though critical interaction with several false antitheses posed by a well-meaning but unnecessary overcorrection to our current post-Christian ministry context, a fair amount of space in each chapter of part two is devoted to constructive theology that is, ironically, somewhat deconstructive in nature. (7) The subtitle of each chapter in part two begins with *toward,* revealing that the goal of each of these chapters, and the book as a whole, is to start the project of forging a missional orthodoxy, not to complete it entirely.

What we will learn is that the widely held notion that there are many people living in our post-Christian culture who are turned off to organized religion but interested in spirituality is more than a baseless cliché. Support for this assertion is found in a *Newsweek* article titled "In Search of the Spiritual," which describes "a world of 'hungry people, looking for a deeper relationship with God,'" and makes the point that within contemporary society "'spirituality,' the impulse to seek communion with the Divine, is thriving."[8] Despite the post-Christian nature of our current ministry context, the Spirit of mission really does seem to be working in people's lives, readying them for an encounter with the risen Christ.

What are we evangelicals (traditional, missional and emerging) going to do with this ministry opportunity? While we must not continue to do business as usual, neither should we feel the need to choose between an arrogant, contextually insensitive, demanding orthodoxy, and one that

---

[8]Jerry Adler, "In Search of the Spiritual," *Newsweek,* August 28, 2005, www.newsweek.com/id/147035.

is so generous and accommodating that it fails to function as an orthodoxy at all. The best way for us to do justice to Paul's concern that ministry be contextualized so that as many as possible might be saved (1 Cor 9:20-22), while also giving heed to Jude's concern that we contend earnestly for the faith that was once for all entrusted to the saints (Jude 3), is to roll up our sleeves and forge a missional orthodoxy.

ACKNOWLEDGMENTS

For a number of reasons this has been a challenging book to write. It's precisely because the process has been so daunting that I am especially appreciative of some key contributions made by several people along the way.

First of all, I want to express my deep gratitude for the invaluable assistance rendered by the two editors who worked on this book. Dr. Gary Deddo acquired the project on behalf of IVP Academic and helped shape the first and second drafts. David Congdon inherited the project after Gary moved on from IVP and contributed greatly to the final version. My university colleagues will verify that I am in the habit of freely acknowledging that this is a much better book because of the involvement of both Gary and David. Though I alone must be held responsible for any flaws the book possesses, I am very grateful for the assistance provided by those talented editors (and copyeditors) at IVP Academic whom I consider my publishing partners.

I also want to direct thanks to those many Vanguard University students who, having interacted with the material that would become this book, offered me valuable feedback regarding its coherence, relevance and utility. One group of students in particular is owed some special acknowledgement. Ben Blush, Adam De La Vega, Ike and Roxanne Eilers, Christina Gaddis, Scott Glisson, Nancy Hamilton, Benjamin Hurst, Julie Jenkins, Michelle Landin, Adorina and Arbella Moshava, Robert Nguyen, Curtis Weigel and the late Randy Mesquite were grad students who worked their way through an early version of the manuscript and ended up providing some invaluable input. I am also grateful for those undergraduate students whose enthusiasm for their professor's labor of love kept me encouraged during the lengthy process of the book's composition, revision and production.

Also deserving of my deep thanks are some Vanguard University colleagues. Dr. Rich Israel, my good friend and department chair, was very supportive throughout the process. Likewise, Vanguard University provost Dr. Jeff Hittenberger provided me with more encouragement than he probably realizes. Conversations about matters theological and missional with fellow religion professors Dr. Ed Rybarczyk, Dr. Frank Macchia, Dr. Greg Austring and Dr. Doug Petersen also proved to be very helpful. And, once again, I must tip my hat to the staff of the Vanguard University library: Dr. Alison English, Mel Covetta, Mary Wilson, Pam Crenshaw, Elena Nipper and Jack Morgan. The eager willingness of these folks to help me locate important resources was of great assistance.

In addition, I must acknowledge the contribution my wife Patti has made to this work. Her support of my sense of call to try to make a difference for Christ in the church and the world is what makes my writing endeavors possible. Simply put, without her loving encouragement, patient endurance and practical assistance, this book would never have been.

Finally, I want to express my sincere gratitude to my "dialogue partners" in this work: Marcus Borg and Brian McLaren. All three of us have something in common: a genuine desire to provide our current ministry context with a compelling vision of the Christian faith. Though we possess differing convictions regarding the essence of the Christian gospel and how it should be contextualized in our place and day, I want to acknowledge that interacting with the theological work of these two talented authors has had an impact on me, precipitating within me a deeper degree of reflection on the nature of God's kingdom and instilling a sense of need for a gospel presentation that is at once humble in manner, modest in scope and faithful to both the biblical text and missional task. It's my hope that this book, while it does not hesitate to highlight some important differences, ends up building bridges rather than walls between our respective visions, contributing to a greater unity between Christians evangelical, missional and emerging. To the degree this goal is realized, the challenge that writing this book has represented will have been worth it and, perhaps ironically, both of my dialogue partners will deserve part of the credit.

PART ONE

The Foundation of a Missional Orthodoxy

1

NEEDED

A Theology Both Missional and Orthodox

It is a basic premise of this book that all Christian theology should be missional, focusing on what God is up to in the world through his Son Jesus Christ and the Holy Spirit.[1] Missiologist Christopher Wright has asserted that "mission is not just one of a list of things that the Bible happens to talk about, only a bit more urgently than some. Mission is, in that much-abused phrase, 'what it's all about.'"[2] A biblically informed theology cannot help but include a focus on mission.

However, an even more basic reason why all theology should be missional is the missionary nature of God.[3] According to some of the best theological minds, mission is not just something God does, it is who he is. There is a "sendingness of God" that is "evident within the trinity itself."[4] Indeed, not only has God sent the Son and the Spirit into the

---

[1]Craig Van Gelder and Dwight J. Zscheile, *The Missional Church in Perspective: Mapping Trends and Shaping the Conversation* (Grand Rapids: Baker, 2011), pp. 26-27.

[2]See Christopher J. H. Wright, *The Mission of God: Unlocking the Bible's Grand Narrative* (Downers Grove, IL: InterVarsity Press, 2006), p. 22.

[3]See the chapter "Our God Is a Missionary God" in John Stott, *The Contemporary Christian* (Downers Grove, IL: InterVarsity Press, 1992), pp. 321-26, as cited in Wright, *Mission of God*, p. 24n2. See also See Van Gelder and Zscheile, *Missional Church*, pp. 27, 32-33, 52; John G. Flett, *The Witness of God: The Trinity, "Missio Dei," Karl Barth, and the Nature of Christian Community* (Grand Rapids: Eerdmans, 2010), pp. 4-5, 30, 35-44; David J. Bosch, *Transforming Mission: Paradigm Shifts in Theology of Mission* (Maryknoll, NY: Orbis, 2011), p. 400.

[4]George R. Hunsberger, "Proposals for a Missional Hermeneutic: Mapping the Conversation" (January 28, 2009), http://gocn.org/resources/articles/proposals-missional-hermeneutic-mapping-conversation. See also Van Gelder and Zscheile, *Missional Church*, pp. 52-53; Flett, *Witness of God*, p. 5.

world to achieve his purposes, but angels, prophets, his Word and the church as well.[5]

This observation that "God is a God of mission" who "sends the community of faith into the world" to participate in his mission—an observation that is at the heart of what has become known as the missional conversation—should tremendously affect the theological endeavor.[6] This is what I mean when I say that all theology should be missional in nature. Indeed, as a biblical and practical theologian influenced by the missional conversation, I suggest that *the goal of any so-called missional theology should be to help communities of believers participate in God's missional purposes by contextualizing the Christian message for their particular cultural locations toward the goal of representing the reign or kingdom of God within them.* Put differently, since the purpose of the church should be to participate in what God is up to in its community rather than merely striving to meet its own institutional needs and those of its members, the purpose of theology should be to help the local church enable its members, both corporately and individually, to be the people of God—that is, faithful witnesses to Christ and his kingdom in their homes, neighborhoods, workplaces and the community as a whole.[7]

All too often, however, Christian theology is done without God's mission in mind or in a way that fails to do justice to the witness to

---

[5]Flett, *Witness of God*, p. 42. See also Bosch, *Transforming Mission*, p. 399; Ross Hastings, *Missional God, Missional Church: Hope for Re-Evangelizing the West* (Downers Grove, IL: IVP Academic, 2012), pp. 77-78.

[6]Michael Barram, "The Bible, Mission, and Social Location: Toward a Missional Hermeneutic," *Interpretation* 61 (January 2007): 43. See also Van Gelder and Zscheile, *Missional Church*, pp. 52-53.

[7]Darrell Guder writes: "The primary task of a missional hermeneutic [i.e., missional theology] then is to provide a particular congregation the formation it needs to be able both to live out its gathered life and its scattered life faithfully." Darrell Guder, "Missional Hermeneutics: The Missional Vocation of the Congregation," *Mission Focus: Annual Review* 15 (2007): 138. Yet another way of grounding Christian ministry in the nature of God is more theological than exegetical in nature. This approach focuses on the Trinity's interpersonal relationships. According to this line of missional thinking, "the church is called to 'echo' in time the communion that is God's life in eternity: she is 'called to be a being of persons-in-relation which receives [her] character as communion by virtue of [her] relation to God and so is enabled to reflect something of that being in the world.'" Flett, *Witness of God*, p. 25. Citations are from Colin Gunton, *The Promise of Trinitarian Theology*, 2nd ed. (London: T & T Clark, 2003), p. 12. Thus, in addition to a focus on the sending nature of God, a missional theology might also seek to tease out the implications of God's communal nature for the missional endeavor, as well as for the traditional theological loci.

Christ presented in Scripture. With respect to the former possibility, a theology that is intended simply to encourage church members in their faith convictions and provide them with biblical support for their liturgical practices, as valid as these goals are, cannot be considered missional. Neither is a theology missional which fails to recognize that, given the contextual nature of all theologizing,[8] every generation of theologians must converse with the biblical texts in a fresh way so as to be led by the Spirit toward a renewed, vital recontextualization of the gospel message that will be compelling to their generation given its specific modes of intellection and expression, as well as the particular existential and religious questions it ponders.

However, with regard to the latter possibility (failing to do justice to the witness to Christ presented in Scripture), it is equally important to recognize that there is a crucial difference between *contextualizing* the gospel for a contemporary ministry context and *accommodating, assimilating* or *conforming* the gospel to a cultural location, altering the very essence of the Christian message to make it more palatable or acceptable per the prevailing zeitgeist. It is because of this latter possibility that this book seeks not simply a missional *theology*, but a missional *orthodoxy* as well—a compelling presentation of the Christian faith and life that, while doing justice to the practice of ministry contextualization modeled for us by the apostle Paul (1 Cor 9:20-22), also pays heed to the biblical exhortation to contend for the faith once for all entrusted to the saints (Jude 3). This, in a nutshell, is what a theology that is both missional and orthodox is about.

But let's be clear, the orthodoxy presented in these pages is *not* intended to function as a criterion for establishing evangelical identity (i.e., who gets to be called an evangelical and who does not) or for establishing one's missional credentials (i.e., who is really doing missional ministry and who is not). Rather, the real need at present is for a *missional orthodoxy*—a vision of the Christian faith that, precisely because it seeks to be faithful to both the biblical text and the mis-

---

[8]See Dean Flemming, *Contextualization in the New Testament: Patterns for Theology and Ministry* (Downers Grove, IL: InterVarsity Press, 2005), p. 298; Bruce J. Nicholls, *Contextualization: A Theology of Gospel and Culture* (Vancouver: Regent College Publishing, 1979), pp. 25-26, 38-40.

sional task, can be used by the Spirit of mission to enable a missional faithfulness and fruitfulness on the part of Christ's followers in our time and place.[9] The primary purpose of the book is to offer the Christian community a rough outline of what such a missional orthodoxy might look like.[10]

CHRISTIAN ORTHODOXY AND THE SWING OF THE PROVERBIAL PENDULUM

This theological project is made necessary by the fact that the story of Christian belief is filled with accounts of radical swings of the proverbial pendulum. Over the years, Christian theologians have tended to overreact back and forth from one extreme theological perspective to the other: from the traditional/conservative to the progressive/liberal and then back again. To put it simply: overcorrections happen![11]

However, against this tendency toward overreaction or overcorrection we have this word of warning uttered by the Preacher of Ecclesiastes:

> It is good to grasp the one
> > and not let go of the other.
> Whoever fears God will avoid all extremes. (Eccles 7:18)

Keeping this sage advice in mind, a major theological controversy that has implications for how we evangelicals engage in missional ministry centers on the very notion of a Christian *orthodoxy* or "right belief." Is there is such a thing, and if so, of what is it composed, and how should it function in an increasingly postmodern, post-Christian culture? Some of the questions currently being debated back and forth with regard to this issue are:

---

[9]With respect to the need for a missional theology to be faithful to the biblical text, see Darrell Guder's encouragement in *Be My Witnesses: The Church's Mission, Message and Messengers* (Grand Rapids: Eerdmans, 1985), p. 8.

[10]Throughout this book, and especially in the final two chapters, is discussion of how missional orthodoxy (right belief) and missional orthopraxy (right practice) work together to comprise what is occasionally referred to here as a *missionally faithful vision of the Christian faith.*

[11]Theologians Roger Olson and D. A. Carson also refer to the theological overreactions produced by the swing of this proverbial pendulum. See Roger Olson, *The Mosaic of Christian Belief: Twenty Centuries of Unity and Diversity* (Downers Grove, IL: IVP Academic, 2002), p. 23; and Donald A. Carson, *Becoming Conversant with the Emergent Church* (Grand Rapids: Zondervan, 2005), p. 234.

- Is what a person *believes* important to God, or only how he or she *behaves*?[12]

- Should missional ministry include an attempt to help people believe certain things—to embrace certain doctrines that derive from the Scriptures and that have been widely held by Christians through the centuries?[13]

- Is there such a thing as Christian dogma—biblical doctrines that are authoritative, non-negotiable, absolutely crucial to the Christian faith?

- If there is such a thing as Christian dogma, do all doctrines derived from Scripture fall into this category, or only some? If only some, which ones, and why these?

- How important is it that we do our best to think and teach "rightly" about doctrines that do not seem to constitute Christian dogma per se? To what degree might the doctrines that comprise Christian dogma inform a proper belief with regard to other Christian doctrines?[14]

---

[12]For a brief, cogent discussion of why many churches eager to reach "postmodern truth-seekers" are known to demonstrate an "antipathy toward doctrine," see Mark DeVine, "Can the Church Emerge Without or with Only the Nicene Creed" in *Evangelicals and Nicene Faith*, ed. Timothy George (Grand Rapids: Baker, 2011), pp. 181-82. See also Brian McLaren's discussion of doctrine as an "imperial product" that needs to be "deconstructed" in *Why Did Jesus, Moses, the Buddha, and Mohammed Cross the Road? Christian Identity in a Multi-Faith World* (New York: Jericho Books, 2012), pp. 101-2.

[13]I have in mind here universally affirmed doctrines such as those included in the Niceno-Constantinopolitan Creed. In support of this, Scot McKnight has written: "I now see the creeds, especially the Apostles' Creed and the Nicene Creed, or the Niceno-Constantinopolitan Creed, as fundamental to the faith of all Christians." See Scot McKnight, *The King Jesus Gospel: The Original Good News Revisited* (Grand Rapids: Zondervan, 2011), p. 63. That said, I wish to emphasize from the outset of this work my agreement with the view that the legitimacy of any creed is dependent on its compatibility with the Bible (see DeVine, "Can the Church Emerge?" p. 181). Thus, the purpose of this work is not to call for a faithfulness to the creeds but to the Scriptures that gave rise to the creeds.

[14]It is not uncommon for theologians to assert that "orthodoxy itself is the lens through which we see theology." See Scot McKnight, "Review: Brian McLaren's 'A New Kind of Christianity,'" *Christianity Today*, February 26, 2010, www.christianitytoday.com/ct/2010/march/3.59.html. See also Mark Galli, "Proof of a Good God: 'Crucified Under Pontius Pilate,'" *Christianity Today*, April 5, 2012, www.christianitytoday.com/ct/2012/april/crucified-under-pilate.html, for an example of how an element of the Nicene Creed, precisely because it is grounded in Scripture, can prove useful in a discussion of a thorny theological problem. See also how Van Gelder and Zscheile affirm the fact that the doctrine of the Trinity "is now being reasserted increasingly as the framework within which other doctrines are explored and explained" (Van Gelder and Zscheile, *Missional Church*, p. 105).

- How is a Christian orthodoxy to be presented to an increasingly post-modern, post-Christian society that tends to be distrustful of such truth-claims?[15] Is it possible to promote such a thing as "right belief" without doing so in a demanding, strident, "dogmatic" tone of voice? Or must we feel the need to embrace an "orthodoxy" that is so accommodating to our cultural context that it ends up functioning as no orthodoxy at all?

All of these questions have proponents on both ends of the spectrum, from the far right to the far left, from a traditional or conservative perspective to one that is much more progressive or liberal. Thus, some Christians seem to suggest that it is crucial to one's salvation to believe rightly about a host of doctrines they see presented in the Bible. Other Christians counter that *believing* is not the point of Christianity at all; how we *behave* is what ultimately matters, regardless of our beliefs.

Allow me to illustrate these two extreme positions on the pendulum's arc with a couple of stories. Several years ago, when I was a young pastor with a newly completed M.Div. degree, I had an interesting encounter with a young man who had yet to complete his theological education at another (apparently rival) seminary. This seminarian, just a couple of years younger than I, was the son of a neighborhood friend who had essentially adopted my wife Patti and me. It was obvious that this next-door neighbor admired us, and we certainly appreciated his friendship and the homeowner wisdom he poured into our lives. He would often speak of his son away at seminary, indicating how much he looked forward to our meeting him. Finally, the day arrived. Unfortunately, it did not turn out to be the happy experience my neighbor had in mind.

Still standing in the entry way of my home, the first words out of the young seminarian's mouth formed the question: "How could you go to a seminary where all the professors have such a low view of Scripture?"

Though I was more than a little surprised by the abrupt, polemical nature of this query, I was also concerned for my neighbor—the seminarian's father—who had a shocked, concerned look on his face as well.

---

[15]See DeVine, "Can the Church Emerge?" p. 182.

So, I very calmly offered in reply that I had not studied with any professors who possessed a low view of Scripture.

The shake of his head and the look on his face told me that my young guest was not buying it. Indeed, he went on to state rather boldly that he did not see how anyone could graduate from a seminary so steeped in theological bankruptcy without coming away from the experience with a terribly low view of Scripture.

Again, trying to make peace for the sake of my neighbor, I simply said, "Well, let me put it to you this way: I love the Lord Jesus just as you do."

He shot back, "I doubt it! Besides, a Mormon or Jehovah's Witness could say the same thing."

Taking another tack, but becoming genuinely frustrated at this point, I said, "No, I can assure you that if both of us were to draw up statements of faith they would line up nicely with each other."

"No, they wouldn't!" he snapped.

I then asked, "How would they differ?"

He explained that my faith statement would be missing any reference to a particular doctrine that is peculiar to his faith tradition. My response was to point out that I was familiar with this doctrine. "But are you suggesting that this peculiar doctrine possesses soteriological significance?" I asked. (In other words, I inquired as to whether he meant to suggest that the embrace of this particular doctrine is crucial to a person's experience of salvation.)

His reply was unequivocal: "Absolutely!" he said.

Immediately, I answered back, "Well, if that's the case, then not even John Calvin was saved." I assumed that this would be significant for this young churchman-in-training whose faith tradition was so thoroughly rooted in the theological work of the great Protestant Reformers.

He smiled and said simply, "Well, we make allowances for Calvin."

The implication was clear. He was saying in effect that his sense of orthodoxy was such that John Calvin might be granted an exception for not holding to the particular doctrine at issue, but not me. I was on the outside of the circle of the saved!

Though I changed the subject for the sake of my next-door neighbor, the rest of the conversation was obviously strained. As I recall, we never left the entry way of my home. It stands to reason, does it not, that it would be difficult for me to "chat it up" with someone who had just insisted that I not only possessed a deficient view of Scripture, but that because I did not belong to his particular ecclesial community (and adhere to the confession of faith held dear by it), I was bereft of salvation as well?[16]

I would eventually go on to write a book on the topic of Pharisaism and fundamentalism (i.e., dogmatism, judgmentalism, separatism, etc.) in evangelical churches.[17] Experiences such as this one explain why.

But this is only one side of the story. In one of the theology courses I teach every semester at a Christian liberal arts university, I make sure that my ministry-bound students interact critically with a wide spectrum of theological responses to the cultural zeitgeist currently exercising a huge influence in the Western world. These responses range from a very conservative, fundamentalist approach, to the work of a mainline Protestant theologian whose influence among some evangelicals seems to be gaining ground.[18] In his book *The Heart of Christianity*, Marcus Borg boldly contrasts an "earlier" vision of the Christian faith (which for him is largely an indiscriminate blend of traditional evangelicalism and Christian fundamentalism) with what he calls the "emerging" vision or paradigm.[19] According to Borg's emerging paradigm, the Christian life should not focus on faith as "believing" but on faith as "beloving" in-

---

[16]Theologian E. J. Carnell once referred to Christian fundamentalism as "orthodoxy gone cultic" because of the manner in which its adherents feel the need to go to the mat over doctrines the Bible does not heavily emphasize, and because of their commitment to separate from those who do not agree with their doctrinal idealism. E. J. Carnell, *The Case for Orthodox Theology* (Philadelphia: Westminster Press, 1959), p. 113, as cited in Roger E. Olson, "A Postconservative Evangelical Response [to Fundamentalism]" in *Four Views on the Spectrum of Evangelicalism*, ed. Stanley N. Gundry, Andrew David Naselli and Collin Hansen (Grand Rapids: Zondervan, 2011), pp. 63, 65.

[17]Gary Tyra, *Defeating Pharisaism: Recovering Jesus' Disciple-Making Method* (Downers Grove, IL: InterVarsity Press, 2009).

[18]For example, in his review of Brian McLaren's *A New Kind of Christianity*, Scot McKnight draws parallels between some of McLaren's theological conclusions and those held by Marcus Borg (see McKnight, "Review").

[19]Borg, HC xi. See also Borg, SC 10-11, 231-38; and Borg and Wright, MJ 10-17. However, even though I will use the term *emerging* to describe Borg's vision, I recognize that his version of the emerging paradigm cannot be equated with the theological perspectives of all those who consider themselves part of the emerging church movement.

stead.[20] Indeed, Borg is sharply critical of the way the earlier version of the Christian faith focuses so much on the need to believe certain things to be true. He sets up this critique with a personal narrative of his own. The story he tells has to do with a conversation he once had with a woman sitting next to him on a plane. In the course of the conversation, the woman made the statement: "I'm much more interested in Buddhism and Sufism than I am in Christianity." When Borg asked her why, she said: "Because they're about a way of life, and Christianity is all about believing." According to Borg, she continued, "I don't think beliefs matter nearly as much as having a spiritual path and following a way."[21]

Commenting on this exchange, Borg goes on to express some essential solidarity with this woman's sentiment, lamenting the fact that

> her statement reflects the most common understanding of the word "faith" in modern Western Christianity: that faith means holding a certain set of "beliefs," "believing" a set of statements to be true, whether cast as a biblical teaching or doctrines or dogma. Indeed, this understanding of faith is central to the earlier paradigm. Most people today, in the church and outside of it, take it for granted that Christian faith means believing a set of Christian beliefs to be true.[22]

Borg then draws a sharp contrast between a Christianity of the "head" and a Christianity of the "heart," suggesting that we can either be one or the other but, of course, it is the latter we should choose.[23] According to this prolific author and the emerging version of Christianity he is promoting, the concern of many Christians through the ages to believe rightly about who God is, what he is up to, and what he desires for and demands of the people he has created is pretty much a colossal case of missing the point of what Christianity is all about.

Two real life stories. Two very different ways of thinking about what lies at the heart of Christianity. Which position should we embrace? In which direction should we lean?

What we have before us is a *false antithesis*—the idea that with regard

---

[20]Borg, HC 40-41; see also Borg, SC 115-24.
[21]Borg, HC 25.
[22]Ibid. See also Borg, GWNK 2; and Borg, SC 11, 14.
[23]Borg, HC 26.

to the matter at hand we only have two options from which to choose.[24] The reality is that while there is such a thing as a true antithesis (an either-or issue that allows for only two possible responses), false antitheses abound. This is especially true in discussions surrounding religion and politics where rigid party lines between conservatives and liberals exist and the tactic to win converts to one's point of view by presenting a caricature of the opposing perspective seems to work so well. Despite all the ferocious rhetoric to the contrary, most disputations between hardcore conservatives and liberals (whether religious or political) allow for a third alternative—an "answer" to the false antithesis that does a much better job of responding to the matter at hand precisely because it seeks to do so in a measured, nuanced and, hence, responsible manner. Wise is the person who recognizes a false antithesis and refuses to fall prey to it by lurching toward one extreme position or the other!

So, as it concerns the question of a Christian orthodoxy, yes, there is a type of Christian fundamentalism (i.e., a nominalism-producing creedalism or confessionalism) that so emphasizes correct doctrine that it might actually hold that, because of grace, how one behaves does not matter as long as one gives mental assent to the "right" confession or set of beliefs. And, yes, there is also a Christian liberalism that seems to advocate a religious relativism which holds that what one believes is immaterial as long as he or she is sincere in these beliefs and is being enabled by them to work for a more just, humane, environmentally sustainable world. Both of these extreme options are problematic. The good news, however, is that, as Ecclesiastes 7:18 reminds us, we do not have to choose between these two extreme views. As an alternative to an overly elaborate and strident orthodoxy or no orthodoxy at all, there is one that strives to be *humble* in manner, *modest* in scope and *faithful* to both the text and the task. This is the main message of this book: We do not have to fall prey to this false antithesis; there is such a thing as a *missional orthodoxy*.

---

[24]Also referred to as a "false dichotomy." Note that my focus on the phenomenon of a false antithesis parallels Roger Olson's use of the phrases "unnecessary bifurcations," "false alternatives" and "absolute antithesis" (see Olson, *Mosaic of Christian Belief*, pp. 23, 25). Note also D. A. Carson's use of the phrases "manipulative antithesis," "absolute antithesis" and "false antithesis" in *Becoming Conversant*, pp. 94, 98, 108, 119, 234.

THE NEED FOR A MISSIONAL ORTHODOXY

If there was ever a time for evangelicals to resist the wide swings of the pendulum by forging a humble, modest, missionally faithful orthodoxy that can function as a compelling alternative to both a fighting fundamentalism and a too-accommodating liberalism, that time is now.

Taking our cue from the apostle Paul, we evangelicals have always been about the mission. But Paul's missional practice was to contextualize the ministry of the gospel depending on the sociocultural conditions of any given ministry location, as 1 Corinthians 9:20-22 makes clear:

> To the Jews I became like a Jew, to win the Jews. To those under the law I became like one under the law (though I myself am not under the law), so as to win those under the law. To those not having the law I became like one not having the law (though I am not free from God's law but am under Christ's law), so as to win those not having the law. To the weak I became weak, to win the weak. I have become all things to all people so that by all possible means I might save some.

At its heart, a missional approach to ministry is all about contextualization—all about asking the question: What is the Holy Spirit up to in this ministry location and how can we, as a missional community formed by the Spirit of mission,[25] cooperate with it? Therefore, I suggest that the Bible's emphasis on the contextualization of the gospel virtually mandates a missional response of some kind to our current ministry context. It is incumbent on contemporary evangelical church leaders and members to do their best to *exegete* (i.e., seek to fully understand) their ministry contexts so that they might offer to the people living and working within them a compelling presentation of the Christian message.

Of course, it's one thing to acknowledge that the biblical call to contextualize requires a missional response. But this still leaves open the question: Why a *missional orthodoxy?* The answer to this crucial query derives from an awareness of the fact that, given the particulars of our

---

[25]See Darrell L. Guder, *The Continuing Conversion of the Church* (Grand Rapids: Eerdmans, 2000), pp. 68, 146.

current ministry context and our commitment to do justice to Jude 3, not just any kind of contextualization will do. In chapter two we will take a hard look at some of our contextualization options. Here the focus will be on some of those ministry-context particulars that seem to mandate a certain kind of missional response.

The post-Christian dynamic. All the indications are that the societies in the West are rapidly becoming more and more post-Christian, perhaps even anti-Christian, in their orientation. This shift toward a post-Christian orientation is especially prevalent among (though by no means limited to) the members of the emerging generations. A recent *Los Angeles Times* article indicated that about seventy-five percent of Americans between the ages of eighteen and twenty-nine now consider themselves "spiritual but not religious."[26] Many of these millions of young adults can be considered post-Christian in the sense that they possess some prior experience in Christian churches. Indeed, according to research conducted by the Barna Group and reported in David Kinnaman's book *You Lost Me: Why Young Christians Are Leaving the Church . . . and Rethinking Faith,* nearly three out of every five young Christians (fifty-nine percent) disconnect either permanently or for an extended period of time from church life after age fifteen.[27]

In a *Christianity Today* article titled "The Leavers: Young Doubters Exit the Church," author Drew Dyck writes, "Among young adults in the U.S., sociologists are seeing a major shift taking place *away* from Christianity. A faithful response requires that we examine the exodus and ask ourselves some honest questions about why."[28] Dyck then marshals forth some rather distressing statistics which, when taken together, serve to

[26]Phillip Clayton, "Letting Doubters in the Door," *Los Angeles Times,* March 25, 2012, http://articles.latimes.com/2012/mar/25/opinion/la-oe-clayton-emergingchurch-20120325. Throughout this work I will make reference to the post-Christian realities at work in America. Support for the idea that these same realities are at work in Canada can be found in Ann-Margret Hovespian, "Quebec: Canada's Prodigal Province," *Christianity Today,* April 26, 2012, www.christianitytoday.com/ct/2012/may/quebec-prodigal-province.html.

[27]The Barna Group, "Six Reasons Young Christians Leave Church," September 28, 2011, www.barna.org/teens-next-gen-articles/528-six-reasons-young-christians-leave-church. See also David Kinnaman, *You Lost Me: Why Young Christians Are Leaving the Church . . . and Rethinking Faith* (Grand Rapids: Baker Books, 2011).

[28]Drew Dyck, "The Leavers: Young Doubters Exit the Church," *Christianity Today,* November 19, 2010, www.christianitytoday.com/ct/2010/november/27.40.html.

demonstrate the reality of the post-Christian dynamic:

> Among the findings released in 2009 from the American Religious Identi-
> fication Survey (ARIS) . . . the percentage of Americans claiming "no re-
> ligion" almost doubled in about two decades, climbing from 8.1 percent in
> 1990 to 15 percent in 2008. The trend wasn't confined to one region. Those
> marking "no religion," called the "Nones," made up the only group to have
> grown in every state, from the secular Northeast to the conservative Bible
> Belt. The Nones were most numerous among the young: a whopping 22
> percent of 18- to 29-year-olds claimed no religion, up from 11 percent in
> 1990. The study also found that 73 percent of Nones came from religious
> homes; 66 percent were described by the study as "de-converts." . . .
>
> Other survey results have been grimmer. At the May 2009 Pew Forum
> on Religion and Public Life, top political scientists Robert Putnam and
> David Campbell presented research from their book *American Grace*, re-
> leased last month. They reported that "young Americans are dropping out
> of religion at an alarming rate of five to six times the historic rate (30 to 40
> percent have no religion today, versus 5 to 10 percent a generation ago)." . . .
>
> There has been a corresponding drop in church involvement. Ac-
> cording to Rainer Research, approximately 70 percent of American youth
> drop out of church between the age of 18 and 22. The Barna Group esti-
> mates that 80 percent of those reared in the church will be "disengaged"
> by the time they are 29.[29]

Obviously, such statistics indicate the need for present and future
evangelical church leaders to engage in some serious reflection.[30] As
someone who works with this demographic nearly every day, I offer the
concern that it is one thing for millions of young adults, in the process
of their psychological individuation into separate selves, to spend some

---

[29]Ibid.

[30]In support of this assertion, New Testament scholar James Brownson writes: "Two realities are
readily apparent to Christians as they examine the present situation of Christianity in its North
American context: First, the increasing marginalization in North American culture of Christian faith in general and of the Christian church in particular must call forth from Christians a
fresh vision for what it means to be a Christian and to be the Christian church in our post-
Christian setting. Second, Christians also believe that the Christian faith offers good news and
hope for our situation, good news that must be lived out and proclaimed with courage and
wisdom." James Brownson, "Speaking the Truth in Love: Elements of a Missional Hermeneutic," February 8, 2011, http://imissional.org/wp-content/uploads/2010/07/Elements-of-a-
Missional-Hermeneutic-Brownson.pdf (p. 479).

time away from an institution they felt forced to participate in growing up (i.e., the church).[31] It is another, however, for many of these millions of young adults to go on to adopt alternative forms of spirituality, essentially rejecting the truth claims of historic Christianity in the process. I had a discussion just today with a young man who, although about to graduate from a Christian university, has no use for the church or the Christianity he has experienced in it. Indeed, this young man who grew up in church is now not only post-Christian, but anti-Christian as well! The question is: Why? Why are there so many people living all around us who, though spiritually hungry, nevertheless consider themselves "over" Christianity and "done" with the church?

Conservative Christianity's image problem. Though some sociological research has suggested that we American evangelicals do not, in fact, have an image problem after all,[32] my personal experience and academic research indicates otherwise.[33] And mine is not the only voice expressing this concern. The same point is made in David Kinnaman's *unChristian: What a New Generation Really Thinks about Christianity . . . and Why It Matters.* On the basis of a three year study that included "more than a dozen nationally representative surveys (reflecting thousands of interviews)" and a series of interviews with "a representative sample of sixteen- to twenty-nine-year olds," along with interviews of "hundreds of pastors and church leaders,"[34] Kinnaman offers the following disturbing conclusions:

> Our research shows that many of those outside of Christianity, especially younger adults, have little trust in the Christian faith, and esteem for the lifestyle of Christ followers is quickly fading among outsiders. They admit their emotional and intellectual barriers go up when they are around Christians, and they reject Jesus because they feel rejected by Christians.[35]

---

[31]For some excellent advice about what churches can do to be proactive about mitigating this problem, see Kinnaman, *You Lost Me.*

[32]See Bradley E. Wright, "Americans Like Evangelicals After All," *Christianity Today,* August 5, 2011, www.christianitytoday.com/ct/2011/august/americans-do-like-evangelicals.html.

[33]See chapter three of Tyra, *Defeating Pharisaism.*

[34]David Kinnaman, *unChristian: What a New Generation Really Thinks About Christianity . . . and Why It Matters* (Grand Rapids: Baker, 2007), p. 15.

[35]Ibid., p. 11.

Painful encounters with the faith also have a strong influence on what a person thinks of Christianity. In fact, we discovered that one-fifth of all outsiders, regardless of age, admitted they "have had a bad experience in a church or with a Christian that gave them a negative image of Jesus Christ." This represents nearly fifty million adult residents of this country—including about nine million young outsiders—who admit they have significant emotional or spiritual baggage from past experiences with so-called Christ followers. Church leaders are not unaware of this issue. Among pastors of Protestant churches, three-quarters said they often encounter people whose negative experiences create major barriers to their openness to Jesus.[36]

Sadly, it really is true that, as Kinnaman puts it, "Christianity has an image problem"[37]—one which a good number of scholars attribute to the fact that there is too much Pharisaism and fundamentalism at work within too many traditional evangelical churches.[38] To the degree that many members of the emerging generations associate such attitudes and actions as legalism, judgmentalism, separatism, dogmatism, pugilism and hypocrisy with conservative churches, traditional evangelicals will

---

[36]Ibid., pp. 31-32.

[37]Ibid., p. 11.

[38]Other works that argue that there yet remains in evangelicalism a strong vestige of some of the negative aspects of Christian fundamentalism (dogmatism, legalism, judgmentalism, separatism, pugilism, etc.) include: Robert Webber, *Common Roots: A Call to Evangelical Maturity* (Grand Rapids: Zondervan, 1978), pp. 57, 64; Donald Bloesch, *The Evangelical Renaissance*, 19-23 (Grand Rapids: Eerdmans, 1973); Donald Bloesch, *The Future of Evangelical Christianity* (Colorado Springs: Helmers & Howard Publishers, 1988), pp. 92-97; Donald Dayton, *Discovering an Evangelical Heritage* (Peabody, MA: Hendrickson Publishers, 1976), pp. 1-7; Joel Carpenter, *Revive Us Again: The Reawakening of American Fundamentalism* (New York: Oxford University Press, 1997), pp. 237-38; Christian Smith, *American Evangelicalism: Embattled and Thriving* (Chicago: University of Chicago Press, 1998), p. 14; Stanley Grenz, *Renewing the Center: Evangelical Theology in a Post-Theological Era* (Grand Rapids: Baker, 2000), pp. 15-16, 81-84; Richard Mouw, *The Smell of Sawdust* (Grand Rapids: Zondervan, 2000), pp. 24-25; Eddie Gibbs and Ryan K. Bolger, *Emerging Churches: Creating Christian Community in Postmodern Cultures* (Grand Rapids: Baker, 2005), pp. 239-328; Roger Olson, *Reformed and Always Reforming: The Postconservative Approach to Evangelical Theology* (Grand Rapids: Baker, 2007), p. 68; Dan Kimball, *They Like Jesus But Not the Church: Insights from Emerging Generations* (Grand Rapids: Zondervan, 2007); and Kinnaman, *You Lost Me.* Furthermore, the following works all speak of the deleterious effects of a Christian Pharisaism in particular at work in the lives of too many conservative Christians and churches: John Fischer, *12 Steps for the Recovering Pharisee (Like Me)* (Minneapolis: Bethany, 2000); Tom Hovestol, *Extreme Righteousness: Seeing Ourselves in the Pharisees* (Chicago: Moody, 1997), pp. 12, 35, 45; Kathleen Kern, *We Are the Pharisees* (Scottdale, PA: Herald Press, 1995), pp. 81-101. Timothy Keller, *The Reason for God: Belief in an Age of Skepticism* (New York: Dutton, 2008), pp. 52, 56-59, 178-79.

increasingly find themselves feeling that they are swimming upstream as they engage in ministry contextualization.

The impact of postmodernity. Furthermore, though I am convinced that some aspects of the advent of postmodernism actually create opportunities for missional ministry (I'll have more to say about this later), it is also true that more and more American adults (even many evangelical church members) are tending toward an embrace of three ideological commitments often viewed as entailments of the postmodern perspective—epistemological relativism, moral relativism and religious relativism.

At the risk of greatly oversimplifying things, I suggest that we think of postmodernism as the view that all knowledge of the world in which we live is the result of a *cultural linguistic constructivism.*[39] That is, according to the postmodern perspective, we do not really experience the world (reality and truth) as it is; we experience our perceptions of the world. Our respective understandings of reality and truth (our worldviews) have to be constructed (hence the term *constructivism*). Furthermore, one theory suggests that the formation of a worldview cannot happen without a cognitive framework—a collection of concepts and categories that enable us to process our sense perceptions of the world around us and turn these raw perceptions into knowledge. Postmodern theory insists that each of us comes by this cognitive framework via language (hence the term *linguistic*).[40] However, for postmodernism, all of the concepts and categories we end up using to construct our knowledge of the world are illusions. They do not exist in the real world, only in our artful mental constructions of it. For example, consider the category of "leaf." In the real world there is no such thing as "leaf," only real leaves, many of which do not match the categorical ideal that exists in our heads. As well, the words we use to describe the world do not really

---

[39]I am indebted to Jim Fidelibus for this helpful way of summarizing the heart of the postmodern understanding of worldviews; see his "Being of Many Minds: The Postmodern Impact upon Psychotherapy" in *The Death of Truth,* ed. Dennis McCallum (Minneapolis: Bethany House, 1996), pp. 146-47.

[40]Put simply, the idea here is that the same rules of grammar within a language that enable its speakers to form meaningful sentences also enable its speakers to form a meaningful view of the world. Or, to put it in even stronger terms, the rules of grammar at work in a language actually govern the manner in which its speakers form their view of the world.

connect with the world, they just point to other words. Words are arbitrary sounds to which we assign meanings. There is no hard metaphysical connection between a word (in any language) and what it signifies. Thus, it is argued, our supposed "knowledge" of the world is actually an endless progression of words pointing to other words, never really making contact with reality itself. The *hard* postmodernist contends that the cumulative effect of philosophical arguments such as these is the conviction that our worldviews are nothing more than illusory linguistic constructions. We are, so to speak, imprisoned within language—a language that comes to us via the culture in which we are raised (hence the term *cultural*). *The end result of a "hard" postmodernism is a thoroughgoing perspectivalism that relativizes truth to each cultural group and, ultimately, to each individual worldview constructor.*

Now, as indicated above, the postmodern perspective goes on to produce three ideological commitments which present certain problems for embracing historic Christian orthodoxy.

- *Epistemological relativism* is the idea that since no culture is in touch with *reality* as it really is, all worldviews (thought of as cultural creations) are equally valid and therefore no one culture's take on reality should be considered any more accurate or authoritative than that of any other.[41]

- *Moral relativism* is the idea that just as no one culture is in touch with the "truth" about reality, no one culture is in touch with the "truth" about *morality* either. Every culture has its own morality that it passes on to its members, and no one culture's understanding of morality should be considered any more accurate or authoritative than that of any other.

- *Religious relativism* is the idea that just as no one culture's take on reality or morality is any more accurate than that of any other, the

---

[41]Stanley J. Grenz and John R. Franke are careful to point out that not all postmoderns are philosophical relativists; see their *Beyond Foundationalism: Shaping Theology in a Postmodern Context* (Louisville, KY: Westminster John Knox, 2000), p. 19. This is why many scholars make a distinction between "hard" and "soft" postmodernism. For example, see Millard Erickson, *Postmodernizing the Faith: Evangelical Responses to the Challenge of Postmodernism* (Grand Rapids: Baker Books, 1998), p. 19; and Carson, *Becoming Conversant*, p. 104.

same is true when it comes to *spirituality;* all religions (also thought of as cultural creations) are equally valid and no one religion is more "true" or salvific than any other.

It does not take an advanced degree in theology to be able to figure out that given conservative Christianity's current image problem, our culture's increasing embrace of these three ideological commitments serves as a huge obstacle to a "business as usual" ministry approach by traditional evangelicals in this time and place.

What all this means is that as it relates to doing missional ministry in an increasingly postmodern, post-Christian context, our manner matters![42] Not intending to discount the convicting work of the Holy Spirit, I will suggest that *any presentation of the gospel evocative of an arrogant, self-righteous, strident version of Christian orthodoxy is going to have trouble even being heard by the members of our post-Christian culture, especially those from the emerging generations.* The young man I referred to earlier, who though having been raised in the church now possesses a virulent anti-Christian perspective, is a heartbreaking case in point.

THE NATURE OF A MISSIONAL ORTHODOXY

Earlier in this chapter I suggested that what is needed in our place and time is an orthodoxy that strives to be *humble* and *modest* as well as *faithful* to both the text and the task. Though chapter two will provide an extended discussion of why a missional orthodoxy is the *best* of several possible theological responses to our current ministry context, I want to first explain why an orthodoxy that strives to be *faithful* to both the text and the task needs to be *humble* and *modest* as well. Here I will also present a brief but important discussion of the distinction that needs to be made between the missional and emerging church movements.

Why a humble orthodoxy. I have already endeavored to make clear

---

[42]Brownson makes essentially the same point: "At the same time, that truth of the gospel—if indeed it is the gospel's truth—is always spoken in love. It is never spoken for the purpose of political advancement or domination, but in the hope that each person and community might discover its true voice and its own distinctive experience of full humanity as the gospel takes root in fresh and diverse ways. *How* we speak is as important to our missional vocation as *what* we speak" (Brownson, "Speaking the Truth," p. 503).

that for this or any orthodoxy to stand a chance of proving compelling in our increasingly postmodern, post-Christian environment, a humble rather than arrogant or strident *manner of presentation* is required.[43] It is my privilege to teach a couple of courses each semester from my university's core curriculum. Teaching these courses provides me with the opportunity to impact the lives of students from various majors who are at various places in their spiritual journey. Frankly, even though I work at a Christian university, some of the students I have in class each semester do not come from Christian homes, nor do they consider themselves Christ-followers. The one thing nearly all my students have in common, however, regardless of where they are in their spiritual journey, is the influence of postmodernity on their lives.

To the degree the young people I interact with each day are indicative of the sensibilities at work in the culture at large, I feel emboldened to put forward three observations that might inform an understanding of how best to conduct ministry in our post-Christian context. First, it is apparent to me that one of the most pungent effects of postmodern thought on the members of our society, especially those who belong to the emerging generations, is a real disdain for haughty, arrogant, coercive presentations of truth claims. Second, however, many if not most of the young adults in post-Christian America, while much influenced by postmodernism, are not studied, hard-core epistemological relativists.[44] Third, many young adults in the West, despite the influence of postmodernity, actually do not mind being told that something is true, if (1) the one making the truth claim seems humble, sincere and willing to dialogue rather than demagogue,[45] and (2) they have reason to believe

---

[43]David Bosch writes regarding the impact of the emergence of postmodernity on mission: "There is no longer any room for the massive affirmations of faith which characterized the missionary enterprise of earlier times, only for a chastened and humble witness to the ultimacy of God in Jesus Christ" (Bosch, *Transforming Mission*, p. 354).

[44]Ross Hastings observes: "It seems that most ordinary people in Western society would be unable to articulate a coherent postmodern way of thinking and being, but may best be described as holding fragmented belief systems" (Hastings, *Missional God*, p. 57).

[45]Perhaps the following observation made by Robert Schreiter with respect to how "truth" is assessed in cultures where meaning is a matter of social judgment is applicable in our own ministry context. Schreiter writes: "Propositional truth might be seen as a necessary but not sufficient condition for establishing intercultural truth. Many peoples of the world have that sense already. They will not believe what strangers say until they see how strangers live." See Robert J.

that through the exchange they might discover something that is *authentic, transcendent, real.*

This emphasis on the importance of humility to a missionally faithful lifestyle should come as no surprise. The Bible is pregnant with passages that call for an attitude of humility not only toward God[46] but also toward other believers[47] and those outside the faith community as well.[48] Speaking pragmatically now, it is my contention that we should keep this biblical emphasis on humility in mind when we come across those passages where the apostle Paul encourages his readers to be intentional about living their lives in such a way as to be missionally beneficial rather than detrimental (e.g., Col 4:5-6; 1 Thess 4:11-12; 1 Tim 3:7), and as we ponder Peter's well-known ministry exhortation: "But in your hearts revere Christ as Lord. Always be prepared to give an answer to everyone who asks you to give the reason for the hope that you have. *But do this with gentleness and respect*" (1 Pet 3:15, emphasis added). And yet, before we move on, I feel the need to make clear that the call to exercise humility in our ministry approach is rooted in more than mere ministry pragmatism. It is grounded also in a theological awareness that as fully devoted followers of Christ, we are called to live our lives as *servants* (not lords) of both *reality* and our *neighbors.*

I am anticipating a more thorough discussion of this theme in the excursus appended to the next chapter when I state here that as servants of *reality* we must continually keep in mind that all of our formulations of the truth fall short of the reality; no formulation is equivalent to the reality. Thus the reality will always exceed our ability to articulate it. We will, as the philosopher of science Michael Polanyi reminds us, always know more than we can tell.[49] This is why we are servants of reality, attempting to serve it better and better by our witness to it in words and in

---

Schreiter, *The New Catholicity: Theology Between the Global and the Local* (Maryknoll, NY: Orbis Books, 1997), pp. 41-42.

[46]For example, 2 Chron 7:14; Is 66:2; Dan 10:12; Mic 6:8; Zeph 2:3; Jas 4:6, 10; 1 Pet 5:6.

[47]For example, Eph 4:2; Phil 2:3; Col 3:12; 1 Pet 3:8; 5:5.

[48]For example, Tit 3:2; Jas 3:13. Though my focus in this section is on the need for a *horizontal, presentational* humility toward other human beings, it should be acknowledged that a missional orthodoxy also requires a *vertical, confessional* humility before God (see DeVine, "Can the Church Emerge?" pp. 182-83).

[49]Michael Polanyi, *The Tacit Dimension* (Chicago: University of Chicago Press, 1966), p. 4.

deeds. The kind of theology and epistemology (or understanding of how we acquire knowledge) I advocate in this work demands that we adopt the posture of the lifelong learner, engaged in an ongoing dialogue, conversation, interaction with reality as we humbly allow reality to master us rather than vice versa.[50] Therefore, it really is inappropriate for us to engage in public theologizing in a haughty, arrogant manner as if we possessed an impeccable intellectual mastery of all the theological realities at work in the world.[51]

As servants of our *neighbors*, we are called most basically to respect them (1 Pet 2:17). This involves listening to them, caring for them, not regarding ourselves as superior to them. It also means never making use of coercive, forceful, manipulative means, even when it comes to the rhetoric we utilize in our interactions with them.[52] Christian humility (and wisdom) requires that we give the other room to seek and find rather than to have truth forced on them. Thus we must be patient as we minister to others, recognizing that they cannot leap to confidence. Even when it comes to something as important as ministering the gospel, we must treat others the same way we would want to be treated (see Mt 7:12). While most of us would always want others to tell us the truth, we would hope this could be done in a way that is neither coercive nor condescending. Since this is the way we would want the truth to be told to us, we are obligated by Christ to offer the truth to others in just the same manner.

To take the issue of humility yet a step further, I will also make reference here to the concepts of *hospitality* and *reciprocity*, which are playing an increasingly significant role in the missional conversation. A missional reading of Luke 10:1-12 (where Jesus gives ministry instructions to the seventy-two disciples sent out ahead of him) yields the ministry principle that in an attempt to forge the types of relationships with post-Christians necessary for an adequate contextualization of the

---

[50]David Bosch refers to the need for humility and self-criticism in his discussion of a modified realism in *Transforming Mission*, pp. 368-69.

[51]See George R. Hunsberger, "The Missional Voice and Posture of Public Theologizing," *Missiology* 34, no. 1 (2006): 22, as cited in Van Gelder and Zscheile, *Missional Church*, p. 143. See also Bosch, *Transforming Mission*, pp. 190-91.

[52]See Hastings, *Missional God*, p. 151.

gospel,[53] it is wise not only to show hospitality to the other, but to request it as well. Commenting on this passage, missional authors Craig Van Gelder and Dwight Zscheile assert that "the disciples were to enter deeply into the lives of the Samaritans' culture. Hospitality in mission here is reversed—not offering hospitality *to* the stranger but seeking the hospitality *of* the stranger, with all the vulnerability that implies."[54] They go on to make the important point that:

> Relying on the hospitality of the community to which you have been sent—especially in the radically vulnerable way that Jesus commands the disciples to do—changes the terms of the missionary encounter. . . . Whatever you offer in the way of sharing the peace, healing, or proclaiming the good news of the kingdom is shared in a relationship of reciprocity, mutuality, and vulnerability.[55]

It is important to note how God models this kind of missional humility for us in sending his Son into the world completely dependent on the hospitality of the human race. If we are to imitate the example of Christ in ministering the message of the kingdom to our world, this will call for more than a willingness on our part to get up close and personal with those who are not like us. There may be times when we are led by the Spirit to humbly ask the stranger to whom we long to minister to minister to us in some way first (cf. Lk 19:1-9; Jn 4:4-42)![56]

And yet, as astounding as the notion of mutual hospitality in ministry might be, the dynamic of reciprocity goes even further. Not to oversimplify, but this ministry principle suggests that as we invite the members of a "target" culture to read the Scriptures with us, we may find that our own understanding of them is impacted by the experience. Once again, Van Gelder and Zscheile explain:

> Reading the Scriptures with people in relation to their particular context can be a freeing experience for those sent in mission as well as for those who are

---

[53]Chapter two will provide a more in-depth discussion of what is involved in an "adequate" contextualization of the gospel for ours or any ministry context.

[54]Van Gelder and Zscheile, *Missional Church*, p. 132.

[55]Ibid., p. 133.

[56]See Gary Tyra, *The Holy Spirit in Mission: Prophetic Speech and Action in Christian Witness* (Downers Grove, IL: IVP Academic, 2011), pp. 12-13, 190-91.

new to the faith. The Spirit works in and among us in these encounters. From this perspective, we should anticipate learning something about the gospel from the cultures of others. The Word and the Spirit provide the critical elements that challenge syncretism and accommodation, which are always dangers, in the cross-cultural encounter. Yet the Word and the Spirit also make possible the reciprocity that opens us for renewal.[57]

My own ministry experience bears witness to this kind of reciprocity. Over the years my understanding of how the Jesus story constitutes really good news for God's world has been taken to new, deeper levels as a result of my hearing and wrestling with the kinds of questions which new and even non-Christians have brought to me and the biblical text. I have grown in my own walk with Christ as a result of conversing, studying and praying with others, even those who were not yet professing believers.

The bottom line behind this discussion of a missional hospitality and reciprocity is that in order for any of this to take place, an attitude of genuine rather than pretended humility is required. Moreover, if we want our presentations of the gospel to be faithful to both the biblical text and the missional task, we simply must keep in mind my previous observation that as it relates to doing missional ministry in an increasingly postmodern, post-Christian context, our manner matters![58]

Why a modest orthodoxy. The sentiments expressed above notwithstanding, at the end of the day the message matters as well. The term *evangelicalism* indicates that at the heart of the movement is a conviction regarding the importance of believing the gospel message, the *evangel* (see Rom 1:5; Gal 5:6; Eph 2:8-10; 1 Thess 1:3; Jas 2:20-22).

In his book *A New Kind of Christianity,* Brian McLaren offers a critique of this evangelical emphasis on believing that drips with sarcasm. He writes: "Whatever the final judgment will be, then, it will not involve God . . . scanning our brains for certain beliefs like products being

---

[57]Van Gelder and Zscheile, pp. 134-35. See also David Bosch's discussion of the concept of "interculturation" in Bosch, *Transforming Mission,* pp. 466-68.

[58]Tacit support for the idea of a humble orthodoxy can be found in Miroslav Volf's helpful and accessible discussion of what is involved in sharing wisdom (giving witness) well in our contemporary ministry context. See Miroslav Volf, *A Public Faith: How Followers of Christ Should Serve the Common Good* (Grand Rapids: Brazos, 2011), pp. 99-117.

scanned at the grocery checkout."[59] The point is taken. However, the truth is that, perhaps due to the fact that at the heart of humanity's Fall was an act of disbelief that led to disobedience (Gen 3:1-4), there are many biblical passages scattered throughout the Bible which indicate how important it is to God for human beings to *believe*,[60] and to do so in the sense of both mental assent and existential trust (e.g., see Ps 78:22). The Greek verb *pisteuō* ("I believe") appears in various forms in the Gospel of John no less than ninety-eight times. Nearly all of the passages in the fourth Gospel which encourage belief in Christ (or his name) are meaningless unless they imply a belief in certain propositions concerning him, which in turn produces the capacity for existential trust. This is especially the case with respect to those familiar passages that somehow associate believing in Jesus with the act of placing one's faith in the proposition that he is the Son of God,[61] such as:

> "Yes, Lord," she replied, "I believe that you are the Messiah, the Son of God, who is to come into the world." (Jn 11:27)

> But these are written that you may believe that Jesus is the Messiah, the Son of God, and that by believing you may have life in his name. (Jn 20:31)

So, naive or not, I offer that there is a Christian orthodoxy (right belief) that, according to the New Testament Scriptures, should be *contended for* (Jude 3) rather than *distorted* (Acts 20:30), *suppressed* (Rom 1:18), *exchanged* (Rom 1:25), *rejected* (Rom 2:8; Tit 1:14), *not agreed to* (1 Tim 6:3-5), *not acknowledged* (2 Tim 3:7), *opposed* (2 Tim 3:8), *wandered away from* (2 Tim 2:18; Jas. 5:19) or *turned away from* (2 Tim 4:4). Furthermore, the New Testament also indicates that there is a body of teaching—a set of core doctrines—so important, so crucial to the Christian faith, that it must be continually proclaimed, affirmed, defended and guarded. For instance, in his ministry instructions to Titus, the apostle Paul indicated that a necessary attribute of an elder for the

---

[59]McLaren, NKC 204.
[60]For example, see Gen 15:6; Ps 78:21-22, 32-33; 106:24-27; Mk 16:15-16; Jn 3:14-16, 18, 36; 5:24; 6:35; Rom 3:22; 4:1-4, 9-12, 18-25; 10:5-15; 1 Cor 1:21; Gal 3:7, 22; Eph 1:18-20; 1 Thess 2:13; 4:9-10; 1 Tim 4:1-3; Heb 10:35-39; 1 Pet 2:7-8; 1 Jn 5:13.
[61]For more on this, see George E. Ladd, *A Theology of the New Testament* (Grand Rapids: Eerdmans, 1993), pp. 307-8.

local church is an ability and willingness to "hold firmly to the trustworthy message as it has been taught, so that he can encourage others by sound doctrine and refute those who oppose it" (Tit 1:9). Indeed, Paul goes on to exhort Titus himself, saying: "You, however, must teach what is appropriate to sound doctrine" (Tit 2:1).[62]

Thus, the question is not: Does the Bible support the idea of a Christian dogma—a set of doctrines that, because they constitute the heart of the Christian message, deserve a dogmatic defense? Rather, the proper question is: Which of the many doctrines derived from Scripture deserve this dogmatic status? For the Bible also refers to some beliefs and doctrines which biblical scholars and theologians call *adiaphora* (i.e., indifferent or disputable matters) precisely because one's position on them is not critical to the experience of salvation (e.g., see Rom 14). The recognition that the New Testament itself makes a distinction between doctrine and dogma leads me to suggest that *a missional orthodoxy that is modest rather than overreaching in terms of its scope*[63] *will focus on those few doctrines which the Bible itself insists are crucial to the experience of salvation.* To be even more specific, I am suggesting that there are four soteriologically crucial beliefs that constitute Christian dogma precisely because they lie at the very heart of biblical Christianity:

1. Jesus is both God and human

2. Jesus' death on the cross possessed an atoning significance[64]

3. Jesus rose bodily from the grave

4. Jesus is now Lord of all[65]

There are, of course, other biblical doctrines that are basic to or

---

[62]Other passages that exhort toward a doctrinal faithfulness include Jn 8:31-32; 1 Cor 11:2; 2 Thess 2:15; 1 Tim 3:9; 4:6, 13, 16; 6:20-21; 2 Tim 1:13-14; 2:15-18; 3:14-17; 4:2-3, 7; Tit 1:9-14; 2:1-2; 1 Jn 2:20-27; and 2 Jn 1:7-11.

[63]In a similar vein, Darrell Guder refers to the need to "approach with modesty the task of gospel definition" (*Be My Witnesses*, pp. 77-78).

[64]For a discussion of why the doctrine of Christ's atoning death should be considered an element of Christian dogma despite the fact that it is not a formal article in the Nicene Creed, see DeVine, "Can the Church Emerge?" pp. 190-95.

[65]On (1), see Jn 20:31; 1 Jn 5:5, 11-12; 2 Jn 1:7-9; on (2), see 1 Cor 15:1-3; 1 Jn 2:2; 4:10; on (3), see Rom 10:9-10; 1 Cor 15:1-5; and on (4), see Rom 10:9-10; 14:9-12; 1 Cor 12:3; Phil 2:9-11; Heb 3:1, 15.

derive from these four (e.g., the virgin birth, Jesus' miracles, the return of Christ, the final judgment). These other beliefs are important and should be included in our preaching and teaching. Together, all of these doctrines fill out a biblically informed vision of the Christian faith. However, since there are no biblical passages which explicitly indicate that a belief in these ancillary doctrines is crucial to salvation, I suggest that we do not include them in that set of beliefs we categorize as Christian dogma.[66] Once again, the great need before us at this time is not for an orthodoxy that merely identifies, but one that inspires: a missional orthodoxy that, precisely because it is humble and modest as well as faithful to both the biblical text and the missional task, can be used by the Spirit of mission to cause many of our post-Christian peers to take another look at the claims of Christ.[67] My concern is that if our understanding of Christian dogma goes beyond the explicit call in Scripture to believe just a few things in order to be saved, we will overreach and begin to contend with each other over such things as the precise timing of Jesus' return, the proper way to govern a church, the

---

[66]At the end of the day, all four of the theologians contributing to the book *Four Views on the Spectrum of Evangelicalism* end up suggesting that evangelicals need to remain faithful to historic Christian orthodoxy. They differ on (1) the emphasis they place on the importance of adhering to doctrines considered dogma; (2) those doctrines they put forward as Christian dogma; and (3) how this dogma is to be determined since evangelicalism lacks a magisterium (i.e., an official dogma-determining body whose pronouncements are binding on all evangelicals). See Stanley N. Gundry, Andrew David Naselli and Collin Hansen, eds., *Four Views on the Spectrum of Evangelicalism* (Grand Rapids: Zondervan, 2011). Over against the views put forward by the four contributors to this work, I want to suggest that an understanding of Christian dogma that is biblically faithful and that does not require some sort of evangelical magisterium will maintain that some doctrines should be considered dogma simply and precisely because the Bible itself indicates that embracing them (in terms of both mental assent and existential trust) is critical to the experience of Christian salvation.

[67]In anticipation of the criticism that what I am proposing is simply Christian fundamentalism in a new dress, I contend that besides the fact that the list of christological doctrines presented here differs from the "fundamentals" presented in the booklet series published between 1910 and 1915 that gave the movement its name (see Christian Smith, *American Evangelicalism: Embattled and Thriving* [Chicago: University of Chicago Press, 1998], p. 6), there is another crucial difference. Referring to the "five 'fundamentals' of American conservative Protestant faith," Robert Schreiter reminds us that "the inerrancy of Scripture, the virginal conception of Jesus, substitutionary atonement, the bodily resurrection of Jesus, and his bodily return in the Second Coming—were chosen not because they summed up the essence of the Christian faith but because they most contradicted modernist sensibility. The reconstruction of 'true faith' in fundamentalism chooses selected items to serve as boundary markers of who is in and who is out" (Schreiter, *New Catholicity*, p. 21). As I have endeavored to make clear, this is not goal of the orthodoxy presented in this work.

nature of divine election, and so on. In this, as in every other area of life, we must ever be on guard against an innate human tendency to want to be in control.[68] At the same time, I believe that it is possible to strive to do justice to Jude 3 without attempting to control the Christian message. The key is to limit our understanding of dogma to those doctrines which the Scriptures themselves emphasize as being crucial to Christian salvation.[69] Thus, while I am willing to make the suggestion that a *little* fundamentalism never hurt anyone, I am just as willing to indict as wrongheaded and missionally unhelpful the tendency among some Christians to feel the need to go to the mat *with other Christians* over every doctrine derived from the Bible.[70] This is what I mean when I suggest that a missional orthodoxy will be modest rather than overreaching in terms of its scope.

THE DIFFERENCE BETWEEN MISSIONAL AND EMERGING

Some readers may be wondering at this point how the emerging church movement fits into the picture. After all, is it not the desire of the emerging church movement to frame the gospel in a fresh way that

---

[68]See the discussion, "Sin as Control," in Guder, *Continuing Conversion,* pp. 74-77, 87, 90, 97.

[69]I want to go on record, if only by way of footnote, asserting that the soteriological criterion I am putting forward as that which constitutes Christian dogma is not necessarily rooted in the idea that the Christian gospel is all about the saving of individual souls, nor does it necessarily produce such a view. Both Scot McKnight and Darrell Guder argue passionately against such a gospel reductionism. At the same time, it is worth noting that both McKnight and Guder, in their own ways, argue that the heart of the Christian gospel centers in the same christological doctrines that I mention. For his part, McKnight grounds the four Gospels in something he refers to as the "apostolic gospel," especially as it is articulated in 1 Corinthians 15:3-5 with Paul's very clear and concise re-presentation of several key christological doctrines. See McKnight, *King Jesus Gospel,* pp. 46-50, 61, 64-65, 68-69, 89-91. Likewise, Darrell Guder states that the apostle Paul "may have defined the gospel in its most succinct form with the words 'Christ died for our sins in accordance with the scriptures' (1 Cor 15:3). . . . The apostolic assertion in 1 Corinthians that 'Jesus' death for our sins and his resurrection by God constitute the center of the gospel of Christ" (Guder, *Continuing Conversion,* pp. 40-41). "The incarnation, death, resurrection, and ascension of our Lord are the central events of salvation history . . . the content of the gospel" (Guder, *Be My Witnesses,* p. 14). Both of these opponents of a gospel reductionism seem to agree that there is a doctrinal core to the Christian *kerygma* that centers in the four christological doctrines the Bible portrays as crucial to the experience of Christian salvation.

[70]To be fair, fundamentalist theologian Kevin Bauder asserts that there is a difference between fundamentalism and the fundamentalist movement, and that there is more than one kind of fundamentalism, not all versions of which manifest the tendency toward overactive dogmatism. See Kevin T. Bauder, "Fundamentalism," in Gundry, Naselli and Hansen, *Four Views on the Spectrum,* pp. 40-49.

proves compelling to a postmodern, post-Christian crowd? Is there not a distinction to be made between the emerging church movement and the more liberal "emerging paradigm" of Marcus Borg? If so, do we really need a *missional* orthodoxy? Hasn't the case for a *generous* orthodoxy already been made? Aren't missional and emerging the same thing?

From the outset, I want to commend anyone who, out of concern to reach our post-Christian peers, endeavors to contextualize the Christian gospel in a compelling manner without assimilating it to the socio-cultural sensibilities at work in contemporary culture. The truth is that many leaders of emerging churches want to do just this, albeit with a special focus on the members of the emerging generations.

Furthermore, I want to be sensitive to those many members of the emerging church movement who will no doubt resist the idea that Marcus Borg's emerging vision of the Christian faith and life is reflective of their theological perspective. At the heart of the emerging movement is a desire to contextualize the gospel for folks dramatically impacted by *postmodernism* in particular. In their authoritative work, *Emerging Churches,* Eddie Gibbs and Ryan Bolger define emerging churches as "communities that practice the way of Jesus within *postmodern* cultures."[71] Though Borg makes the claim that his emerging paradigm is a product of "Christianity's encounter with the modern and postmodern world,"[72] most observers place him squarely in the traditional Protestant liberal camp, operating with anti-supernaturalistic assumptions that are more modern than postmodern in orientation.[73] The way Borg associates his emerging vision of Christianity with mainline Protestantism only serves to reinforce this categorization.[74]

But this leaves us still wondering about some of the other questions posed above. Specifically, if not everyone in the emerging movement would own Borg as a representative spokesman, and if the emerging

---

[71]Gibbs and Bolger, *Emerging Churches,* p. 44 (emphasis added).
[72]Borg, HC xii.
[73]For example, see Scot McKnight, "Review"; and Gary Dorrien, "American Liberal Theology: Crisis, Irony, Decline, Renewal, Ambiguity," *Cross Currents* 55, no. 4, www.crosscurrents.org/dorrien200506.htm (accessed September 22, 2012).
[74]Borg, HC xii, 6-7, 13, 44, 86, 92, 99, 104, 120, 159, 196, 213.

movement is marked by a commitment to do ministry in a postmodern culture, what need is there for a book that focuses on a *missional orthodoxy*? Again, aren't missional and emerging the same thing?

Several important observations related to these two questions need to be made here.

There is more than one way to be missional. The first problem with equating "missional" with "emerging" is that it fails to take into account that there is more than one way to conceive of missional ministry. Van Gelder and Zscheile refer to two major alternative missiologies that emerged in the mid-twentieth century:

> These alternative ecumenical and evangelical missiologies are still very much at work within the church today, where each movement continues to express high levels of suspicion toward the other. The ecumenical approach seeks to attend primarily to a larger theological understanding of mission, especially the mission of the Triune God, leaving many evangelicals concerned that evangelism is being diluted or lost. The evangelical approach seeks to attend primarily to obeying the Great Commission and thereby focuses especially on Christology and human obedience, leaving many ecumenicals concerned that a holistic gospel is being compromised. The introduction of the missional church conversation, along with earlier initiatives, helped to provide for some bridging, with ecumenicals becoming more aware of evangelism's role in the discussion and evangelicals beginning to reconceive mission in light of the mission of the Triune God. [75]

Though this quote suggests that one of the contributions of the missional church conversation has been some "bridging" between ecumenicals and evangelicals, the fact that the authors did not intend to suggest that everyone flying the missional banner speaks with one voice is indicated by the map portraying the various "branches" or categories of missional conversation partners their book provides.[76] According to this "map," the main issue distinguishing the various branches has to do with whether the *missio Dei* (God's mission) and reign of God are understood in a "specialized" sense (i.e., God working in the world through

---

[75]Van Gelder and Zscheile, *Missional Church*, p. 25.
[76]Ibid., pp. 10-11, 67-98.

the church) or in a "generalized" sense (i.e., God working in the world beyond the church through secular history). For their part, the authors, hoping to "bring greater clarity to the missional church conversation,"[77] propose an integration of these perspectives: "The church participates in God's continuing creation and redemptive mission."[78] However, this laudable call for a synthesis notwithstanding, the fact is that currently there is more than one way of being missional—with significant differences between them. Such an observation makes a simple equation of the missional and emerging movements impossible.

Neither is the emerging church movement monolithic. Second, just as there is more than one way of being missional, there are also numerous versions of what it means to be emerging. Here is one take-away from a *Christianity Today* article provocatively titled "Five Streams of the Emerging Church: Key Elements of the Most Controversial and Misunderstood Movement in the Church Today."[79] According to the article's author, New Testament scholar Scot McKnight, there is not only a distinction to be made between emerging churches and the Emergent movement,[80] but also between various types of emerging Christians differentiated primarily by the degree to which a postmodern worldview and post-evangelical approach to theology is embraced.[81]

Missional authors Ed Stetzer and David Putnam have also made the point that not all segments of the emerging church are the same:

---

[77]Ibid., pp. 12-14.

[78]Ibid., p. 57.

[79]See Scot McKnight, "Five Streams of the Emerging Church: Key Elements of the Most Controversial and Misunderstood Movement in the Church Today," *Christianity Today*, January 9, 2007, www.christianitytoday.com/ct/2007/february/11.35.html.

[80]McKnight explains: "To prevent confusion, a distinction needs to be made between 'emerging' and 'Emergent.' Emerging is the wider, informal, global, ecclesial (church-centered) focus of the movement, while Emergent is an official organization in the U.S. and the U.K." Having identified the organization as "Emergent Village," McKnight goes on to offer the following stipulation: "While Emergent is the intellectual and philosophical network of the emerging movement, it is a mistake to narrow all of emerging to the Emergent Village" (McKnight, "Five Streams").

[81]McKnight offers that "the vast majority of emerging Christians are evangelical theologically. But they are post-evangelical in at least two ways": (1) they are suspicious of systematic theology, wary of the idea that any one theology gets it absolutely right; (2) the question of who is "in" and who is "out" pains them (McKnight, "Five Streams").

What is called the "emerging church" appears to have forked in three directions. One fork takes the same gospel in the historic form of church but seeks to make it understandable to the emerging culture. A second stream takes the same gospel but focuses on questioning and reconstructing much of the form of church. While the third stream and more extreme approach focuses on questioning and revisioning the gospel and the church. For the purpose of this discussion we will look at these three forks the Relevants, Reconstructionists, and Revisionists.[82]

According to Stetzer and Putnam, it is possible to distinguish between emerging church leaders based on the degree to which they advocate for a revision of the gospel and the church. Such an analysis lends support for the notion that there is within the emerging church movement a fair amount of diversity over some pretty important matters. If it is true that there is more than one way of being emerging, just as there is more than one way of being missional, how can a simple equation of the two movements be possible?

Mutual misgivings between members of the two movements. Because both the missional and emerging movements are committed to a contextualization of the story of Jesus for our current post-Christian culture, it is easy to see why they might be conflated. However, a third observation worth noting is that members of both movements have gone on record, expressing some serious concerns regarding the ministry practices of those in the opposing camp.

For example, after expressing appreciation for many of the attributes of emerging churches, missional church advocates Alan Roxburgh and Scott Boren feel the need to make the following distinction:

> The emergent and missional streams, however, are not necessarily the same thing. Many emergent churches seem to be new forms of attractional churches that have little sense of their neighborhoods or the missional nature of the church. The church has long sought to do church services and events in relevant ways to attract different segments of society—the seeker service being the most prominent in its aim to reach

---

[82]Ed Stetzer and David Putnam, *Breaking the Missional Code: Your Church Can Become a Missionary in Your Community* (Nashville: Broadman & Holman, 2006), p. 188.

middle-class Baby Boomers. Some emergent churches are leading in the missional conversation, charting new paths for the rest of us. But the category of emergent and the imagination of missional are two different things.[83]

Van Gelder and Zscheile make a similar observation when they express concern that—along with the church renewal movement (1960s and 1970s), the church growth movement (1970s and 1980s), the church effectiveness movement (1980s and 1990s) and the church health movement (1990s and 2000s)—the emerging church movement (1990s and 2000s) can function as just another way to "help the church remain successful within a changing context."[84] This pragmatic emphasis on strategy and technique can, say these missional experts, betray a failure on the part of some emerging church leaders to "attend first to the identity/nature of the church before seeking to address its purpose/mission."[85] These (and other) missional authors find it troubling when any type of church, whether evangelical or emerging, evidences a preoccupation with ministry pragmatism at the expense of a more profound theological reflection on the nature and purpose of the church.[86]

The distinction between emerging and missional churches drawn by Stetzer and Putnam reflects a different concern. The main critique these two evangelical missional authors level at some (not all) forms of the emerging church has to do with a willingness to revise the ministry

---

[83]See Alan J. Roxburgh and M. Scott Boren, *Introducing the Missional Church: Why It Matters, How to Become One* (Grand Rapids: Baker, 2009), pp. 53-54.

[84]Van Gelder and Zscheile, *Missional Church,* p. 8.

[85]Ibid., p. 9.

[86]At the heart of the missional movement is the premise that "what the church *is* must deeply inform what the church *does*" (Van Gelder and Zscheile, *Missional Church,* p. 64). Of course human beings act in mission, but it is crucial to understand that since God is the primary agent in mission, the church is obligated to take its ministry cues from him. Rather than doing things and then hoping God will bless their activities, the church should be asking: What is God doing, how would he have us participate with him in it? According to Van Gelder and Zscheile, "Getting the sequence right is crucial for allowing God's person and power to become fully operative within the life and ministry of the church. The sequence flows as follows: The church *is.* The church *does* what it is. The church *organizes* what it does" (p. 64). This missional concern regarding ministry agency seems to be grounded in the observation that churches that get the just-stated sequence wrong have been too willing and able to serve their own agendas when engaging in "mission" rather than attending to the purposes of God in the world.

message in a manner that fails to "maintain biblical integrity."[87] Their concern is that it is possible to overcontextualize the gospel, so to speak, for the emerging culture, resulting in a ministry message that does not accurately reflect the heart of God.

And just as it is possible to find participants in the missional camp expressing concerns over the beliefs and ministry behaviors of emerging church leaders, the converse is also true. In a well-known blog post titled "Dan Kimball's Missional Misgivings," the emerging church pastor and author expressed his concern over the lack of disciple making going on in many missional churches. Kimball's critique deserves a fairly full recitation:

> Not long ago I was on a panel with other church leaders in a large city. One missional advocate in the group stated that younger people in the city will not be drawn to larger, attractional churches dominated by preaching and music. What this leader failed to recognize, however, was that young people were coming to an architecturally cool megachurch in the city—in droves. Its worship services drew thousands with pop/rock music and solid preaching. The church estimates half the young people were not Christians before attending.
>
> Another outspoken advocate of the house church model sees it as more missional and congruent with the early church. But his church has the same problem. After fifteen years it hasn't multiplied. It's a wonderful community that serves the homeless, but there's no evidence of non-Christians beginning to follow Jesus. In the same city several mega-churches are seeing conversions and disciples matured.
>
> I realize missional evangelism takes a long time, and these churches are often working in difficult soil. We can't expect growth overnight.
>
> But given their unproven track records, these missional churches should be slow to criticize the attractional churches that are making a measurable impact. No, I am not a numbers person. I am not enamored by how many come forward at an altar call. In fact, I am a bit skeptical. But I am passionate about Jesus-centered disciples being made. And surprisingly, I find in many large, attractional churches, they are.[88]

---

[87]Stetzer and Putnam, *Breaking the Missional Code,* pp. 187-91.

[88]See Dan Kimball, "Dan Kimball's Missional Misgivings," December 2, 2008, www.outofur.com/ archives/2008/12/dan_kimballs_mi.html. See also missional author Alan Hirsch's sympathetic

So, first, there is more than one way of being missional; second, neither is the emerging church movement monolithic; and third, mutual misgivings exist between members of the two movements. The cumulative force of these three observations should be sufficient to put to rest the idea that the emerging and missional movements are synonymous. Still, I have yet to explain why, though I view the emerging church movement overall as a comrade rather than a competitor in the gospel contextualization endeavor, I believe that there is enough of a difference between missional and emerging to warrant a book that spells out why what is needed in our place and time is a missional orthodoxy that is faithful, humble and modest rather than one that is simply generous.

THE BOOK'S SECONDARY PURPOSE

A *secondary* purpose of *A Missional Orthodoxy* is to build some bridges between the traditional evangelical, missional and emerging church movements. In the preface, I indicated my belief that the tensions which exist between members of these three communities seem to center in varying understandings of the nature of the Christian gospel and what constitutes an adequate and appropriate contextualization of it for an increasingly postmodern, post-Christian culture. This observation is foundational to my sincere hope that the missional orthodoxy presented in this work can serve to produce a greater sense of unity and collegiality among many members of all three groups. In apparent agreement with this concern for consensus is Darrell Guder who, making use of a familiar metaphor, writes:

> Our theological movement tends to be like a pendulum, swinging from one side to another. And the extremes at both sides are narrow understandings of the gospel, bent on separating the inseparable, not the broad and comprehensive middle road that draws all of these important emphases together into a consensus on the whole gospel. Such consensus would be marked by a fundamental accord as well as by diversity of method and expression that the whole church experiences as enriching.

---

but critical response to Kimball's posting. Alan Hirsch, "Alan Hirsch's Response to Dan Kimball's Missional Misgivings," December 11, 2008, www.outofur.com/archives/2008/12/dan _kimballs_mi.html.

Understandable as this pendulumlike tendency is, we must learn in our theological work to view what we do as part of a much larger whole. We must view our particular work as a contribution to the understanding of a much bigger gospel. We must be very careful that we are not, again, taming and domesticating the gospel by reducing it to the manageable limits of a particular theological approach or system, or a particular cultural, social, or political interest.[89]

A key to achieving the kind of unity (but not uniformity) of which Guder speaks is a mutual embrace of a missional orthodoxy that strives to be humble in manner, modest in scope and faithful to both the text and the task. I am convinced that there is a way of contextualizing the story of Jesus that does justice to both 1 Corinthians 9:20-22 (the call to contextualize) and Jude 3 (the need to contend earnestly for the faith once for all delivered to the saints)!

Toward this end, I write as an *evangelical* with a heart open to a biblically informed *missional* approach to ministry. My principal conversation partners will be the *emerging* paradigms put forward by theologian Marcus Borg (primarily in *The Heart of Christianity*)[90] and emergent author and provocateur Brian McLaren (primarily in *A Generous Orthodoxy*).[91] Though once again it would be a mistake to put the theologies of Borg and McLaren in the same category, both of these

---

[89]See Guder, *Be My Witnesses*, pp. 228-29.

[90]Other works by Borg that will be referred to in this book include *Speaking Christian: Why Christian Words Have Lost Their Meaning—and How They Can Be Restored* (New York: HarperOne, 2011); *Meeting Jesus Again for the First Time: The Historical Jesus and the Heart of Contemporary Faith* (New York: HarperOne, 1994); *The God We Never Knew: Beyond Dogmatic Religion to a More Authentic Contemporary Faith* (New York: HarperOne, 1997); *Reading the Bible Again for the First Time* (New York: Harper One, 2001); and Marcus Borg and N. T. Wright, *The Meaning of Jesus: Two Visions* (San Francisco: HarperSanFrancisco, 1999).

[91]Brian McLaren, *A Generous Orthodoxy* (Grand Rapids: Zondervan, 2004). Please note that since this work is currently available in both hardcover and paperback editions, and because these editions differ in their pagination formatting, I will cite two sets of page number references. The first set refers to the hardcover edition; the second set, placed in brackets, refers to the paperback. Other works by McLaren that will be referenced include *A New Kind of Christianity: Ten Questions That Are Transforming the Faith* (New York: HarperOne, 2010); *Everything Must Change: When the World's Biggest Problems and Jesus' Good News Collide* (Nashville: Thomas Nelson, 2007); *The Secret Message of Jesus: Uncovering the Truth That Could Change Everything* (Nashville: Thomas Nelson, 2006); *More Ready Than You Realize* (Grand Rapids: Zondervan, 2002); *A New Kind of Christian* (San Francisco: Jossey-Bass, 2001); and *Why Did Jesus, Moses, the Buddha, and Mohammed Cross the Road? Christian Identity in a Multi-Faith World* (New York: Jericho Books, 2012).

gifted writers in their own ways offer the Christian community a vision of the Christian faith that differs in some important respects from the one held by most traditional evangelicals.

In the very first paragraph of the preface of *The Heart of Christianity*, Borg indicates that his purpose in writing is to describe two very different visions of Christianity—two different answers to the question: What does it mean to be a Christian? He goes on to indicate: "In this book, I describe two quite different answers to this question. The first is an earlier vision of Christianity; the second, an emerging vision."[92]

For his part, McLaren is famous for his assertion of the need for "a new kind of Christianity" and that "everything must change."[93] But while Borg tends to be a bit more straightforward in his approach, acknowledging his openness to the classical theological liberalism so often associated with mainline Protestantism (and stating frankly his opposition to some doctrines considered cardinal to evangelicals), McLaren is by his own admission much more obscure or "unclear" in the various theological positions he takes.[94] While this deliberate attempt at being less than clear suits his purpose of provoking conversation,[95] it also raises questions. It is not simply mean-spirited, cranky fundamentalists who are concerned that the versions of the Christian faith put forward by some emergent leaders like McLaren are not as careful as they need to be with respect to Jude 3.

To be more specific, it is my sense that the tension that exists between the traditional evangelical and emerging church movements corresponds with the doctrinal differences that result when emergent leaders like Brian McLaren seem to make theological moves that parallel those prescribed by liberal theologians such as Marcus Borg.[96] In a nutshell, the concern is that

---

[92]See Borg, HC xi.

[93]See McLaren, NKC; and McLaren, *Everything Must Change*.

[94]See McLaren, GO 23 [27].

[95]Ibid., pp. 22-23 [27].

[96]For example, see Scot McKnight's frank but fair review of Brian McLaren's *New Kind of Christianity*. McKnight offers this concluding statement: "Alas, *A New Kind of Christianity* shows us that Brian, though he is now thinking more systemically, has fallen for an old school of thought. I read this book carefully, and I found nothing new. It may be new for Brian, but it's a rehash of ideas that grew into fruition with Adolf von Harnack and now find iterations in folks like Harvey Cox and Marcus Borg. For me, Brian's new kind of Christianity is quite old. And the problem is that it's not old enough." See Scot McKnight, "Review." Other emergent leaders I associ-

some champions of the emergent vision have, like Borg, *overcorrected* to our current post-Christian ministry context, allowing the pendulum to swing a bit too far in the direction opposite of Christian fundamentalism toward a position that approximates an assimilating liberalism.[97]

Thus, given the popularity of McLaren among many emerging church leaders, it seems to me that for the tension between the traditional evangelical and emerging church communities to be resolved, any possible parallels between the emerging theologies of McLaren and Borg need to be explored with the goal of identifying when and where they really do exist, and also when and where it only seems like they do. Where there are actual parallels that produce significant theological differences between the traditional evangelical and emergent movement, the question then is: *Must we actually choose between the so-called "earlier" and "emerging" paradigms? Or is there a third alternative that, because it strives to be faithful to both the text and the task, is something the Spirit of mission can use to produce an even greater degree of missional faithfulness and fruitfulness in our place and day?*

Though it may be naive to think so, my hope is that the missional orthodoxy presented here will resonate with many members of the traditional evangelical, missional and emerging church communities, making it possible for us to achieve a greater sense of spiritual if not ecclesial unity. This in turn can enable us to pour even more of our energies into a contextualization of the gospel that can actually succeed at reaching our post-Christian peers for Christ at this critical juncture in human history.

THE METHOD TO MY MESSAGE

It is my intention, therefore, in this pendulum-taming, bridge-building work to interact with these two thoughtful, talented and influential proponents of emerging paradigms in a focused, fair and irenic—though not uncritical—manner. Indeed I will devote a fair amount of space in chapters three through ten to analyzing the theological perspectives of

---

ate with McLaren in terms of the direction of their theological trajectories include Rob Bell, Doug Pagitt, Tony Jones and Peter Rollins.

[97]See the excursus at the end of chapter two of this work for an in-depth discussion of some possible reasons for what I am referring to as the liberal/emergent overcorrection to our post-Christian context.

my dialogue partners. The goal of these analyses is not to engage in polemics per se. Rather, while affirming the desire of both authors to present to our post-Christian peers a compelling vision of the Christian faith and doing my best to differentiate between the emerging visions they offer, my aim is to proffer a third, missional alternative to the *overcorrections* that each writer has put forward. Many Christians, especially those who hail from very conservative churches, have never been exposed to the work of theologians whose positions reflect the more liberal side of the pendulum's arc. It has been my experience that students and church members from the emerging generations tend to consider it an intriguing and invaluable experience to engage in a careful study of the positions put forward by my two dialogue partners and to think more deeply and biblically about what they believe and why. I am hopeful that the majority of my readers will feel the same way.

That said, I want to stipulate from the outset that I consider many of the emerging paradigm's critiques of fundamentalism (and the epistemological foundationalism that feeds it)[98] to be valid. For missional reasons these critiques must be paid some serious attention. There really is too much dogmatism, legalism, judgmentalism, pugilism, separatism and so on going on in traditional evangelical churches!

At the same time, in the process of mounting their critique of Christian fundamentalism, some of those promoting the emerging vision have put forward some false antitheses that require readers to choose between caricatures of the earlier (traditional) perspective and winsome presentations of the emerging view. This method of argumentation, while often effective, is not really honest and is ultimately not helpful as a means of promoting missional faithfulness and fruitfulness. For all of the popular appeal of an overcontextualized Christian message, at the end of the day I am not convinced that it is one that leads to a genuinely saving faith in Christ and holistic experience of his kingdom.

All of this leads to the basic methodological premise of this work.

---

[98]For example, see Dave Tomlinson, *The Post-Evangelical,* rev. ed. (Grand Rapids: Zondervan, 2003), pp. 92-93; John Franke, "Christian Faith and Postmodern Theory: Theology and the Nonfoundationalist Turn," in *Christianity and the Postmodern Turn: Six Views,* ed. Myron B. Penner (Grand Rapids: Brazos, 2005), pp. 105-21; McLaren, *New Kind of Christian,* pp. 54-59; McLaren, *More Ready,* p. 131.

Because of my conviction that a missional orthodoxy can and should function as a bridge-building alternative to the emerging, missional and evangelical approaches to theology and ministry, I propose that by working our way through the various false antitheses (which vividly portray the eccentric positions at both ends of the theological spectrum) put forward by my two dialogue partners, we will be able to sketch the rough contours of a biblically and missionally faithful alternative.[99]

The next chapter will focus on various contextualization options and demonstrate why I believe the one associated with a missional orthodoxy can produce the kind of missional faithfulness and fruitfulness God desires and deserves. In the process, I will present the case that the contextualization approaches utilized by my two dialogue partners end up failing the biblical and missional faithfulness tests.

However, before I conclude this first chapter, I want to underscore once again how crucial it is for all evangelicals (traditional evangelicals in particular) to reckon with the possibility that the cultural sensitivity at work in the theologizing of both Borg and McLaren is something all evangelicals should pay attention to. Though we may end up feeling the need to nudge their theological conclusions toward a greater fidelity to the biblical witness, this does not mean that we cannot gain some crucial insights as to what is going on in the hearts and minds of our post-Christian peers and, therefore, what some of the existential issues are that a biblically *and* missionally faithful contextualization of the gospel will need to address in order to prove compelling.

Those of us who consider ourselves traditional evangelicals really do need to learn how to be more missional and emerging. It might help if we were to gain a better understanding of what a truly adequate and appropriate contextualization of the gospel involves. It is toward just such an endeavor that we turn our attention now.

---

[99]This dialectical approach is reminiscent of the one suggested by David Bosch who wrote: "It is only with the force field of apparent opposites that we shall begin to approximate a way of theologizing for our own time in a meaningful way" (Bosch, *Transforming Mission*, p. 376). Shults reveals a similar approach: by "engaging representatives from both [the analytical and continental philosophical] traditions, I hope to show how we can work together" (Shults, *Postfoundationalist Task*, p. xii).

2

OUR CURRENT MINISTRY CONTEXT

Searching for the Right Response

Though it may be naive to do so, I have indicated that this book's primary aim is to articulate a vision of the Christian faith and life that, because it strives to be faithful to both the biblical text and missional task, is something the Spirit of mission can use to invite many of our post-Christian peers to take another look at Christ and his church. I also suggested that a secondary purpose of this work is to attempt to build several bridges between the traditional evangelical, missional and emerging church communities. Ironically, in order to accomplish the goal of relieving at least some of the tension that seems to exist between some members of these three movements, we must first become acutely aware of where the real rather than imagined pinch points are. Such an understanding is crucial if we want to deal with the issues of disagreement that are substantial rather than superficial, and if we are going to begin speaking to rather than past one another.

Again, not to oversimplify, my sense is that much of the tension among the three movements seems to center in their significantly different understandings of what constitutes an adequate and appropriate contextualization of the Christian faith for an increasingly postmodern, post-Christian culture. Theoretically at least, if members of the three movements were to come to terms regarding a contextualization process they all felt comfortable with, a lot of the suspicion and acrimony would be alleviated, and energies could be invested in gospel proclamation and demonstration rather than polemics.

This is why, before examining how a missional orthodoxy might treat each of the traditional theological loci (see part two), it seems wise to discuss the topic of gospel contextualization and attempt to explain what it is and isn't, and how and why the traditional evangelical, missional and emerging communities differ in their approaches to it. Though it may be a naive hope, I would like to think that as we engage this topic we might discover that the missional orthodoxy I am proposing has what it takes missiologically and epistemologically, as well as theologically, to enable these three important movements to become real colleagues rather than competitors in the ministry contextualization endeavor.

THREE MAIN CONTEXTUALIZATION OPTIONS

I am not a missiologist by training, but I will offer that despite the fact that "there is no shortage of terms used to describe the activity of relating the gospel to local cultures and contexts,"[1] it is possible to discern within the emerging/missional literary corpus at least three very basic understandings of what it means to contextualize the gospel for a given ministry context. At the risk of gross oversimplification, I will suggest that between two noncontextualizing options—the essential *refusal to contextualize* the message that is often at work in Christian fundamentalism and an *abject assimilation* of the faith that is often associated with Christian liberalism—the three contextualization options currently at work in our post-Christian context can be labeled as *contextualization (indigenization), recontextualization* and *accommodation.*[2]

As figure 2.1 indicates, I suggest that these three legitimate gospel contextualization options (indigenization, recontextualization and accommodation) can be placed on a continuum that reflects not only their

---

[1]Dean Flemming, *Contextualization in the New Testament: Patterns for Theology and Ministry* (Downers Grove, IL: InterVarsity Press, 2005), p. 18. See also David J. Bosch, *Transforming Mission: Paradigm Shifts in Theology of Mission* (Maryknoll, NY: Orbis, 2011), p. 431.

[2]Missiologist Lamin Sanneh seems to offer implicit support for the idea that there are two non-contextualizing options that need to be avoided when, speaking of mission and syncretism in the expansion of Christianity in the earliest era, he writes: "While ascetic renunciation was not a viable option, assimilation saddled Christianity with the problem of cultural compromise." Lamin Sanneh, *Translating the Message: The Missionary Impact on Culture* (Maryknoll, NY: Orbis Books, 2009), p. 43.

position between the two noncontextualizing possibilities, but also their concerns vis-à-vis faithfulness to the biblical text on the one hand and the missional task on the other. I am suggesting further that in a general sense it is possible to associate each of these three contextualization options with a tendency toward either theological conservatism or theological liberalism. Before proceeding to a brief analysis of these three basic understandings of contextualization, I need to carefully articulate four crucial presuppositions at work in my approach to this topic.[3]

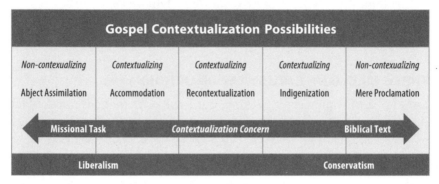

Figure 2.1.

First, despite any postmodern concern regarding the limits of language and totalizing, imperialistic metanarratives, the theological realism that I will advocate later in this chapter asserts that it is indeed possible to communicate the gospel in a cross-cultural manner that does justice to both the biblical text and the missional task. Darrell Guder insists that "the translatability of the gospel is a basic theme of missiological thought and practice."[4] Guder goes on to provide an explanation for this cross-cultural translatability, implicitly demonstrating his own embrace of a theological realism:

---

[3]See the discussion of the importance of the "pre-understanding" the interpreter brings to the biblical text in general and the question of how the gospel should be interpreted in particular in Bruce J. Nicholls, *Contextualization: A Theology of Gospel and Culture* (Vancouver: Regent College Publishing, 1979), pp. 39-45.

[4]Darrell L. Guder, *The Continuing Conversion of the Church* (Grand Rapids: Eerdmans, 2000), p. 78. In turn, Guder bids his readers to take note of Lamin Sanneh's work on the translatability of the Christian message in Sanneh, pp. 1-129. See also Craig Van Gelder, *The Ministry of the Missional Church* (Grand Rapids: Baker, 2007), p. 61; Ross Hastings, *Missional God, Missional Church: Hope for Re-Evangelizing the West* (Downers Grove, IL: IVP Academic, 2012), p. 166.

Confession of faith in all languages is possible because of the distinctive character of God's action, as it leads to faith. God's self-communication takes the form of incarnation in history, events in which God encounters us and enables us to recognize that it is God who speaking and acting. . . .

By the gift of God's Spirit, this witness may be translated into every human setting, since Jesus may be met and known in every human setting. The particularity of Jesus, a man in the first century Jewish culture of Palestine, can be translated into the particularity of every other culture and place. . . . The Word continues to become flesh as it is witnessed to. This is possible because he, this particular man Jesus, is risen and alive, and "all authority in heaven and on earth has been given to [him]" (Matt. 28:18).[5]

Second, my conviction is that as we strive to contextualize the Christian message for a target audience, the goal should be a presentation of the gospel that is *compelling* as well as *comprehensible*.[6] Obviously at work in the contextualization process is the desire to enable the members of a target audience to understand the message being presented to them. But mere comprehension, as important as it is, is not the only goal. A presentation can be comprehensible without proving compelling. A fully adequate approach to gospel contextualization will also be marked by the missionary's desire for the members of the target audience to hear the Christian message as *good news*—such good news that it must be embraced and acted on at all costs (see Mt 13:44-46), despite whatever new countercultural beliefs and behaviors it calls for. Further, what makes for a compelling presentation is not only its coherence, but its *existential relevance and impact* as well. The Christian

---

[5]Guder, *Continuing Conversion*, pp. 80-81. At the same time, of course, the gospel's translatability also means that the Christian faith can take on various culturally impacted forms as it is lived out in various settings. This sometimes produces a certain uneasiness in Christian missionaries concerned to maintain the integrity of the Christian message (see ibid., pp. 90-92). As will be indicated below, the key is to distinguish between preserving the core doctrines that lie at the heart of the gospel and embracing a culturally impacted understanding of the way the gospel functions as good news within a particular ministry context (along with the contextually sensitive manner in which the Christian faith is to be lived out by members of that context so that it becomes their own).

[6]Guder speaks of the need for the church's witness to the world to be "understandable" and "credible." See Darrell Guder, "Missional Hermeneutics: The Missional Vocation of the Congregation," *Mission Focus: Annual Review* 15 (2007): 141.

message should address the existential questions and needs of the members of the target audience in a way that justifies its being touted as "good news" despite the way it will inevitably present certain challenges to the current way of life within the cultural context.[7] Indeed, as New Testament scholar Dean Flemming argues, a biblically informed understanding of gospel contextualization will

> refer to the dynamic and comprehensive process by which the gospel is incarnated within a concrete historical or cultural situation. This happens in such a way that the gospel both comes to authentic expression in the local context and at the same time prophetically transforms the context. Contextualization seeks to enable the people of God to live out the gospel in obedience to Christ within their own cultures and circumstances.[8]

I will address the incarnational and transformational aspect of genuine gospel contextualization later on in this chapter. For now, let me simply say that what all this means is that a simple *translation* of a gospel tract, portion of Scripture (e.g., the Gospel of John) or rendering of the Christ-event (i.e., Jesus' birth, life, death, resurrection, current high-priestly ministry and eventual return) into the local vernacular is not going to constitute a full contextualization of the gospel. *The Christian gospel has not been fully contextualized until the reasons why the Christ-*

---

[7]Speaking of the advent of "contextual theology" within missional rather than academic settings, Robert Schreiter explains that "without reducing theological expression to a mere reflection determined by context, theologians in these settings came to realize that, if Christianity was to engage the hearts and minds of believers, then it must take the context that shapes their lives and in which their communities are rooted much more intentionally and seriously." Robert J. Schreiter, *The New Catholicity: Theology Between the Global and the Local* (Maryknoll, NY: Orbis Books, 1997), pp. 1-2. At the same time, Schreiter is careful to reiterate that "theology must not be reduced to context in a crude contextualism, for then it is likely to lose its critical edge as it becomes simply a product of its surroundings. The relation to context is always one of intimacy and distance at the same time. It must be rooted in the context, yet be able to take stock of the context at the same time" (pp. 3-4). Karl Barth makes essentially the same point when he asserts that though the process of contextualization requires a sensitivity to the felt needs among the members of the target audience, the gospel must not be accommodated to these felt needs. Indeed, genuine Christian mission will at times tell "man to his face, that he misunderstands his own deep needs." See Karl Barth, "Questions Which 'Christianity' Must Face," *The Student World* 25, no. 1 (1932): 96-98, as cited in John G. Flett, *The Witness of God: The Trinity, "Missio Dei," Karl Barth, and the Nature of Christian Community* (Grand Rapids: Eerdmans, 2010), p. 85. See also my discussion of "The Global Growth of Pentecostalism as an Expression of Missional Faithfulness" in Gary Tyra, *The Holy Spirit in Mission: Prophetic Speech and Action in Christian Witness* (Downers Grove, IL: IVP Academic, 2011), pp. 105-7.
[8]Flemming, *Contextualization*, p. 19.

event or story of Jesus spells good news for the members of the target au-
dience, despite the challenges to the socio-cultural-religious status quo its
acceptance involves, have been made crystal clear. Thus, doing theology
(speaking and writing about who God is, what he is up to, what he wants
for and from his creation, and how human beings should respond to
him) is necessarily involved in the contextualization process, as Paul's
presentation of the gospel before the meeting of the Areopagus in
Athens makes clear (see Acts 17:16-34).

Third, it is not uncommon for contemporary discussions of contextualization to make the point that the gospel must not be reduced, in
Flemming's words, to "a set of prefabricated formulations that can be
carried about and unpacked for all situations."[9] Instead, he argues, the
gospel has to do with "the transforming story of God's self-giving love
revealed above all in the life, death and resurrection of Jesus Christ" and
that "the gospel is too pregnant with meaning to be confined to a single
set of terms or images, or to one way of telling the story." Indeed,
Flemming asserts that "when we listen to the New Testament witness to
Christ, what we hear is not a theological monotone but a chorus of different voices." He goes on to cite with approval the idea that the New
Testament provides us with a collection of "Holy Spirit-inspired 'contextualizations'" that "allow the one gospel to be expressed and applied in a
variety of ways, using language, images and ideas that make sense to the
audience."[10] According to Flemming, "This pattern of context-sensitive
theologizing legitimates—even mandates—appropriate theological diversity in our own time. The multitextured gospel story must be told and
lived out in flexible forms as it engages new contexts. Otherwise, it will
never be truly understood or embodied."[11]

At the same time, Flemming also acknowledges that because there is
"one gospel,"[12] there is such a thing as "a genuine representation of the

---

[9]Flemming, *Contextualization*, p. 296.
[10]Ibid., p. 297. The reference to "Holy Spirit-inspired contextualizations" is from David J. Hes-
selgrave and Edward Rommen, *Contextualization: Meanings, Methods and Models* (Grand Rapids: Baker, 1989), p. 236. See also Guder, *Continuing Conversion*, pp. 92-96.
[11]Flemming, *Contextualization*, p. 297. See also the chapter titled "The Challenge of Reductionism" in Guder, *Continuing Conversion*, pp. 97-119.
[12]Flemming, *Contextualization*, p. 297.

gospel" that we must be careful not to stray away from in our attempts at doing contextual theology.[13] He articulates this crucial contextualization concern in this way:

> Where do we draw the line of demarcation between genuine contextualization and inappropriate syncretism that compromises the "truth of the gospel" (Gal 2:5, 14)? How do we recognize when the story being told is no longer the gospel story? It is not always easy to discern when theological innovation is healthy and when it is not.[14]

This raises the question that is at the heart of the idea of a missional *orthodoxy:* By what criterion do we arrive at an understanding of what constitutes a *genuine* representation of the gospel?

For his part, Flemming points readers back to the gospel itself as that which "provides coherence to the New Testament witness" despite its "many diverse voices."[15] He then defines the gospel: "Fundamentally, the gospel is news of what has happened. It proclaims what God *has done* in Jesus' life and ministry, death and resurrection, and what God *will do* to bring Jesus' saving mission to a consummation."[16] According to Flemming, "This Christ-centered story of God's intervention in human history is told explicitly in the Gospels and is assumed, interpreted and expanded in the other New Testament writings."[17] At the same time, "the New Testament writers do not seem to be interested in precisely defining the boundaries of what is genuine theology and what is not. They offer no definitive articulation of the gospel to use as a template and no single attempt to summarize the gospel story as a whole."[18] These statements by themselves can make it sound as though the primary criterion we possess for assessing the faithfulness of a gospel contextualization is some sort of implicit understanding of "the central gospel proclamation of what God has done in Christ."[19]

---

[13]Ibid., p. 298.

[14]Ibid., p. 302.

[15]Ibid., p. 300.

[16]Ibid. See also the excellent examination of the thesis that "the fundamental certainty of biblical faith is the fact that there is good news about God," in Guder, *Continuing Conversion,* pp. 28-48.

[17]Flemming, *Contextualization,* p. 300.

[18]Ibid., p. 303.

[19]Ibid. David Bosch seems also to suggest that there is something about the gospel's intrinsic functioning as a "sign of contradiction" vis-á-vis every culture that should allow it to function

However, from my perspective there is a problem with defining a genuine representation of the gospel simply as one that stays true to the "one coherent story" as it is portrayed in Scripture. This approach does not seem to take into consideration the possibility of contemporary church leaders failing to agree on what that "one coherent story" is really about. As the remainder of this book will demonstrate, the truth is that the influence of both modernity and postmodernity has been huge, affecting even the way theologians understand the nature of the gospel and the kingdom of God that is at the center of Jesus' proclamation and demonstration.

Furthermore, it is hard for me *not* to find in the New Testament much more of a "definitive articulation of the gospel" than some are willing to acknowledge. For example, in 1 Corinthians 15 we read:

> Now, brothers and sisters, I want to remind you of the gospel I preached to you, which you received and on which you have taken your stand. By this gospel you are saved, if you hold firmly to the word I preached to you. Otherwise, you have believed in vain. For what I received I passed on to you as of first importance: that Christ died for our sins according to the Scriptures, that he was buried, that he was raised on the third day according to the Scriptures, and that he appeared to Cephas, and then to the Twelve. After that, he appeared to more than five hundred of the brothers and sisters at the same time, most of whom are still living, though some have fallen asleep. Then he appeared to James, then to all the apostles, and last of all he appeared to me also, as to one abnormally born. (1 Cor 15:1-8)

The way Paul refers to the "gospel" in this passage certainly seems to suggest that *he intended to provide his readers with a definitive articulation of at least the heart of it.* Yes, the fact that he refers in verse 2 to "the word I preached to you," implies that there was a larger message which he summarizes here. But at the very least this passage indicates that, for Paul, the historical facts of Jesus' death, burial and resurrection are at the center of *his* gospel message.[20]

---

as a safeguard against theological assimilation. See Bosch, *Transforming Mission*, p. 466.

[20]The fact that Paul uses phrases such as "my gospel" (Rom 2:16; 16:25; 2 Tim 2:8) and "this gospel" (1 Cor 15:2; Eph 3:7; Col 1:16; 2 Tim 1:11) may indicate that there were other versions

On the basis of such passages I have specified four christological doctrines that I believe constitute the very heart of the Christian faith *precisely because the Scriptures themselves indicate their importance to Christian salvation.* By way of review, these four crucial christological verities are (1) Jesus is both God and human;[21] (2) Jesus' death on the cross possessed an atoning significance;[22] (3) Jesus rose bodily from the grave;[23] and (4) Jesus is now Lord of all.[24] These four christological truths render the Christ-event—Jesus' birth, ministry, death, resurrection, current high-priestly ministry and eventual return—as good news for the entire cosmos. They underwrite the gospel or story of Jesus in such a way that without them, the gospel loses its impact; the story of Jesus loses its significance for both Israel and the world at large.[25]

That a crucial connection exists between the christological verities and the Christian faith is indicated by the fact the rest of the New Testament seems to indicate a general apostolic consensus regarding the manner in which the Jesus story spells good news for the world as a whole. What unites this shared understanding of the significance of the Jesus story is a common commitment to the four christological truths. None of the apostles denied Jesus' deity, the atoning nature of his death, his bodily resurrection or his present lordship. Instead, these themes were reflected time and again in their writings and, we presume, in their preaching.

At the same time, the apostolic correspondence in the New Testament indicates that the precise manner in which the Jesus story spells good news could be articulated a bit differently given the unique set of circumstances at work in each ministry context (Rome, Corinth, Galatia,

---

of the gospel at work in Paul's day. Of course, according to Gal 1:6-9, we also know that Paul considered these other versions of the gospel to be false—actual perversions of the gospel that he summarizes here in 1 Cor 15 and alludes to in Gal 1:1-5.

[21]See Jn 20:31; 1 Jn 5:5, 11-12; 2 Jn 1:7-9.

[22]See 1 Cor 15:1-3; 1 Jn 2:2; 4:10.

[23]See Rom 10:9-10; 1 Cor 15:1-5.

[24]See Rom 10:9-10; cf. Rom 14:9-12; 1 Cor 12:3; Phil 2:9-11; Heb 3:1, 15. For a discussion of why the doctrine of Christ's atoning death should be considered an element of Christian dogma despite the fact that it is not a formal article in the Nicene Creed, see Mark DeVine, "Can the Church Emerge Without or with Only the Nicene Creed?" in *Evangelicals and Nicene Faith,* ed. Timothy George (Grand Rapids: Baker, 2011), pp. 190-95.

[25]Guder, *Continuing Conversion,* pp. 29-30, 44-48.

Ephesus, etc.). Thus, the way the apostle Paul preached the gospel in Asia (Acts 13:13-41) was much different than the way he did so in Athens (Acts 17:16-30), even though at the heart of both messages were either explicit or implicit allusions to the christological verities.

How do we reconcile what appears to be the apostles' shared embrace of these christological truths with the freedom they exercised in how they articulated the significance of the Jesus story within various ministry contexts? The answer is *not* to suppose that the New Testament lacks a definitive articulation of the meaning of the gospel, but to make a necessary distinction between the christological principles that empower the Jesus story and the contextually sensitive manner in which that story is presented as good news for different audiences.

A careful read of the epistolary literature reveals that a common commitment to the four christological truths is precisely what *provides coherence* among the various ways the New Testament authors contextualized the Jesus story.[26] Therefore, while we do indeed possess a certain flexibility in how we understand and declare the way the Jesus story spells good news for different cultural settings, the *essential* meaning of the gospel is not up for grabs. The apostolic presentations of the gospel in the New Testament are contextualizations, but not just any contextualizations. There is an authoritative aspect to the apostolic understanding of the good news as revealed in these various contextualizations. We therefore possess enough of a definitive articulation of the gospel in the New Testament to take 1 Corinthians 15:2 and Jude 3 seriously. Our contextualizations of the gospel can and should be both culturally sensitive and canonically informed. How we present the gospel must not only be true to the Jesus story, but also to the apostolic consensus regarding the gospel, which centers in those christological principles that underwrite the Jesus story.

Figure 2.2 demonstrates that (1) the christological verities are at the heart of the Jesus story; (2) all the apostles possessed a common commitment to a Jesus story empowered by the christological verities; and (3) our missional presentations of the gospel should therefore strive to

---

[26]Flemming, *Contextualization*, pp. 297, 300.

communicate to various ministry contexts how the Jesus story spells good news for them in unique and culturally particular ways, while also calling for an existentially effective embrace of the four christological verities.

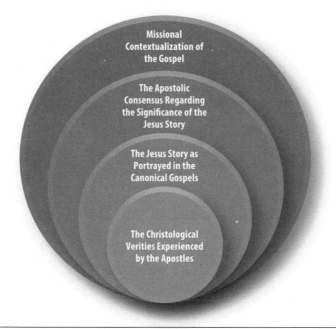

Figure 2.2. The relationship between the christological verities and the gospel

Support for this understanding of the relationship between the christological truths and the gospel that must be contextualized in a missional manner is not without support from some prominent theological and missiological voices. Scot McKnight grounds the Gospels in the apostolic gospel, especially as it is articulated in 1 Corinthians 15:3-5 with Paul's very clear and concise re-presentation of several key christological doctrines.[27] According to Robert Schreiter, the "central message" of

---

[27]Scot McKnight, *The King Jesus Gospel: The Original Good News Revisited* (Grand Rapids: Zondervan, 2011), pp. 46-50, 61, 64-65, 68-69, 89-91. Furthermore, even though McKnight agrees with the emphasis on the gospel as story, he can also say that "I now see the creeds, especially the Apostles' Creed and the Nicene Creed, or the Niceno-Constantinopolitan Creed, as fundamental to the faith of all Christians." Indeed, he goes on to stipulate that "'creed' and 'gospel' are intimately connected, so intimately one can say the creed is the gospel" (p. 63). This

Christianity is about "the passion, death and resurrection of Jesus Christ."[28] Darrell Guder states that the apostle Paul "may have defined the gospel in its most succinct form with the words 'Christ died for our sins in accordance with the scriptures' (1 Cor 15:3),"[29] and with "the apostolic assertion in 1 Corinthians that 'Jesus' death for our sins and his resurrection by God constitute the center of the gospel of Christ."[30] Moreover, when summarizing the ministry message, Guder seems to allude to each of the four christological verities, demonstrating how important they are to God's overarching purposes:

> This good news is rooted in God's self-disclosure as loving, saving, reconciling, and redeeming. The incarnation of Jesus is the climax of that self-disclosure. Jesus' message of the kingdom of God, the cross and resurrection, and the basic confession that Jesus is the Savior and the Lord who is bringing in the kingdom all define the evangel. That evangel is the heart of Christian mission.[31]

Flemming himself implies that a doctrinal core lies at the heart of the Jesus story when he cites, as an indication of the gospel's coherence, "Paul's bedrock confession that Christ died for our sins and was raised according to the Scriptures (1 Cor 15:3-4), Peter's witness to the Roman God-fearer Cornelius (Acts 10:34-43) and Revelation's song in praise of the Lamb who was slain to redeem the nations (Rev 5:9)."[32] According to Andrew Walls, it is first and foremost a common commitment to some central beliefs regarding the "ultimate" and "final" significance of "the person of Jesus called the Christ" that provides remarkable continuity in the way various cultures throughout history have manifested their respective understandings of and devotion to the Christian faith.[33] Finally, Bruce Nicholls likewise speaks

---

leads him to conclude that "denial of the creed is tantamount to denying the gospel itself because what the creeds seek to do is bring out *what is already in the Bible's gospel*" (p. 65, emphasis original).

[28]Schreiter, *New Catholicity,* p. 38.

[29]Guder, *Continuing Conversion,* p. 40.

[30]Ibid., p. 41.

[31]Ibid., pp. 1-2.

[32]Flemming, *Contextualization,* p. 300.

[33]Andrew F. Walls, *The Missionary Movement in Christian History: Studies in the Transmission of Faith* (Maryknoll, NY: Orbis, 1996), pp. 6-7.

of the possibility of a "gospel core" that is essentially "trans-cultural" in nature.[34]

In sum, while I agree with Flemming that we should take our contextualization cues from what is modeled for us in the New Testament,[35] I am suggesting that we must also take seriously the apostolic consensus regarding the gospel. While a theoretical difference can be made between the four cardinal christological verities and the Jesus story as it is portrayed in the four Gospels—or even between the Jesus story and any presentation of how it constitutes good news in a particular ministry situation—a faithful contextualization of the gospel will either explicitly or implicitly include both aspects. Each particular audience will be called to embrace (both mentally and existentially) the four cardinal christological commitments and to live the life of love that follows from them (see 1 Jn 3:23).[36]

To be sure, these doctrines do not possess any sort of magical saving power. What I am presenting here is neither a fideism nor a creedalism, neither a mysticism nor a scholasticism. Rather, it is the Jesus of the doctrines—the Jesus we encounter when we embrace in a theologically real way the verities behind these doctrines—who saves us.[37] Indeed, it is the effect of these four christological commitments on the lives of individuals and the cultures they inhabit that affords the story of Jesus its remarkable transformational capacity.[38] The incarnated verity behind

---

[34]Nicholls, *Contextualization*, p. 38.

[35]Ibid., pp. 15-16, 23-24, 296-300, 321.

[36]Thus, though David Bosch seems to indicate that there is something about the "gospel" or "word of Christ" that must not be allowed to "become culture's prisoner" (Bosch, *Transforming Mission*, p. 466; see also Walls, *Missionary Movement*, pp. 8-9), I wish he would have been more careful to distinguish between an apparent gospel essence that is transcultural and all subsequent *theologizing about the gospel* that is ineluctably contextual. Bosch writes: "The relationship between the Christian message and culture is a creative and dynamic one, and full of surprises. There is no eternal theology, no *theologia perennis* which may play the referee over 'local theologies'" (Bosch, *Transforming Mission*, p. 466).

[37]Guder, *Continuing Conversion*, pp. 81-82.

[38]Andrew Walls reminds us of "the impossibility of separating an individual from his social relationships and thus from his society" and of the fact that it is this recognition that has produced within Christian history the "desire to indigenize"—to find a way to "live as a Christian and yet as a member of one's own society" (Walls, *Missionary Movement*, p. 7). At the same time, "Along with the indigenizing principle which makes his faith a place to feel at home, the Christian inherits the 'pilgrim principle,' which whispers to him that he has no abiding city and warns him that to be faithful to Christ will put him out of step with his society; for that society

these four christological doctrines makes a missional orthodoxy both possible and necessary.[39]

This leads me to me to a fourth crucial presupposition. As the following analysis of the three most basic approaches to gospel contextualization will indicate, in the minds of the New Testament writers there is an essential relationship between several crucial christological commitments and the gospel. This makes it both possible and necessary to distinguish between the *assimilation* of the gospel and its *accommodation*. This distinction may seem arbitrary since some scholars will use "accommodation" and "assimilation" to refer to the same thing—that is, the complete capitulation of the gospel to the plausibility structures at work in a ministry context, a syncretizing of the Christian message with the religious, moral and political sensibilities prevalent within the culture.[40] Precisely how an accommodation of the gospel differs from its assimilation, and why both are problematic, will be spelled out below.

Now that I have made explicit the "pre-understanding" that I bring to the discussion,[41] let's proceed now to a brief analysis of each of the contextualization options.

The idea of indigenization. I know from personal experience that

---

has never existed, in East or West, ancient time or modern, which could absorb the word of Christ painlessly into its system" (p. 8). See also Guder, *Continuing Conversion*, pp. 84-85; Hastings, *Missionary God*, p. 148.

[39]Not surprisingly, I tend to view any sort of antithesis between the four christological verities and the reality of Jesus as dubious. What I am advocating is a biblically informed, Spirit-empowered christological realism which strives to do justice to the many invitations/exhortations we find in the New Testament to believe into *(eis)* Jesus and the many passages that seem to indicate that what we believe about Jesus is of paramount importance. For instance, I wonder if taken together passages such as Jn 2:23-25 and Jn 16:25-31 might indicate a concern on the part of Jesus that we know him for who he truly is. Seeing him as a mere prophet, even one who can work wonders, is not enough. A real relationship with the real Jesus requires that we know who he really is. Put differently, real, saving faith involves an existentially effective commitment to the verities because the real, saving Jesus is the Jesus of the verities. Any other Jesus is a "false Christ" (cf. Mt 24:24), likely belonging to a false gospel (Gal 1:6-9). Thus, while I will certainly acknowledge that the christological doctrines are not themselves the object of our faith, I will insist that because they are by God's design the means by which we encounter the object of our faith, they are indispensable to the gospel. A missional orthodoxy will therefore attempt to provide an "answer" to any proposed antithesis between the real Jesus and the christological verities concerning him.

[40]For more on the concept of a plausibility structure, see Lesslie Newbigin, *The Gospel in a Pluralist Society* (Grand Rapids: Eerdmans, 1989), pp. 8-11, 95-102. See also Bosch, *Transforming Mission*, p. 368; Hastings, *Missional God*, pp. 38-39, 61.

[41]See Nicholls, *Contextualization*, pp. 39-45.

when some evangelicals speak of contextualizing the gospel, they really have a form of *indigenization* in mind. This understanding of the contextualization process naively assumes that while ministry methods might vary from context to context, the gospel message can and should remain absolutely pristine. Once again, when I refer to the *gospel message,* I am not speaking about the doctrinal core at the heart of the Christian gospel, but *the way these core christological doctrines play out as good news in God's world and what the Christian life should look like in light of this good news.*[42]

The idea behind indigenization is that the missionary possesses a pristine and therefore impeccable grasp of the *gospel message* and that its contextualization amounts to a "clothing of the gospel in traditional cultural elements which facilitates its communication in a relevant way" to the target audience.[43] Missing from the indigenization approach is any serious "attempt to allow the whole context, including the social and political dimensions of a culture, to influence the way in which the gospel is expressed."[44] More than that, the indigenization approach does not take into account the possibility that interacting with the sociocultural ethos of a culture might lead to an improved understanding of what God is up to in the world or enable us to see something about ourselves that may be limiting our understanding of how the Christ-event plays out as good news in God's world as a whole, and this part of God's world in particular.[45] I will have more to say about the paradigmatic ministry story related in Acts 10 momentarily. For now I simply want to point out that it was apparently after a fairly brief period of interaction in the home of Cornelius with some pre-Christian (Gentile) hearers of the gospel message that the apostle Peter was led by the Spirit to say: "I now realize how true it is that God does not show favoritism but accepts from every nation the one who fears him and does what is

---

[42]For more on the diverse ways the Christian faith has found expression over the years, see the chapter titled "Culture and Coherence in Christian History," in Walls, *Missionary Movement,* pp. 16-25.

[43]John Corrie, "Mission and Contextualization," www.trinity-bris.ac.uk/assets/files/articles/corrie_mission_and_contextualisation.pdf (accessed September 30, 2012).

[44]Ibid.

[45]See Guder's discussion of "Translation as Continuing Conversion of the Church," in *Continuing Conversion,* pp. 87-92.

right" (Acts 10:34-35). Apparently God used Peter's interaction with the members of a particular ministry context to help him better understand how the core christological doctrines at the heart of the Christian faith play out as good news in the world. This in turn shaped Peter's ministry practice within that context, particularly as he began baptizing Gentile converts into the community of faith. Again, I am not suggesting that the four cardinal christological doctrines can ever be legitimately absented from the Christian faith. However, there seems to be more to the contextualization of the gospel than simply altering the means by which the Christ-event is communicated. Though well intentioned, the indigenization process of contextualization ultimately fails the missional faithfulness test.

The fine line between accommodation and assimilation. On the opposite side of the contextualization spectrum is the dynamic of *accommodation*. As I am using the term,[46] an "accommodation" of the gospel message does not amount to an abject *assimilation* of the Christian faith—that is, it does not involve a *complete* capitulation to the sociocultural sensibilities at work in a ministry context in a way that those core christological doctrines are either abandoned or neologized due to their supposed implausibility or the manner in which they give offense.[47] But I do want to suggest that the accommodation understanding of contextualization falls just short of a complete capitulation to the intellectual, moral, political and religious sensibilities at work in the target culture. There is only a fine line separating these two ministry approaches.

According to my definition, an accommodation of the gospel occurs when, as a result of paying more attention to the "voice" of the target culture than to Scripture and the history of its interpretation,[48] we feel the need not only to *re-vision* the gospel message,[49] but to *rehabilitate* it

---

[46]As an indication of how important it is to define one's terms in this discussion, David Bosch uses the term *accommodation* to describe the Roman Catholic version of indigenization. See Bosch, *Transforming Mission*, pp. 458-63.

[47]In truth, the assimilation process as I describe it is no contextualization of the Christian gospel at all. This is why both classical liberalism and Christian fundamentalism, for reasons that differ greatly, both fail at rendering to God a missional faithfulness.

[48]Bruce Nicholls likewise warns against this missional move. See Nicholls, *Contextualization*, pp. 27, 51-52.

[49]I am indebted to the late Stanley Grenz for the idea of a "revisioned" understanding of the

as well. It is not that our interaction with the target culture has helped us see something about God or ourselves that we had not seen before. Rather, our interaction with the culture has caused us to conclude that there is something dreadfully wrong with the gospel message that has been proclaimed by the church from the beginning of its existence until now. *This felt need to rehabilitate the gospel has the effect of producing a vision of the Christian life that is overly influenced by the sociocultural sensibilities at work in the target culture.* Though there is an attempt to justify this missional move on the basis of a "new" or "fresh" understanding of the "true" significance of the Jesus story, absent from this new iteration of the gospel is (1) a comprehensive and coherent consideration of *all* the components of the Jesus story (i.e., his birth, life, death, resurrection, present high-priestly ministry and eventual return); (2) attention to the crucial significance of the four christological doctrines to the Jesus story; and (3) a sufficient degree of humility regarding how the church has through the ages understood the very basic manner in which the Jesus story spells good news for God's world. *Though well-intentioned, the accommodation understanding of contextualization errs in paying more attention to the sociocultural sensibilities at work in the ministry context than to the biblical text.* While this does not result in an abject assimilation of the gospel to the cultural zeitgeist of the ministry context, it can produce eccentric versions of the Christian message which, in my opinion, ultimately fail the biblical faithfulness test.

Why a recontextualization of the gospel is required. As figure 2.1 indicates, in between indigenization and accommodation is the process of *recontextualization.* The concept of recontextualization, as I envision it,[50] is based on a number of important realizations. (1) "The Christian faith never exists except as 'translated' into a culture."[51] (2) While the cardinal christological verities that lie at the heart of the Christian faith

---

Christian message in light of current contextual realities that falls short of either a reformulation or rehabilitation. See Stanley J. Grenz, *Revisioning Evangelical Theology: A Fresh Agenda for the 21st Century* (Downers Grove, IL: InterVarsity Press, 1993).

[50]As will be indicated below, the way I make use of the concept of recontextualization differs somewhat from understandings put forward by other contributors to the missional conversation.

[51]Bosch, *Transforming Mission*, p. 438.

are essential and immutable, an understanding of how the Christ-event plays out as good news may (must) be articulated differently from culture to culture, context to context. (3) The contextualization process therefore involves the *doing of theology* (thinking, speaking, writing about God) toward the goal of crafting a comprehensible and compelling presentation of the gospel message for a given cultural context. (4) All such *theologizing toward a presentation of the gospel message* is inherently contextual in nature since the missionary is impacted both by his or her own cultural location and the one to which he or she is seeking to present the gospel.[52] (5) Indeed, the *theologizing* of the magisterial Reformers, the church fathers and even the biblical authors themselves can be thought of as contextual in nature since all their thinking, speaking and writing about God occurred within particular historical and cultural locations.[53] (6) It is naive, therefore, to assume that prior to the contemporary contextualization endeavor the missionary was in touch with a pristine, *acultural* understanding of the *gospel message* (i.e., how the Christ-event plays out as good news in God's world)[54] that needed simply be adorned in traditional cultural garb in order to make it comprehensible and compelling to an indigenous audience.[55] (7) While always guarding against assimilation and accommodation, a truly compelling contextualization requires a *re-contextualization* of the Christian message involving a fresh consideration of the Christian gospel in light of the modes of intellection, sociocultural realities and existential and religious questions at work in the target culture.[56] (8) Ongoing recontextualizations of the Christian message must occur lest a too-conservative approach allows the gospel message to be held captive to a contextualization exercise that took place in an earlier day and at another place (e.g., the understanding of the gospel message produced by the scholastic successors of Luther and Calvin in Western Europe

---

[52]See Nicholls, *Contextualization*, pp. 53-54. See also Walls, *Missionary Movement*, p. 10.

[53]See Flemming, *Contextualization*, p. 298; Nicholls, *Contextualization*, pp. 25-26, 38-40.

[54]See Nicholls, *Contextualization*, pp. 53-54.

[55]See David Bosch's comprehensive critique of the indigenization understanding and practice of contextualization in Bosch, *Transforming Mission*, pp. 458-63.

[56]Bosch makes the assertion: "The Christian faith must be rethought, reformulated and lived anew in each human culture, and this must be done in a *vital* way, in depth and right to the cultures' roots" (Bosch, *Transforming Mission*, p. 463).

during the years following the Protestant Reformation). (9) For a contextualization of the gospel to prove genuinely compelling, it must involve an identification-differentiation-transformation process which calls for the missionary to do more than simply *translate* the gospel. The message must be *incarnated* within the cultural setting at great risk to the missionary him- or herself. It is only after identifying with the members of a target culture, seeking to genuinely understand them and their culture from the inside-out,[57] that the difference-making (i.e., transformational)[58] aspects of the gospel can be communicated (through both prophetic speech and action) in a compelling manner.[59]

Once all nine of these important realizations are given due consideration, the conclusion more and more missional and emerging evangelicals are arriving at is this: *In reality, it is not simply the ministry method and manner that are shaped by the contextualization process but the message as well (though not the doctrinal core that lies at the heart of the message).*[60] The process of recontextualization therefore speaks of "fresh

---

[57]See Alan Hirsch, *The Forgotten Ways: Reactivating the Missional Church* (Grand Rapids: Brazos, 2006), p. 144.

[58]Citing the work of Pedro Arrupe, David Bosch writes: "Inculturation's concern . . . is to become 'a principle that animates, directs, and unifies the culture, transforming it and remaking it so as to bring about a 'new creation.' The focus, then, is on the 'new creation,' on the transformation of the old, on the plant which, having flowered from its seed, is at the same time something fundamentally new when compared with that seed" (Bosch, *Transforming Mission,* p. 466). It should be pointed out, however, that Bosch is not here affirming the idea that the contextualized gospel becomes a "new creation" but that its contextualization results in the transformation of the target culture into a new creation. See also Guder, *Continuing Conversion,* pp. 84-85.

[59]Though I have a more person-to-person dynamic in mind when I refer to the transformational effect of prophetic speech and action, Ross Hastings seems to have a more corporate and culture-wide dynamic in mind when he states: "One of the key prophetic roles of the missional church, however, is to poke holes in cherished intellectual assumptions that undergird secular culture. The Spirit may be at work to unsettle people and draw them to repentance of their culture's idolatries" (Hastings, *Missional God,* p. 52). For a variation on this theme, see Bruce Nicholls' discussion of the "two-way process of contextualizing the Word in a specific cultural location." The main difference is the way Nicholls uses the terms "renunciation" and "distancing" rather than "differentiation," and rightly points out that for a genuine identification to take place, the missionary must adopt a prophetic posture toward her own culture as well as the one she is seeking to impact with the gospel (Nicholls, *Contextualization,* pp. 50-51). See also Robert Schreiter's helpful discussion of what makes for a good communication event in *New Catholicity,* pp. 34-39.

[60]Referring to the recontextualization process as "inculturation," David Bosch points to the advocacy of a "dynamic equivalence" model of translation by the Consultation on Gospel and Culture sponsored by the Lausanne Committee on World Evangelization held in 1978 in Wil-

hearings" of the gospel that can lead to *both* methodological and theological innovations as we engage in cross-cultural ministry. Such Spirit-driven innovations are simply necessary for the gospel to do its transformational work in the lives of people inhabiting the many diverse cultures that make up the "world" for which Christ died (see Jn 3:16-21).

To be clear, while I am arguing that perhaps we evangelicals need to be a bit more open than we have in the past to the idea that a "fresh hearing" of the gospel in light of one's contemporary ministry context might lead to both theological and methodological innovations, I am not suggesting that such innovations will relate to the doctrinal core that is at the very heart of the Christian faith. Moreover, I contend further that for the recontextualization exercise to be considered faithful to the biblical text, any theological innovations that occur as a result of fresh considerations of the gospel in light of the contemporary ministry context will be justified only on the basis of a *theological antecedent* clearly present in God's Word. For example, the story told in Acts 10:1-18 of Peter's *new theological conviction* (that the gospel is meant for Gentiles as well as Jews) and *new ministry practice* (preaching to and baptizing Gentiles) possessed a theological antecedent in the form of discrete Old Testament passages that convey God's concern for the Gentiles as well as the Jews.[61] The presence of this theological antecedent in the Old Testament Scriptures was important to the apostolic community, as Acts 15:13-18 makes clear. Thus, Peter's theological and methodological ministry innovations were actually *the result of the Holy Spirit illuminating truth that was already included in Scripture,* not his speaking new truth to Peter that possessed no prior biblical precedent.

At first glance, it might appear that it is nothing more than this sort of spiritual illumination that Brian McLaren and other emergent leaders have in mind. However, a second look at how McLaren states his case for

---

lowbank, Bermuda as an indication of a Protestant, even evangelical, embrace of this post-indigenization understanding of contextualization.

[61]See Ray Anderson, *The Soul of Ministry: Forming Leaders for God's People* (Louisville, KY: Westminster John Knox Press, 1997), pp. 17-24, 124-28. See also Christopher J. H. Wright, *The Mission of God: Unlocking the Bible's Grand Narrative* (Downers Grove, IL: InterVarsity Press, 2006), pp. 454-500, for a comprehensive study of the Old Testament's focus on God's mission as it relates to "the nations."

a continual *reform* of the ministry message indicates that *his locus for a theological antecedent is not the Scriptures as a whole, but a distinctive understanding of Jesus' gospel of the kingdom in particular*—a discrete understanding of Jesus' message that, prior to our time, no one in the history of the Christian movement may have embraced or even imagined, but that is now being brought to light by the Holy Spirit. McLaren writes:

> Each of these new challenges and opportunities requires Christian leaders to create new forms, new methods, new structures—and requires them to find new content, new truths, new meaning to bring to bear on the new challenges. These new messages are not incompatible with *the gospel of the kingdom Jesus taught*. No, they are inherent in it, but previously undiscovered, unexpressed, perhaps unimagined. *Jesus' original message* was pregnant with all that they would need, but there was much Jesus said, that they could not yet bear to hear, and so Jesus would send the Spirit of truth to guide them into all truth as they needed it and were ready to bear it.[62]

Though appreciative of much that McLaren has to say in all his books, I am concerned that this slight change of focus from the Scriptures as a whole to the way a given faith community might be "led" to reinterpret Jesus' kingdom message at least potentially opens the door to theological innovations that could actually be at odds with the apostolic witness.[63] This concern is heightened by McLaren's willingness in later works to suggest that Jesus' ministry message has essentially been misunderstood by large segments of the church throughout the history of the Christian movement.[64] Furthermore, while I certainly want to affirm the ongoing role of the Holy Spirit to help Christ's followers better understand what Jesus was and is about (see Jn 16:13-15; 1 Cor 2:6-16; 1 Jn 2:20-27), my concern is that if we completely untether this illuminating work of the Spirit from the canon as a whole and the way the church has historically understood the ministry message of Jesus, we may open the door to the

---

[62]McLaren, GO 192-93 [215], emphasis added.

[63]The reader may recall how a previously cited excerpt from Ed Stetzer and David Putnam, *Breaking the Missional Code: Your Church Can Become a Missionary in Your Community* (Nashville: Broadman & Holman, 2006), p. 188, expressed concern over this very possibility.

[64]See Brian McLaren, *The Secret Message of Jesus: Uncovering the Truth That Could Change Everything* (Nashville: Thomas Nelson, 2006).

possibility of faith communities "hearing" the Spirit say things to them in their day that fail to do justice to the exhortation found in Jude 3 to contend for the faith that was once for all entrusted to the saints.[65]

There has to be a way to do justice to both concerns: to effectively re-contextualize the gospel in our post-Christian context (the missional task) while at the same time remaining faithful to the historic, apostolic understanding of the Christian message (the biblical text). While the Scriptures are made up of culturally located speech about God, they are not just another contextualization of the gospel! Dean Flemming speaks of the "distinctive and authoritative character of New Testament theologizing as the expression of divine revelation."[66] In a like manner Bruce Nicholls writes of "the nature and function of the cultural conditioning in the biblical revelation, where the sovereignty of God is at work in a way that is unique."[67] Inspired by the Spirit of God, the biblical documents exercise an authority in the lives of Christian missionaries in two senses: (1) The product of the recontextualization endeavor must resonate not only with the story of Jesus as portrayed in Scripture, but with

---

[65]Support for the need to differentiate between the notions of "new truth" and "progress in Christian teaching" can be found in Thomas C. Oden, "The Faith Once Delivered: Nicea and Evangelical Confession," in *Evangelicals and Nicene Faith*, ed. Timothy George (Grand Rapids: Baker, 2011), p. 18.

[66]Flemming, *Contextualization*, p. 296.

[67]Nicholls, *Contextualization*, pp. 25, 45-48. Thus, while agreeing that there is no acultural understanding of how the Jesus story plays out as good news for the world, I am arguing against the widely embraced notion originated by Friedrich Schleiermacher that "there never was a 'pure' message, supracultural and suprahistorical" (see Bosch, *Transforming Mission*, p. 432). I am suggesting that because the apostolic community possessed a unified understanding of the four christological verities, the fact that each of the discrete passages which refer to them possessed a peculiar *Sitz im Leben* need not imply that their meaning is up for grabs based on our own contextual locatedness. Bosch himself, though he acknowledged that all theology is contextual, also warned against "an uncritical celebration of an infinite number of contextual and mutually exclusive theologies"; the idea that "each scriptural text is . . . so deeply shaped by its context that it actually constitutes an isolated theological world in itself" (p. 437); the "danger of [the] absolutism of contextualism" (p. 438); the idea that the message of the gospel is something "we derive *from* contexts" rather than "something we bring *to* contexts" as the *"norma normans*, the 'norming norm'" (p. 440, emphasis original); and "allowing the context to determine the nature and content of theology for that context" (p. 442). Thus, I am committed to the idea, rooted in my embrace of a theological and critical realism, that it is possible through the Holy Spirit to indwell the biblical texts in a way that allows us to arrive at a "good enough" understanding of how the apostles themselves understood the four christological verities. See Andrew Walls's related discussion of the Christian's "adoptive past" in Walls, *Missionary Movement*, p. 9.

the christological verities also presented in Scripture (e.g., 1 Cor 15:1-8), which render that story as good news for all creation. (2) The Spirit-inspired and illuminated Scriptures possess the authority to *empower* Christ's followers to do what the recontextualization process calls for—that is, "incarnate" the story of Jesus within a particular culture in a comprehensible, compelling and comprehensive manner which, while seeking to *understand* rather than *condone* or *condemn* the status quo, ends up transforming it as new believers begin to allow Jesus to live out his life of love through them within their cultural setting.[68]

THEOLOGICAL RESPONSES TO THE CURRENT CULTURAL ZEITGEIST

So, how does this discussion of the three main gospel contextualization options inform the possibility of some bridge-building between the emerging, missional and traditional evangelical movements? In the previous chapter I made a passing reference to the idea that it is possible to conceive of a spectrum of theological responses to the cultural zeitgeist currently at work in the Western world (which is a blend of modernism and postmodernism).[69] Figure 2.3 portrays this spectrum with special attention to the phenomenon of postmodernism.

As figure 2.3 indicates, theologians reply to the philosophical currents that presently exercise a huge influence in our ministry context in a variety of ways, ranging from a very conservative, traditional, arguably fundamentalist, essentially noncontextualizing response (which I have labeled "repudiation"), to several evangelical/post-evangelical, contextualizing responses (labeled "toleration," "incarnation" and "accommodation" respectively), to the more classically liberal, assimilating response ("capitulation").[70] It is a thesis of this book that one of these responses is more theologically appropriate and therefore better

---

[68]According to Guder, "Scripture is appropriately read and interpreted as the Spirit-empowered testimony that equips God's people for their mission, that is, for their incarnational witness" (Guder, *Continuing Conversion,* p. x).

[69]See Hastings, *Missional God,* p. 60.

[70]See the similar categorization of responses to postmodernity in Shults, *Postfoundationlist Task,* p. xiii. Though the typology offered by Shults highlights only three responses—*de*constructive (affirming), *paleo*-constructive (rejecting) and *re*constructive (discerning, reconfiguring)—we both end up advocating for what Shults refers to as a "middle way" (see pp. 11-12, 17-19, 25-81).

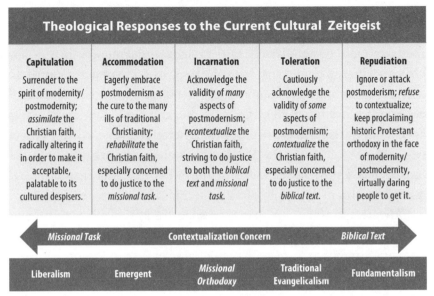

Theological Responses to the Current Cultural Zeitgeist				
Capitulation	**Accommodation**	**Incarnation**	**Toleration**	**Repudiation**
Surrender to the spirit of modernity/ postmodernity; *assimilate* the Christian faith, radically altering it in order to make it acceptable, palatable to its cultured despisers.	Eagerly embrace postmodernism as the cure to the many ills of traditional Christianity; *rehabilitate* the Christian faith, especially concerned to do justice to the *missional task.*	Acknowledge the validity of *many* aspects of postmodernism; *recontextualize* the Christian faith, striving to do justice to both the *biblical text* and *missional task.*	Cautiously acknowledge the validity of *some* aspects of postmodernism; *contextualize* the Christian faith, especially concerned to do justice to the *biblical text.*	Ignore or attack postmodernism; *refuse* to contextualize; keep proclaiming historic Protestant orthodoxy in the face of modernity/ postmodernity, virtually daring people to get it.

Missional Task   **Contextualization Concern**   *Biblical Text*

| Liberalism | Emergent | Missional Orthodoxy | Traditional Evangelicalism | Fundamentalism |

Figure 2.3.

able to offer our post-Christian contemporaries a compelling presentation of the Christian faith which, while sensitive to sociocultural sensibilities, nevertheless remains consonant with the faith that was "once for all entrusted to the saints" (Jude 3).[71] This, of course, is the "incarnation" response, as indicated by its placement at the center of the spectrum. This middle position suggests that of the five response models portrayed, the one associated with a missional orthodoxy best resists the wide swing of the pendulum as it relates to the task of doing theology and ministry in a post-Christian context. In order to demonstrate why this particular theological response or ministry model should be considered preferable to the others, the strengths and weaknesses of each approach with respect to the dynamic of gospel contextualization will be explored.

The "repudiation" response. There are some theologians whose response to the advent of postmodernism is either to ignore or simply say

---

[71]For a thoughtful and passionate essay which encourages evangelicals living in an era marked by "increasing syncretism" and "radical pluralism" to take the exhortation of Jude 3 seriously, see Oden, "Faith Once Delivered," pp. 3-19.

no to it.[72] Some advocates of this response emphasize the importance of a strict loyalty to a particular confession or creed in the face of both modernity and postmodernity. Others suggest that the way forward for both theology and ministry is to go back to a premodern approach, trusting in the inherent authority and hence power of theological and ecclesiastical tradition. In either case, the call here is for churches to keep doing business as usual, proclaiming a historic version of the gospel (e.g., the one crafted by the Nicene theologians, or perhaps one of the confessions forged in the wake of the Protestant Reformation), and doing ministry in an equally classic, traditional manner.

One strength of the "repudiation" response is its laudable commitment to the idea that the gospel message is inherently powerful and needs no human assistance in terms of its essential relevance to this or that ministry context. Another strength lies in its commitment to the idea that there is a doctrinal core to the gospel of Jesus Christ and the coincidental concern to resist the perennial temptation to compromise the gospel as it is proclaimed in varying ministry locations. However, sometimes a strength taken to an extreme can morph into a weakness. Indeed, to the degree that the "repudiation" response is driven by a radical concern to preserve *at all costs* a classical understanding of Christian faith and practice, it appears to be a form of Christian fundamentalism.[73]

From a missional perspective, perhaps the biggest problem with Christian fundamentalism is its reticence—its essential unwillingness, really—to contextualize the gospel for our current ministry context. In

---

[72]For example, see the evaluation and critique of the negative responses to postmodernism advocated by theologians David Wells, Thomas Oden and Francis Schaeffer in Millard Erickson, *Postmodernizing the Faith: Evangelical Responses to the Challenge of Postmodernism* (Grand Rapids: Baker Books, 1998), pp. 23-82.

[73]Likewise, Shults refers to the *paleo*-constructive response to postmodernism as "fundamentalist" in nature. Such a response, says Shults, calls for the contemporary church to "reject or ignore the challenge of postmodernity and appeal to an earlier premodern era in which truth and knowledge were allegedly unproblematic" (Shults, *Postfoundationalist Task*, p. xiii). In addition, I offer that a slavish devotion to the classics can also be motivated by the need to believe that we are in touch with religious behaviors (i.e., liturgical practices) that are superior to all others as evidenced by their long history of use. This conviction affords the worshipper a sense of certainty and control with respect to his or her standing before God. I contend that such a craving for certainty and control, grounded in the need for a sense of psychological safety before God, is at the heart of religious fundamentalism/Pharisaism. See Gary Tyra, *Defeating Pharisaism: Recovering Jesus' Disciple-Making Method* (Downers Grove, IL: InterVarsity Press, 2009), pp. 70-73.

my opinion, the repudiation response does not take seriously enough how post-Christian, perhaps even anti-Christian, many members of our current ministry context have become. As stated previously, we simply must awaken to the fact that there are increasing numbers of people living all around us who, though spiritually hungry, nevertheless consider themselves "over" Christianity and "done" with the church. Millions of these young adults are moving on to other, more eclectic forms of spirituality. Do we sufficiently recognize how difficult it is to win people back to a "sincere and pure devotion to Christ" (2 Cor 11:1-4) once they have embraced spiritual eclecticism? I completely understand the thought behind the repudiation response's commitment to the classics. But given the biblical call to contextualize and the statistics about the increasing number of post-Christians all around us,[74] can we afford to keep doing theology and ministry the same way year after year, counting on the fact that those who are "destined" to become Christians will somehow find their way into our churches and to our altars? Besides, doesn't everyone deserve to hear a compelling presentation of why the Christ-event spells good news for them in particular (cf. 1 Cor 9:20-22)? I am afraid that the reluctance of this very conservative response to engage in any serious attempt at the contextualization of the gospel for our current ministry context ironically fails not only the missional faithfulness test but the biblical faithfulness test as well.[75]

The "capitulation" response. On the opposite side of the spectrum in figure 2.3 is the "capitulation" response. As an evangelical committed to taking Jude 3 seriously, I struggle with this response's willingness to simply assimilate the message of Christianity to the plausibility structures and religious, moral and political sensibilities prevalent within our

---

[74]See chapter one, pp. 36-38.

[75]When I refer to the "repudiation" response, I do not have in mind emerging churches that endeavor to emulate the liturgical practices of the ancient church. At work in most of these congregations is not a strident insistence on a "correct" form of worship. Rather there is an awareness that due to the effects of modernity and postmodernity on contemporary culture and a corresponding disappointment with traditional and "seeker-sensitive" evangelical worship services, many post-Christians who return to the church find engagement in classical forms of worship to best enable an experience of the transcendent. Because this focus on ancient liturgical practices is generated by a sensitivity to a religious sensibility at work in a target audience, such a missional move can be viewed as a form of ministry contextualization rather than a repudiation of the need for it.

current ministry context.[76] The dynamic of syncretizing or trying to blend or harmonize the Christian faith with the zeitgeist at work in a target culture has a long history, going back beyond Schleiermacher's neologizing of key Christian concepts so as to make them acceptable to the cultured despisers of Christianity in eighteenth- and nineteenth-century Europe[77] to the gospel-distorting work of the Gnostics in the third and fourth centuries and all the way back to the apparent attempt of some of the Corinthian church leaders to blend the Christian faith with their previous religious and cultural commitments.[78] While I want to commend anyone who possesses the desire to help people connect with Christ, I cannot condone the capitulation approach. In a manner even more problematic than the repudiation response, this ministry tack also fails both the biblical and missional faithfulness tests.

The "toleration" response. Moving back across the spectrum in the direction of the conservative swing of the pendulum, we find the "toleration" response (see figure 2.3). Not all evangelicals, not even all traditional evangelicals, consider it appropriate to simply ignore the advent of postmodernism.[79] As a matter of fact, one of the strengths of this response to the cultural zeitgeist is its willingness to acknowledge that there is some validity to the epistemological challenge presented by the postmodern turn. Though it is probably not a majority of traditional evangelical church leaders who would go so far as to embrace a soft postmodernism (as I do), I suspect that the numbers of those

---

[76]For more on the dynamics of cultural and theological syncretism, see Nicholls, *Contextualization*, pp. 28-34.

[77]I am referring here to the practice of infusing new meaning into old, familiar concepts so as to update them and salvage them for use in the contemporary era. For example, see the way Schleiermacher redefines such concepts as "miracle," "revelation," "inspiration," "prophecy," "grace" and "true belief" in Friedrich Schleiermacher, *On Religion: Speeches to Its Cultured Despisers* (New York: Harper and Row, 1958), pp. 88-90.

[78]Scattered throughout Gordon Fee's magisterial commentary on 1 Corinthians are references to the idea that at least some of the Corinthian church members were tempted to interpret their new Christian faith as a new form of *sophia* or *philosophia* and the implications this syncretizing had for theology and ethics. See Gordon Fee, *The First Epistle to the Corinthians* (Grand Rapids: Eerdmans, 1987), pp. 8, 11, 14-15, 49, 57, 67-68.

[79]One example who comes to mind is evangelical theologian D. A. Carson who, though wary of the degree to which he feels that the emerging church movement has allowed itself to be overly influenced by postmodernism, nevertheless acknowledges that some aspects of the postmodern turn possess some epistemological validity and even value, and appears to advocate (as I do) a "soft postmodernism" (Carson, *Becoming Conversant*, pp. 106, 108, 110-12, 115-24, 192).

willing to do so are increasing, especially among the younger members of the movement.

Another strength of this response is that due to the evangelical movement's commitment to mission in general and enthusiastic participation in the church renewal, growth, effectiveness and health movements in particular, there is strong support here for some form of gospel contextualization. Finally, given the evangelical movement's commitment to biblical authority, there is a concern here to do justice to Jude 3 as the contextualization process occurs.[80]

But I have two big questions with regard to the toleration response. First, is the kind of contextualization that many evangelical churches engage in (i.e., indigenization) sufficient to overcome the image problem that exists in our post-Christian ministry context? Second, does an indigenization approach to gospel contextualization have what it takes to function in a truly compelling and comprehensive (i.e., transformational) manner over against the strength of the current cultural zeitgeist? As we have seen, the impact of postmodernism and its three entailments (epistemological, moral and religious relativism) on our culture has been huge. Furthermore, the juggernaut effect of the current cultural zeitgeist has actually been exacerbated by a discipleship deficit in way too many traditional evangelical churches.[81] It pains me as an evangelical to say that, based on hundreds of interactions I have had over the years with university students who have been severely disappointed by their experience in traditional evangelical churches, we cannot consider the toleration response adequate for the ministry task at hand. Despite its laudable commitment to remain faithful to the biblical text, in my opinion it does not merit a passing grade with respect to the missional faithfulness test.

The "accommodation" response. Moving once again across the spectrum in the direction of the pendulum's swing to the more liberal side, we find the "accommodation" response (see figure 2.3). I have al-

---

[80]Darrell Guder speaks of the need for missional theology to be worked out under the "tutelage and control" of the scriptural witness. See Darrell Guder, *Be My Witnesses: The Church's Mission, Message and Messengers* (Grand Rapids: Eerdmans, 1985), p. 8.

[81]For a discussion of the discipleship deficit, see Tyra, *Defeating Pharisaism*, pp. 194-97. See also Hirsch, *Forgotten Ways*, pp. 103-4.

ready indicated that I view the vast majority of emerging church leaders as comrades rather than competitors in the gospel contextualization endeavor. The commitment of many of these leaders to do theology and ministry in such a way as to present a biblically faithful gospel to the members of the emerging generations deserves the support of every evangelical Christian who is more concerned about the making of disciples than the maintenance of ecclesiastical traditions.

My concern, however, is that some influential members of the emergent movement may have adopted a gospel contextualization approach that is less faithful to the biblical text than seems wise or appropriate. Some advocates of the accommodation response may be guilty of listening more to the voice of the cultural context than the one speaking to them from Jude 3. As we have seen, this has produced a contextualization process that calls for a *rehabilitation* of the Christian message rather than a prayerful, Spirit-enabled re-visioning that keeps both the text and the task (and the history of biblical interpretation) in mind. This is anything but a distinction without a difference. In point of fact, perhaps more than any other *it is this issue that generates the greatest amount of tension between traditional evangelicals and some members of the emerging church movement*. Indeed, given the importance to the rest of this book of what I am referring to as the liberal/emergent overcorrection to our post-Christian ministry context, it is worth taking time to explore some plausible reasons for it. It's for this reason that I have appended to this chapter an excursus that explores not only some possible reasons for the liberal/emergent overcorrection, but also the philosophical/theological perspective that underwrites a compelling alternative to it. I cannot indicate strongly enough how important it is that this excursus material be given some careful consideration before the reader proceeds any further in this chapter. Doing so will put the reader in a better position to appreciate the bridge-building possibilities provided by a missional orthodoxy and the "incarnation" response to the current cultural zeitgeist associated with it.

The "incarnation" response. Having surveyed the other four responses to the current cultural zeitgeist, as well as the detailed discussion of the liberal/emergent overcorrection presented in the excursus appended to this chapter, we are now in a position to fully appreciate the response that, because it is the one most faithful to the missionary nature of God, does the best job of remaining faithful to both the biblical text and missional task (and for that reason can serve as a bridge between the traditional evangelical, missional and emerging church movements). In his promotion of an "inculturation" model of contextualization, David Bosch specifies that it "consciously follows the model of the *incarnation.*"[82] Andrew Walls asserts that at the heart of the contextualization process as ordained by God is a "translation principle" rooted paradigmatically in Christ's incarnation.[83] Darrell Guder emphasizes the crucial importance of "the incarnation of Christ and the continuing enfleshment of the gospel" by means of Jesus' disciples and the church.[84] More than one missional author has referred to Christ's incarnation as the best way to understand what is involved in the contextualization of the Christian faith in a new location.[85] *Incarnation* is perhaps the theological term that best captures the way Jesus himself envisioned how his story would be contextualized into new cultural locations. In his high priestly prayer, Jesus says to his Father: "As you sent me into the world, I have sent them into the world" (Jn 17:18). Similarly, some of Jesus' final words to his disciples were, "As the Father has sent me, I am sending you" (Jn 20:21). It is no wonder then that Bosch stipulates that "the kenotic and incarnational dimension of authentic inculturation is mentioned again and again in all theological traditions."[86]

---

[82]Bosch, *Transforming Mission,* pp. 464-65, emphasis original. See also Hastings, *Missional God,* p. 38.

[83]Walls, *Missionary Movement,* pp. 26-36.

[84]See Guder, *Be My Witnesses,* pp. 24-32.

[85]For example, see Hastings, *Missional God,* pp. 38, 82, 148-89; Darrell Guder, ed., *Missional Church: A Vision for the Sending of the Church in North America* (Grand Rapids: Eerdmans, 1998), pp. 11, 14; Alan J. Roxburgh and M. Scott Boren, *Introducing the Missional Church: Why It Matters, How to Become One* (Grand Rapids: Baker, 2009), p. 32; Michael Frost and Alan Hirsch, *The Shaping of Things to Come: Innovation and Mission for the 21st-Century Church* (Peabody, MA: Hendrickson Publishers, 2003), pp. 35-41; Hirsch, *Forgotten Ways,* pp. 128-29, 131-47; Ed Stetzer, "Why We Should Use the Term 'Incarnational Mission' (Part 1)," June 20, 2011, www.edstetzer.com/2011/06/incarnational-mission-part-1.html; Ed Stetzer, "Incarnational Mission (Part 2)," July 21, 2011, www.edstetzer.com/2011/07/incarnational-mission-part-2.html; Ed Stetzer, "Incarnational Mission (Part 3)," July 25, 2011, www.edstetzer.com/2011/07/incarnational-mission-part-3.html.

[86]Bosch, *Transforming Mission,* p. 465.

The corpus of missional literature is replete with discussions of the nature of incarnational ministry. The best ones, in my opinion, are those that take John 20:21 into consideration and endeavor to identify how Jesus, the incarnate Christ, went about contextualizing the good news during his earthly ministry. One of my favorite descriptions is this:

> The most effective witness the church makes will always be in the lives of those who in Christ's name bury themselves in the lives and struggles of another people, missionaries who serve the people, learn to speak their language, develop the capacity to feel their hurt and hunger, and who learn to love them personally and individually.[87]

Commenting on this brief but pungent definition, Ed Stetzer explains:

> Incarnationalism speaks of identifying with and living among the people God has sent us to. The incarnation was about the Word taking on flesh, but in taking on flesh Jesus didn't live an isolated life divorced from the culture. He lived with and among people in such a way that his words and actions made sense to a specific people group. He was in many senses one of them, while remaining distinct as the Son of God.[88]

I have already asserted that for a contextualization of the gospel to prove genuinely compelling to a person or group of persons, it must involve an identification-differentiation-transformation process. The end goal of Jesus' incarnational ministry was not merely to identify with sinful humanity but to heal, transform and re-create it. That Jesus did this by burying himself deeply within a particular historical cultural context while maintaining his integrity as the divine Son of God should be instructive for us who are sent to do ministry in his name. By working in union with the risen and ascended Christ through the Spirit,[89] the

---

[87]This quote is by M. Theron Rankin, a former president of what is now the International Mission Board of the Southern Baptist Convention, cited in Alan Neely, "Incarnational Mission," in *The Evangelical Dictionary of World Mission* (Grand Rapids: Baker Academic, 2000), p. 475, cited in Stetzer, "Incarnational Mission (Part 2)."

[88]Stetzer, "Incarnational Mission (Part 2)."

[89]See Hastings, *Missional God*, p. 82. For a provocative discussion of the need for Christ's followers engaged in missional ministry to follow the lead of the Spirit and to be careful to direct the attention of hurting people to Christ rather than themselves, see J. Todd Billings, "The Problem with 'Incarnational Ministry,'" *Christianity Today*, August 10, 2012, www.christianitytoday.com/ct/2012/july-august/the-problem-with-incarnational-ministry.html.

end goal of our "incarnational" attempts at ministry should be to see individuals and cultures transformed into the likeness of Christ and the kingdom of God. But, once again, *only after identifying with the members of a target culture, seeking to genuinely understand them and their culture from the inside-out,* can the difference-making (i.e., transformational) aspects of the gospel be communicated (through both prophetic speech and action) in a compelling manner. Just as the incarnation of Christ was not optional in God's saving economy, neither is the incarnational method of contextualizing the gospel.

CHRISTOLOGICAL SUPPORT FOR THE INCARNATION RESPONSE

The ways in which local churches can and should function in an incarnational, kingdom-representing manner within their ministry contexts will be addressed in chapters nine and ten of this book with their respective treatments of ecclesiology and eschatology. In what remains of this chapter, I will provide a theological justification for the "incarnational" response to the current cultural zeitgeist over against those I have labeled as "repudiation," "toleration," "accommodation" and "capitulation." In a nutshell, I argue that because the "incarnation" response does the best job of doing justice to both the christological verities and the cultural realities at work in various ministry contexts, it should be viewed as the ministry method most faithful to the incarnational nature of the Christ of the gospel. For this reason, it is the one that best facilitates Christ's redemptive, transforming work among the people living in—and the sociocultural dynamics at work in—any culture in which it is embedded.

The Chalcedonian Controversy. In *The Mosaic of Christian Belief,* Roger Olson reminds us that at Chalcedon in A.D. 451, the fourth ecumenical (universal) council of Christian bishops developed a christological affirmation that "culminated a long controversy among Christians and became the orthodox statement on Christology for all Christians (Eastern Orthodox, Roman Catholic, most Protestants) for more than fifteen hundred years."[90] The doctrine of the Trinity, in which the deity of

---

[90]Roger Olson, *The Mosaic of Christian Belief: Twenty Centuries of Unity and Diversity* (Downers Grove, IL: IVP Academic, 2002), p. 226. My intent here is not to argue that the Chalcedonian

Christ is affirmed, had already been formulated in the Nicene Creed which was first adopted at the Council of Nicaea (325) and then revised at the Council of Constantinople (381).[91] The christological issue that was resolved at Chalcedon had to do with how the two natures of Christ (human and divine) related to one another. Really, there were two primary christological questions prompting the Chalcedonian Creed (or Definition). First, some early Christian leaders and thinkers "questioned whether a person could be both truly human and truly divine and really be one person."[92] Second, other early church fathers "questioned whether a divine-human person could have dual natures or whether such a one must be a third something—a hybrid of divinity and humanity."[93]

At the risk of oversimplifying, I suggest that these two questions were prompted by the fact that the Gospels present a Jesus who, on the one hand, "grew in wisdom" (Lk 2:52), but on the other hand, also knew what people were thinking (Mt 9:4; Lk 9:47), what their motives were (Mt 22:18), what they intended to do (Jn 6:15) and what events would transpire in the future (Jn 18:4). *How do we understand Jesus as human and divine at the same time?* The theological affirmation forged at Chalcedon and designed to address this christological quandary reads as follows:

> Following, then, the holy fathers [of the Nicene Council and Council of Constantinople], we unite in teaching all men to confess the one and only Son, our Lord Jesus Christ. This selfsame one is perfect both in deity and also in humanness; this selfsame one is also actually God and actually man, with a rational soul and a body. He is of the same reality as God as far as his deity is concerned and of the same reality as we are

---

Creed possesses some sort of binding authority, but simply to point out its longstanding and widespread influence on the theologizing of the Christian movement. That said, even though all theological creeds are historically and culturally conditioned contextualizations of the Christian faith, to the degree that the ecumenical creeds reflect biblically informed attempts by communities of Christian theologians to articulate the nature and significance of the christological verities and the Jesus we experience through an existentially impactful embrace of them, they should not be dismissed out of hand simply because of their historical and cultural particularity. In other words, the fact that the Chalcedonian Creed has exercised such an abiding and pervasive influence on Christian theologizing should give us pause before we disregard its counsel.

[91]Ibid., p. 137.
[92]Ibid., p. 225.
[93]Ibid.

ourselves as far as his humanness is concerned; thus like us in all respects, sin only excepted. Before time began he was begotten of the Father, in respect of his deity, and now in these "last days," for us and on behalf of our salvation, this selfsame one was born of Mary the virgin, who is God-bearer in respect of his humanness. [We also teach] that we apprehend this one and only Christ—Son, Lord, only-begotten—in two natures; [and we do this] without confusing the two natures, without transmuting one nature into the other, without dividing them into two separate categories, without contrasting them according to area or function. The distinctiveness of each nature is not nullified by the union. Instead, the "properties" of each nature are conserved and both natures concur in one "person" and in one *hypostasis* [subsistence, entity]. They are not divided or cut into two *prosōpa* (individual persons), but are together the one and only and only-begotten Logos of God, the Lord Jesus Christ. Thus have the prophets of old testified; thus the Lord Jesus Christ himself taught us; thus the Symbol of the Fathers [Nicene Creed] has handed down to us.[94]

The theological significance of the Chalcedonian definition. While the controversy and the conciliar response to it might at first strike the modern Christian as much ado about nothing, its significance is real. For reasons related to both revelation and redemption,[95] it was important to the church fathers gathered at Chalcedon to affirm a union, rather than a division or conflation, of the two natures of Christ. Indeed, the christological assertion at the heart of the Chalcedonian definition is referred as the *hypostatic union.*[96] According to Olson:

> *Union* refers to the union of two natures; *hypostatic* refers to the one person of the Son of God, the Logos who became human in the incarnation through the Holy Spirit and Mary. Thus, *hypostatic union* is the belief in a perfect union of two distinct but never separate natures—one human and one divine—in one integral eternal divine person. . . . They [the fathers and bishops of Chalcedon] never intended this model to be an explanation of the mystery of the incarnation; rather they intended it

---

[94]John H. Leith, ed., *Creeds of the Churches: A Reader in Christian Doctrine from the Bible to the Present,* rev. ed. (Richmond, VA: John Knox Press, 1973), pp. 35-36, cited in ibid., pp. 226-27.
[95]Olson, *Mosaic of Christian Belief,* pp. 236, 242.
[96]Ibid., p. 227.

to be a paradoxical protection of the mystery against rationalizing explanations that effectively destroy the mystery.[97]

It appears that even in the early centuries of the Christian movement, the perennial temptation to fall prey to a false antithesis had to be resisted. Thus, the Chalcedonian creed calls for the faithful to maintain a delicate balance as it relates to Christ's two natures. This biblically derived christological affirmation enjoins a "both-and" rather than "either-or" understanding of Jesus' divinity and humanity. To be more precise, *union without conflation* was and is the key to what Olson elegantly refers to as "a paradoxical protection of the mystery against rationalizing explanations that effectively destroy the mystery."

The "rationalizing explanations" to which Olson refers took the form of a number of alternative views of Jesus that, because they threatened to destroy the mystery of the incarnation (thus emptying the Jesus story of its revelatory and redemptive power),[98] precipitated the theological controversy addressed at Chalcedon.[99] While a thorough analysis of these alternative perspectives is beyond the scope of this work,[100] I will suggest that these alternative views fall into four categories, each occupying its own place on the arc of the proverbial pendulum on either side of the orthodox position. Figure 2.4 portrays this spectrum of christological perspectives regarding the dual nature of Christ.

On the far right side is *docetism* (Greek *dokēsis,* "appearance," and *dokein,* "to seem"),[101] a christological view that denied Jesus' humanity. This view, which circulated mainly in Gnostic circles, insisted that Jesus Christ only *seemed* to have a human body and only *appeared* to suffer

---

[97]Ibid.

[98]I want to underscore here that "the protection of the mystery" aimed at by framers of the creed had to do with much more than a desire to maintain the integrity of an aesthetically appealing theological concept. Instead, the community of patristic theologians that forged the Chalcedonian definition recognized on the basis of Scripture that the ability of Jesus Christ to function in a truly efficacious manner in terms of both revelation and redemption depended on his being both God and human at the same time, his two natures in union without conflation.

[99]Olson, *Mosaic of Christian Belief,* pp. 232-38.

[100]For such an analysis, see Roger E. Olson, *The Story of Christian Theology* (Downers Grove, IL: IVP Academic, 1999), pp. 205-49.

[101]Carl E. Braaten, Robert W. Jenson and Gerhard O. Forde, *Christian Dogmatics,* vol. 1 (Minneapolis: Fortress Press, 1984), p. 499.

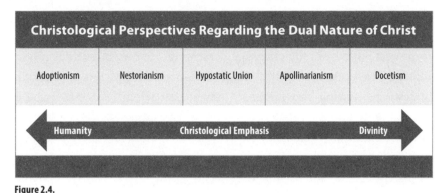

Christological Perspectives Regarding the Dual Nature of Christ

| Adoptionism | Nestorianism | Hypostatic Union | Apollinarianism | Docetism |

Humanity ◄─── Christological Emphasis ───► Divinity

Figure 2.4.

and die."[102] According to Carl Braaten, Robert Jenson and Gerhard Forde:

> The gnostic influence, orienting in general from Oriental spirituality, regarded matter as evil and the flesh as unreal. Therefore, when God became man and the Word became flesh in the person of Jesus the Christ, this was only apparently so. For docetism, the divinity of Christ posed no problem; it could hardly be emphasized enough. In its view, however, the Son of God could not really become human. The human life of Jesus evaporated into a cloud of divinity.[103]

On the far left side of the pendulum's swing is *adoptionism,* a position which denied the divinity of Jesus. Several groups of early Christians took this position. For instance, the Ebionites were Jewish, nontrinitarian disciples who held that while Jesus was the Christ, he was a mere man, the natural son of an earthly father and mother, divinely chosen to function as the Jewish messiah.[104] In addition to the Ebionites, Olson explains that the Syrian bishop Paul of Samosata and his followers "believed that Jesus Christ was only human but a very special human—one 'adopted' by God as his special prophet and 'son.'"[105]

Just right of the center of the spectrum is *Apollinarianism,* which takes its name from its primary promoter, Apollinarius, an early bishop of the church in Laodicea. This view is actually representative of a collection of related perspectives (Eutychianism, monophysitism), all of which tended

---

[102]Ibid.
[103]Ibid.
[104]Ibid., pp. 499-500.
[105]Olson, *Mosaic of Christian Belief,* p. 233.

to conflate the two natures of Christ in such a way as to place a greater emphasis on his divinity at the expense of his humanity. The concern was to protect Jesus from the charge of possessing what we in our day might refer to as a "split personality." Thus Apollinarius, suspicious of any talk of Jesus possessing two natures[106] taught that while Jesus possessed a human body and soul (in the sense of an animating life force), he was without a human rational mind. In Jesus of Nazareth, "the place for a human rational soul or spirit (i.e., mind) was filled by the divine Logos/ Word, the eternal Son of God, the second person of the Trinity."[107] While this seemed to explain why the human Jesus could know what other people were thinking, it had the effect of presenting a Jesus who lived his earthly existence, in Olson's words, as "God in a bod."[108]

The reason for the concern of Apollinarius and others was the chris-tological perspective located just left of the center of the pendulum's arc—a view known as *Nestorianism,* named after its chief proponent, Nestorius, the Antiochian patriarch (super-bishop) of Constantinople. This view, essentially a trinitarian version of adoptionism,[109] pictured Jesus as a divine-human being who

> was actually a "moral union" of two persons like a perfect marriage. The eternal Son of God entered into a unique relationship with the human Jesus Christ from the latter's very beginning in the virgin Mary. What was born of Mary, however, was only the human one—the Son of David. Throughout his life on earth the human one and divine one worked en-tirely in concert with each other although only the human one was born, experienced limited knowledge, grew in wisdom, suffered and died. The divine one, the Word of God/Logos/Son of God, performed the miracles and remained untouched by any weaknesses, frailties, suffering, increase in knowledge and wisdom or death.[110]

Nestorius had issues with the idea that a human, Mary, could give birth to the Son of God. In the end, it was because Nestorianism, well-meaning though it might have been, seemed to reduce Jesus to "a man

---

[106]Ibid., p. 235.
[107]Ibid., p. 236.
[108]Ibid.
[109]Ibid., p. 237.
[110]Ibid.

in a special kind of relationship with God" that the leaders of the early church met in Ephesus in A.D. 431 and condemned this christological perspective as a heresy.[111]

As we have already seen, one of the lessons of the history of theology is that overcorrections happen! In the case of the theological controversy addressed at Chalcedon, the trajectories had ranged back and forth across the christological spectrum from those views which tended to deny or downplay Jesus' humanity to those which tended to deny or downplay his divinity. Finally, the church fathers arrived at a "unified and unifying Christology" which affirmed "Jesus Christ as God incarnate; one unified person—the eternal Son of God equal with the father; of two distinct but never separate natures, human and divine."[112]

The missiological significance of the Chalcedonian definition. Why this history lesson? What does Christology have to do with missiology?[113] I suggest that these four alternatives to the orthodox doctrine of the hypostatic union (i.e., the incarnate Christ) are roughly analogous to the four alternatives to the incarnation response to the current cultural zeitgeist: repudiation, toleration, accommodation and capitulation. In other words, just as the early Christians struggled with how to properly understand the relationship between the divine and human natures in Jesus Christ, a controversy exists today as to the proper way to relate the divine

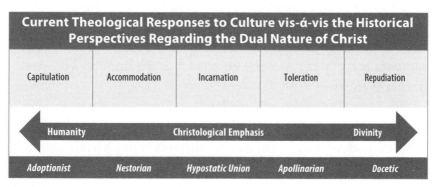

Figure 2.5.

---

[111]Ibid.

[112]Ibid., p. 241.

[113]For more support for the idea that a missional ecclesiology/missiology must be informed by christology, see Hirsch, *Forgotten Ways*, pp. 94, 99, 142-43, 153-54n9, 277.

and human components of the ministry contextualization task—the Christian gospel (at the center of which are the four christological verities) and the distinctive, real-life attributes of various human cultures.

With this idea in mind, figure 2.5 portrays the associations I make between the spectrum of theological responses to the cultural zeitgeist currently at work in the Western world and the historic positions regarding the two natures of Christ.

Just as it is important for reasons related to revelation and redemption to embrace a particular understanding ("union without conflation") of the incarnate Christ's two natures (human and divine), the same is true with respect to an adequate and appropriate engagement in missional ministry. The contextualization of the gospel necessarily involves two components. The divine component is the gospel itself, at the heart of which are the christological verities. The human component is comprised of the "conditions on the ground," the matrix of sociocultural realities at work in each slightly unique ministry locale. When contextualizing the gospel for various human cultures, it is possible to fail to do justice to either the christological verities or the cultural realities. Despite our best intentions, we seem to possess a persistent tendency to deny or downplay one or the other in our missional endeavors. But this is surely what must *not* happen if the transformation of individuals and cultures is to occur!

An entire book could well be devoted to the task of expounding on the proposed associations displayed in figure 2.5. What follows is a brief description of each, along with some indication of why the "incarnation" response is the better choice with respect to the ministry contextualization endeavor.

The *capitulation* approach can be considered *adoptionist* because it abjectly denies the divine side of the contextualization coupling—the christological verities. In succeeding chapters it will become apparent that there are some missionally minded folk who embrace a non-trinitarian adoptionist, essentially ebionitic, understanding not only of Jesus Christ, but of Christian mission as well.[114] Just as the second-century

---

[114]Referred to by Braaten, Jenson and Forde as the "left wing" of christology, "'Ebionitism' is the name of a widespread christological teaching of the second century that presented Jesus as a mere man, denying his divinity altogether." Stemming mainly from Jewish circles, "for the

Ebionites denied the essential deity of Jesus and embraced an adoptionist Christology, even so there are contemporary theologians who feel no need to maintain any sort of genuine commitment to the christological verities (which they consider to be insurmountable stumbling blocks to people in our Western ministry context), viewing Jesus as a mere human being who serves as a marvelous, extraordinary example of a God-centered life.

Olson correctly links christological adoptionism with "modern liberal Protestant Christianity."[115] One does not have to be a fighting fundamentalist to possess the conviction that the capitulation response's abject assimilation of the gospel to the current cultural zeitgeist so as to make the Christian faith more acceptable to its current crop of cultured despisers is an option that has rightly been rejected by the majority of Christians throughout the history of the movement. In the same way that a merely human Jesus fails in terms of the divine revelation and universal redemption clearly spoken of in the New Testament Scriptures, so a ministry message that offers the world nothing more than an inspiring example of someone who, because of an extraordinary God-consciousness, lived as a person for others, fails to possess the kind of spiritual power required to transform human hearts and subvert human cultures toward an embrace of kingdom values. At the end of the day, the capitulation response fails with respect to both a missional and biblical faithfulness. A serious attempt to do justice to both 1 Corinthians 9:20-22 (the missional task) and Jude 3 (the biblical text) cannot help but move the pendulum from the far left side of the spectrum, further to the right. But how far should we allow the pendulum to swing in that direction?

The *repudiation* approach can be considered *docetic* because it tends to deny the significance of the human side of the contextualization coupling—the cultural realities. Braaten, Jenson and Forde refer to docetism as "the perennial heresy of the 'right wing' in christology."[116] Just as his-

---

Ebionites, Jesus was certainly the Messiah, the Christ, but he was only a man. He could not be God. Impossible! They also denied the virgin birth. Jesus was born the natural son of an earthly father and mother, Joseph and Mary" (Braaten, Jenson and Ford, *Christian Dogmatics,* 1:499-500).

[115]Olson, *Mosaic of Christian Belief,* p. 234.

[116]Braaten, Jenson and Ford, *Christian Dogmatics,* 1:499.

toric docetism denied the possibility that the divine Logos could have actually taken on human flesh and contended that he only appeared to do so, the repudiation response rejects the idea that the Christian faith and life can and should look different when embraced and lived out in various cultural contexts. A docetic approach to ministry contextualization essentially rejects the incarnation of the gospel into various cultural forms, insisting instead on a rigid adherence to one classical form and expression of Christian life and worship that should be replicated in every time and place.

While I appreciate how the repudiation response strives to do justice to Jude 3, its understanding of the Christian faith lacks a necessary nuance. Failing to make the important distinction between dogma and doctrine, the fundamentalism at the heart of this response tends toward an orthodoxy that is too elaborate in terms of scope (a strident, over-developed creedalism or traditionalism) and less than humble in how it is held and proffered to others (a Christian Pharisaism). Failing to take seriously Paul's exhortation in 1 Corinthians 9:20-22 to keep contextualizing the gospel for various human cultures, this unbalanced, essentially docetic approach to Christian life and ministry attaches too much importance to maintaining a commitment to historic, classical, supposedly pristine *expressions* of both the *message* and *method*.

The *incarnation* response offers a better approach. With regard to the *message,* this response understands the danger of allowing the Christian gospel to be held captive to a contextualization endeavor that took place in a prior era and at another location. Though a commitment to the christological verities must never change, each ministry context deserves a fresh incarnation or revisioning of the gospel—a *contextually sensitive* articulation of why the members of this particular cultural locale should consider the Christ-event to be amazingly good news despite any challenges its acceptance will produce to the way they are currently living.

An important component of the missional impulse that makes a docetic response to human cultures untenable is the conviction that the Spirit of mission is actually at work in various human cultures, prior to the arrival of the Christian missionary, preparing the members of that culture to hear and appreciate the gospel once it is proclaimed to them.[117] The missional orthodoxy I associate with the incarnation response believes this is true even with respect to the advent of postmodernity. Ross Hastings speaks for many missional evangelicals:

> I believe we can feel positive about the mission in this era insofar as we can see evidence of windows that the Spirit has created with postmodernity for receptivity to the gospel. There is a new openness to spirituality. There is a hunger for intimacy born of much domestic brokenness, and particularly the absence of fathers, as a result of the drivenness for success and its symbols. There is an emotional authenticity about this generation that is very much consonant with gospel values, and a refreshing change from the emotional pharisaism one often finds in the church. There is a distrust of metanarratives, which are considered oppressive, and yet the nature of Christianity, understood rightly, is not oppressive. Furthermore, the concern for the poor that characterizes many postmoderns, inspired by popular artists, creates opportunities for many to sense the appeal of Jesus who became poor, lived among the poor and proclaimed a gospel for the poor.[118]

In a way that neither the repudiation nor toleration responses allow, the incarnation response leans into the various ways that postmodernity can actually facilitate a fruitful engagement in missional ministry. While remaining loyal to the Jesus of the verities, the incarnation response seeks to recognize and cooperate with what the Spirit of mission is up to in a ministry environment that he has not given up on—its increasingly post-Christian nature notwithstanding!

Furthermore, with regard to the *method,* the incarnation response recognizes, on the basis of 1 Corinthians 9:20-22, that very few ecclesial traditions and missional methods should be considered sacrosanct. The recontextualization process calls for both theological and methodological innovation toward the goal of developing *compelling presentations of the gospel* and *culturally informed expressions of Christian community.* Though our rock-bottom commitment to the Jesus of the

---

[117]Ross Hastings actually points out the failure on the part of many fundamentalist evangelicals to reckon with this possibility (see Hastings, *Missional God,* p. 45).
[118]Ibid., pp. 57-58.

verities should never change, it is crucial that both our ministry message and method experience an ongoing, culturally sensitive revisioning and retooling, so that, as Paul put it, "by all possible means [we] might save some" (1 Cor 9:22).

The bottom line is that because of its essentially docetic philosophy of ministry, the repudiation response, like the capitulation response, ultimately fails both the biblical and missional faithfulness tests. The incarnation response, with its commitment to taking both 1 Corinthians 9:20-22 and Jude 3 seriously, is therefore a better option—one which I hope some of my conservative evangelical colleagues will seriously consider.

The *toleration* approach can be considered *Apollinarian* because it tends to downplay the significance of the human side of the contextualization coupling—the cultural realities. Roger Olson asserts that something akin to the Apollinarian view that Jesus lived out his earthly existence as "God in a bod" seems to be the "popular default Christology of many untutored Christians."[119] When Olson refers to "untutored Christians," I think he has in mind the members of churches in which a certain amount of anti-intellectualism is still in play. I know from my experience in the classroom that many students from traditional evangelical or Pentecostal-charismatic churches struggle at first when challenged to think through what it means to say that Jesus was fully human. These discussions can seem at first to be irreverent, if not blasphemous.

Eventually, however, most of my students progress toward the realization that a "God in a bod" Christology is incompatible with a thoughtful, biblically informed understanding of soteriology. Referring to Apollinarianism, Olson is careful to point out:

> The church fathers recognized this is a very serious mistake that could eventually undermine salvation itself for, as Gregory of Nazianzus declared, "What God has not assumed [taken to himself in incarnation] is not saved." That is, if Jesus Christ is the mediator between God and humanity and if the incarnation is itself necessary for salvation, then the incarnate Savior Jesus Christ must have had full and complete humanity and full and complete deity—two unmutilated, complete and perfect natures.[120]

---

[119]Olson, *Mosaic of Christian Belief*, p. 236.
[120]Ibid.

In the same way that something more than a "God in a bod" Christology is necessary for salvation, the Christian church must do more than *tolerate* its cultural setting, including postmodernity, if its ministries are to have any genuine effect. A penetration of culture is called for if the church is going to do more than merely talk about being spiritual salt and light. The toleration response to the current cultural zeitgeist fails the missional faithfulness test precisely because of its reticence to adequately engage the realities of human culture while still maintaining its embrace of the christological verities.

The goal of an adequate missional engagement with human culture is the same as Jesus' incarnation: identification, differentiation, transformation. My work with members of the emerging generations has shown me that, due to the impact of postmodern philosophy and culture and their deep disappointment with traditional evangelicalism, they have become amazingly cynical about all things Christian. In order to entice them to take another look at Christ, something more is needed than a rehearsal of the four spiritual laws (our being careful to utilize colloquial speech and pop-cultural references notwithstanding). What is required is a gospel recontextualization—a fresh retelling of the story of Jesus that, while maintaining a commitment to the four christological verities at the heart of the Christian faith, is profoundly shaped by an empathetic understanding of their deepest fears and aspirations. We must do more than tolerate the impact of postmodernism. Taking seriously the identification, differentiation and transformation dynamics that are a huge part of the incarnation response, someone from the evangelical world needs to come alongside these angry, confused, hurting post-Christian young adults and serve them. Someone must enter into their lives, build the kind of humble, reciprocal relationships that provide psychological air to breathe and allow them to open up to a genuine dialogue regarding the radical claims of Christ and an encounter with his transformational Spirit. In other words, someone needs to engage in some empathic listening, recognizing that in between a condoning and condemning response to their anti-Christian vitriol is the possibility of simply understanding it and loving them anyway. We are never more like the incarnate Christ than when we seek first to understand the pain of the other before we attempt to minister to them. Indeed, my experience has been that a close relationship exists between a willingness to gain such an understanding and our experience of the Spirit-imparted ability to speak and act prophetically into the life of a post-Christian peer in a way that is both missionally faithful and fruitful.[121] The incarnation response embraces and employs the identification-differentiation-transformation process involved in a genuine contextualization of the gospel in a way that the toleration response does not.

One of my hopes is that not a few evangelical students or church members reading this book will catch the vision of a missional orthodoxy and will make the quality decision to move from the toleration to the incarnation response. We need more and more representatives of the evangelical movement to prayerfully surrender their theological imaginations to the Spirit of mission so that he might empower them to articulate the story of Jesus in fresh, innovative ways that succeed at both the missional and biblical faithfulness tests.

The *accommodation* approach can be considered Nestorian because it tends to downplay the divine side of the contextualization coupling—the christological verities. I hope that some leaders and members of emerging churches will likewise see the value of the incarnation response and gravitate toward it. Actually, my sense is that the leaders of the vast majority of emerging churches are doing this right already— engaging rather than repudiating or tolerating culture—building relationships, listening empathically, allowing their theological imaginations free reign to come up with innovative ministry methodologies that have the potential to impact people who would probably never darken the door of a traditional evangelical church. It takes a huge amount of courage and commitment to launch and maintain a ministry approach that no one has tried before. The response these young ministry innovators deserve from the rest of the evangelical community is one of respect and support.

---

[121]Similarly, Bruce Nicholls writes: "But distancing must be followed by identification with the receptor's culture. . . . The incarnation is the absolute model of this identification involving both renunciation and identification. There will be no real cross-cultural communication apart from identification. It begins as an attitude of the mind (Phil 2:5) and leads on to the practice of costly servanthood (Phil 2:5-8). This is the missionary calling of the church, the price to be paid for true contextualization" (Nicholls, *Contextualization*, p. 51).

That said, my concern is that some of these ministry innovators, due perhaps to the influence of some emergent authors, may be guilty of adopting an essentially Nestorian approach to missional ministry. This occurs when well-intentioned church leaders pay more attention to the cultural sensibilities at work in our post-Christian context than to biblical passages such as John 20:31; 2 John 1:7-9; 1 Corinthians 15:1-8 and Romans 10:9-10, which underscore the crucial importance of believing and trusting in particular things about Jesus so as to experience the salvation the Bible talks about so much.[122]

As long as the four central christological doctrines are not vitiated by some fresh understanding of how the story of Jesus plays out as good news for the members of a cultural context, then great! If, however, out of some sense of need to *rehabilitate* the gospel, an author or church leader feels the freedom to even flirt with the idea that perhaps one or more of these four christological verities is not really crucial to the Christian faith and life, then we have a problem. As indicated previously, there is a fine line between the accommodation and assimilation methods of gospel contextualization (see figure 2.1). It might seem to some that it is only a fine line that separates the accommodation and recontextualization approaches as well.[123] Should someone mistakenly conclude that only subtleties distinguish these three contextualization approaches, it might be tempting to "play it safe" and ride the pendulum in the opposite direction toward the indigenization or even "mere proclamation" contextualization methods. But that would be an overcorrection to an overcorrection! No, the responsible move is to do the hard work of nuancing between the indigenization, recontextualization and accommodation approaches and thereby find our way to the incarnation response.

---

[122]Speaking of the importance of the notion of salvation to the Christian faith and, therefore, to Christian missiology, David Bosch writes: "Salvation is indeed a fundamental concern of every religion. For Christians, the conviction that God has decisively wrought salvation for all in and through Jesus Christ stands at the very center of their lives. After all, the very name Jesus means 'Savior.' . . . It follows from this conviction that the Christian missionary movement has been motivated, throughout its history, by the desire to mediate salvation to all. The 'soteriological motif' may indeed be termed the 'throbbing heart of missiology' since it concerns the 'deepest and most fundamental question of humanity'" (Bosch, *Transforming Mission*, p. 402).

[123]Actually, I believe the difference between accommodation and recontextualization is hugely significant!

Referring to ideas originally expressed by Lesslie Newbigin, missional authority Darrell Guder speaks of the need for Christians to be able to "live bilingually . . . speaking both the language of faith and translating that language into our lives and actions in our various mission fields."[124] There will be some participants in the missional conversation who will not be satisfied with my understanding of the dynamic of recontextualization. Still I contend that this type of recontextualization is in complete accord with the conviction of many that we dare not attempt to be translators of the gospel without possessing the kind of "scriptural literacy" that enables us to do so in a faithful manner.[125] Because the "incarnation" response to the current cultural zeitgeist requires us evangelicals to live bilingually, it succeeds with respect to both the biblical and missional faithfulness tests. Precisely because of its position in the middle of the pendulum's arc, the missional orthodoxy associated with the incarnation response has what it takes to bridge the divide that exists between many members of the traditional evangelical, missional and emerging church movements. It really is possible for us to do more than merely talk about being comrades rather than competitors in the ministry contextualization endeavor.

In the chapters that follow we will examine the eight traditional theological loci in light of the false antitheses put forward by the liberal/emergent overcorrection to our post-Christian ministry context. Our approach will be to allow a theological realism that takes seriously the missionary nature of God to help us arrive at "answers" to these false dichotomies. This, in turn, will enable us to avoid a fighting fundamentalism on the one hand and a too-accommodating liberalism on the other. My hope is that the end result of these eight discussions will be a vision of the Christian faith and life that not only functions as common ground between traditional, missional and emerging evangelicals, but also invites many of our post-Christian peers to take another look at Christ and his church. Ultimately, that is what a missional orthodoxy is all about.

---

[124]Guder, "Missional Hermeneutics," p. 140.
[125]Ibid.

EXCURSUS: THE LIBERAL/EMERGENT OVERCORRECTION AND REALIST ALTERNATIVE TO IT

Throughout this book I refer to the liberal/emergent overcorrection. In this excursus I explore some possible reasons for this overcorrection and then go on to explain how a theological and critical realism provides a compelling alternative to it. Since the theological and critical realist perspective described in the next few pages functions as a key component of the missional orthodoxy proffered in the remainder of this work, it's crucial that this excursus material be given some careful, thoughtful consideration.

Some possible reasons for the liberal/emergent overcorrection. While I will not claim to know the heart motives of those promoting the emergent vision of the Christian faith, a careful read of the literature produced by and about them can provide some indications of why they have felt it necessary to follow the swing of the pendulum toward an approach that entails an accommodation of the gospel to our postmodern, post-Christian culture extending beyond a simple contextualization or even a biblically informed recontextualization.[126]

A frustration with fundamentalism. One possible explanation for this understandable, but still lamentable, overcorrection is that many of those promoting the emergent paradigm have been hurt by previous encounters with Christian fundamentalism. A careful read of the literature (books, articles and blogs) describing the emergent impulse will reveal that a significant stimulant for it has been an aversion to the fundamentalist attitudes and behaviors still prevalent in too many conservative congregations and denominations. For example, in *Emerging Churches,* which may be the authoritative work on the topic, Eddie Gibbs and Ryan Bolger note that a significant number of emerging church leaders report having been profoundly disappointed, frustrated or wounded by the fundamentalist attitudes and practices they experi-

---

[126]"On the left wing of the emerging movement, we can discern an unintended lapse into patterns of theologizing reminiscent of Protestant liberalism. Here the Bible, along with every other theological resource, may be exploited in search of support for the advance of values and often unacknowledged 'doctrines' that shape and animate core convictions and goals, but the community of faith remains answerable to nothing outside itself" (DeVine, "Can the Church Emerge?" pp. 184-85).

enced within traditional evangelical churches. Of the fifty stories re-counted in the fascinating and helpful appendix, over half of them contain fairly explicit references to such attitudes and behaviors.[127]

Clearly there is more than a sense of frustration driving the coura-geous ministry leadership at work in many emerging churches. But could it be that in back of much of the emergent disappointment with traditional evangelical Christianity and promotion of the emerging paradigm is a latent but poignant sense of frustration with Christian fundamentalism?[128]

A concern over conservative politics. Perhaps another cause for disap-pointment among those advocating the emerging paradigm has to do with the political conservatism they associate with conservative evan-gelical Christianity.[129] Reports given in books such as Dan Kimball's *They Like Jesus but Not the Church* suggest that the disdain which at least some young adults harbor for traditional conservative churches may have as much to do with their distaste for conservative politics as with any concern over an outdated or inauthentic style of ministry.[130]

This is a real issue that needs to be talked about. The fact is that a person's engagement in the heady world of politics can become not only all-consuming but all-determining as well. This is true for those on both sides of the political aisle. My concern is that the theological convictions of way too many Christians derive more from the dynamic of political partisanship (conservative or liberal) than the influence of Scripture. Thus, while sympathetic to the emergent concern that too many evangelical churches have allowed themselves to be co-opted by

---

[127]Eddie Gibbs and Ryan K. Bolger, *Emerging Churches: Creating Christian Community in Post-modern Cultures* (Grand Rapids: Baker, 2005), pp. 239-328. For similar descriptions of disen-chantment, see Dave Tomlinson, *The Post-Evangelical*, rev. ed. (Grand Rapids: Zondervan, 2003), pp. 23, 26-27, 30, 53-56; and Dan Kimball, *They Like Jesus but Not the Church: Insights from Emerging Generations* (Grand Rapids: Zondervan, 2007). Both of these works reference the frustration some members of the emerging generations have with the idea that one must possess politically conservative views in order feel at home in traditional evangelical churches.

[128]D. A. Carson has likewise explored this thesis. See Carson, *Becoming Conversant*, pp. 14-25, 85-86.

[129]For example, see McLaren, NKC 6-7; McLaren, GO 15-16 [19-20], 45 [51]n14, 61 [68], 116 [128], 119 [131], 138 [152], 233-34 [263-64]; 245-46 [277-78]; Borg, HC 138-46; Roger E. Olson, *Reformed and Always Reforming: The Postconservative Approach to Evangelical Theology* (Grand Rapids: Baker Academic, 2007), p. 8; Jim Wallis, *The Politics of God: Why the Right Gets It Wrong, and the Left Doesn't Get It* (San Francisco: HarperSanFrancisco, 2005).

[130]Dan Kimball, *They Like Jesus*, pp. 73-95.

a particular political party, I must at the same time insist that a vision of the Christian faith that is faithful to both the biblical text and missional task will not be overly influenced by any political agenda, whether left or right.

The need for a more palatable paradigm. Yet another possible reason for the liberal/emergent overcorrection is the conviction that in an increasingly postmodern, post-Christian world, a presentation of the earlier, more traditional version of Christianity is simply not sustainable as a missional approach.

Representing the liberal perspective, Marcus Borg has gone on record as saying that the earlier (traditional) understanding of Christianity is "unpersuasive" to millions of contemporary Americans and "no longer works" for them.[131] This observation appears to have produced within Borg what is undoubtedly a well-meaning sense of need to assimilate the teachings of historic Christianity to the contemporary culture so as to create a version of the faith that is not a "stumbling block" to the sensibilities of contemporary post-Christians.[132] He writes, "The issue isn't that one of these visions of Christianity is right and the other wrong. Rather, the issue is functionality, whether a paradigm still works."[133] Since there is little or no need in Borg's emerging paradigm for the concept of "right belief," his argument is that even radical changes in the message we Christians present to the world are justified on the grounds that they are necessary in order to do "evangelism" among the millions of post-Christians living around us.[134]

What does the freedom Borg feels to change the message of Christianity in order to make it more acceptable to our post-Christian peers have to do with the emergent movement? In *A Generous Orthodoxy,* Brian McLaren makes what appears to be a similar assertion:

> Our message and methodology have changed, do change, and must change if we are faithful to the ongoing and unchanging mission of Jesus Christ. In other words, I believe that we must be *always reforming,*

---

[131]Borg, HC 18. See also Borg, GWNK 2.
[132]Borg, HC 18. See also McLaren, GO 16 [20], 39-40 [44-45], 92 [100].
[133]Borg, HC 18. See also Borg, SC 17-20.
[134]Borg, HC 18.

not because we've got it wrong and we're closer and closer to finally "getting it right"' but because our mission is ongoing and our context is dynamic. From this viewpoint "getting it right" is beside the point; the point is "being and doing good" as followers of Jesus in our unique time and place, fitting in with the ongoing story of God's saving love for planet Earth."[135]

So, according to at least some of the leaders of the emergent version of the Christian faith, in order to be missionally effective in our current ministry context, we simply must (contrary to the kind of contextualization at work in the toleration response) be willing to not only contemporize our ministry methods, but the message as well. Given what McLaren (like Borg) has to say about "getting it right" being "beside the point," some crucial questions arise: What kind of changes to the message does the emergent paradigm have in mind? Are we merely talking about changes in our understanding and presentation of how the story of Jesus plays out as good news for our contemporary culture, or might these accommodation-inspired changes go deeper than that to affect those christological doctrines that form the very heart of the Christian faith? Borg's writings clearly indicate that he is open to both kinds of changes to the gospel if necessary for "contextualization" in the contemporary era. The kinds of changes McLaren has in mind seem for the most part to be limited to the former type. However, because of his penchant for theological speech that is deliberately obscure and imprecise, McLaren can, here and there, be interpreted as maintaining an openness to the latter type as well.

What are we to make of this? Given McLaren's influence in the emerging church community it seems appropriate to wonder whether he, for missional purposes, actually considers it acceptable to disavow (or even downplay) any of the four christological verities or if he only pretends to do so in order to provoke conversation and push the pendulum in a less fundamentalist direction. The final possible reason I will offer for the liberal/emergent overcorrection to our post-Christian context may help us better understand the willingness of some post-evangelicals to make these Borg-like theological moves.

---

[135]McLaren, GO 191-92 [214], emphasis original.

An eccentric epistemology leading to a different view of doctrine. I suspect that yet another explanation for the tendency of some emergent authors to travel in a theological trajectory that leads toward assimilation rather than recontextualization may have to do with the degree to which the promoters of the new paradigm have embraced a hard postmodern epistemology—an eccentric epistemology that ultimately promotes an actual aversion to doctrine or, at the very least, a view of how doctrine functions that differs dramatically from the classical one.[136]

In the previous chapter I offered a simple overview of the culturally conditioned perspectivalism that is postmodernism. At this point I want to delve a bit deeper into the realm of epistemology—that branch of philosophy that focuses on how we actually gain knowledge. My hope is that this brief discussion will possess some explanatory power as to why some Christians on both the left and the right are willing to promote some rather radical swings of the theological pendulum.

First, an epistemological model known as *classical foundationalism* asserts that a certain and objective knowledge of the world around us is possible because the knowledge edifice rests on a foundation of indubitable first order truths that can be "proved" through rational argument.[137] In other words, this perspective suggests that it is possible for human knowers, through rational means, to gain certain, objective knowledge of reality, including the realm of theology. Of course, one of the problems with a hard foundationalism is that it can produce a fighting fundamentalism—Christians cocksure that they have the truth about all things theological in their back pockets!

Over against this extreme view is the equally extreme nonfoundationalist (really antifoundationalist) epistemological perspective. As we have already seen, a *hard postmodernism* (cultural linguistic constructivism)

---

[136]See DeVine, "Can the Church Emerge?" pp. 184-86. Unfortunately I cannot devote as much space to this subject as it deserves, but I will at least attempt to offer a broad overview.

[137]Christian philosopher Nicolas Wolterstorff explains that the goal of foundationalism is "a body of theories from which all prejudice, bias, and unjustified conjecture have been eliminated. To attain this, we must begin with a firm foundation of certitude and build the house of theory on it by methods of whose reliability we are equally certain." Nicolas Wolterstorff, *Reason Within the Bounds of Religion* (Grand Rapids: Eerdmans, 1993), p. 28. See also Stanley J. Grenz and John R. Franke, *Beyond Foundationalism: Shaping Theology in a Postmodern Context* (Louisville, KY: Westminster John Knox, 2000), pp. 23, 30.

insists that a certain, objective knowledge of reality is impossible because all knowledge is necessarily relative to each knower's historically and culturally conditioned perspective. As time and culture are constantly changing, so is each culture's perspective of reality. According to postmodern thought, truth itself should be thought of as ever changing, completely relative to each culture's (or individual's) unique perspective.[138]

This essentially relativistic perspective on the nature of truth explains why some Christians, having taken the cultural-linguistic turn, have also come to view Christian doctrines merely as cultural creations of discrete Christian communities, or as Kevin Vanhoozer describes them, "articulations of the implicit grammatical rules that govern the community's speaking and thinking about God."[139] Here theology is grounded in ecclesiology rather than vice versa. Rather than a theology derived from the self-revelation of God presented in Christ and the Scriptures that witness to him informing the beliefs and practices of the church, it is held that doctrines merely articulate the logic of why each church (or family of churches) engages in its unique ecclesial practices.[140] Therefore, ac-

---

[138]Please note that Grenz and Franke use "nonfoundationalism" and "postfoundationalism" as synonyms (*Beyond Foundationalism*, pp. 28-29). Vanhoozer is careful to make a distinction between his postfoundational project and "those nonfoundationalist approaches that conceive knowledge as a web, net, or mosaic of belief." Apparently including the work of Grenz and Franke in this critique, Vanhoozer goes on to express his concern by saying: "In a web of beliefs, no one belief is more important than any other. Moreover, beliefs may be revised under pressure from experience. Indeed, in many nonfoundationalist accounts of knowledge, it is not a set of beliefs but the believing community that is considered 'basic' insofar as the web or mosaic of belief is borne along, and revised by, traditions and communities of inquiry." Kevin J. Vanhoozer, *The Drama of Doctrine: A Canonical Linguistic Approach to Christian Theology* (Louisville, KY: Westminster John Knox Press, 2005), p. 293; see also p. 293n3, which references Grenz and Franke, *Beyond Foundationalism*, p. 47.

[139]Vanhoozer, *Drama of Doctrine*, pp. 6-7. Vanhoozer goes on to wonder "whether such an approach has more of sociology than of theology about it. Does doctrine refer to God, or does it merely describe how members of the Christian community talk about God? If church practices serve as both source and norm for theology, how can we ever distinguish well-formed practices from those that are *deformed?* Kathryn Tanner accurately states the problem: '[P]ostliberal talk of describing the internal logic of first-order practices strongly suggests that second-order theology does nothing more than uncover a logic internal to those practices themselves.' It is important to recognize that there is something in the nature of theology's subject matter—God, the gospel—that resists being designated as mere 'local custom.'" Ibid., p. 7, citing Kathryn Tanner, *Theories of Culture: A New Agenda for Theology* (Minneapolis: Fortress Press, 1997), p. 74.

[140]Vanhoozer, *Drama of Doctrine*, pp. 6-7. Furthermore, for a telling discussion of how those promoters of the emerging paradigm who pride themselves on being doctrine-free are actually neck-deep in "doctrine-like convictions or values that characterize emerging church aspira-

cording to the emerging version of this "postliberal" perspective,[141] Christian doctrines can and should experience a rehabilitation from generation to generation and culture to culture so as to enable each Christian community to function relevantly in its unique time and place.

Thus it is argued by Christian nonfoundationalists (i.e., those promoting the emerging paradigm) that what is needed is a Christian orthodoxy that is flexible and generous rather than rigid and dogmatic. Furthermore, McLaren, while critical of the narcissistic motive behind some people's embrace of pluralistic relativism, has suggested that perhaps an embrace of it should be seen as a dangerous but necessary medicine—a "needed chemotherapy"—something the church should submit to for a season in order to emerge into something "beyond and better" than the old way of being Christians and doing church. To be more precise, McLaren speaks of a "pluralistic phase" that perhaps the church should not "stop short" of but rather "go through" and eventually "pass beyond."[142]

Now I, for one, find it difficult to comprehend how one passes through and beyond a phase of "pluralistic relativism." How does one emerge from an embrace of relativism into some sort of non- or postrelativism? It seems as if McLaren is suggesting that the way to steer the pendulum toward a balanced position between extremes (a noble goal) is to purposefully push the pendulum in an eccentric direction. At best, this simply doesn't make sense. At worst, it betrays the embrace of a hard postmodernism (something McLaren seems to disavow). I understand and agree with McLaren's concern over a fighting fundamentalism. But could it be that, ironically, the emerging paradigm McLaren is promoting has, like the one put forward by Borg, fallen prey to a false antithesis? *Perhaps we do not have to ride the pendulum all the way*

---

tion related to culture, authenticity, mystery, modesty, and community," see DeVine, "Can the Church Emerge?" pp. 186-88.

[141]Postliberalism is associated with the work of theologians such as George A. Lindbeck, Hans W. Frei, David H. Kelsey, William C. Placher and Ronald F. Thiemann. For more on postliberalism, a good place to start is George Lindbeck, *The Nature of Doctrine: Religion and Theology in a Postliberal Age* (Louisville, KY: Westminster John Knox, 1984). See also the helpful treatment of Lindbeck's theology in Robert C. Greer, *Mapping Postmodernism: A Survey of Christian Options* (Downers Grove, IL: IVP Academic, 2003), pp. 64-68, 142-57.

[142]See McLaren, GO 286-87 [325-26].

toward an embrace of a pluralistic relativism in order to avoid a fighting fundamentalism. Perhaps there is a third alternative between hard foundationalism and anti-foundationalism that does not involve an embrace of pluralistic relativism for any amount of time.[143]

A critical and theological realism. As suggested above, the foundationalist epistemological model is usually associated with modernity, religious fundamentalism and traditional evangelicalism,[144] while the nonfoundationalist model is typically associated with postmodernity and the emergent/post-evangelical paradigm.[145] Some have suggested that an alternative to these two extreme epistemological views is postfoundationalism (also known as a critical or modified realism), which insists that while our perceptions of reality are indeed conditioned by our historical and cultural contexts, it is still possible to reach beyond these contexts to arrive at a "sufficient, good enough" knowledge of the world around us.[146]

---

[143]It is worth noting that McLaren cites the work of David Bosch several times in *A Generous Orthodoxy*. This may indicate that his argument for a temporary embrace of a pluralistic relativism so as to emerge into something "beyond and better" may have been influenced by Bosch's discussion of "paradigm shifts in theology" (see Bosch, *Transforming Mission*, pp. 189-91). As part of this discussion, Bosch argues for a middle ground, so to speak, between the "mutually exclusive categories of 'absolute' and 'relative'" (p. 190). But it seems to me that the "middle ground" Bosch goes on to describe actually has to do with the manner in which our theological positions are held and proffered to others, rather than the nature of truth itself. According to Bosch, we do not have to choose between insisting that we currently possess the only valid understanding of a theological topic or acquiescing to the idea that any view is valid as long as it is held with sincerity. We steer a middle course between these two extreme positions, says Bosch, when we maintain a commitment to our current perspective on the matter while also being open to the possibility that, because our theological knowledge is currently less than perfect (see 1 Cor 13:12), we may someday come across another perspective that seems to do a better job of making sense of the data. Therefore, we must be open to paradigm shifts occurring in our theologizing when it becomes apparent to us that someone else's theological map is actually more accurate than the one we have been promoting (p. 191).

[144]Actually, scholars have pointed out that classical theological liberalism is likewise owing to a classical foundationalist epistemology. For example, see Nancey Murphy, *Beyond Liberalism and Fundamentalism: How Modern and Postmodern Philosophy Set the Theological Agenda* (Valley Forge, PA: Trinity Press International, 1996), pp. 12, 15-35.

[145]Grenz and Franke, *Beyond Foundationalism*, p. 46. See also McLaren, GO 286 [325].

[146]For example, see Vanhoozer, *Drama of Doctrine*, 286-91, 293-305; and Kevin Vanhoozer, "Pilgrim's Digress: Christian Thinking on and About the Post/Modern Way," in *Christianity and the Postmodern Turn: Six Views*, ed. Myron B. Penner (Grand Rapids: Brazos, 2005), pp. 88-89. See also the extended discussion of a post-foundationalism that serves as a relational ("both-and" rather than "either-or") "middle way" alternative to a dogmatic foundationalism and a skeptical nonfoundationalism in Shults, *Postfoundationalist Task*, pp. 11-12, 17-19, 25-81. See also the seminal work in J. Wentzel van Huyssteen, *Essays in Postfoundationalist Theology* (Grand Rapids: Eerdmans, 1997).

One postfoundationalist approach argues that, contrary to the way cultural-linguistic constructivism explains the acquisition of the cognitive framework necessary for the development of one's worldview, the truth is that as human infants and children *indwell,* bump around within, learn to speak and adapt to the physical and social worlds around them, this rudimentary interaction with reality produces a *tacit knowledge.* In other words, it creates a knowledge they do not know that they know or would not be able to explain to others—a subsidiary, below-the-radar awareness of the way things are, an "implicit knowledge" on which they rely in all their "explicit operations."[147] It is, therefore, not simply the acquisition of language, but rather this *holistic indwelling* of the world (physical and social) that allows human beings to acquire the cognitive framework necessary to assimilate real, trustworthy, if not perfect knowledge of the way the world works and how to best navigate their way in and through it.[148]

Trinitarian theologians who have embraced a critical realist epistemology go on to suggest that the same dynamic holds true with regard to the acquisition of spiritual knowledge. The *theological realism* I will be affirming throughout this book asserts that God is the most real entity in the universe[149] and that, with the *incarnation of Christ* and *outpouring of the Holy Spirit,* the trinitarian God has made it possible for those "in Christ" to know and interact with him in a real rather than merely conceptual, abstract or ideal manner.[150] As the members of a

---

[147]Thomas F. Torrance, "The Place of Michael Polanyi in the Modern Philosophy of Science," *Ethics in Science and Medicine 7* (1980): 60, as cited in Elmer Colyer, *How to Read T. F. Torrance: Understanding His Trinitarian and Scientific Theology* (Downers Grove, IL: InterVarsity Press, 2001), p. 335; see also p. 337.

[148]Torrance writes: "Indwelling is a holistic, significantly informal, integrative and heuristic process of investigating a field of inquiry. As this inquiry develops, our minds begin to assimilate the internal constitutive relations embodied in what we seek to know." Thomas F. Torrance, *Transformation and Convergence in the Frame of Knowledge: Explorations in the Interrelations of Scientific and Theological Enterprise* (Grand Rapids: Eerdmans, 1984), p. 114, as cited in Elmer Colyer, *How to Read T. F. Torrance*, p. 336. See also Colyer's treatment of how Torrance's concept of a "personal knowledge" avoids being merely subjective (ibid., pp. 342-44, 357) and David Bosch's brief overview of a "modified realism" (Bosch, *Transforming Mission*, pp. 368-69).

[149]God is not only the ultimate reality out of which everything in the cosmos derives its being (Acts 17:28; Rev 4:11), he is also the means by which all perceptive beings possess the capacity for knowledge of the real world around them (Ps 36:9; Jn 1:3-4).

[150]According to T. F. Torrance, "Everything hinges on the reality of God's *self*-communication to

Christian community[151] bump around in the "world" presented in the pages of the Spirit-inspired Scriptures,[152] as they engage in a spiritually disciplined, communal indwelling of the biblical narratives (and through them the grand, overarching story of redemption), slowly but surely the Holy Spirit helps them acquire a "cognitive framework," which the apostle Paul referred to as the "mind of Christ" (1 Cor 2:16; cf. 1 Jn 2:20-27).[153] Since Jesus Christ is, as the author of Hebrews put it, "the radiance of God's glory and the exact representation of his being" (Heb 1:3), the knowledge he provides of who God is and what he is about is spot on in terms of its fidelity. As T. F. Torrance has famously asserted, "What God is antecedently and eternally in himself he really is toward us in the concrete embodiment of his Truth in Jesus Christ the word made flesh."[154] All that is required, then, for a *real* knowledge of God and what he is up to in the world is our grace-enabled acquisition of the cognitive concepts and categories fitting to the divine subject matter—God's self-revelation.[155] It is through this God-

---

us in Jesus Christ, in whom there has become incarnate, not some created intermediary between God and the world, but the very Word who eternally inheres in the Being of God and is God, so that for us to know God in Jesus Christ is really to know him as he is in himself. It is with the same force that attention is directed [in the work of the church fathers] upon the Holy Spirit, whom the Father sends through the Son to dwell with us, and who, like the Son, is no mere cosmic power intermediate between God and the world, but is the Spirit of God who eternally dwells in him and in whom God knows himself, so that for us to know God in his Spirit is to know him in the hidden depths of his divine Being." T. F. Torrance, *Reality & Evangelical Theology* (Downers Grove, IL: InterVarsity Press, 1999), p. 23.

[151]See the treatment of Torrance's understanding of "the role of the church in theology" in Colyer, *How to Read T. F. Torrance*, pp. 352-55.

[152]Thomas F. Torrance, *Reality and Scientific Theology* (Edinburgh: Scottish Academic Press, 1985), pp. 83-84, as cited in Colyer, *How to Read T. F. Torrance*, p. 351, see also pp. 352-53, 356-57; T. F. Torrance, *Reality & Evangelical Theology*, pp. xv, 48-49.

[153]See also Ps 119:99; Lk 2:46-47, 52. Kurt Anders Richardson describes Torrance's version of this indwelling of Scripture: "We do not pretend to be the original readers of the Bible, nor do we ignore the distance between the times and spaces of the original writings and our own. Instead, through continual practice of reading and rereading and meditating on the words of Scripture, with the guidance of the Holy Spirit and the witness of the foundational doctrines of Christianity, believers acquire living and relational knowledge of God in each generation of the church." Kurt Anders Richardson, "Foreword: Introducing Torrance—Wonder over the Intelligibility of God," in Torrance, *Reality & Evangelical Theology*, p. xv. See also Lesslie Newbigin's crucial discussion of what it means to indwell the biblical text and the implications for missional ministry in Newbigin, *Gospel in a Pluralist Society*, pp. 97-102.

[154]Torrance, *Reality & Evangelical Theology*, p. 141. See also Karl Barth, *Church Dogmatics* 1/1 (Edinburgh, T & T Clark, 1936), pp. 350-51, cited in Hastings, *Missional God*, p. 101.

[155]What I have in mind here are theological concepts such as creation, fall, redemption, restora-

commissioned, Christ-centered, Spirit-enabled, *theologically real* cognitive framework that we find access to spiritual wisdom—that is, real,
trustworthy, if not perfect, knowledge (see 1 Cor 13:12) of the way the spiritual world works and how to best navigate our way in and through it.[156]

To be more specific, the fact that we currently "see but a poor reflection as in a mirror" and know only "in part" means that no human
theologizing this side of heaven should be considered impeccable. Because the divine reality always exceeds our statements about it, all theological speech must be judged by how well it points to the reality to
which the witness of Scripture directs us—the Jesus who confronts us in
and through the four christological verities. This is where the distinction
between dogma and doctrine proves crucial. All doctrines, like maps of
reality, can be updated to more faithfully refer to this divine reality. This
is why no single theology, not even any one extra-biblical creedal formulation, should ever be considered final.

Still, a theological realism holds that because God, by the Spirit through
the Scriptures, is in touch with the church, dogma has been delivered.
Thus, those carefully and prayerfully crafted creedal formulations that

---

tion, grace, mercy, holiness, justice, sin, substitution, election, messiah, judgment, faithfulness, repentance, discipleship and kingdom. While I suppose an awareness of the four christological verities will be acquired through the biblical indwelling experience, I am not suggesting
that the four verities are the "cognitive concepts and categories" required for spiritual knowledge. These commitments are the product of spiritual knowledge, not prerequisites for it.

[156]According to T. F. Torrance, we must move away from the dualist epistemological construct
that pits the subjective against the objective as if we exist merely in a human/world epistemological environment (field). Actually, our environment is triadic—God/human/world. The
creator God, who himself is intrinsically rational, has invested rational capacities in the human
species precisely so that we may come to know the rationality inherent in both the universe
and the God who created it. This means that our present epistemological condition is not
subject/object but object/object accountable to God the one true Subject (*Reality & Evangelical
Theology*, pp. 27-30). That the one true Subject has, via the incarnation, entered into our epistemological environment (field) and spoken revelatory words to the creatures he desires to be
in relationship with has implications for our ability to know God as he really is. This important
insight provides support for my thesis that there exists a third alternative to the false antithesis
between a belief that human rationality can through logical deduction arrive at certain, objective knowledge of the real and the antithetical view that absolutely no real knowledge of anything is possible due to the historically and culturally conditioned (subjective) status of the
human knower. To reiterate my position, God himself is the really real, the fountain of all life
and light/knowledge (Acts 17:28; Rev 4:11; Ps 36:9; Jn 1:3-4). Via the incarnation of God into
the world through Jesus Christ, real knowledge of God (and his view of the world) is at least
theoretically possible to those followers of Christ willing to *indwell* the biblical documents
designed by God to make revelation of himself to human creatures possible.

were designed specifically to articulate Christian dogma and that have garnered a wide consensus from segments of the church located far and wide in terms of time and geography, should be seriously consulted and only overturned or even modified when there is an overwhelming consensus that such changes are warranted. Such warrant is based on the degree to which these proposed theological changes actually improve our understanding and experience of the central reality presented in sacred Scripture, namely, the character of God as revealed in and through the Jesus we experience by means of an existentially authentic embrace of the four christological verities. In other words, what orients all contemporary theological statements are not their cultural circumstances, but the divine reality itself known in Jesus Christ. The most helpful theological statements offered by any generation's theologians can and should be selected or coined from the current cultural-linguistic setting. But these culturally conditioned theological statements cannot set the criteria or provide the norm for the church's doctrinal commitments. The fact that there are central realities revealed in and through the four christological verities— that is, Christian dogma—which orient and gives relative value to all theological speech (including Christian doctrines) is a crucial element of a theological humility that also allows for theological conviction.[157]

The critical-realist epistemological perspective has been associated with what some refer to as post-postmodernism.[158] For the sake of clarity, I will sometimes use the term *soft postmodernism* and suggest that a commitment to such a perspective, especially when combined with an embrace of the theological realism discussed above, constitutes a *measured* rather than an overreacting/overcorrecting response to a fighting fundamentalism and the epistemological foundationalism that feeds it. In other words, we do not have to choose between a classical foundationalist epistemology that facilitates the fundamentalist's arrogant embrace of a demanding orthodoxy, and an abjectly nonfoundationalist epistemology that relativizes truth and engenders an assimi-

---

[157]I am especially indebted to one of this book's editors, Dr. Gary Deddo—whose familiarity with the work of T. F. Torrance is extensive—for some of the language utilized in this and the preceding paragraph.

[158]See Robert C. Greer, *Mapping Postmodernism: A Survey of Christian Options* (Downers Grove, IL: IVP Academic, 2003), pp. 3, 6-7, 22-24, 64, 180, 182, 201, 206, 211-15, 217, 228-31, 251.

lation or accommodation of the gospel to the sociocultural sensibilities at work in each generation's ministry context.[159] There is a postfoundationalist, critical-realist, *soft-postmodern* epistemology which, when combined with an embrace of a biblically-informed theological realism, can empower Christ's followers to fruitfully *recontextualize* into any cultural context a gospel that transcends every cultural context while at the same time remaining true and *faithful* to its meaning as understood by the original apostolic community.

---

[159]For more on the distinction between foundationalist dogmatism and nonfoundationalist relativism, as well as the "middle way" offered by postfoundationalism, see Shults, *Postfoundationalist Task,* pp. 31-42.

PART TWO

The Forging of a
Missional Orthodoxy

3

REVELATION AND PREPARATION

Toward a Missionally Orthodox
Doctrine of the Bible

Once, while teaching a course on Christian ethics, I was moderating a discussion of some important social moral issues when a student raised his hand and asked in frustration: "Professor Tyra, why do you keep bringing the Bible into this?" Ever since this ironic exchange took place it has been my practice to issue a disclaimer at the beginning of all my theology courses: *I will be bringing the Bible into this!* There is a sense in which this chapter functions for this book as such a disclaimer.

Most theology textbooks begin with a *prolegomenon* which usually includes a discussion of the nature of Scripture and its relation to doing theology as a whole. For some theologians this move is indicative of a foundationalist mindset which holds that the entire theological edifice must be built on the bedrock of some proffered "proofs" regarding the inspiration and reliability of Scripture. They think a weak foundation will cause the edifice to collapse.

However, just because a theological work leads with a discussion of the nature of Scripture and its role vis-à-vis the theological task does not mean that the author is a *hard* foundationalist.[1] The nonfoundationalist theologian John Franke has pointed out that the term "foundationalism" can have more than one meaning and that there is a

---

[1]See F. LeRon Shults, *The Postfoundationalist Task of Theology: Wolfhart Pannenberg and the New Theological Rationality* (Grand Rapids: Eerdmans, 1999), p. 30.

sense in which nearly all theologians can be considered foundation-
alists. He writes:

> In its broadest sense, foundationalism is merely the acknowledgement
> that not all beliefs are of equal significance in the structure of knowledge.
> Some beliefs are more "basic" or "foundational" and serve to give support
> to other beliefs that are derived from them. Understood in this way,
> nearly every thinker is in some sense a foundationalist, rendering such a
> description unhelpful in grasping the range of opinion in epistemological
> theory found among contemporary thinkers.[2]

This idea that some Christian beliefs are basic to others explains why
I have chosen to focus the first chapter of the second part of this work on
bibliology. It is not because I am taking a hard foundationalist approach.
It is because I am convinced of the God-given and absolutely irre-
placeable role Scripture plays in giving us a unique and direct knowledge
of the same Reality its authors knew and to which they bore faithful
witness. In short, since it is singularly revelatory of the God to whom it
refers, I am committed to forging an orthodoxy that is faithful to the
biblical text as well as the missional task. With respect to the need for a
missional theology to be faithful to Scripture, Darrell Guder writes:

> With regard to the mission and work of the church, the nature of faith
> remains the same—it is faith, not sight. But it is to be *informed* faith, faith
> that is truly a response to God's actions and words, and not a conviction
> we have conjured up in ourselves to meet our needs. . . . Therefore, as we
> seek to work out our understanding of the mission of the church today,
> we want to be careful to work from the scriptural witness, under its tu-
> telage and control.[3]

Specific to the missional orthodoxy proposed in this work is my suggestion that, because there are some contemporary voices calling for the
historic gospel to not only be re-envisioned but *rehabilitated* as well, we

---

[2]John Franke, "Christian Faith and Postmodern Theory: Theology and the Nonfoundationalist
Turn," in *Christianity and the Postmodern Turn: Six Views,* ed. Myron B. Penner (Grand Rapids:
Brazos, 2005), pp. 108-9. Shults makes the same observation and clarifies why and how Pannenberg can and cannot be considered a foundationalist (see Shults, *Postfoundationalist Task,*
pp. 7-8). See also the way Shults clarifies his own use of the term *post*-foundationalism (p. 27).
[3]Darrell Guder, *Be My Witnesses: The Church's Mission, Message and Messengers* (Grand Rapids:
Eerdmans, 1985), p. 8.

must *think deeply and biblically* about each and every *reformulated* doctrine being urged on the Christian community by those promoting the emerging vision of the faith. One of these reformulated doctrines has to do with the Bible itself. In their respective presentations of the emerging version of the heart of Christianity, both of my dialogue partners—Marcus Borg and Brian McLaren—discuss the nature of Scripture and its role in the Christian life. Though these discussions differ from each other somewhat, it is my contention that between them several significant false antitheses are presented. This chapter will examine these false antitheses, providing biblically and theologically informed alternatives to them which I believe can contribute to the development of a missionally faithful bibliology.

THE ORIGIN OF SCRIPTURE: DIVINE OR HUMAN

In what sense is Scripture sacred, the Word of God? This is an important question that from the outset can either unite or divide evangelicals (traditional, missional and emerging).

Borg on the Bible's origin. One of the antitheses put forward by Marcus Borg in *The Heart of Christianity* has to do with the nature and thus the authority of the Bible. Borg asserts that there are two main ways of viewing the Bible: the earlier paradigm's view that it is "a divine product with divine authority" and the emerging paradigm's perspective that the Bible is "a human response to God."[4] The problem for Borg is that "contemporary biblical literalism—with its emphasis on biblical infallibility, historical factuality, and moral and doctrinal absolutes—is an obstacle for millions of people."[5] Contrary to the earlier paradigm's problematic view of the Bible, Borg states forthrightly that, according to the emerging perspective, "the Bible is a human product, not a divine product."[6] The Bible is the human response of two historical communities (ancient Israel and the early church) to God, merely indicating "how *they* saw things . . . how *they* saw their life with God," and revealing

---

[4]Borg, HC 15. However, he does allow for a theoretical distinction between harder and softer forms of the literalism at work in the earlier paradigm's bibliology (pp. 8-9). See also Borg, RBA 4-11, 21-26.

[5]Borg, HC 43. See also Borg, RBA 23-26.

[6]Borg, HC 45.

only "*their* laws and ethical teachings, *their* prayers and praises, *their* wisdom about how to live, and *their* hopes and dreams."[7] There is no thought here of the Bible as God's self-revelation as traditionally understood. Such a notion is adamantly dismissed when Borg states unequivocally that the Bible "is not God's witness to God (not a divine product), but *their* [Israel and the early church's] witness to God."[8]

But Borg seems to be guilty of some incoherence, if not self-contradiction, here. On the one hand, he asserts that the Bible is a human product that is "sacred" only in the sense that the Christian community has come to consider it so,[9] but on the other hand, he allows that "the Bible is a means of divine self-disclosure."[10] On the one hand, Borg is willing to refer to the Bible as the "word of God," but on the other hand he insists that this idiom is acceptable only as long as it is intended to refer to the Bible's status and function, rather than its origin.[11] The bottom line for Borg seems to be that while God can use the words of the Bible to speak to individuals in a sacramental manner,[12] it is still an entirely human product.[13] According to this reformulated doctrine of Scripture, the concepts of biblical infallibility and inerrancy, so important to the earlier paradigm's view of the Bible, are unnecessary modern inventions.[14] These concepts only apply if there is some sense that the content of the Bible actually comes from God, a view Borg steadfastly rejects.

Thus, what we end up with, really, is the need to choose between a bibliology from above, which emphasizes the divine participation in biblical inspiration, and a bibliology from below, which emphasizes the human component in the inscripturation process. Contrasting the way

---

[7]Ibid., emphasis added.

[8]Ibid., emphasis added.

[9]Ibid., pp. 47-48. See also Borg, RBA 28-30.

[10]See Borg, RBA 34.

[11]Ibid., pp. 33-34.

[12]Borg, HC 57-59. See also Borg, RBA 31-33.

[13]See Borg, SC 58-59.

[14]Borg attempts to convince his readers that the earlier paradigm's view of the Bible, rather than being classical or historic, is actually the result of the deformative effect of the influence of modernism. He insists that ideas such as biblical infallibility and inerrancy did not even appear until the seventeenth century and have been "insistently affirmed by some Protestants" only since the nineteenth and twentieth centuries (Borg, HC 11; see also Borg, RBA 6-7).

the earlier and emerging paradigms view the origin, interpretation and function of the Bible—as well as the implications for the Christian life produced by each of these antithetical bibliologies—Borg concludes: "So different are these two views of Christianity that they almost produce two different religions, both using the same Bible and language. Our time of two paradigms is virtually a tale of two Christianities."[15]

Actually, I heartily agree with Borg's assertion that the way we view the nature and authority of the Bible will dramatically shape our vision of the Christian faith. I also concur with the idea that God can use the words of Scripture to speak to his people in a sacramental manner. What I feel the need to challenge is the premise that we must choose between the two radically antithetical takes on Scripture which Borg puts before us.[16]

McLaren's take on the origin of Scripture. For his part, Brian McLaren begins his brief treatment of bibliology in *A Generous Orthodoxy* by affirming his belief that the Bible is inspired by God.[17] It is apparent that McLaren wishes to reassure his readers of his high regard for the Bible.[18] The question is: Does this emergent leader provide the members of the traditional evangelical, missional and emerging church communities with enough common ground here for a sense of theological and ministry unity to emerge? This is a debatable issue since the rest of his chapter titled "Why I Am Biblical" seems to be filled with caveats regarding what his affirmation of the divine inspiration of the Bible actually means. My sense is that McLaren presents a view of Scripture which while not overtly affirming Borg's antithesis, can be interpreted in such a way as to sound somewhat sympathetic to it.[19] Though I understand and agree with many of McLaren's concerns about how the Bible has been approached and utilized by conservative Christians over the years, given the importance of the Scriptures to the gospel contextualization process, I wish he would have been a little less vague and relativ-

---

[15]Borg, HC 15.
[16]For a more in-depth treatment of this particular theme see N. T. Wright, *The Last Word: Beyond the Bible Wars to a New Understanding of Scripture* (San Francisco: HarperSanFrancisco, 2005).
[17]McLaren, GO 159 [177].
[18]Ibid.
[19]An examination of McLaren's later works tends to confirm rather than belie this suspicion. For example, see McLaren, NKC 67-97.

izing in the way he presents his view of the Bible's origin and authority.[20] The theological realism that I believe is crucial to a holistic experience of God and his kingdom is dynamically connected to a certain view of sacred Scripture. My concern is that McLaren's bibliology does not adequately lead young, impressionable readers toward embracing such a view. In fact, it might do just the opposite.

To be more specific, two principal questions come to my mind regarding McLaren's explanation of why he is "biblical." The first question has to do with McLaren's treatment of the claims the Bible makes for itself. Here McLaren refers to only one passage, 2 Timothy 3:14-17:

> But as for you, continue in what you have learned and have become convinced of, because you know those from whom you learned it, and how from infancy you have known the Holy Scriptures, which are able to make you wise for salvation through faith in Christ Jesus. All Scripture is God-breathed and is useful for teaching, rebuking, correcting and training in righteousness, so that the servant of God may be thoroughly equipped for every good work.

While this is a fine passage to cite when considering what the Bible has to say about its own origin and authority, still I am led to wonder whether any treatment of this topic can afford to ignore 2 Peter 1:20-21, a similarly-themed passage in the New Testament: "Above all, you must understand that no prophecy of Scripture came about by the prophet's own interpretation of things. For prophecy never had its origin in the human will, but prophets, though human, spoke from God as they were carried along by the Holy Spirit."[21] Though this passage focuses on the prophetic portions of Scripture in particular, I offer that its reference to the biblical authors being "carried along" by the Spirit can apply to other portions of Scripture as well (see Heb 1:1; Acts 1:15-20). At the very least, this possibility seems to merit a discussion in any attempt at a biblically informed bibliology.

---

[20]Likewise, McLaren provides a brief, vague and relativizing treatment of biblical inspiration and authority in NKC 83.

[21]New Testament scholar George Ladd refers to 2 Peter 1:20-21 as "one of the classic statements about inspiration in the entire Bible." George E. Ladd, *A Theology of the New Testament* (Grand Rapids: Eerdmans, 1993), p. 652.

A second question is prompted by the ambiguous way McLaren describes the biblical inspiration process. Despite his stated commitment to a view of biblical inspiration that avoids an overemphasis on either its divinity or humanity,[22] the analogy he uses to explain what it means to say that the Bible is God-breathed is so vague as to be somewhat perplexing. In the end, it proves to be relativizing as well.

McLaren's argument is that the Bible is inspired in the sense that God is its "ultimate Creator" (though not its immediate "pro-creator"), just as God is the *ultimate* Creator (though not the immediate pro-creator) of all human beings.[23] Such a conception of inspiration can connote the idea that there is some sort of deistic distance between God and the Bible—that is, that the biblical documents are for all intents and purposes the product of natural and historical forces only *remotely* related to God in that they were *originally initiated* by him. Though McLaren's attempt to argue for a human element in the inscripturation process is understandable, the way he makes his case may actually support a view that, because it does not do sufficient justice to the sense of *inspirational immediacy* suggested by passages such as 2 Peter 1:20-21, sends the pendulum too far in the direction of a Bible-as-human-response doctrine of Scripture. Thus, the second question which McLaren's brief treatment of bibliology brings to mind is: *Doesn't the idea that God is simply the ultimate Creator of the Bible in the same way that he is the ultimate Creator of all human beings minimize the idea that the Scriptures came about through the direct and special inspiration of the Spirit?* Where is the Holy Spirit in McLaren's view of biblical inspiration? His bibliology seems to lack any discussion of the role of the Spirit in the inscripturation process. Since the Bible itself is more specific than this when discussing the role of the Spirit in the process of biblical inspiration, should we not attempt to be as well?

Perhaps I am being too critical by suggesting that the unnecessarily brief and vague way McLaren makes his case regarding the origin of Scripture might be indicative of a reformulated doctrine of the Bible that ultimately fails to pass the biblical-faithfulness test. However, theo-

---

[22]McLaren, GO 162-63 [180-81].
[23]Ibid., pp. 161-62 [180].

logian John Stackhouse has likewise indicated that he is "not terribly sympathetic" to McLaren's "agenda of raising more questions than he satisfactorily answers."[24] Furthermore, Roger Olson observes that, as in the case of John Locke (one of the primary promulgators of Deism), it is possible to *neglect* Christian dogma without actually *denying* it.[25] Thus I suggest that the very subtle, accommodating theological move whereby a proponent of the emerging paradigm merely neglects without actually denying those biblical doctrines considered problematic to our post-Christian peers can result in a version of the Christian faith that, like Deism, is not faithful to the biblical text. What is more, such an accommodating theological move may produce a version of the Christian faith that (again like Deism) proves to be short-lived and ultimately more of a hindrance than a help to the missional task. In other words, my concern is that McLaren's bibliology, while not overtly denying the concept of *inspirational immediacy,* at the very least tends to neglect it, and does so in such a way as to at least insinuate the same sort of false dichotomy put forward by Borg.[26]

A theologically "real" view of the Bible's origin. This, then, brings us back to Borg and his assertion that we must choose between his characterizations of how the earlier and emerging paradigms view the Scriptures, between a bibliology from above and one from below. As an alternative to this idea, I suggest that biblical inspiration occurs in an incarnational, holistic, theologically realistic manner.

It is true, as Borg points out, that the earlier paradigm doesn't hesitate to refer to the Bible as the "word of God."[27] Perhaps this is due to the fact that the phrase "word of God" appears so often in the Bible. For instance, in Matthew 15:1-6, Mark 7:5-13 and John 10:34-35, Jesus refers to the Old Testament Scriptures collectively as the "word of God," and in Romans 3:2, the apostle Paul does the same. Luke 5:1 and John 3:34

---

[24]John G. Stackhouse, "A Generic Evangelical Response [to Confessional Evangelicalism]" in *Four Views on the Spectrum of Evangelicalism,* ed. Stanley N. Gundry, Andrew David Naselli and Collin Hansen (Grand Rapids: Zondervan, 2011), p. 109.

[25]Roger Olson, *The Mosaic of Christian Belief: Twenty Centuries of Unity and Diversity* (Downers Grove, IL: IVP Academic, 2002), p. 60.

[26]This view finds some support in the equally ambiguous manner in which McLaren depicts the Bible's inspiration in McLaren, NKC 83.

[27]Borg, HC 7. See also Borg, SC 57.

call Jesus' teaching the "word of God," and the rest of the New Testament often refers to the Jesus story as a whole as the "word of God" (e.g., Acts 6:7; 8:14; 11:1; 12:24; 13:46; Phil 1:14; 1 Thess 2:13). This explains why we evangelicals are fond of referring to the Bible as a whole as the *Word of God*.

But does this mean, as Borg suggests, that we must choose between a bibliology from above and one from below? I do not think so.

The prologue to the Gospel of John famously refers to Jesus himself as the "Word" (Jn 1:1-18). Thus, it is not uncommon for evangelicals to refer to the Bible as the *written* word of God, and to Jesus as the *living* Word of God.[28] I would not be the first to suggest that it is possible to see a conceptual analogy between these two expressions of the "word of God."[29] In the same way that the Bible clearly teaches that Jesus the *living Word* is both divine and human at the same time (cf. Jn 1:1 and Jn 1:14),[30] can we not construe a similar union of the divine and human in the *written Word*?[31] If, within his creation, God can work in such a way as to bring into coordination distinctly divine and human elements in the person of the incarnate Christ ontologically (i.e., two natures forming one *hypostasis* in the person of Jesus), surely he can do the same with the inspired, God-breathed Scriptures epistemologically (i.e., divine knowledge and human understanding forming a union that is the biblical witness).[32] To

---

[28]For example, see Karl Barth, *Dogmatics in Outline* (New York: Harper and Row, 1959), p. 17; Donald Bloesch, *Spirituality Old & New: Recovering Authentic Spiritual Life* (Downers Grove, IL: IVP Academic, 2007), p. 86; Donald Bloesch, *A Theology of Word and Spirit: Authority and Method in Theology* (Downers Grove, IL: IVP Academic, 1992), p. 195; N. T. Wright, *Simply Christian: Why Christianity Makes Sense* (San Francisco: HarperSanFrancisco, 2006), p. 181.

[29]For example, see Peter Enns, *Inspiration and Incarnation: Evangelicals and the Problem of the Old Testament* (Grand Rapids: Baker Academic, 2005). Even Borg alludes to this dual use of the phrase "word of God" in the Bible, though, ironically, he does so not to inspire confidence in the Scriptures as God's revelation, but to minimize its authority when compared to the revelation in Christ. See Borg, SC 62-63. McLaren adopts a similar approach, pitting the revelation found in Jesus the living Word and the revelation found in the Bible against each other not only to distinguish them from one another but to diminish the value of the revelation found in the Bible. See McLaren, NKC 115-16.

[30]I am anticipating here the discussion of Christology in chapter five of this work.

[31]See Donald G. Bloesch, *Holy Scripture: Revelation, Inspiration and Interpretation* (Downers Grove: IL: InterVarsity Press, 1994), p. 41.

[32]Note, however, that the analogy between the living and written expressions of the Word of God, though valid, is asymmetrical. Jesus himself is the ontological reality. Scripture is revelational or, we might say, epistemological. Since the ontological orders and grounds the epistemological, how we know depends on what or who we are gaining knowledge of. Thus, the onto-

put it differently, despite the fact that Jesus' body may have manifested some physical uniqueness (e.g., distinctive facial feature, unique gait, left-handedness) or even imperfection (e.g., pockmark, scar, facial asymmetry), he was nevertheless able to provide his hearers with a faithful revelation of who God is and what he is about (Heb 1:3). In the same way, despite the very real human characteristics observable in its various texts (e.g., authors' vocabularies, linguistic capacities, unique personalities, pre-modern understanding of the cosmos, cultural conditioning), the Bible is able, due to the inspiring and illuminating work of the Spirit, to provide its readers with a faithful witness to Christ.

This is a crucial proposition. Earlier in this work I referred to T. F. Torrance's observation that "what God is antecedently and eternally in himself he really is toward us in the concrete embodiment of his Truth in Jesus Christ the word made flesh." Torrance goes on to say that "in Jesus Christ God has so communicated himself in our humanity that human words are taken to speak for God, and therefore it is in and through Jesus Christ that our human words may rightly and properly speak of God—insofar, that is, as they are rooted in the Mystery of Christ the incarnate Truth."[33] Torrance is not simply asserting here that all human speech about God needs to be christological in its ground and goal in order to be accurate. He is also arguing that because of the incarnation and the inspiring work of Christ's Spirit, it is possible for God to use the speech of fallible human beings, causing it to "rightly and properly speak of God."

Furthermore, this revelatory dynamic is at the very heart of the prophetic phenomenon to which the Scriptures bear consistent witness: the Holy Spirit supernaturally enables human beings to speak to God or about him to others in ways that are doxologically and missionally

---

logical is primary; the revelational/epistemological is secondary. So there is an asymmetric analogy between who Jesus is as the God-Human and how he makes himself known through the medium of Scripture. To argue that Jesus and the Bible are analogous is not to suggest that the Bible is divine and deserving of worship the way Jesus is. It is only to suggest that the Bible's origin is owing to an inspirational immediacy not present in Borg's bibliology and not sufficiently apparent in McLaren's.

[33]T. F. Torrance, *Reality & Evangelical Theology* (Downers Grove, IL: InterVarsity Press, 1999), pp. 141-42.

faithful.[34] This is not to say that contemporary prophetic utterances share the status of sacred Scripture, but simply that the inscripturation process involved an inspiration dynamic analogous to the prophetic phenomenon where the Spirit of God enables fallible human beings to speak faithfully to or on behalf of God. The amazing reality is that God is pleased to use specific, certain, particular human beings in specific, certain, particular times to effect divine revelation that is timeless in nature. The biblical authors, prophetic and apostolic, are given a particular calling and gift to function as authoritative human witnesses to the reality of who God is and what God has done. Though care must be taken to distinguish between two distinct works of the Spirit—the inspiration of the biblical writers and the illumination of its interpreters and hearers (the latter work depending upon the former)—a similar prophetic dynamic is at work in both. God seems to have a penchant for enabling prophetic activity.

On the basis of a full appreciation of the implications of Christ's incarnation and the advent of the Holy Spirit for the purpose of divine revelation, I am led to ask: Why must we choose between a bibliology from above and one from below? *A theological realism not only allows for but actually mandates an incarnational understanding of biblical inspiration analogous to the union of the distinctly divine and human elements in the Christ-event.* This theologically coherent, missionally compelling bibliology holds that the same God who revealed himself via the incarnation of Christ was able also to inspire fully conscious human Scripture composers, copyists, compilers and canonists before, during and after the Christ-event to produce a set of written documents—the *written Word*. While maintaining the real humanity of its cadre of human authors (including their personalities, worldviews, even ethnocentric biases), the written Word still succeeds at pointing people to the *living Word,* Jesus Christ, and the divine self-revelation and reconciliation available through him. While this view of inspiration stops short of insisting that each and every word of the original autographs was divinely

---

[34]For a fuller discussion of the connection between the prophetic phenomenon and the mission of God, see Gary Tyra, *The Holy Spirit in Mission: Prophetic Speech and Action in Christian Witness* (Downers Grove, IL: IVP Academic, 2011), especially p. 22n24.

dictated, it does hold that some were[35] and that those that were not still reflect the respectful but resolute influence of the Holy Spirit on the motivation and intellection of the human authors. To go beyond this biblically faithful view of the origin of Scripture would violate our commitment to an orthodoxy that is modest in scope rather than overreaching. But, on the other hand, to suggest that the Bible is less than the inspired word of God would be indicative of a reformulated doctrine of the Bible that fails the faithfulness test!

The bottom line is that though this incarnational view of biblical inspiration, like the incarnation itself, possesses an element of mystery (paradox)[36] and is obviously problematic for a nontrinitarian such as Marcus Borg,[37] it is nevertheless a valid, biblically informed and theologically coherent alternative to the Bible-as-divine-product versus Bible-as-human-response antithesis.[38] Furthermore, the fact that the emerging generations, due to the impact of postmodernism, are more open than their forebears to the phenomena of paradox and mystery, is all the more reason why this view should be the cornerstone of a biblically and missionally faithful doctrine of the Bible. I am convinced that an incarnational, theologically real view of the Bible's origin and authority is one that many members of the traditional evangelical, missional and emerging church communities can and should get behind!

---

[35]For example, see Ex 34:27-28; Is 8:1; 30:8; Jer 30:1-2; 36:2; Hab 2:2; Acts 1:15-20; 7:37-38; Rev 1:11, 19; 2:1, 8, 12, 18; 3:1, 7, 14; 14:13; 19:9; 21:5.

[36]The ambiguities attached to this understanding of the origin of Scripture are due to the mystery inherent in the notion of a divine-human hypostasis rather than to a deliberately vague manner of presentation. Indeed, in another work, in a subsection titled "Why Our Perspective Needs to Be Either-Or," Borg explicitly rejects the notion that the Bible can be seen as "*both* divine and human" because of the "confusion" he insists this paradoxical view creates (see Borg, RBA 26-28, emphasis original). Put in christological terms, Borg disregards the possibility of a "hypostatic union" of the divine and human elements which the incarnational theory of biblical inspiration posits. Emphasizing the confusion that would result from a "Nestorian" disunion between the human and divine natures, Borg opts for an "Ebionitic" understanding of divine revelation: "Thus the lens I am advocating does not see the Bible as a whole as divine in origin, or some parts as divine and some as human. It is *all* a human product, though generated in response to God. As such, it contains ancient Israel's perceptions and misperceptions of what life with God involves, just as it contains the early Christian movement's perceptions and misperceptions" (p. 27).

[37]See chapter four of this work for more on this. Borg ends up affirming an essentially modalistic understanding of the "threefoldness" of God. See Borg, SC 212-15. He writes, "God is one (Christians are monotheists), and God is known to us in three primary ways" (p. 215).

[38]Tacit support for this conclusion can be found in N. T. Wright, *Simply Christian*, pp. 180-84.

THE NATURE OF SCRIPTURE:
AN ENCYCLOPEDIA OR STORYBOOK

It goes without saying that how we view the nature of the Bible will affect our approach to it and that how we approach the Bible is crucial to our experience with it. Therefore, another very important false antithesis is the one which suggests that we must choose between approaching the Bible as a "storehouse of facts" or as an album of inspiring stories.

For sure, the Bible is filled with stories. Moreover, the cumulative effect of all the biblical documents is to present the world with a grand narrative—the story of the world's creation, fall, redemption and restoration. Only within the context of this overarching biblical story is the full meaning of the Jesus story adequately appreciated.

However, while some traditional evangelical theologians have perhaps not sufficiently emphasized the role of narrative in God's self-revelation in Scripture, it is quite common for emergent authors to over-correct, virtually denying that the Bible presents truths in the form of propositions as well.[39]

McLaren's concern. For example, though Brian McLaren never explicitly states that the Bible is void of propositional truth, his caustic references to the practice of treating the Bible as a "look-it-up encyclopedia of timeless moral truths"[40] or of "confusing the genre of ancient biblical narratives with the modern genres of political constitution or moral dictionary or religious blueprint"[41] can certainly give that impression.[42]

---

[39]For a remarkably strident critique of the overemphasis on narrative in the biblical interpretation approaches of emergent church leaders such as Rob Bell, Brian McLaren and Doug Pagitt, see Leslie Leyland Fields, "The Gospel Is More Than a Story: Rethinking Narrative and Testimony," *Christianity Today* (July 16, 2012), www.christianitytoday.com/ct/2012/july-august/the-gospel-is-more-than-a-story.html.

[40]McLaren, GO 171 [190].

[41]Ibid., p. 170 [189]. See also McLaren, NKC 83.

[42]Indeed, McLaren's entire theological project is based on a radically new reading of the "overarching story line of the Bible" (see McLaren, NKC 34-45). Such a fresh reading changes everything for McLaren, as his books make clear. There is no doubt that McLaren is an ingenious and talented author who has put forward some clever, if radical, hermeneutical proposals. Though his critique of the Greco-Roman soul-sort narrative, which he says dominates and distorts the traditional evangelical understanding of the biblical story, has its own critics (e.g., see Scot McKnight, "Review: Brian McLaren's 'A New Kind of Christianity,'" *Christianity Today*, February 26, 2010, www.christianitytoday.com/ct/2010/march/3.59.html), he is right to encourage Christians to consider the possibility that our hermeneutical lenses have been overly influenced by certain philosophical, religious and political presuppositions. The irony is that McLaren's

Now, my own custom is to warn my students against approaching the Bible with an "I-It" rather than an "I-Thou" mindset. This is, of course, a reference to the work of philosopher Martin Buber and his book *I and Thou*.[43] Applied to this discussion, the idea is that we can approach Scripture either as an "It" to be studied, handled, or managed, or as a "Thou" to interact with respectfully as the medium of God's self-revelation, open to the possibility that doing so will exercise a life-transforming effect on us.

T. F. Torrance speaks of how fundamentalism's failure on this score—that is, its tendency to approach the Bible as an "I-It" relationship—causes the Bible to be "treated as a self-contained corpus of divine truths in propositional form endowed with an infallibility of statement which provides the justification felt to be needed for the rigid framework of belief within which fundamentalism barricades itself."[44] These are some strong but necessary words of warning. Ironically, a high view of Scripture calls for us to be careful *not* to so equate God's self-revelation with the biblical text that the book becomes merely a thing to be mastered, rather than the means by which God masters us.

Contra McLaren. So, I really do understand McLaren's concern over how we approach Scripture. But, contra McLaren, I acknowledge that along with many meaning-laden, inspiration-rich stories, the Bible is also full of passages that either explicitly or implicitly exhort the reader to place his or her faith in the veracity of a certain proposition. Consider, for example, the following:

---

overemphasis on the narrative element in Scripture to the neglect of its propositional content means that his over-politicized re-read of the biblical story line is just as liable to being errantly influenced by hermeneutical presuppositions as the older view. The question then is this: Does the overarching story line of the Bible proposed by McLaren or Borg (or N. T. Wright, for that matter) do sufficient justice to *all* of the Bible's content? Or does it require that we wink at—ignore—certain elements of Scripture that do not seem to fit, especially those crucial ideas which, because of their narrative-clarifying importance, the biblical authors were careful to communicate in a propositional rather than poetic manner? The danger of overemphasizing the narrative element in Scripture is precisely this: everything hinges on how we see the story and therefore on the presuppositions—philosophical, religious and political—that we bring with us to the hermeneutical task. While we cannot free ourselves completely of our presuppositions, the task of having to do justice to *both* the narrative *and* propositional elements of Scripture can mitigate a tendency to read those presuppositions into the biblical story.

[43]See Martin Buber, *I and Thou* (New York: Scribner, 2000).

[44]See Torrance, *Reality & Evangelical Theology*, p. 17.

Jesus said to her, "I am the resurrection and the life. The one who believes in me will live, even though they die; and whoever lives by believing in me will never die. Do you believe this?"

"Yes, Lord," she replied, "I believe that you are the Messiah, the Son of God, who is to come into the world." (Jn 11:25-27)

Jesus performed many other signs in the presence of his disciples, which are not recorded in this book. But these are written that you may believe that Jesus is the Messiah, the Son of God, and that by believing you may have life in his name. (Jn 20:30-31)

If you declare with your mouth, "Jesus is Lord," and believe in your heart that God raised him from the dead, you will be saved. (Rom 10:9)

Brothers and sisters, we do not want you to be uninformed about those who sleep in death, so that you do not grieve like the rest of mankind, who have no hope. For we believe that Jesus died and rose again, and so we believe that God will bring with Jesus those who have fallen asleep in him. (1 Thess 4:13-14)

And without faith it is impossible to please God, because anyone who comes to him must believe that he exists and that he rewards those who earnestly seek him. (Heb 11:6)

Of course, giving mental assent to a proposition should also lead to existential trust. Indeed if it were not presented in such a pseudo-antithetical manner, the distinction Marcus Borg makes between faith as *assensus* (mental assent) and *fiducia* (existential trust) could be hugely helpful.[45] But existential trust cannot arise without mental assent in some sort of proposition first.[46] Thus, according to the apostle Paul, an existential trust in the lordship of the risen Christ necessarily entails a belief in the proposition that God has raised him from the dead (Rom 10:9).

What we seem to find in Scripture is a grand narrative in which discrete stories and propositional teaching are so closely interwoven that to

---

[45]Borg, HC 24-32. See also Borg, GWNK 169-71.
[46]New Testament scholar George Ladd affirms the idea that faith in *(pisteuo eis)* Christ, while calling for a "personal identification" with him, includes "intellectual assent" and "affirmations" about him. See Ladd, *Theology of the New Testament*, pp. 307-8.

fail to do justice to either makes the whole incomprehensible and void of life-transforming power. Thus, the idea that we must choose between viewing the Bible as *either* a storehouse of facts *or* as some sort of inspired storybook is yet another false antithesis that can and should be avoided.[47]

INTERPRETING SCRIPTURE:
LITERAL-FACTUAL OR MERELY METAPHORICAL

Another issue that might stand in the way of a greater unity between traditional, missional and emerging evangelicals is the manner in which the Bible is actually interpreted.

Borg's concern. In the process of forming the antithesis between the earlier and emerging views of the Bible (which is crucial to the argument of *The Heart of Christianity*), Marcus Borg suggests that the earlier view is captive to a "literal-factual" approach to Scripture.[48] This *implies* that many (if not most) traditional evangelicals feel the need to interpret the Bible in a doggedly literalistic manner.

The fact is that not all evangelicals do this. But even if this were true, it would be one thing if Borg's alternative simply called for Christians to recognize that the presence of metaphorical passages in the Bible mandates that at least some biblical texts be interpreted figuratively rather than literally. This would be a measured response to a problematic her-

---

[47]McLaren suggests that an alternative to seeing the scriptures as an "authoritative constitution" or as a "collection of human literature" is to view the Bible as an "inspired library" that functions as a sort of catalyst for conversation through which God reveals himself (McLaren, NKC 83). Though he argues that the "inspired library" perspective can be seen as a third alternative to the other two options (which it is), I still find it insufficient as an adequate, missionally faithful "answer" to the antithesis McLaren puts forward. As we have seen, the Bible presents us with passages which suggest that there is truth presented in the apostolic proclamation of the Christian message that should be *contended for* (Jude 3) rather than *wandered away from* (2 Tim 2:18; Jas. 5:19) or *turned away from* (2 Tim 4:4). In other words, the apostolic witness should be seen as in some sense *authoritative!* See Thomas C. Oden, "The Faith Once Delivered: Nicea and Evangelical Confession," in *Evangelicals and Nicene Faith,* ed. Timothy George (Grand Rapids: Baker, 2011), pp. 4-5. Because of my aversion to the Pharisaism which so easily springs up within evangelical communities of faith, I am somewhat sympathetic to McLaren's admonition against treating the Bible as an authoritative constitution. Still, I am uneasy with the way the notion of spiritual authority is virtually absent from McLaren's presentation of the Bible as an inspired library. Perhaps we should worry less about finding a metaphor that pictures what we believe the nature of the Bible to be and focus more on actually allowing it to function in our lives in a manner consistent with apostolic practice and encouragement.
[48]Borg, HC xii, 15. See also Borg, SC 21-26, 107-8.

meneutical tendency.[49] But Borg's proposal constitutes a serious over-correction. Pushing the pendulum too aggressively in the opposite direction of a hyper-literalist approach to the Bible, he writes:

> The emerging paradigm sees the Bible metaphorically, by which I mean its "more-than-literal," "more-than-factual," meaning. It is not very much concerned with the historical factuality of the Bible's stories, but much more with their meanings. It is not bothered by the possibility that the stories of Jesus' birth and resurrection are metaphorical rather than literally factual accounts. It asks, "Whether it happened this way or not, what is the story saying? What meanings does it have for us?"[50]

Now, Borg's subsequent discussion of how truth can be communicated via metaphor is very helpful, something more conservative Christians should contemplate lest we succumb to the temptation to equate metaphor with *myth* in the worst sense of that word.[51] That said, Borg's overemphasis on a merely metaphorical interpretation of Scripture merits censure. Based on the overall way Borg utilizes Scripture in laying out his vision of the heart of Christianity, I suggest that the name for his approach to the Bible should not be "more-than-literal, more-than-factual" but rather "rarely-if-ever-literal because not-likely-factual."[52] It is one thing to suggest, as many reputable biblical scholars do, that the meaning and spiritual value of the books of Job or Jonah do not depend on their historical facticity; it is another to suggest that the doctrine of Christ's bodily resurrection need not possess the historical facticity on which the apostle Paul based its veracity (1 Cor 15:9-19).[53] Christ's resurrection is a doctrine that is at the heart of Christianity precisely because its embrace is central to the experience of Christian salvation (see Rom

---

[49]N. T. Wright qualifies what it means to take the Bible literally: "Many churches, including my own, have retained the Reformer's emphasis on the 'literal sense' of scripture, not in the sense of 'taking everything literally' but in the sense of 'discovering what the writers meant' as opposed to engaging in free-floating speculation. As I pointed out earlier, the 'literal sense' means the sense originally intended; thus, ascertaining the 'literal sense' of a parable involves recognizing it *as* a parable, not an anecdote about something which actually happened. Getting at the original sense of scripture is an ongoing task for scholar, preacher and ordinary reader alike" (N. T. Wright, *Last Word*, p. 135).

[50]Borg, HC 13-14. See also Borg, SC 26-33.

[51]Borg, HC 49-56.

[52]See Borg and Wright, MJ 3-4.

[53]Borg, HC 112-13. See also Borg, SC 110-11; Borg, GWNK 93; and Borg and Wright, MJ 130-35.

4:23-25; 10:9; 1 Cor 15:1-8). Thus, as it relates to the goal of forging a missional orthodoxy that strives to be faithful to the text as well as the task, a rejection of this doctrine's facticity is nothing less than a fatal error.

To reiterate, it appears that once again Borg has created for his readers a false antithesis. They must *either* interpret every statement in the Bible in a literal-factual manner (the earlier paradigm) *or* reject biblical literalism entirely and approach the Bible as a culturally conditioned text that, while merely a human product, is somehow so infused with metaphorical "truth" that it can function for them in a sacramental manner, allowing them to connect or make contact with God.

Contra Borg. In response to this proposed antithesis, I suggest that it is not necessary for evangelicals to choose between a slavish devotion to a literal-factual interpretation of Scripture and an approach that tends to view all biblical stories as mere metaphors. Rather, we can and should approach the Bible *realistically*, taking it very seriously (though not always literally) in the process. At the least, this realistic manner of biblical interpretation means that we must assume the responsibility to nuance our approach to the Bible, interpreting some passages quite literally and others more figuratively based on their literary genre (e.g., poetry, parable, apocalyptic). This might just give new meaning to that famous exhortation provided by the apostle Paul to his ministry protégé: "Do your best to present yourself to God as one approved, a worker who does not need to be ashamed and who correctly handles the word of truth" (2 Tim 2:15).

At an even more basic level, a *realistic* approach to the Bible means that we assume there is a reality greater than the text itself—a reality which the text, as a sign, seeks to direct us toward and even disclose to us. Inspired by the Holy Spirit, the words of the biblical text do not simply refer to ideas or other words or concepts, but to a personal reality—a divine reality who is eager to make contact with us. A realistic approach to the Bible expects an intimate, interactive, transformational experience of the God who is the ultimate reality from which all physical, spiritual and virtual realities derive. Once again, the spiritual hunger at work in our ministry context in general,[54] coupled with the desire of the

---

[54]See Ross Hastings, *Missional God, Missional Church: Hope for Re-Evangelizing the West* (Downers Grove, IL: IVP Academic, 2012), p. 57.

emerging generations in particular to experience something transcendent, makes this theologically real approach to the Scriptures a compelling missional alternative, something that all evangelicals (traditional, missional and emerging) can and should embrace.

USE OF SCRIPTURE:
PEDAGOGICAL CLUB OR SELF-HELP INSTRUMENT

The idea that the Scriptures aim to put us in touch with a divine reality will not only influence how we approach them but how we make use of them as well. This is yet another issue that can either unite or divide traditional, missional and emerging evangelicals.

Scripture as sacrament: Some common ground. We have already noted Marcus Borg's suggestion that the Bible may function in the lives of Christians in a sacramental manner. Likewise, philosopher Jamie Smith speaks of the possibility of the Scriptures being "read and encountered as a site of divine action, as a means of grace, as a conduit of the Spirit's transformative power."[55] Roger Olson makes a similar assertion when he states that "the Bible is the sacrament of God's Word because, although in one aspect it is a human book of human words and sentences, it is also a material channel of God's grace and is uniquely used by God to bring people into transforming encounter with God that informs and changes them."[56] Finally, affirming a sacramental approach to and use of Scripture and actually suggesting a missional connection in the process, theologian Donald Bloesch writes:

> In its classical setting evangelical theology is sacramental, but in its varied expressions in history it has often taken the form of a rationalizing of divine revelation. I contend that evangelical theology will regain its vitality and relevance when it rediscovers the sacramental understanding of truth, authority and revelation—an understanding found not only in the Bible itself but in the fathers of the church through the ages, particularly in the mainstream of the Protestant Reformation.[57]

---

[55]James K. A. Smith, *Desiring the Kingdom: Worship, Worldview and Cultural Formation* (Grand Rapids: Baker Academic, 2009), p. 135.
[56]Olson, *Mosaic of Christian Belief,* p. 106.
[57]Bloesch, *Holy Scripture,* pp. 44-45.

Thus, as it relates to a sacramental use of Scripture, there is apparently some common ground between the emerging and earlier paradigms which many contemporary evangelicals are willing to embrace. However, while Borg offers no rationale for how the Bible as a purely human response to a noninterventionist God (see chapter four below) can function in this sacramental manner, I offer (from the perspective of a theological realism that sees a conceptual analogy between the living and written expressions of the Word of God) that just as the living Word—the God-man, Jesus of Nazareth—serves as the "primary sacrament" (primary connection) between God and man,[58] so (in a secondary sense) may the Spirit-inspired but humanly authored written Word provide a point of contact between the believer and Christ.

As for Bloesch's suggestion that the missional vitality of evangelicalism may hinge on the recovery of the sacramental understanding of theology and the Scriptures, Smith suggests this dynamic occurs when the Scriptures are heard and read in a worship context.[59] While Smith seems to have a fairly formal liturgical worship setting in mind, it has been my experience that the same dynamic can also occur in less formal settings, whenever Christ's followers gather to engage in a humble, prayerful, meditative study of the Bible, open to the experience of a realistic, existentially meaningful encounter with the Spirit of the living God.[60] Indeed, given our culture's hunger and thirst for spiritual experience, one of the most missionally effective moves a community of Christians can make is to encourage pre- and post-Christians to join them in corporate times of Scripture study with the goal of experiencing something transcendent—not just information or inspiration, but actual transformation as well.

Scripture as sacrament: The only use? So the problem is not with the idea that the Bible might function as a sacramental means toward one's spiritual formation, but with the suggestion that this is the *only* proper

---

[58]See Ray Anderson, *The Soul of Ministry: Forming Leaders for God's People* (Louisville, KY: Westminster John Knox Press, 1997), pp. 167-69.

[59]Ibid.

[60]For more on this, see Gary Tyra, *Christ's Empowering Presence: The Pursuit of God Through the Ages* (Downers Grove, IL: InterVarsity Press, 2011), pp. 176-78.

use of the Bible.[61] While this motion is put forward by Borg, it finds a "second," so to speak, in McLaren's work. Indeed, in *A Generous Orthodoxy*, McLaren seems to set up a false antithesis regarding the proper use of Scripture when he writes:

> It's no surprise then that biblical Christians have thrived when we've used the Bible with the goal of becoming good people who, because we follow Jesus, do good works in God's good world. And we have languished and wandered when we have used the Bible as a weapon to threaten others, as a tool to intimidate others and prove them wrong, as a shortcut to being know-it-alls who believe the Bible gives us all the answers, as a defense of the status quo—none of these being the use Paul the apostle wanted Timothy, his protégé, to make of the Scriptures.[62]

I agree with McLaren that sometimes we evangelicals have been too harsh, dogmatic and pugilistic in our apologetic, polemical and pastoral uses of the Bible. However, McLaren seems to be overcorrecting here and creating a false antithesis in the process. Especially when viewed in the context of the book as a whole, it is easy to interpret this passage in such a way as to hear McLaren insisting that the *only* proper use of the Bible is as a means of personal growth toward becoming good people engaged in the task of making the world a better place, and that it is simply inappropriate for Christians to use the Bible in a corrective manner vis-à-vis other folks.

But what about the one Pauline passage that McLaren cites in his treatment of Scripture (2 Tim 3:14-17) with its reference to certain particular functions of Scripture? "All Scripture is God-breathed and is useful for *teaching, rebuking, correcting and training* in righteousness, so that the servant of God may be thoroughly equipped for every good work." McLaren does address this issue, if only in an oblique manner, when he offers a paraphrase of this Pauline passage that serves to steer his readers away from the idea that the apostle expected Timothy to use the Bible to teach, rebuke, correct or train *others*. Notice McLaren's use of the second person pronoun *you* here:

---

[61]See N. T. Wright's discussion of why the Scriptures should be thought of as "more than a devotional aid" in *Last Word*, pp. 32-34.
[62]McLaren, GO 165 [183].

The Bible, [Paul] says, is good for equipping people to do good works. It does so specifically through teaching (telling *you* what is true and right), rebuking (helping *you* see where you've gone wrong), correcting (guiding *you* on how to get on the right track again), and training in justice (educating *you* in the skills of staying on the right path).[63]

The subtle implication here is that we might use the Bible on ourselves in a corrective manner, but not in the lives of others. But what are we supposed to do with those biblical passages that state rather unequivocally that the followers of Christ are to behave toward one another in correcting, rebuking, admonishing, encouraging and commanding ways?

Preach the word; be prepared in season and out of season; correct, rebuke and encourage—with great patience and careful instruction. (2 Tim 4:2)

This saying is true. Therefore rebuke them sharply, so that they will be sound in the faith. (Tit 1:13)

These, then, are the things you should teach. Encourage and rebuke with all authority. Do not let anyone despise you. (Tit 2:15)

Let the message of Christ dwell among you richly as you teach and admonish one another with all wisdom through psalms, hymns, and songs from the Spirit, singing to God with gratitude in your hearts. (Col 3:16)

As I urged you when I went into Macedonia, stay there in Ephesus so that you may command certain people not to teach false doctrines any longer. (1 Tim 1:3)

Obviously, these passages do not give evangelicals a license to function toward one another as arrogant, pugnacious, self-righteous know-it-alls. But neither do they suggest that we are never to use the Bible in a way that challenges bad theology or behavior! If Timothy himself ever wrestled with the swing of the pendulum as it relates to the issue of the proper use of the Bible, I suspect that a measure of poise and equilibrium was likely achieved in his life and ministry when he came across these words from the apostle's pen:

---

[63]Ibid., p. 164 [182], emphasis added.

> And the Lord's servant must not be quarrelsome but must be kind to everyone, able to teach, not resentful. Opponents must be gently instructed, in the hope that God will grant them repentance leading them to a knowledge of the truth, and that they will come to their senses and escape from the trap of the devil, who has taken them captive to do his will. (2 Tim 2:24-26)

Does this passage not reflect Paul's commitment to a humble, modest orthodoxy that is at once faithful to both the biblical text and the missional task?

THE MISSIONAL IMPACT OF A BIBLICALLY FAITHFUL BIBLIOLOGY

Both Marcus Borg and Brian McLaren seem to suggest that a reformulation or rehabilitation of the Christian doctrine of the Bible is necessary because the earlier paradigm's approach to and use of Scripture has become an insurmountable stumbling block to missional ministry in the modern/postmodern West. But is this true? Convinced that it is not, I wish to conclude this chapter with a brief but important discussion of how and why a biblically faithful doctrine of the Bible can impact an engagement in missional ministry in positive ways.

My dialogue partners' missional angst. We have already noted McLaren's concern that too many traditional evangelicals are guilty of using the Bible as a weapon toward others in a polemically pugilistic manner. According to Borg, our pre- and post-Christian peers find unacceptable certain ecclesial practices which he insists derive from the earlier paradigm's understanding of Scripture: rejection of science, subordination of women, negative attitude toward gays and lesbians, preoccupation with conservative personal righteousness more than compassion and justice, and promotion of Christian exclusivism.[64] Borg goes on to indict the earlier paradigm's wholesale embrace of all the implications of a too-literal interpretation of Genesis 1–11, the God-approved slaughter of the Canaanites, the divine approval of human slavery, the idea "that God cares (or has ever cared) about whether we

---

[64]Borg, HC 3, 15-16.

wear garments made of two kinds of cloth," the idea "that the second coming of Jesus will involve the destruction of most of humankind," and the idea "that Jesus is the only way of salvation, and that people can be saved only by believing that he literally died for our sins."[65] There are some beliefs included in this list that even some missional and emerging evangelicals would gladly own, and others that even those evangelicals traditional in orientation would eschew. Though Borg never states that *all* traditional evangelicals engage in *all* these practices and hold to *all* these beliefs, his antithetical method of argument implies as much.

Reasons for resisting this extreme swing of the pendulum. Both Borg and McLaren appear absolutely convinced of the need for a reformulated doctrine of the Bible. But does effective evangelism in an increasingly postmodern, post-Christian culture require that evangelicals follow the swing of the pendulum toward the emergent view of the origin, nature, interpretation and use of Scripture? There are a couple of reasons why I do not think so.

First, while interpreting the Bible hyperliterally and then using it to club others in a harsh, dogmatic manner is not acceptable behavior in a postmodern, post-Christian world, a biblically faithful view of the Bible needs not be this way. A missionally orthodox doctrine of the Bible holds that the Scriptures (1) are both divinely inspired and humanly produced; (2) contain truth presented in the form of both proposition and story; (3) should be interpreted in a discerning, realistic manner; and (4) should be utilized as a means of gospel proclamation and spiritual formation in the lives of others as well as our own. There is nothing about this balanced, missionally faithful alternative to the emerging paradigm's reformulated doctrine of Scripture which mandates that the Bible be interpreted hyperliterally and then used as a weapon to beat others into submission.

Second, I have already indicated that my experience has been that most of the post-Christians living around us are not studied, committed epistemological relativists.[66] They do not mind being confronted with a

---

[65]Ibid., pp. 43-44.
[66]See Hastings, *Missional God*, p. 57.

truth claim if this confrontation occurs within the context of a loving relationship, reflects a concern for authenticity, is marked by humility and offers the prospect of an encounter with something truly transcendent. Many members of the emerging generations are, in fact, desperately eager to have someone shoot straight with them, especially if the message being proclaimed holds promise for an experience of something or someone that is real, holy and true.[67]

Thus, contrary to Borg's premise that only the emergent paradigm can be evangelistically effective in our time and place, the way is actually clear for thoughtful evangelicals of all stripes (traditional, missional and emerging) to offer pre- and post-Christians a bibliology that is both theologically coherent and missionally compelling. While we will not attempt to provide the spiritually hungry with irrefutable "proofs" of such things as the divine inspiration of Scripture and the Bible's reliability, we can and should (1) provide them with many intellectual and existential reasons why they should "taste and see" for themselves just how inspired and reliable the sacred Scriptures are (Ps 34:8) and (2) invite them to spend some time prayerfully studying (engaging in a spiritually disciplined indwelling of) the Scriptures along with us, sincerely opening themselves to the experience of God's self-revelation in the process (Jn 1:37-39, 44-46; 4:42).[68]

Furthermore, during these times of corporate Scripture study, we evangelicals should model for these inquirers good rather than bad exegesis and make them aware of those hermeneutical principles and practices that will enable them to avoid being scandalized by the problematic practices and teachings that Borg points out and erroneously

---

[67]Support for this notion can be found in various sources. For example: Kenda Creasy Dean, *Almost Christian: What the Faith of Our Teenagers Is Telling the American Church* (New York: Oxford University Press, 2010), pp. 4, 17, 36, 90-91, 159-60, 173; Kenda Creasy Dean and Ron Foster, *The Godbearing Life: The Art of Soul Tending for Youth Ministry* (Nashville: Upper Room Books, 1998), p. 9; Sarah Arthur, *The God Hungry Imagination: The Art of Storytelling for Postmodern Youth Ministry* (Nashville: Upper Room Books, 2007), pp. 29, 50; and Dan Kimball, *The Emerging Church: Vintage Christianity for New Generations* (Grand Rapids: Zondervan, 2003), pp. 116, 144-45.

[68]Once again, we engage in a spiritually disciplined indwelling of the Scriptures when we interact with them by means of several different spiritual disciplines (study, prayer, worship, community, service, etc.) all at the same time and with the goal of ongoing existentially meaningful, spiritually transformational experiences with the risen Christ in view.

attributes (if only by way of implication) to the entire evangelical community. These principles might include:

- The inspiration process as organic rather than mechanical

- The amazing unity of the biblical story[69]

- The idea of progressive revelation—that is, for various reasons God did not dump the whole truckload of spiritual truth or knowledge of his will on any generation of humanity until the time of Christ

- The principle of testamental differentiation—that is, when the two testaments conflict, it is the New Testament that trumps the Old and not vice versa[70]

- The logic of election—that is, why it made sense for God to choose one nation with whom to interact in a self-revelatory manner for the sake of the whole world[71]

In my experience, when a community of Christ-followers prayerfully models these kinds of hermeneutical principles and practices for those studying Scripture with them, all the supposedly insurmountable problems for ministry that Borg and McLaren associate with the earlier paradigm's understanding of the Bible begin to fade.[72]

---

[69]For an insightful discussion regarding the "theological coherence" of the Bible, "including the relationship of the Testaments," see David Filbeck, *Yes, God of the Gentiles Too: The Missionary Message of the Old Testament* (Wheaton, IL: Billy Graham Center, 1994), p. 10, as cited in Christopher J. H. Wright, *The Mission of God: Unlocking the Bible's Grand Narrative* (Downers Grove, IL: InterVarsity Press, 2006), p. 51. Wright summarizes his own discussion of the theological coherence provided the Bible by its missional focus when he states that "the whole Bible renders to us the story of God's mission though God's people in their engagement with God's world for the sake of the whole of God's creation" (ibid.).

[70]For more on this hermeneutical principle, see Gilbert Bilezikian, *Christianity 101: Your Guide to Eight Basic Christian Beliefs* (Grand Rapids: Zondervan, 1993), pp. 17-19. See also N. T. Wright, *Last Word*, p. 125.

[71]For more on this hermeneutical principle, see Lesslie Newbigin, *The Gospel in a Pluralist Society* (Grand Rapids: Eerdmans, 1989), pp. 80-88. See also Wright, *Mission of God*, pp. 65, 262-64.

[72]Additional resources for the task of answering Christianity's critics in a missionally faithful manner include: David T. Lamb, *God Behaving Badly: Is the God of the Old Testament Angry, Sexist and Racist?* (Downers Grove, IL: InterVarsity Press, 2011); Paul Copan, *Is God a Moral Monster: Making Sense of the Old Testament God* (Grand Rapids: Baker Books, 2011); Sean McDowell, ed., *Apologetics for a New Generation: A Biblical and Culturally Relevant Approach to Talking About God* (Eugene, OR: Harvest House Publishers, 2009); Paul Copan and William Lane Craig, eds., *Contending with Christianity's Critics: Answering New Atheists and Other Objec-*

We evangelicals have a reputation for being people of the Book, but we should also strive to be people of the Spirit of the Book! We should possess an empowering confidence in the Holy Spirit's faithfulness to work in a convicting, convincing manner as we invite pre- and post-Christians to "taste and see" for themselves just how inspired and reliable God's Word is by spending some time prayerfully studying (indwelling) sacred Scripture along with us.

On the one hand, we may be surprised at how many people around us will respond well to such an invitation if it is graciously given. On the other hand, it should come as no surprise at all when we see the lives of such spiritual inquirers being changed as a result of this Scripture-indwelling experience. I know it can happen. It happened to me. I suspect that it probably happened to most of my readers as well. Unless I miss my guess, the best explanation for why anyone would be reading these words right now is because they have had a personal, life-changing encounter with the Book, and the Spirit that inspired it. In all likelihood, it was not a set of rational arguments for the inspiration and reliability of Scripture that motivated most of us to devote our lives to Christ; it was the experience of having our worlds rocked by the trinitarian God who has revealed himself in a powerful way through both his living and written Word. This theologically realistic experience is precisely the aim of a missionally faithful bibliology. The Spirit of mission has provided us with a powerful resource as we witness to Christ and represent his kingdom in an increasingly postmodern, post-Christian environment. As the author of Hebrews put it, "For the word of God is alive and active. Sharper than any double-edged sword, it penetrates even to dividing soul and spirit, joints and marrow; it judges the thoughts and attitudes of the heart" (Heb 4:12-13). A missionally faithful bibliology does not require that we rehabilitate our doctrine of the Bible. We just need to let the Word of God do its work in us, and then cooperate with the Spirit of mission as he en-

---

tors (Nashville: B & H Academic, 2009); Paul Copan, *When God Goes to Starbucks: A Guide to Everyday Apologetics* (Grand Rapids: Baker Books, 2008); and Paul Copan and William Lane Craig, eds., *Passionate Conviction: Contemporary Discourses on Christian Apologetics* (Nashville: B & H Academic, 2007) .

ables us in creative ways to help our post-Christian peers come into intimate contact with it.

The next chapter will turn to theology proper—the doctrine of God. The bad news is that more false antitheses that serve to divide rather than unite await our consideration. The good news is that "answers" to these faux antitheses are at hand.

4

GREAT AND GOOD

Toward a Missionally Orthodox Doctrine of God

Theologian Roger Olson observes that "throughout the history of Christian thought about God's nature and attributes the pendulum has swung between emphasis on God's *greatness* and emphasis on God's *goodness*."[1] He goes on to claim that "if ever in any locus of Christian belief a false polarity is noticeable it is here." In other words, Olson is aware of how common (and unnecessary) it is for Christian thinkers to overemphasize either the greatness or goodness of God.

This is a serious problem not only for professional theologians but for lay theologians as well. Every reflective human being is a theologian in the sense that we all have a basic conviction of whether a God exists and, if so, what this God is like.[2] During my three decades of work in the local church and the classroom, I can attest to the fact that a person's theology matters! Many counseling sessions have required that I help a parishioner or student explore how a biblically inaccurate understanding of God was contributing to a serious problem in his or her life. Furthermore, validating Olson's observation, my experience has shown that the theological deficiencies at work in the hearts and minds of most church members and students have to do with an unbalanced emphasis on either God's greatness or his goodness. A biblically accurate under-

---

[1]Roger Olson, *The Mosaic of Christian Belief: Twenty Centuries of Unity and Diversity* (Downers Grove, IL: IVP Academic, 2002), pp. 111-12, emphasis original. See also p. 124.

[2]See Andrew F. Walls, *The Missionary Movement in Christian History: Studies in the Transmission of Faith* (Maryknoll, NY: Orbis, 1996), p. 10.

standing of the character of God is absolutely crucial to the Christian life and hence to the missional task!

Both of my dialogue partners, Marcus Borg and Brian McLaren, suggest that because God is ineffable it is hard to speak of him with any degree of precision.[3] Still, they both proceed to suggest that there are two distinct, mutually exclusive views of God that we must choose between—the God of the earlier paradigm and the God of the emerging version of the Christian faith. While each of these emerging authors seems to be motivated by the desire to put forward a view of God that possesses a greater missional impact, my concern is that their doctrines of God actually tend to aggravate rather than alleviate the pastoral problems mentioned above and ultimately serve to work against what God is up to in the world.

This chapter will identify the theological antitheses employed by Borg and McLaren in their respective attempts to articulate an emergent vision of God. It will also explore some important theological themes that need to be affirmed in response to these proffered antitheses if our doctrine of God is to prove faithful to both the biblical text and the missional task.

ANTITHESES IN MARCUS BORG'S DOCTRINE OF GOD

Chapter four of Borg's *The Heart of Christianity* is devoted to a discussion of theology proper. His antithetical approach to the topic is clearly evident as he writes, "In North American Christianity today, there are two very different ways of thinking about God, two very different understandings of God. To a large extent, they correspond to the earlier paradigm and emerging paradigm."[4]

According to Borg, these two theologies differ in two main respects: (1) the way God relates to the world and (2) God's character. These two fundamental theological issues are clearly connected and will dramatically affect what Christians believe God is up to in the world and therefore how they approach each day of their lives. The impact of such theological reflection can be enormous! The problem is that as Borg

---

[3]Brian McLaren, GO 154 [171]; Borg, HC 70. See also Borg, SC 74.
[4]Borg, HC 61.

treats these two issues, several antitheses are brought to the fore.

God "out there" versus God "right here." Borg makes it clear that the primary polarity inherent in the two paradigms has to do with their respective views of the *God-world relationship*. He identifies the earlier paradigm's perspective as "supernatural theism," and the emerging view as "panentheism."[5] While supernatural theism envisions God as a person-like being separate from the world he created, panentheism "imagines God as *the encompassing Spirit* in whom everything that is, is."[6] Borg insists that an embrace of panentheism does justice to both divine transcendence—the God who is "the more"—and immanence— the God who is "right here."[7] However, despite this insistence, Borg's promotion of the God "right here" over the God "out there" perspective[8] cannot help but emphasize God's immanence over his transcendence.[9] The irony is that, though Borg places the accent on God's immanence rather than his transcendence, his theology proper ends up resembling a deism that forthrightly denies that the Creator of the world is a person-like being with personal characteristics who intervenes in human history in any sort of providential manner.[10] Indeed, Borg's theology proper, when conceived of in a consistent manner, does not seem to allow for the possibility of Christ's followers interacting with God as a loving, heavenly *Abba* (Father) in a genuinely intimate, interactive manner. Obviously, this understanding of God runs counter to the day-to-day theological realism that I am advocating.

Divine intervention versus divine intention and interaction. Borg goes on to insist that the main difference between supernatural theism and panentheism has to do with the issue of divine intervention. When describing supernatural theism, Borg alludes to the idea of a God "out there" intervening in human history in spectacular events, "especially those associated with Jesus: his birth, miracles, death, and resurrection." Borg goes on to observe that "supernatural theists generally

---

[5]Ibid., p. 65. For a much more extensive treatment of panentheism, see Borg, GWNK 31-52.
[6]Borg, HC 65-66, emphasis original; see also pp. 70, 155; Borg, GWNK 12, 35-36, 72.
[7]Borg, HC 66.
[8]Ibid.
[9]See Borg, SC 68-73.
[10]Ibid., p. 73.

affirm that God continues to intervene to this day, especially in response to prayer."[11]

Borg proceeds to stipulate that the panentheism he is promoting does
not picture the encompassing Spirit as "intervening" in the affairs of the
world in the ways just described. Instead, Borg avers, "Rather than
speaking of divine intervention, panentheism speaks of divine intention
and divine interaction. Or, to use sacramental language, it sees the
presence of God 'in, with, and under' everything—not as the direct
cause of events, but as a presence beneath and within our everyday
lives."[12] Despite all of his attempts to indicate otherwise, the theological
image generated by Borg is that of a benevolent life-force in which the
universe exists. Miracles in general, and those that take the form of
divine providence in the lives of God's covenant partners in particular,
are simply ruled out.[13]

While Borg allows for the possibility that prayer can be effective, he
insists that this effect is not the result of divine intervention into the
world's affairs by the personal God of the Bible.[14] Instead, Borg's view
seems to be that prayer works in an extraordinary yet ultimately natural
manner,[15] evidently on the basis of some mysterious relationship between prayer-energy and physical matter. But at the same time that he
affirms a power in prayer, Borg unequivocally denies the idea that prayer
brings about any sort of divine intervention in the events that take place
in our world. Apparently, while it is bad form to claim to know how
prayer works (doing so is "an act of intellectual pride"),[16] it is permissible to claim to know how it does not.

To be fair, Borg's insistence on a non-interventionist understanding
of God seems to be driven by a concern to protect the divine presence
from the charge of either incompetence or capriciousness. The problem
of evil—how a God who is supposedly both great and good can allow

---

[11]Borg, HC 65.
[12]Ibid., pp. 66-67.
[13]A belief in the miraculous and its importance to the Christian faith is something Borg relegates
to the earlier paradigm. See ibid., pp. 9, 53, 65, 81.
[14]Ibid., p. 67. See also Borg and Wright, MJ 66.
[15]Borg, HC 197.
[16]Ibid.

such things as the Holocaust to occur in our world—is definitely an issue with missional significance. The problem of evil is a topic of great concern to many of our post-Christian peers. Borg's approach to this topic is to argue that since the encompassing Spirit that is God does not intervene in the world, it really cannot be held to blame for what we humans do to one another.[17] While space will not allow for a thorough response here to the problem of evil and Borg's apologetic tack regarding it, the question of whether it is necessary or wise to follow his lead in this regard will be addressed later in this chapter.

"Wholesale God" versus "retail God." Yet another antithesis proffered by Borg contrasts the divine reality ("ultimate reality") as it really is (the "wholesale God") with the ways various religions portray it (the "retail God").[18] This antithetical pairing provides Borg with a framework for his discussion of whether God should be thought of as a "person-like being with personal characteristics" or merely as a divine "presence" for which Christians use "personal language."[19] Borg indicates that while he considers it acceptable to use personal language when referring to the divine presence, he cannot accept the idea that God is a person-like being.[20] Borg is convinced that to think of God in a personal manner opens the door to supernatural theism and all the problems associated with the idea that a personal God actually intervenes in the affairs of this world.[21]

Throughout *The Heart of Christianity* Borg tends to be highly selective in his use and citation of Scripture. Borg cites only one biblical passage in support of his panentheistic understanding of God: "'For in him we live and move and have our being.' As some of your own poets have said, 'We are his offspring'" (Acts 17:28). Still, despite the paucity of explicit biblical support for this theological perspective, he insists that panentheism is not only more biblical and orthodox than supernatural theism,[22] it is the preferred way to view the God-world relationship

---

[17]Ibid., p. 67.
[18]Ibid., pp. 71-73.
[19]Ibid.
[20]Ibid., p. 72.
[21]Ibid.
[22]Ibid., p. 69.

since the alternative is simply "no longer compelling and persuasive."[23]

Borg seems to have within himself the hermeneutical and revelatory key as to when and where to affirm, deny or overlook the biblical witness, for clearly these criteria derive from sources other than the biblical record. Whatever these criteria are, for Borg they constitute definitive revelation rather than Scripture. How could Scripture function as genuine revelation for Borg since he assumes that there is no divine personal intervention? Borg's theology proper does not allow for the possibility of God providentially providing a human witness to his identity and purposes.

"God of requirements and rewards" versus "God of love and justice." Borg goes on in his antithetical treatment of theology proper to claim that there are also two basic ways of speaking of *God's character:* "God as a God of requirements and rewards" and "God as a God of love and justice."[24] Borg portrays the "God of requirements and rewards" as an "ancient king," a "lawgiver and judge who has requirements that must be met."[25] Viewing God in this way, Borg suggests, reduces the Christian life to a matter of sin management,[26] with Jesus' death "understood as the sacrifice that makes forgiveness and salvation possible."[27]

Over against this, Borg puts forward what he considers to be a better alternative: the God of love and justice.[28] Choosing once again to be

---

[23]Ibid.

[24]Ibid., p. 75. See also Borg, SC 77-83, where Borg contrasts God as "punitive and threatening" with God as "gracious, loving and compassionate," and then suggests that there is really no way for these antithetical understandings of his character to be reconciled—i.e., "combined" (p. 82).

[25]Borg, HC 75.

[26]Though Borg does not actually use the phrase "gospel of sin management," this concept, made popular by Dallas Willard, is referenced more than once by McLaren (see GO 48 [54] n18, 126 [139]). The irony is that Willard actually speaks of two "gospels of sin management," one promoted by those of the theological right that focuses on individual sins, and one promoted by those on the theological left that focuses on social sins and structural evils. Nowhere, to my knowledge, does Willard deny that individual sins need to be atoned for. See Dallas Willard, *The Divine Conspiracy: Rediscovering Our Hidden Life in God* (San Francisco: HarperSanFrancisco, 1998), pp. 41-58. For a more in-depth discussion of the effect which a "monarchical model" of God has on the Christian life, see Borg, GWNK 62-71.

[27]Borg, HC 75.

[28]Borg indicates that he has chosen to "leave unaddressed" the issue of "whether these two ways are complete contrasts or whether they can be combined" (Borg, HC 75). But just because an author acknowledges that what he or she is putting forward might be a false antithesis does not somehow make it something other than a false antithesis.

highly selective in his citation of Scripture, Borg focuses his attention
exclusively on those passages which speak of God as a lover—someone
who, because he loves everybody and everything, is very concerned
about how we human beings treat one another and the non-human
world in which we live.[29]

Borg also exercises some selectivity in the way he portrays God's
passion for justice. Depicting justice simply as love for the other—especially the marginalized other—Borg focuses all of his attention on
God's very real concern for the rights of the poor and the politically
oppressed. He passes over all biblical passages indicative of the fact that
because at the heart of the biblical concept of justice (Hebrew: *ṣedeq,
ṣĕdāqâ;* Greek: *dikaiosynē*) is the idea of fairness, equity, righteousness,
right judgment, justice and judgment can go hand in hand. For instance, Psalm 9:7-8 reads:

> The LORD reigns forever;
> > he has established his throne for judgment.
> He rules the world in righteousness
> > and judges the peoples with equity.

Unfortunately, Borg also ignores those passages which evidence a
connection between God's commitment to *justice* and the *requirement*
of an atoning sacrifice for human sin. For example, speaking of Jesus,
the apostle Paul wrote:

> God presented Christ as a sacrifice of atonement, through the shedding
> of his blood—to be received by faith. He did this to demonstrate his
> righteousness, because in his forbearance he had left the sins committed
> beforehand unpunished—he did it to demonstrate his righteousness at
> the present time, so as to be just and the one who justifies those who have
> faith in Jesus. (Rom 3:25-26)

That Borg intends these two theological conceptions of the character
of God—the God of requirements and rewards and the God of love and
justice—to be viewed as antithetical is beyond question. He goes so far
as to suggest that these divergent views of God's character lead to drasti-

---

[29]Ibid., pp. 75-76.

cally different takes on the nature of the Christian life.[30] The implication is that Borg's readers must choose between a view of God that focuses simply and solely on the management of their own sins (the God of requirements and rewards), or a theological perspective that promises to transform them into more compassionate, relationally capable, grace-embracing and grace-extending human beings (the God of love and justice). This is a rather egregious false antithesis.

Furthermore, though Borg refers here and in several other places to the possibility of a transformational relationship with God that makes us more relationally capable and available toward fellow human beings,[31] he never offers an explanation as to how it is possible to be in a loving, personal relationship with a "sea of being,"[32] the essentially impersonal divine presence that is the "encompassing Spirit." In one particularly telling passage Borg states: "We are in a covenantal relationship with 'what is.'"[33] Consider what Borg is suggesting: the possibility of a *covenantal* relationship with "ultimate reality," "Being itself," and "isness without limitation."[34] But since the concept of covenant (Hebrew *bĕrît*) as portrayed in Scripture involves a word of unconditional promise that calls for personal trust in a personal agent to fulfill the promise, how is this possible given Borg's theology proper? While the theological realism I espouse has no problem accepting that some aspects of our relationship with God will in this life remain mysterious (1 Cor 13:12),[35] it is clear that the biblical narrative as a whole ascribes to God not just the attribute of intentionality but personality as well. Indeed, both personality and intentionality are crucial to the covenant-cutting dynamic. Borg does not offer his readers an adequate explanation as to how a *covenant* with "what is" is to be conceived.

Furthermore, Borg's concept of the divine foreshadows some crucial

[30]Borg, HC 76.
[31]Ibid., pp. 36, 40-41, 57, 60, 72, 73, 75-77, 103-4, 120, 180, 188, 190, 198, 222.
[32]Ibid., pp. 217-18.
[33]Ibid., p. 73.
[34]Ibid., p. 71.
[35]See Ross Hastings, *Missional God, Missional Church: Hope for Re-Evangelizing the West* (Downers Grove, IL: IVP Academic, 2012), p. 102.

issues related to his Christology. If God is in Christ revealing himself to humanity, he does so as a divine person, as *personal* in a way analogous with us. Thus Borg has no room in his theological project for an incarnation. An impersonal God would never become incarnate—indeed, he could not!

"God of law" versus "God of grace." Going forward, in a very important theological move, Borg asserts that "another way of putting this same contrast is the God of law versus the God of grace."[36] He then proceeds to argue once again that these two antithetical images of God produce two profoundly different, antithetical conceptions of the Christian message and the Christian life. According to Borg, the earlier paradigm views the Christian message as bad news that focuses on the reality of a final judgment. Thus the Christian life is all about *requirements* and getting ready to go to heaven someday. "This is Christianity as a religion of threat, anxiety, and self-preservation."[37] But, of course, there is a radical alternative. We can, insists Borg, choose rather to view the Christian message as good news—an "invitation into a new life here and now, one that transforms us personally and seeks to transform life in this world."[38]

A God of law versus a God of grace? The Christian message as bad news versus the Christian message as good news? A gospel of sin management versus a gospel of moral transformation? A Christian life based on fear and focused on one's own eternal destiny versus a Christian life of love focused on making the world a better place here and now? Do we really have to choose between these binary couplings as if they were mutually exclusive options, or do they constitute a series of false antitheses?[39] The swing of the pendulum between what are truly nonexclusive possibilities could not be more apparent than in Borg's treatment of theology proper. Yes, the way we view the God-world relationship and his character will impact the way we approach the Christian

---

[36]Borg, HC 71.
[37]Ibid., p. 77.
[38]Ibid. See also Borg, GWNK 157.
[39]See Darrell Guder's discussion of how Karl Barth assesses and then dismisses both of these antithetical, ultimately reductionistic understandings of the gospel. Darrell L. Guder, *The Continuing Conversion of the Church* (Grand Rapids: Eerdmans, 2000), pp. 121-25.

life. But embracing the truncated, either-or understanding of God promoted by Borg will lead us away from the Bible's clear, no-nonsense
theological realism and toward an approach to the Christian life that
lacks the holism and missional faithfulness which a more biblically informed theology proper can produce.[40]

ANTITHESES IN BRIAN MCLAREN'S DOCTRINE OF GOD

Because there is no discrete chapter in *A Generous Orthodoxy* devoted
to a discussion of theology proper,[41] McLaren's doctrine of God must be
teased out of his treatment of several different topics. This, combined
with his acknowledged belief that "clarity is sometimes overrated"[42] and
his disdain for the use of "code words" that might help readers know
where he stands on certain crucial theological issues,[43] means that it can
be somewhat difficult to discern with precision all the details of
McLaren's doctrine of God.

I have already pointed out that even though both of my dialogue
partners make reference to the concept of God's ineffability (i.e., human
language cannot portray him adequately), each proceeds to pit an earlier
understanding of God against an emerging one. For sure, the doctrines
of God put forward by Borg and McLaren are not one and the same. The
biggest difference is that in some places McLaren uses language that is
connotative of classical Christian trinitarian theism. Obviously, this is
no little disparity. Still, in his own way McLaren, like Borg, presents an
antithesis between earlier and emerging theological paradigms, implicitly suggesting the need to choose between them.

"God A" versus "God B." McLaren's typology of a "God A" and "God
B" is fairly famous. According to McLaren, God A is "a single, solitary,
dominant Power, Mind or Will," while God B is "a unified, eternal, mys-

---

[40]Law and grace are not antithetical as Borg insinuates. Because God is gracious he has given
humanity the law which reflects not only his divine character but the divine wisdom we need
to navigate our way through this fallen world. God's grace is also responsible for the gifts of
Christ's sacrifice and the leadership of the Holy Spirit that together make it possible for us to
fulfill the "righteous requirements of the law" (see Rom 8:1-4).

[41]McLaren is not hesitant to express his lack of appreciation for a systematic approach to doing
theology (see McLaren, GO 151-52 [168-69], 219-20 [245-46], 286 [325], 289-91 [329-31]).

[42]Ibid., p. 23 [27].

[43]Ibid., pp. 69-70 [77-78].

terious, relational community/family/society/entity of saving Love."[44]
The way McLaren develops this antithesis is more than a little reminiscent of the way Borg contrasts a "God of requirements and rewards"
with a "God of love and justice," and a "God of law" (also referred to as
"the monarchical model of God")[45] with a "God of grace." Like Borg,
McLaren argues that these differing conceptions of God will greatly
affect how Christians understand the Christian message and the
Christian life.[46]

However, McLaren makes a unique move in the presentation of his
God A versus God B antithesis. The christological context of McLaren's
exposition of this binary theological typology indicates that he associates God A with the way God was understood prior to the Christ
event and God B with *the way the church came to think of God,* "after a
few centuries of reflecting on God as revealed and experienced through
Jesus (in the context of some major controversies with varied forms of
Greek philosophy)."[47] This would seem to suggest that God A is the way
the people of Israel and even the earliest Christians would have viewed
the God of the Bible, with God B evolving or *emerging* over the span of
several centuries following Christ's time on earth. Is McLaren suggesting that the "God A" view derives from what the Old Testament has
to say about the divine, while the "God B" perspective emerges from a
reflection on the more Christ-focused documents of the New Testament? If so, might this bifurcation of the Bible and its message imply

---

[44]McLaren, GO 76 [84-85]. McLaren develops this antithesis more fully in *A New Kind of Christianity,* actually giving these two depictions of deity different names: the Greco-Roman *Theos* vs.
the Hebrew-Aramaic *Elohim* or *Jesus' Abba* (See McLaren, NKC 42-45, 47-49, 54, 65, 98-99,
108, 128, 194, 239, 266-68, 272, 278).

[45]Borg, HC 75.

[46]The radical reconstruction of Christianity in *A New Kind of Christianity* owes much to McLar-
en's differentiation between two conceptions of God (see McLaren, NKC 42-45, 47-49, 54, 65,
98-99, 108, 128, 194, 239, 266-68, 272, 278).

[47]Indeed, the way McLaren describes the Trinity suggests that for him it is a doctrinal development grounded in the theological reflections and experiences of the church fathers rather than
something that is actually inherent within Scripture (see McLaren, GO 76 [84-85]). In another
place, McLaren hints at an evolutionary difference in the way God is portrayed in the Old and
New Testaments when he writes: "This full, radiant, glorious experience of God in Jesus Christ
eventually revolutionized the whole concept of God, so that the word *God* itself was reimagined
through the experience of encountering Jesus, seeing him act, hearing him speak, watching him
relate, and reflecting on his whole career" (GO 73 [82], emphasis original).

a huge discontinuity between the God of Moses and the God of Jesus? Is maintaining this discontinuity really a crucial component of an effective recontextualization of the message of Christianity for our post-Christian context?

Fairness and a desire for accuracy requires that we keep in mind that McLaren couches his God-A-versus-God-B antithesis within a discussion of how to speak of God without making him seem like a patriarchal, chauvinistic despot.[48] Like Borg, McLaren seems to want to rehabilitate the reputation of the God of the Bible for his post-Christian readers.[49] Thus, as part of an extended apology for using masculine pronouns for God and Jesus (an apology in the sense of both expressing remorse and explaining his action), McLaren makes the point that to see Jesus as the "Son of God" actually provides a new, improved impression of what God is like. Instead of seeing him as "a loud, bullying macho general," we witness a "vulnerable baby." Rather than attribute to God an "angry dominance that threatens with suffering," we behold in Jesus a "loving faithfulness that suffers instead." According to McLaren: "If Jesus truly reveals and images God, this vision of God is vastly different from the tough, macho judge and angry male potentate that many people think of when they think of God."[50]

Note how similar McLaren's description of God A is to Borg's depiction of the "God of law" as an "ancient king" and a "lawgiver and judge."[51] While I really do understand McLaren's apologetic motive for his God-A-versus-God-B antithesis, my concern is that, whether he intends it or not, this antithetical approach can leave readers with the impression that God A is the image of deity that derives from the pages of the Old Testament, while God B emerges from a careful reading of the New Testament. From what source would McLaren's *post-Christian* readers most likely have derived the image of God as a "judge" and "potentate," if not from the Old Testament? Though McLaren's desire to disabuse postmodern, post-Christian readers of the "patriarchalism or

---

[48]McLaren, GO 74-77 [82-85].
[49]Ibid., pp. 16 [20], 39-40 [44-45], 92 [100]. See also McLaren, NKC 19-20, 98-118.
[50]McLaren, GO 75 [84].
[51]Borg, HC 75.

chauvinism that has too long characterized Christianity"[52] is understandable (even laudable), is it really an appropriate missional move to portray the God of the Old and New Testaments practically as polar opposites? Could this be an accommodating rather than recontextualizing theological move with some rather profound implications for other aspects of orthodoxy? The bottom line is that, for all the good McLaren intends, his God-A-versus-God-B typology is a bit too redolent of Borg's theological tack in *The Heart of Christianity*.

TOWARD A BIBLICALLY AND MISSIONALLY FAITHFUL (REALIST) DOCTRINE OF GOD

Over against these false antitheses put forward by both Borg and McLaren in their respective treatments of a theology proper, I propose that there are several important realities that must be kept in mind as we forge a biblically and missionally faithful doctrine of God that takes seriously the theological realism proffered in this work.

There is an alternative to the God-out-there versus God-right-here antithesis. According to Borg, the two main theological options at our disposal are a supernatural theism which radically separates God from the world and a panentheism which places the world within God the all-encompassing Spirit. However, N. T. Wright suggests a different cosmological model which contains three options with respect to the God-world relationship rather than just two. Option one, which can take the form of either pantheism or panentheism, "slides the two spaces [heaven and earth] together," making of them "two ways of talking about the same thing."[53] The second option, at work in such belief systems as Epicureanism, gnosticism and deism, "is to hold the two spaces firmly apart," viewing God as radically aloof from the world of human activity.[54] Yet a third option of the God-world relationship sees heaven and earth overlapping in a mysterious but real and significant manner. According to Wright, "Option Three is what we find within classic Ju-

---

[52]McLaren, GO 75 [83].

[53]N. T. Wright, *Simply Christian: Why Christianity Makes Sense* (San Francisco: HarperSanFrancisco, 2006), p. 60. Wright's categorization of panentheism as a form of pantheism, rather than a sufficiently distinct alternative to it, should not go unnoticed.

[54]Ibid., pp. 61-63.

daism and Christianity. Heaven and earth are not coterminous, in this option. Nor are they separated by a great gulf. Instead, they overlap and interlock in a number of different ways."[55]

Wright goes on to argue that it is this third option—an alternative to both the supernatural theism and panentheism described by Borg—that actually enjoys the greatest degree of biblical support. Wright explains, "The Old Testament insists that God belongs in heaven and we on earth. Yet it shows over and over again that the two spheres do indeed overlap, so that God makes his presence known, seen and heard within the sphere of earth."[56] In this vein, Wright takes note of the way the Bible describes occurrences such as Abraham's interactions with God; angels moving back and forth between heaven and earth on Jacob's ladder; Moses finding himself standing on holy ground as he observes the burning bush; the people of Israel being guided and protected by a covering cloud by day and pillar of fire by night; revelatory experiences in the tent of meeting; the awesomeness associated with the ark of the covenant; and the power of prayer offered in or even toward the temple in Jerusalem.[57]

Another line of support for this third option, according to Wright, is that "this sense of overlap between heaven and earth, and the sense of God thereby being present on earth without having to leave heaven, lies at the heart of Jewish and early Christian theology."[58] In other words, it is only against the backdrop of this understanding of the God-world relationship that many Jewish and Christian affirmations make sense. Though Wright does not specify what he has in mind here in terms of Christian affirmations, I would offer such crucial Christian doctrines (christological verities) as Jesus' divinity, atoning death, bodily resurrection and lordship over all (see Jn 20:31; Rom 10:9; 1 Cor 15:1-5).

Finally, Wright observes that "the belief in heaven and earth as quasi-independent but mysteriously overlapping spheres goes a long way toward explaining several otherwise puzzling things in ancient Israelite

---

[55]Ibid., p. 63.
[56]Ibid., pp. 63-64.
[57]Ibid., pp. 64-65.
[58]Ibid., p. 65.

and early Christian thought and life."[59] Wright goes on to elaborate, for example, on how option three best explains the practice of Christian prayer, which is based on the conviction that God can and does intervene in a corrupt world seeking to remedy the human suffering caused by sin.[60]

The relevance of all this for the cultivation of a missionally faithful theology proper should be apparent. Contrary to the assertion made by the proponents of the emerging paradigm, there is an alternative to the God-out-there versus God-right-here antithesis. For Christian faith and practice to make sense, even to post-Christians, it is necessary to proclaim a God who is both at the same time. Once again, I have found that the members of the emerging generations have no problem embracing such a paradoxical proposal. Indeed, such proposals seem to resonate with a deep-seated sense many postmoderns have that the complexities of human existence are due to the fact that at the heart of reality itself is the phenomenon of paradox (rather than chaos)—with paradox being understood as an apparent contradiction that masks a deeper harmony.[61]

A "good enough" knowledge of God is possible, important and desirable. In chapter two I argued for a theological realism which asserts, among other things, that because of the incarnation of Christ and the inspiring and illuminating work of the Holy Spirit, it is possible for human beings to possess a knowledge of God that enables us to interact with him in ways that are real rather than merely conceptual. Scottish theologian T. F. Torrance writes: "Through the incarnation of his Son or Word, and in the Holy Spirit mediated through him, God the Father does not remain closed to us but has opened himself to our human knowing. Through Jesus Christ—as Paul expressed it—and in one Spirit we have access to the Father" (Eph 2:18).[62]

With this in mind, I will offer a tip of my hat to my dialogue partners

[59]Ibid.

[60]Ibid., pp. 65-66.

[61]See Jamie Smith's reference to Mark Noll's treatment of the "doubleness" at work in the "Chalcedonian definition of Christ's identity" in James K. A. Smith, "What Galileo's Telescope Can't See," *Christianity Today*, September 28, 2012, www.christianitytoday.com/ct/2012/september/what-galileos-telescope-cant-see.html.

[62]T. F. Torrance, *Reality & Evangelical Theology* (Downers Grove, IL: InterVarsity Press, 1999), p. 23.

for the way they show restraint in their references to God's ineffability.[63]
Both Borg and McLaren merely associate this concept with a need for
theological humility rather than founding on it an abject theological ni-
hilism (i.e., the conviction that absolutely no knowledge of God is
possible).[64] This restraint is well-founded since, over against the epistemological skepticism produced by the postmodern turn, the writings of
the New Testament assert that it is indeed possible for God's people to
possess a real and salvific—if less than perfect—knowledge of God (and
his Son, Jesus). As cited above, T. F. Torrance references Ephesians 2:18
in this regard, which speaks of both Jews and Gentiles having "access to
the Father" through Christ and the Holy Spirit. In another powerful
passage, Paul writes: "For God, who said, 'Let light shine out of darkness,'
made his light shine in our hearts to give us the light of the *knowledge of
God's glory displayed* in the face of Christ" (2 Cor 4:6, emphasis added).[65]
Furthermore, while Paul's caveats in 1 Corinthians 13:12 (that we currently "see" imperfectly and "know" only in part) seem to emphasize the
need for a theological humility that strives to avoid a natural human
tendency to overly rationalize and dogmatize the Christian faith, still
other New Testament passages seem to refer to our ability to possess a
knowledge of the "truth" about the way things really are.[66] For example,
the prologue to John's Gospel boldly states that "the law was given
through Moses; grace and *truth* came through Jesus Christ" (Jn 1:17-18,
emphasis added). And the introduction to the letter to Titus reads: "Paul,
a servant of God and an apostle of Jesus Christ to further the faith of
God's elect and their knowledge of the *truth*" (Tit 1:1, emphasis added).[67]
Finally, there are still other passages which suggest that there is not only
such a thing as knowable theological truth, but that it is crucial that this

---

[63]See T. F. Torrance's discussion of the difference between *theologia in se* (i.e., God's self-knowledge) and *theologia nostra* (our knowledge of God) in *Reality & Evangelical Theology*, pp. 21-22.
[64]McLaren, GO 155 [171-72]; Borg, HC 70.
[65]Other passages which indicate the possibility of humans possessing a real knowledge of God include Rom 1:28; 2 Cor 2:14; 4:6; 10:5; Eph 4:13; Col 1:10; and 2 Pet 1:2-3, 8.
[66]See Torrance, *Reality & Evangelical Theology*, pp. 12-20, for discussion of the humility appropri-ate to all human knowledge of the universe and the God who created it.
[67]Other New Testament passages that speak of our ability to possess knowledge of the "truth" about the way things really are include: 1 Tim 2:4; 2 Tim 2:25; Heb 10:26; 1 Jn 2:20-21; and 2 Jn 1:1-4.

truth be held on to since it can also be distorted, rejected, exchanged, wandered away from and so on.[68]

Therefore, it is one thing to point out how the ineffability of God urges a more humble, generous, poetic, mystical approach to theology.[69] (As an evangelical with a Pentecostal-charismatic heritage I am no fan of overly conceptualized versions of the Christian faith that find expression in highly dogmatic, hyper-rational, ultra-scholastic theologies which promote a harsh, rigid fundamentalist spirit.) It is another thing, however, to even insinuate that the work of most traditional evangelical theologians, whom McLaren refers to as "prose scholars," is somehow wrongheaded or of minimal value since "the Bible itself contains precious little expository prose."[70] In my opinion, McLaren's harangue against prosaic theology, while not altogether without merit, is itself worthy of critique. Yes, the apostolic letters were situational in their composition,[71] sometimes seem to cite early Christian hymnody (e.g., Phil 2:6-11), and together comprise a part of the larger biblical story. Still, even a cursory perusal of the many biblical passages cited above should suffice to indicate that the Spirit-inspired authors of the New Testament intended to provide their readers with an authoritative theology and often did so in a manner that was more prosaic than poetic.

Besides, as I have already indicated, most of the post-Christians making up our current ministry context are actually quite open to hearing a hope-inspiring, direction-imparting, existentially meaningful spiritual message as long as it is offered in a humble rather arrogant manner. A big part of the good news that we Christians have to offer those around us is that the God who is there is not silent: he is a speaking, self-revealing God who has made himself known through his son Jesus Christ and the Spirit-inspired and illuminated Scriptures that point

---

[68]See Mk 12:14; Lk 20:21; Jn 1:14, 17; 3:21; 4:23-24; 8:32, 40, 44-45; 14:6, 16-18; 15:26; 16:13; 17:17; 18:37; Acts 20:30; Rom 1:18, 25; 2:8; 15:8; 2 Cor 4:2; 11:10; 13:7-8; Gal 2:5, 14; 5:7; Eph 1:13; 4:21; 6:14; Col 1:5-6; 2 Thess 2:9-13; 1 Tim 2:4; 3:15; 4:3; 6:3-5; 2 Tim 2:15, 18, 25; 3:7-8; 4:4; Tit 1:1, 14; Heb 10:26; Jas 1:18; 5:19; 1 Pet 1:22; 2 Pet 1:12; 2:2; 1 Jn 1:6, 8; 2:4, 20-21; 3:19; 4:6; 5:6; 2 Jn 1:1-2, 4; and 3 Jn 1:1, 3-4, 8, 12.

[69]McLaren, GO 155 [171-72].

[70]Ibid.

[71]That is, they were written to address specific real-life drama occurring in first-century churches.

people toward him (Jn 1:14, 18). While no one should ever think they possess an exhaustive knowledge of God, they can believe that, because of his mercy and grace, God has done what is necessary to enable those open to the gracious movement of the Spirit to acquire a knowledge of him that possesses some staggering implications for life both here and now and in the age to come.

The God of the Scriptures is not schizophrenic. While Marcus Borg is careful to concede that the themes of law and grace appear coincidentally in both the Old and New Testaments,[72] both Borg and McLaren still tend to posit a huge disconnect between a God of law and a God of grace. But is such a theological move actually necessary in order to interest post-Christians in the biblical message? Is it really so difficult, as the emerging paradigm suggests, to conceive of a God who—precisely because he is true to his own loving, holy and just nature and desires the very best for and from the people made in his image—has graciously provided his covenant partners with certain behavioral standards while at the same time mercifully making provision for their self-sabotaging missteps? At the risk of oversimplifying a very complex missional matter, even those students of mine most influenced by postmodern thought understand the validity of thinking of God as a divine parent who, because he desires the best for all of his kids, seeks to nurture them in an environment rich with requirements, rewards, love and justice (see Micah 6:8).

Moreover, there is a fine line between clearing up any misconceptions our post-Christian peers may have regarding the best way to interpret what the Bible says about God and endeavoring to *apologize* for the way God is presented in Scripture.[73] This distinction is important because there is a certain similarity between apologizing for God and *attempting to defend his honor.* The latter, problematic activity is typified by those characters in the book of Job who are sarcastically referred to as his "friends" (see Job 13:7-8). Why did these so-called friends of Job end up becoming so very frustrated with him (see Job 8:1-2; cf. Job 13:4; 19:1-3)? Because they tenaciously held to two widespread but erroneous either-

---

[72]See Borg, HC 76.
[73]See McLaren, GO 74-77 [82-85].

or ideas: (1) that human beings live in a black-and-white world where sin is *always* the cause of personal misfortune (see Job 8:1-4; 34:10-12), and (2) that a perfectly predictable God *never,* ever "plays rough" with his kids with a benevolent purpose in mind. Because they firmly embraced these canards, Job's "friends" became extremely impatient, incensed at his reluctance to honor God the way they thought he should (e.g., see Job 11:1-12). But in the end, these defenders of God's honor found themselves indicted for not speaking rightly about God as Job had (Job 42:7-8)!

Could it be that the emergent apologist, eager to rehabilitate God's reputation among post-Christians by bracketing off his requirements and rewards from his commitment to love and justice, might be guilty of a similar either-or approach to the character of God? How ironic is it that those promoting the emerging paradigm might actually have something in common with Job's fundamentalist friends—a sincere but unnecessary felt-need to defend God's honor in the face of some cultured despiser's criticism of his character! Again, it is one thing to help someone better understand what the Bible as a whole actually says about who God is and what he is about; it is another to proffer an erroneous either-or theological construct (i.e., a false antithesis) in order to defend his honor.

The God of the Bible is nothing if not personal and prone to intervene. We have seen that Borg's version of the emerging paradigm seems to present us with the need to choose between devoting ourselves to a personal, Holocaust-causing deity, or an impersonal one that does not intervene in human history at all. Of course, this is a false antithesis. We do not have to make this choice.[74]

According to the Bible, God exists eternally as Father, Son and Holy Spirit—three divine persons in relationship to one another. Many New Testament passages evince the doctrine of the Trinity by referring to all three members of the Godhead.[75] Thus it is not quite true that the church

---

[74]Darrell Guder refers to the presupposition of a noninterventionist God as one that requires the rewriting "of most of the major chapters of Christian theology." See Darrell Guder, *Be My Witnesses: The Church's Mission, Message and Messengers* (Grand Rapids: Eerdmans, 1985), p. 5.

[75]See, for example, Mt 28:19; Lk 3:22; Jn 14:26; 15:26; Acts 2:32-33; 7:55; 1 Cor 12:3-4; 2 Cor 13:14; Eph 2:13-18, 22; 4:4-6; 2 Thess 2:13-14; Heb 9:14; and 1 Pet 1:2.

fathers, having been influenced by Greek philosophical concepts, created the doctrine of the Trinity, reading it into the biblical text. Rather, their wrestling with theological questions while at the same time indwelling the Scriptures resulted in their synthesizing clues latent in the biblical witness and forging a crucial doctrine that made explicit the truth and reality of the God known by the biblical authors.[76]

Furthermore, as C. S. Lewis has famously observed, this trinitarian God depicted in the Bible is not only personal, but "super-personal." Long before the emergent paradigm *emerged* as such, Lewis wrote:

> A good many people nowadays say, 'I believe in a God, but not in a personal God.' They feel that the mysterious something which is behind all other things must be more than a person. Now the Christians quite agree. But the Christians are the only people who offer any idea of what a being that is beyond personality could be like. All the other people, though they say that God is beyond personality, really think of Him as something impersonal: that is, as something less than personal. If you are looking for something super-personal, something more than a person, then it is not a question of choosing between the Christian idea and the other ideas. The Christian idea is the only one on the market.[77]

Behind Lewis' argument seems to be his understanding of a doctrine known as the "social Trinity," in which, as Craig Van Gelder and Dwight Zscheile explain, the triune God

> is conceived as a relational community of equality and mutuality within which the distinctive identity of each person of the Trinity is fully maintained as Father, Son, and Spirit. There is an irreducible otherness within God in relation to each person of the Trinity. This deep interrelated communion of the three persons of the Trinity is often expressed by the word *perichoresis,* which refers to the mutual indwelling within the threefold nature of the Trinity. All three persons of the divine community mutually indwell one another in a relational unity while maintaining their distinct identities.[78]

---

[76]For more on why accurate knowledge of God requires an indwelling of the biblical witness, see T. F. Torrance, *The Trinitarian Faith: The Evangelical Theology of the Ancient Catholic Church* (Edinburgh: T & T Clark, 1988), p. 57.

[77]C. S. Lewis, *Mere Christianity* (San Francisco: HarperSanFrancisco, 2001), p. 160.

[78]Craig Van Gelder and Dwight J. Zscheile, *The Missional Church in Perspective: Mapping Trends*

Lewis was struck, and rightly so, by the fact that the Christian conception of God emphasizes in the extreme God's being personal and relational in his very nature—that "the nature of God is communion."[79] It is a super-personal, hyper-relational God with whom we human beings have to do (cf. Heb 4:13 KJV)![80]

Now, the fact that God's singular being paradoxically involves a community of divine persons eternally relating to one another explains why the Bible presents us with a God who is eager to experience a personal relationship with human beings created in his image.[81] Postmodernity's rejection of modernity's rational, autonomous knower is rightly critical of an overemphasis on the individual. However, this same criticism can tend toward a rejection of individualism as a whole, accompanied by a sometimes radical embrace of communalism. Once again, overcorrections happen! As a result, some of those who promote the emergent vision of the Christian faith are not only highly critical of the individualism they perceive in contemporary evangelicalism, but go beyond this to complain of evangelicalism's emphasis on the concept of a personal relationship with God through Christ. Pointing out that the phrase "personal relationship" is not present in the New Testament witness, some emergent theologians express concern that such language is off-putting to the post-Christians living around us and that such a concept causes many contemporary Christians to become myopic, self-centered and consumerist in the way they live out the Christian faith. McLaren himself evidences this tendency in some sections of *A Generous Orthodoxy*.[82]

Certainly many evangelical Christians have become too individualistic in their walk with Christ and consumerist in their approach to the church. Indeed, the phrase "personal relationship" with God or Christ

---

and Shaping the Conversation (Grand Rapids: Baker, 2011), p. 54.

[79]Ibid., p. 55. Van Gelder and Zscheile are critical not only of the failure of the authors of *Missional Church* to explore the implications of the nature of God as communion, but that "this lack of development continues today in the vast majority of publications that employ a missional understanding, conceiving of the Triune God exclusively as a *sending* God."

[80]For a helpful discussion of "the Trinity and the power of relationality," see Hastings, *Missional God*, pp. 84-93.

[81]Guder asserts that "a special relationship with God" was the very purpose for humanity's creation (*Be My Witnesses*, p. 3).

[82]McLaren, GO 49 [55], 52-53 [59], 55 [62], 59 [66], 99-101 [107-9], 105 [115], 107 [117-18], 202 [227].

does not show up in the pages of the New Testament. But does this mean that the *concept* of a personal relationship with God or Christ is altogether absent from God's word? Is denying or even simply downplaying the idea of a personal relationship with Christ the best way to respond to the problem of Christian individualism?[83]

This is an important issue for Christians who want their faith to be biblically informed. Therefore, I encourage my readers to take a closer look at the biblical text in order to determine whether the authors of the New Testament, nearly two millennia before the advent of modernity's rational, autonomous knower, communicated the *idea* that God is concerned for the spiritual well-being of individuals and desires that individuals enter into and maintain a *personal relationship* with him through Jesus Christ—that is, a personal though not private relationship that most certainly has communal implications. Consider, for example, the many references to "anyone" and "whoever" in Matthew 10:37-42. While this passage gives the impression that the most basic decisions related to Christian discipleship must be made by individuals, they also possess important social implications.

> *Anyone* who loves their father or mother more than me is not worthy of me; *anyone* who loves their son or daughter more than me is not worthy of me. *Whoever* does not take up their cross and follow me is not worthy of me. *Whoever* finds their life will lose it, and *whoever* loses their life for my sake will find it.
>
> *Anyone* who welcomes you welcomes me, and *anyone* who welcomes me welcomes the one who sent me. *Whoever* welcomes a prophet as a prophet will receive a prophet's reward, and *whoever* welcomes a righteous person as a righteous person will receive a righteous person's reward. And if *anyone* gives even a cup of cold water to one of these little ones who is my disciple, truly I tell you, that person will certainly not lose their reward. (Mt 10:37-42, emphasis added)

---

[83]Philip Harrold cites T. F. Torrance as having argued that in the catechetical process the "message of Christ is communicated first and foremost in personal relation to Christ" that "requires a response of self-awareness and self-denial" and issues in "distinct call for personal decision." See Philip Harrold, "Getting to Know Him: Catechesis at Its Very Best Is a Very Personal 'School of Faith,'" *Christianity Today,* September 27, 2012, www.christianitytoday.com/ct/2012/september/getting-to-know-him.html.

This is one of many passages that seem to promote a *biblical individualism*.[84] Indeed, I contend that it was his interaction with biblical passages such as this one, rather than simply the impact of modernity on his thinking, that caused the eminent theologian of the contemporary era, Karl Barth, to define a Christian by saying, "We understand by the Christian a man whom Jesus Christ has called to attachment to Himself, to His discipleship and to living fellowship with Himself, and whom, as we finally say, He has bound and indeed conjoined Himself."[85] It would be hard to imagine a conception of a Christian more evocative of the notion of a personal relationship with Christ than this one. Thus, the idea that at the heart of the Godhead is a community of three persons engaged in a sort of divine dance produced by the eternal, loving interaction between Father, Son and Holy Spirit[86] supports the conviction that *our God is all about the dynamic of interpersonal relationship*. We might even say that he is a hyper-personal, ultra-relational God who is radically interested in a personal (though not private) relationship with each and every human being created in his image. Therefore, when Christians use personal, relational, communal language in reference to God, we are not projecting onto him our personal attributes and capacity for community. Rather, the reason why human beings are both community-capable and community-craving creatures is because we bear the *imago Dei!*

Also, an alternative to the antithesis that God is either an incompetent or capricious Holocaust-causing deity or a divine presence that never intervenes in human history is the biblically informed view of God as not only great and good, but wise and freedom-respecting as well. Though separate and distinct from the world he created, the great and good God of the Bible is not only willing but eager to intervene within it, revealing himself to a fallen creation to reconcile it to himself.

---

[84]Other passages that reflect God's interest in a personal relationship with people created in his image include Mt 16:24-27; Mk 8:38; Lk 15; Jn 7:17; 10:3; 14:23; Rom 10:11; 1 Cor 3:17; 11:29; 16:22; 2 Cor 5:17; Gal 1:15-16; 2:19-21; Phil 4:13; Heb 3:12; 4:1, 10; Jas 1:23-26; 2:14; 2 Pet 1:8-9; 3:9; 1 Jn 2:4-6; 4:8, 15-16; and Rev 3:20-22; 22:12, 17.

[85]Karl Barth, *Church Dogmatics* 4/3.2, trans. G. W. Bromiley (Edinburgh: T & T Clark, 1962), pp. 555-56, as cited in Guder, *Continuing Conversion*, p. 122.

[86]Lewis, *Mere Christianity*, pp. 175-76.

Because God is free in his own being, he has created human beings with a capacity to make free decisions. It was (and is) a colossal and ubiquitous misuse of this capacity to make free moral and spiritual decisions that made divine redemption of the cosmos necessary.[87] The holy or salvation history (German *Heilsgeschichte*) in the Bible is made up of those moments whereby God has acted wisely and mercifully within human history so as to effect its redemption. Thus, to deny divine intervention is to tear at the very fabric of the biblical narrative. As N. T. Wright has so ably indicated, the story of the Bible that emergent authors such as Marcus Borg want to cite (if only selectively) as support for their emerging vision of the Christian faith makes no sense at all if God is merely an all-encompassing Spirit who never intervenes in a fallen, rebellious world in desperate need of redemption. God is not the cause of human evil such as that manifested in the Holocaust, he is the cure! Therefore, Christians need not—must not—deny God's personal and interventionist attributes in order to render him less offensive to a post-Christian culture. The apostle Paul was not ashamed of a gospel message that presents God as a divine interventionist (see Rom 1:16; 3:21-26). He encouraged his ministry protégé Timothy to be likewise unashamed of this interventionist understanding of the gospel story (see 2 Tim 1:8-10). Perhaps we do not need be ashamed either.

Furthermore, the same Bible that portrays God as intervening in human history writ large also has him intervening in the day-to-day lives of individual covenant partners. The notion of divine providence, missing from a naturalistic understanding of the universe, is key to Christians being able to interpret everything that happens to them, whether good or bad, as meaningful and redemptive—something that God can and will ultimately cause to work for their good (see Rom 8:28). I am also convinced that a crucial connection exists between Romans 8:28 and the experience of Christian hope. As Viktor Frankl demonstrated in his book *Man's Search for Meaning*, hope is crucial not only to human flourishing, but to human survival as well.[88] *To the degree that experiencing God as an interventionist is crucial to Christian hope, this is*

---

[87]See Guder, *Continuing Conversion*, pp. 37-38.
[88]Viktor Frankl, *Man's Search for Meaning* (Boston: Beacon Press, 2006), pp. ix, 81.

a theological attribute that Christianity cannot afford to give up no matter how well-meaning (though misguided) the missional motive.

My hope is that this chapter has demonstrated how important our concept of God is to our daily lives and how unnecessary it is to have to choose between a God who is great (in terms of requirements and rewards) and a God who is good (in terms of love and justice). The God of the Bible is great, good and wise as well! This is a theology proper that has missional legs precisely because it is messy, involves paradox, requires a capacity to engage in nuanced (rather than either-or) thinking, and calls for a willingness to walk humbly rather than arrogantly before God (see Micah 6:8). This kind of theological realism is an exciting, coherent, existentially relevant way of understanding God that has what it takes to win both the minds and hearts of many members of the traditional evangelical, missional and emerging communities.

The next chapter will focus on the divine-human person whose birth, life, atoning death, present intercessory ministry and eventual return is at the heart of the gospel story. As with their theology proper, promoters of the emerging paradigm feel the need to redefine the nature and work of Jesus Christ out of deference to both modern and postmodern sensibilities. Is this a wise, necessary missional move, or does it actually eviscerate—cut the very heart out of—historic, biblical Christianity? We shall soon see.

5

LION AND LAMB

I n his book *Delighting in the Trinity: An Introduction to the Christian Faith,* Michael Reeves emphasizes the importance of Christ to Christianity by referring to a sermon once preached by "Charles Spurgeon, the twinkle-eyed master-preacher of the nineteenth century."[1] Said Spurgeon in this sermon:

> The motto of all true servants of God must be, "We preach Christ, and him crucified." A sermon without Christ is like a loaf of bread without any flour in it. No Christ in your sermon, sir? Then go home and never preach again until you have something worth preaching.[2]

I never tire of reminding my students of how important it is that they help their post-Christian peers understand the critical difference between *churchianity*—the way imperfect human beings have "done" church over the years—and real Christianity—what the Bible actually says about the person, message and work of Jesus.[3] It's not genuine Christianity that most of our post-Christian friends and family members

---

[1] Michael Reeves, *Delighting in the Trinity: An Introduction to the Christian Faith* (Downers Grove, IL: IVP Academic, 2012), pp. 83-84.

[2] Charles Spurgeon, "Sermon 2899," in *Metropolitan Tabernacle Pulpit: Sermons* (London: Passmore & Alabaster, 1904), 50:431, cited in Reeves, *Delighting in the Trinity,* p. 84.

[3] Though McLaren does not use these term *churchianity,* he does refer to the dynamic of people continuing to respect Jesus while being disappointed with "those who most used his name" (NKC 7, 20).

have discarded; they've never seen real Christianity. Rather, what most post-Christians in our culture have rebuffed is the church's sometimes egregiously imperfect portrayals of Christianity.

For our purposes here, this distinction I am making between mere churchianity and real Christianity is not intended to downplay the importance of the church, but to emphasize how crucial it is for Christ's followers to think deeply and biblically about who Jesus is and what he is about.

There is a reason why the first ecumenical council at Nicaea focused so much attention on Christology. The doctrine of Christ has tremendous implications for both Christian orthodoxy (right belief and worship) and orthopraxy (right ministry practice).[4] Christianity stands or falls on the person of Christ.

This chapter will reveal that some who promote the emerging paradigm feel the need to *redefine* Jesus in a manner that differs fairly dramatically from the classical (historical) and catholic (universally accepted) view. For example, Marcus Borg begins his presentation of the doctrine of Christ by asserting that there is a significant difference in the way the earlier and emerging paradigms view Jesus: "The emerging paradigm affirms the decisive centrality of Jesus, even as it sees Jesus quite differently than the earlier paradigm does. Its historical, metaphorical, and sacramental approach leads to 'seeing Jesus again,' just as it leads to seeing the Bible and God again."[5]

The need to *see Jesus again* comes through loud and clear in McLaren's writings as well. While this is especially true in his later works,[6] even

---

[4]Amos Yong argues that "when the links between Athanasius's understanding of the person of Christ and the saving works of Christ are made explicit, we can observe how the orthodox doctrine of Christ is interrelated with what we might call orthopraxis—the right practices that (ought to) mark Christian faith and discipleship." Amos Yong, *Hospitality and the Other: Pentecost, Christian Practices and the Neighbor* (Maryknoll, NY: Orbis, 2008), p. 42.

[5]Borg, HC 81. Indeed, the task of redefining Jesus for those who struggle with the traditional view of him is a central theme of Borg's theological project (see Borg, MJA 1-3). The irony is, however, that his contention that many of our contemporaries struggle with the historic view of Jesus himself rather than what Christians have historically done in his name is, as we have seen, at odds with the "I love Jesus, but hate the church (or religion)" sensibility that the latest research attributes to our post-Christian peers.

[6]Such as Brian McLaren, *The Secret Message of Jesus: Uncovering the Truth That Could Change Everything* (Nashville: Thomas Nelson, 2006); *Everything Must Change: When the World's Biggest Problems and Jesus' Good News Collide* (Nashville: Thomas Nelson, 2007); and *A New Kind*

in *A Generous Orthodoxy* McLaren hints at the need for a new perspective on who Jesus is and what he is about. In the first chapter, he describes the seven Jesuses he has come to know in the course of his spiritual journey: the *conservative Protestant* Jesus, the *Pentecostal* Jesus, the *Roman Catholic* Jesus, the *Eastern Orthodox* Jesus, the *liberal Protestant* Jesus, the *Anabaptist* Jesus, and the *liberation theology* Jesus.[7] McLaren strives to make clear that his desire is not to "further distinguish, delineate, or divide" the various groups of Christians who hold these various views of Jesus. Rather, his goal is to "create a hologram: a richer, multidimensional vision of Jesus" that all Christians can embrace.[8] Still, the way he presents these seven Jesuses seems to imply that none of these groups actually sees Christ adequately. Thus, while McLaren might insist that he is simply putting together a comprehensive (rather than novel) picture of Christ, in the end he is advocating a new, emerging, *better* way of conceiving of Christ.[9]

As to why we need to "see Jesus again," Borg is quite forthright in how he differentiates his emerging vision of the Christian faith from the earlier or traditional perspective. Indeed, in a couple of somewhat startling paragraphs Borg boldly asserts that the traditional view of Jesus is simply no longer tenable in today's world. He states that the "earlier image of Jesus and the image of the Christian life that goes with it have become unpersuasive to millions of people in the last century."[10] After

---

of Christianity: Ten Questions That Are Transforming the Faith (New York: HarperOne, 2010).

[7]McLaren, GO 43-67 [49-74].

[8]Ibid., pp. 65-66 [73-74].

[9]In several places, McLaren indicates his ability to affirm the Nicene and Apostles' Creeds (GO 28 [32], 32 [36], 221-22 [250]). However, these statements of affirmation aside, nowhere in this work does McLaren refer to those christological concepts that are at the heart of the Nicene Creed (e.g., the *homoousion* and *hypostatic union* in Christ). Furthermore, McLaren goes on to assert that the core fundamentals of the Christian faith are not doctrinal (and therefore contained in these creeds), but are practical—i.e., "to love God and to love our neighbors" (p. 184 [206]). This is what led theologian John Frame to make the observation that what McLaren presents in *A Generous Orthodoxy* is not really an orthodoxy, but an orthopraxy instead. See John M. Frame, "Review of Brian McLaren, *A Generous Orthodoxy*," March 10, 2012, www.frame-poythress.org/frame_articles/2005McLaren.htm. Borg can likewise endorse the recitation of the classic Christian creeds during worship, though he goes on to insist that a thoughtful modern person should not feel the need when doing so to think that he or she is actually confessing a belief in such doctrines as a literal return of Christ and his resurrection from the dead. See Borg, HC 159; see also Borg, SC 203-12; and Borg and Wright, MJ 153-55.

[10]Borg, HC 81.

providing a fairly accurate summary of the traditional view of Jesus,[11] Borg expresses concern that this perspective calls for people to actually believe that "Jesus is the only Son of God, born of a virgin; that he died for our sins; that he rose physically from the dead; that he will come again; and so forth."[12] According to Borg, "This image of Jesus no longer works for millions of people, both within and outside of the church. For these millions, its literalism and exclusivity are not only unpersuasive, but a barrier to being Christian."[13] He then offers his readers this reason for hope: "But for people who can't accept the older image, the historical-metaphorical approach to Jesus and Christian origins provides a way to take Jesus seriously."[14] So with the goal of making it possible for our post-Christian peers to "take Jesus seriously," Borg offers his readers a new and improved Christology.

Given that one of the stated purposes of *A Generous Orthodoxy* is to provide disaffected Christians some "reasons to stay in,"[15] we might suppose that even though McLaren is less stark in the presentation of his motive, the reformulated Christology he presents in that work (as well as the rehabilitated doctrine of Christ he advocates in later works) is likewise motivated by a concern to be missionally effective. Even though McLaren states that the reason why "so many of us have come close to withdrawing from the Christian community" is "not because of Jesus and his good news,"[16] his reformulated doctrine of Christ makes it clear that this depends on whether we are in touch with the real Jesus or a Pauline perversion of him and his significance.[17]

I suggest that because of the importance of Christ to Christianity, even traditional evangelicals should be open to "seeing Jesus again" in the sense of improving our understanding of him through a fresh reading of the biblical text in light of questions prompted by our current

---

[11]Ibid.
[12]Ibid., p. 82.
[13]Ibid.
[14]Ibid.
[15]McLaren, GO 16 [20].
[16]Ibid.
[17]See ibid., pp. 86 [94], 206-7 [231]. See also McLaren, NKC 138, 142-57, where McLaren makes the argument that it is not so much that Paul perverted the teachings of Jesus, but that commentators have perverted the teaching of Paul, especially the meaning of his letter to the Romans.

cultural context. However, this same importance of Christ to Christianity—the fact that at the heart of the Christian faith are four christological verities[18]—should caution us against a wholesale recasting of Jesus such that our Christology becomes either the product of what Christianity's current crop of cultured despisers is willing to accept about him or the version of him that best suits our political agenda. Therefore, my goal in this chapter is to evaluate the reformulated Christologies proffered by my two dialogue partners over against the classical view of who Jesus is and what he is about in order to allow for the *emergence* of a *nuanced Christology* that strives to be as faithful as possible to both the biblical text and the missional task.

THE THREE ANTITHESES OF MARCUS BORG'S RECONFIGURED CHRIST

In order to make it possible for modern/postmodern people to take Jesus seriously, Borg feels the need to offer his readers a series of stark, either-or christological antitheses.

The pre-Easter versus post-Easter Jesus. The fundamental, overarching antithesis at work in Borg's emerging doctrine of Christ involves a crucial distinction between a "pre-Easter" and "post-Easter" Jesus.[19] According to Borg, "The pre-Easter Jesus is *Jesus before his death.*" This historical Jesus, whom Borg identifies as "a Galilean Jew born around the year 4 BCE and executed by the Romans around the year 30 CE," is "dead and gone; he's nowhere anymore."[20] Borg clarifies, "This statement does not deny Easter in any way, but simply recognizes that the corpuscular Jesus, the flesh-and-blood Jesus, is a figure of the past."[21]

Borg then explains that "the post-Easter Jesus is *what Jesus became after his death . . .* the Jesus of Christian experience and tradition." The post-Easter Jesus is that *image* of him that derives from (1) the way Christians have *thought* to experience him over the years and (2) the

---

[18]See chapter two above, pp. 72-77.

[19]Borg, HC 82-83. Note that Borg's book, *Meeting Jesus Again for the First Time,* provides a much more detailed treatment of this christological distinction so crucial not only to Borg's doctrine of Christ, but his vision of the Christian faith. See also Borg, GWNK 87-104.

[20]Borg, HC 82.

[21]Ibid. See also Borg, SC 86-87; Borg, MJA 20-36; and Borg and Wright, MJ 6-8, 51.

memory of him that has been perpetuated within the "developing traditions of the early Christian movement—in the gospels and the New Testament as a whole, as well as in the creeds."[22] Clearly, Borg is arguing here that the post-Easter Jesus is not *literally* the resurrected and ascended Jesus of the Gospels. We are left with the idea that the post-Easter Jesus is a philosophical *concept* that, for some unexplained reason, can be experienced as a "divine reality of the present"[23] even though, as we have seen, Borg's panentheism also contends that divine intervention does not actually occur in our world.

Jesus human versus Jesus divine. In the process of making this distinction between the pre- and post-Easter Jesus, Borg presents his readers with yet another antithesis. Evidently the pre-Easter Jesus cannot be human and divine at the same time. Furthermore, since the pre-Easter Jesus could not have been both God and human, focusing any attention at all on his supposed divinity necessarily results in an inability to see him as a "credible human being."[24] Borg's argument presumes that any emphasis on Jesus' divinity must necessarily be at the expense of his humanity. Thus, if we want a Jesus who can truly empathize with us in our humanity, we cannot also think of him as divine. In fact, we actually discredit the real Jesus when we ascribe divinity to him, turning him into a God in disguise who performs "parlor tricks"—"walking on water, stilling a storm, feeding a multitude, raising the dead."[25]

Nowhere does Borg consider the possibility that in his incarnation and *kenosis* (self-emptying) an essentially divine Jesus might have laid aside the privileges of his deity (see Phil 2:5-7) in order to live vicariously as a genuine human being whose ministry vocation called him to be genuinely dependent on the Holy Spirit (see Lk 4:1; Mt 12:28). No, according to Borg, we must view the pre-Easter Jesus as *either* a God in disguise performing parlor tricks *or* as real human being who we can actually relate to and seek to emulate.

Furthermore, Borg warns that choosing errantly here will not only

---

[22]Borg, HC 82. See also Borg, SC 87-88; Borg, MJA 9-11, 15-17; Borg, GWNK 97-98, and Borg and Wright, MJ 4-5, 53-54.
[23]Borg, HC 82. See also Borg, SC 87; Borg and Wright, MJ 146; and Borg, GWNK 91-92.
[24]Borg, HC 83.
[25]Ibid.

result in the loss of a pre-Easter Jesus we can identify with, but will cause the post-Easter Jesus to evaporate as well. After all, once one decides to adopt a too literal view of the Gospel's portrayal of Jesus as divine and risen, then one must also accept the notion of Christ's ascension to heaven. But if Jesus has ascended to heaven, Borg's argument goes, then he is no longer here among us and "we lose the living Jesus as a figure of the present who is still here, still an experiential reality today."[26] Borg's argument seems to be that a literally resurrected and ascended Jesus cannot be at God's right hand and present to his people at the same time.

The voice of Jesus versus the voice of the community. To support this distinction between his pre-Easter Jesus and post-Easter Jesus, Borg has to make a distinction between two layers of tradition, both of which, he says, are present in the Gospels.[27] His contention is the same as that proffered by many critical scholars who insist that the biblical materials are essentially unreliable in their record of the life and ministry of Jesus, especially regarding the claims he made about his own ontology (essential being). According to this argument, the church's memory of the pre-Easter Jesus was essentially compromised by "the community's continuing experience of the post-Easter Jesus."[28] While some unmitigated memories of the pre-Easter Jesus remain in the four Gospels, an effort must be made to differentiate between the "voice of Jesus" and the "voice of the community."[29] In other words, the voice of Jesus, as rare as it is in the Gospels, is historically trustworthy. The voice of the community, which forms the bulk of the Gospel story, is not. This amounts to the *a priori* (presumptive) assumption that the vast majority of what the Gospels say about what the real Jesus said, what he did, and who he is has to be taken with a grain of salt.

MARCUS BORG'S EMERGING CONCEPTION OF CHRIST

The three christological antitheses outlined above are fundamental to Borg's reconfigured doctrine of Christ, dramatically impacting the way

---

[26]Ibid., p. 83.
[27]Ibid., p. 84. See also Borg, MJA 21; Borg, GWNK 87-88; and Borg and Wright, MJ 53-58, 146.
[28]Borg, HC 84.
[29]Ibid.

he understands Jesus' ontology, vocation, death and significance.

Jesus' ontology. Based on the distinction he makes between the "two layers of tradition" and their "two voices," Borg goes on to make two big christological moves with regard to Jesus' ontology or essential being. First, he argues that the christological language in the Gospels is post-Easter, meaning that *Jesus never claimed to be divine.* According to Borg, the pre-Easter Jesus did not actually utter the claims to divinity that we find in the canonical Gospels (especially the Gospel of John). Rather, Borg insists that all such "language is post-Easter," the "voice of the community" essentially putting these claims to divinity in the mouth of the Jesus portrayed in the Gospels "decades after Easter."[30]

Borg's second christological move has to do with the proper way to interpret the community-composed christological language we find in the Gospels. According to Borg, *all such language should be interpreted in a metaphorical rather than literal manner.* He argues that obviously Jesus is not literally a lamb or a light, or bread or a word, or so on: "These are all metaphors."[31] The same is true with respect to the most significant self-claim made by Jesus: "Son of God," says Borg, "is a metaphor like the rest."[32] This kind of language simply meant that Jesus had an intimate relationship with God and could represent him with some special sense of authority. This same kind of language could be used for anyone closely connected to God—for example, Israel as a whole or particular Jewish kings and mystics.[33] According to Borg, we err when we read too much into those passages where Jesus is referred to as God's Son.

So, if Jesus is not the incarnate Son of God in a literal, ontological sense, then who or what was he? The way Borg speaks of Christ's ontology in *The Heart of Christianity* can be confusing. Despite the fact that he seems to argue against the notion of Jesus' inherent divinity, he also describes him as "the Word and Wisdom and Spirit of God become flesh" and asserts that "his life incarnates the character of God, indeed, the passion of God."[34] Perhaps while Borg the *critical scholar* is careful

---

[30]Borg, HC 86-87. See also Borg, GWNK 88, 91; and Borg, MJA 109-11.
[31]Borg, HC 87.
[32]Ibid.
[33]Ibid., pp. 87-88.
[34]Ibid.

to maintain the distinction between the "two layers of tradition" and the "two voices," Borg the *professing Christian* will at times describe Jesus in a post-Easter manner, echoing the "voice of the community" and employing confessional language that is reflective of how Christians historically have related to the post-Easter Jesus. Apparently, even though Borg considers the post-Easter Jesus a chimera, this illusion somehow possesses the power to affect professing Christians in an existentially meaningful manner. This is why Borg, echoing the *voice of the Christian community*, is able and willing to describe the *post-Easter* Jesus as "the decisive disclosure and epiphany of what can be seen of God embodied in a human life."[35] But what about the earlier layer of tradition and Jesus' own voice? As we have seen, Borg insists that the pre-Easter Jesus is "dead and gone; he's nowhere anymore . . . the flesh-and-blood Jesus, is a figure of the past."[36] In another work Borg insists that "to deny that the pre-Easter Jesus was God does not diminish Jesus at all. Indeed, it exalts him. He was utterly remarkable—one of the two most remarkable people who ever lived."[37] Thus, the impression Borg gives is that the *pre-Easter Jesus* should be thought of as a mere man who, perhaps more than most, lived a life that was "radically centered in God."[38]

Jesus' vocation. The view that the pre-Easter Jesus was a mere man who lived in a remarkably God-centered manner has implications for Borg's view of Jesus' ministry career. While he speaks of the historical Jesus as a Jewish mystic (holy man),[39] a healer, and a wisdom teacher, Borg's primary vision of the historical Jesus is as a social prophet and "movement initiator" of the same ilk as "the great social prophets of the Hebrew Bible, figures such as Isaiah, Jeremiah, Amos, and Micah."[40] These men, Borg explains, "were God-intoxicated voices of religious social protest against the economic and political injustice of the domination systems of their day."[41] So, according to this view,

---

[35]Ibid. See also Borg and Wright, MJ 54.

[36]Borg, HC 82.

[37]See Borg, SC 96. See also Borg and Wright, MJ 147; and Borg, MJA 32.

[38]Borg, HC 88, 90.

[39]See also Borg and Wright, MJ 59-64.

[40]Borg, HC 91. See also Borg, MJA 30-31, 34, 119; Borg and Wright, MJ 71-76; and Borg, GWNK 90-91, 100, 103, 142.

[41]Borg, HC 91.

"Jesus was a prophet of the Kingdom of God . . . a radical critic of the domination system of his time that channeled wealth to the few and poverty to the many."[42]

Jesus' death. Borg explains the death of Jesus in a way that comports with his view of the historical or pre-Easter Jesus as a radically God-centered human being whose primary ministry vocation was as a social prophet. In response to the question, why was Jesus killed? Borg explains that it was "because he was a social prophet and movement initiator, a passionate advocate of God's justice, and radical critic of the domination system who had attracted a following."[43] In other words, Jesus "was killed because of his politics—because of his passion for God's justice."[44]

According to Borg, when the statement, "Jesus died for your sins," is understood literally rather than metaphorically, it creates significant theological problems.[45] Borg insists that the only real recourse is to conclude that "this interpretation, like the others in the New Testament, is post-Easter and thus retrospective. Looking back on the execution of Jesus, the early movement sought to see a providential purpose in this horrendous event."[46]

So, why did Jesus die?[47] According to Borg, Jesus (the social prophet and movement initiator) died as a tragic result of his attempts to bring down the "domination system" at work in the Jewish temple cultus of his day. Borg insists that temple theology had "claimed an institutional monopoly on the forgiveness of sins" and "access to God."[48] Thus, when members of the Christian community years and decades later began to affirm that "Jesus is the sacrifice for sin," this was merely intended to function as an "antitemple statement" that subverted the temple's claim

---

[42]Ibid.
[43]Borg, HC 91-92. See also Borg and Wright, MJ 81-91.
[44]Borg, HC 92.
[45]Ibid. The essence of Borg's critique of the traditional view of Jesus' death as a substitutionary sacrifice that requires faith in order to be appropriated is that it seems to put a limit on God's ability to forgive and "introduces a requirement into the very center of our life with God: knowing about and believing in Jesus and his sacrificial death" (ibid., p. 94; cf. Jn 6:28-29). See also Borg, SC 99-100; and Borg and Wright, MJ 140-42.
[46]Borg, HC 92.
[47]Borg's understanding of Jesus' death will be discussed in more detail in chapter eight below.
[48]Ibid., p. 94.

to have a monopoly on forgiveness and access to God.[49] Borg asserts that Jesus did not see it as his vocation to literally die for the sins of the world, nor was this the foreordained will or plan of God.[50] Such a "providential" understanding of Jesus' ministry vocation and the meaning of his death has no basis in historical fact but is actually one of many post-Easter, retrospective interpretations.[51]

Over against the assertion that Jesus' death was merely a tragic accident of history are certain New Testament passages which clearly state that Jesus' suffering was at the very heart of his messianic mission, and thus foreordained. Consider, for instance, the following three excerpts from the early sermons of Acts:

> This man [Jesus] was handed over to you by God's deliberate plan and foreknowledge; and you, with the help of wicked men, put him to death by nailing him to the cross. (Acts 2:23)

> Now, fellow Israelites, I know that you acted in ignorance, as did your leaders. But this is how God fulfilled what he had foretold through all the prophets, saying that his Messiah would suffer. (Acts 3:17-18)

> Indeed Herod and Pontius Pilate met together with the Gentiles and the people of Israel in this city to conspire against your holy servant Jesus, whom you anointed. They did what your power and will had decided beforehand should happen. (Acts 4:27-28)

Biblical texts such as these, especially since they seem to reflect some of the most primitive theologizing of the New Testament, make it hard to concur with Borg's dismissal of the "providential" view of Jesus' death—a retrospective interpretation he contends resulted from a long period of theological reflection.

Jesus' significance. We have already seen that one of the features of the earlier paradigm (traditional evangelicalism) that Borg considers untenable in a post-Christian ministry context is its view of the exclusivity of Christ—that in terms of both revelation and reconciliation,

---

[49]Ibid., p. 95.
[50]Ibid. See also Borg and Wright, MJ 79-82.
[51]Borg, HC 92, 95, 100.

Jesus is *the* way to God rather than only *a* way or merely *our* way.[52] Borg's advocacy of a deliteralization of language about Jesus as the Son of God and dying for the world's sins seems to be necessary for him to maintain (1) his relativization of the *revelation* of God to the world in Jesus and (2) his rejection of the idea that the sacrificial, substitutionary death of Christ serves as an exclusive means by which the world is *reconciled* to God (see 2 Cor 5:17-21). With regard to the revelation of God provided by the post-Easter Jesus, Borg asserts that "we can say that he is the decisive revelation of God for us as Christians without needing to say that he is the *only* and *exclusive* revelation of God, as the earlier paradigm affirms."[53] And with respect to the dynamic of reconciliation, Borg indicates that he finds it ironic, given Jesus' career as a social prophet bent on the deconstruction of all human systems of domination, "that the religion that formed around Jesus would within four hundred years begin to claim for itself an institutional monopoly on grace and access to God."[54]

In the end, Borg's position on the significance of Jesus seems to be that the post-Easter Jesus is *a* great example of what it means to live a life radically centered in God—to walk the "path" of "dying and rising" (i.e., dying to self and rising to a life centered in God).[55] But, the fact that Jesus is *a* great example of this path does not mean that he is the only one. Borg contends that the path of dying and rising is at the heart of all the "enduring religions of the world."[56] Indeed, having insisted that all the enduring religions possess their own version of what it means to be "born again" and the means by which this is to be accomplished,[57] he asserts:

> Seeing this commonality between the way of Jesus and the ways of the world's religions is sometimes disconcerting to Christians, given our history of "Jesus is the only way." But the commonality is cause for celebration, not consternation. Not only does it mean, to echo an exclamation in the book of Acts, the Spirit has gone out to Muslims, Buddhists, Jews,

---

[52]Borg's religious relativism will be explored in more detail in chapter nine.
[53]Ibid., pp. 88-89.
[54]Ibid., p. 95.
[55]Ibid., pp. 93, 107-12, 119, 121, 134, 174, 178, 180. See also Borg, SC 101-2.
[56]Borg, HC 119.
[57]Ibid.

Hindus, and so forth, but it also adds credibility to Christianity. When the Christian path is seen as utterly unique, it is suspect. But when Jesus is seen as the incarnation of a path universally spoken about elsewhere, the path we see in him has great credibility.[58]

Thus, according to Borg, the ultimate significance of the post-Easter Jesus is that he is *our* way: the model for Christians of what it means to be born again, a person whose example can be looked to over and over again for fresh inspiration to keep following the path that leads to personal transformation.[59]

CHRISTOLOGICAL PARALLELS BETWEEN
MARCUS BORG AND BRIAN McLAREN

While there are some important differences between the doctrines of Christ proffered by my two dialogue partners, there are some striking similarities as well.[60] I am afraid that in the next few paragraphs my observations may strike some readers as incredibly suspicious, if not cynical. Though I hope this is not the case, it cannot be helped. These are huge issues that are at the very heart of the Christian faith. They must be carefully and courageously explored if any common ground in the area of Christology is to be achieved between the evangelical, missional and emerging church communities.

McLaren on who Jesus is. With regard to Jesus' ontology, McLaren's position is characteristically obscure, making good on his promise to provoke conversation. On the one hand, McLaren affirms a trinitarian understanding of God.[61] On the other hand, his actual Christology is for several reasons somewhat reminiscent of Borg's.

It should be borne in mind that, like Borg, McLaren's desire is to present to postmodern, post-Christian readers a vision of the Christian

---

[58]Ibid.

[59]Ibid.

[60]Indeed, in one of his later works McLaren takes a page from Borg's playbook, building a couple of chapters on Christology around a series of contrasts (i.e., antitheses) between what he refers to as the "conventional" and "emerging" views of Jesus. Brian McLaren, *Everything Must Change: When the World's Biggest Problems and Jesus' Good News Collide* (Nashville: Thomas Nelson, 2007), pp. 77-92.

[61]McLaren, GO 31 [35-36], 55-56 [62-63], 76 [84-85].

faith and life that will not serve as a stumbling block.[62] On the one hand, McLaren's sensitivity to the sociocultural sensibilities at work in our postcolonial, post-Christian ministry context is to be commended. On the other hand, it raises the question: Could it be that it is an over-sensitivity to the *religiously relativistic* sensibilities of our day that explains why McLaren's most basic Christological statement—"God was in Jesus in an unprecedented way"—does not necessarily attribute full divinity to Jesus and is something that Borg[63] or even Friedrich Schleiermacher (the father of liberal theology[64]) could affirm? (As will be pointed out later in this chapter, the issue of Christ's exclusivity is huge among many contemporary post-Christians.)

This explanation finds support in the deliteralizing way McLaren compares the phrase "son of" (as in "son of God") with the phrase "mother of" (as in "mother of all wars").[65] Bringing to mind Borg's insistence that such language should be interpreted metaphorically rather than literally, McLaren's treatment of this crucial christological title seems to suggest that the phrase "Son of God" can simply mean that Jesus *embodies the heart of God* or *carries the essence of God* in the same way that, for instance, the apostles James and John *embodied the essence of thunder* ("sons of thunder"), some people *embody the essence of evil* ("sons of the devil"), or that Jesus also *embodied the essence of what it means to be human* ("son of man").[66] In other words, this is a *functional* way of referring to Jesus as the Son of God rather than an *ontological* declaration. Does such a metaphorical view do justice to the biblical text and the early creeds based on it? The bottom line is that nowhere in *A Generous Orthodoxy* does McLaren clearly state that Jesus is, ontologically rather than merely functionally, the Son of God—the second person of the Godhead having assumed human flesh. I am not asserting that McLaren denies the essential divinity of Christ. I am just pointing

---

[62]Ibid., pp. 16 [20], 39-40 [44-45], 92 [100].

[63]Ibid., p. 69 [77]. One thinks, for example, of Borg's view of Jesus as "a 'spirit person', a 'mediator of the sacred', one of those persons in human history to whom the Spirit was an experiential reality." See Borg, *Meeting Jesus Again*, p. 32. See also Borg, *The God We Never Knew*, pp. 91-92.

[64]For example, see Scot McKnight, "Justification Among the Liberals" (April 13, 2012), www .patheos.com/blogs/jesuscreed/2012/04/13/justification-among-the-liberals/.

[65]McLaren, GO 72 [80].

[66]Ibid.

out the need for some more clarity concerning a crucial christological commitment since any actual divergence in doctrine here would be a deal-breaker in terms of an increased sense of unity between the evangelical, missional and emerging church communities.

New Testament theologian George Ladd once stated that in the history of theological thought, "Son of God" "connotes the essential deity of Jesus Christ. He is the Son of God, i.e., God the Son, the second person of the triune Godhead."[67] This is a clear, precise, no-nonsense articulation of what it means to say that Jesus is the Son of God. Ladd goes on to argue that this is indeed what the authors of the Gospels meant by this designation even though he is fully aware that "this expression was used in the religious literature of Judaism and in the Old Testament with different meanings from that which we customarily recognize."[68] Thus, given the importance of this topic, McLaren's reticence to provide a similarly clear, precise, no-nonsense articulation of how Jesus is the Son of God results in a discussion of who Jesus is that strikes me as inappropriately vague to say the least.

McLaren on what Jesus was about. Another possible parallel between Borg's and McLaren's Christologies is the way they interpret the significance of Jesus' vocation or calling. Like Borg, McLaren expresses reservation at the idea that "Jesus was born to die"—a christological perspective he associates with the conservative Protestant Jesus.[69] This focus on Jesus' death essentially constitutes a marginalization of his life and devolves into a preoccupation with the "justification of the individual" to the neglect of "justice for the many."[70]

Thus, sharing Borg's sense of need to "search for other ways of seeing Jesus,"[71] McLaren enthusiastically affirms a christological perspective which views Jesus as "a prophet who bravely confronts the establishments of power and prestige" and who works to undo "systems of oppression."[72] Obviously, this is reminiscent of Borg's vision of the pre-

---

[67]George E. Ladd, *A Theology of the New Testament* (Grand Rapids: Eerdmans, 1993), p. 158.
[68]Ibid., p. 159.
[69]McLaren, GO 45-49 [51-56].
[70]Ibid., p. 48 [55].
[71]Ibid., p. 49 [55].
[72]Ibid., p. 63 [70-71].

Easter Jesus as a social prophet and movement initiator devoted to the deconstruction of sinful domination systems. While in *A Generous Orthodoxy* this understanding of Christ's vocation is one option among many, in later works McLaren seems to zero in on this as his christological perspective of choice.[73]

I am not at all antagonistic to the idea that Jesus possessed social concerns. I am actually in hearty agreement with Christian political scientist Dennis McNutt's observation that "working for justice in the legal system is an act of high spirituality every bit as much as fasting, praying, paying tithes, or going to the mission field, for this is one way we can love our neighbor."[74] Based on the many biblical passages which either indicate God's passion for social justice or issue a call for his people to pursue it,[75] my conviction is that striving to establish justice in society is an important way Christians may fulfill Jesus' command to love our neighbors as ourselves (Mk 12:30-31). And, according to Matthew 5:13-16, it is also key to our functioning in this world as salt and light, thereby enabling our neighbors to experience a spiritual connection with our heavenly Father. That said, it may be possible out of deference to postmodern, post-Christian sensibilities, to *overpoliticize* and *overtemporalize* Jesus' ministry message and vocation[76] in a way that downplays what the Bible says about Jesus as "the lamb of God who takes away the sins of the world"[77] or purposefully understates the way Jesus' teachings focus on both "this age" and the "age to come."[78] Unfortunately, McLaren seems to make these moves.[79]

---

[73]For example, see McLaren, NKC 127, 131, 135; McLaren, *Everything Must Change*, pp. 77-147; Brian McLaren, *The Secret Message of Jesus: Uncovering the Truth That Could Change Everything* (Nashville: Thomas Nelson, 2006), pp. 4, 9-34.

[74]Dennis McNutt, "Politics for Christians (and Other Sinners)" in *Elements of a Christian Worldview,* ed. Michael Palmer (Springfield, MO: Logion, 1998), p. 418.

[75]For example, see Deut 16:20; Ps 11:7; 106:3; Prov 28:5; 29:7; Is 56:1; Jer 21:12; Amos 5:15, 21-24; Zech 7:9-10; Mt 23:23; Lk 11:42.

[76]I would offer that McLaren's later works *Everything Must Change* and *The Secret Message of Jesus* serve as examples of this tendency to over-politicize and over-temporalize Jesus' ministry message and vocation.

[77]See Jn 1:29; cf. Mt 20:28; 1 Tim 1:15; 1 Jn 2:2; 4:10.

[78]See Mt 12:32; 13:40-43, 47-50; 24-25; Lk 20:34-36.

[79]Furthermore, given McLaren's call for a "generous" orthodoxy and a Christology/soteriology that downplays Jesus' concern about getting individuals to heaven (e.g., see McLaren, GO 86-87 [94-95], 100 [109], 107 [117-18], 112 [122], 160 [178], 237-39 [267-69]), I find it ironic that the

McLaren's understating of the cross. McLaren genuinely seems to possess a sincere, holistic appreciation for what Jesus did on the cross. At the same time, he relativizes the importance of Jesus' sacrificial death by (1) criticizing conservative Protestants for an overemphasis on the cross-work of Christ (due to a myopic, misguided focus on the forgiveness of past sins and a future in heaven) to the neglect of his teaching ministry (which was intended to inculcate a better way to live here and now), and (2) affirming the idea that the "salvation" Jesus effects can be grounded in other aspects of his life and ministry quite apart from his death and resurrection (his incarnation, his teaching and example, and his convening and leading a community of disciples through whom he "confronts the corrupt, compromised religious system and violent, unjust political and economic powers . . . through nonviolent resistance").[80] Furthermore, there is some evidence that McLaren has issues with the concept of a penal substitutionary atonement.[81] As my more complete treatment of McLaren's soteriology in chapter eight will make clear, all of this is somewhat reminiscent of Borg's redefinition of what it means to say that "Jesus died for your sins." And, as we will see, the problem is that it also seems to represent another possible divergence from yet another of the four christological verities that I have suggested constitute Christian dogma—that is, the atoning, sacrificial nature of Christ's death (see Eph 5:1-2; Heb 9:24-28; 10:10-14; 1 Jn 2:2; 4:10). As this issue relates to a missional orthodoxy, we must be very careful. Some overstated language, though perhaps intended to correct a perceived imbalance in the traditional evangelical perspective, could turn into an overcorrection that further fractures rather than heals the unity between traditional, missional and emerging evangelicals. Neither am I convinced that disavowing or even downplaying a substitutionary sacrifice of Christ is necessary for encouraging post-Christians to take another look at Jesus.

McLaren on the importance of confessing Christ as Lord. McLaren is

---

only time in the Gospels when the Greek word *agathos* is translated in the NIV (and other translations) as "generous" rather than merely "good" is at Mt 20:15—the culmination of a parable that focuses on individual rewards in the age to come!

[80]McLaren, GO 62-63 [70-71].

[81]Ibid., pp. 197-98 [220].

famous for asserting, "I don't believe making disciples must equal making adherents of the Christian religion. It may be advisable in many (not all!) circumstances to help people become followers of Jesus *and* remain within their Buddhist, Hindu, or Jewish contexts."[82] Many missionally minded evangelicals would have no problem with the idea of sending baptized believers back into the cultural contexts in order to represent Christ there. But is this what McLaren has in mind? Absent any reference to baptism or participation in a Christian community, McLaren's commitment to helping people become followers of Christ can be interpreted in a Borg-like manner to mean that our goal should simply be to enable people, whatever their religious affiliation, to follow the path of dying and rising, to live their lives the way Jesus did—for the sake of God and others rather than themselves.[83]

My point is not to argue for or against a soteriological inclusivism which posits that it is possible for some to be saved through Christ though never in this life professing faith in him. Personally, I am pretty sure that some folks have been and are being saved though they have not explicitly called on Christ (e.g., "Old Testament saints, infants who die young, and the severely mentally challenged").[84] But fully aware that for some the inclusivist view can include the conviction that "grace operates outside the church and *may be* encountered in the context of

---

[82]Ibid., p. 260 [293].

[83]See McLaren, NKC 161-72. Indeed, in a later work McLaren argues: "So if a Muslim or Hindhu community is destroying Muslims or Hindhus, if it bores them with irrelevance, wastes their time and energy with meaningless and pointless rituals, if it turns them against others and obstructs the common good, I hope a Christian community will open their doors wide and offer sanctuary and healing. How could anyone turn them away? How could anyone refuse them water for baptism? How could anyone refrain from breaking out the bread and wine and welcoming them to the table? But the same must be said when Christians are being destroyed, bored, wasted, or turned hostile by their Christian communities, and other communities (often agnostics or atheists) offer them sanctuary. That's why this saving mission vigorously supports religious freedom, including the freedom to change religions and the freedom to be non-religious, multireligious, or spiritual-but-not-religious." Brian McLaren, *Why Did Jesus, Moses, the Buddha, and Mohammed Cross the Road? Christian Identity in a Multi-Faith World* (New York: Jericho Books, 2012), p. 260. Obviously, I share McLaren's concern regarding dysfunctional Christian churches. But is it not an overcorrection to endorse the idea that it does not really matter what "religion" one belongs to as long as it is helping us become more open toward God and others?

[84]See Daniel Clendenin, "The Only Way: Answering the Argument That All Religions Are More or Less True," *Christianity Today*, January 12, 1998, www.christianitytoday.com/ct/1998/january12/8t1034.html.

other religions,"[85] my desire is simply to encourage those evangelicals (traditional, missional and emerging) who acknowledge the unique soteriological significance of Jesus to ponder these questions. If we are to be faithful in our practice and speech to the divine reality we have encountered in Christ, then how should we express in our language (and our lives) the truth about who Jesus is? What should those who intend to be faithful to Jesus say to others about him? Just how important is it for us to hope and pray that those to whom we minister will be led to make their own confession of Christ as Lord?[86]

As we reflect on these questions, we should keep in mind New Testament passages such as:

> If you declare with your mouth, "Jesus is Lord," and believe in your heart that God raised him from the dead, you will be saved. For it is with your heart that you believe and are justified, and it is with your mouth that you profess your faith and are saved. (Rom 10:9-10)

> Therefore God exalted him to the highest place
>   and gave him the name that is above every name,
> that at the name of Jesus every knee should bow,
>   in heaven and on earth and under the earth,
> and every tongue acknowledge that Jesus Christ is Lord,
>   to the glory of God the Father. (Phil 2:9-11)

> Therefore, holy brothers and sisters, who share in the heavenly calling, fix your thoughts on Jesus, whom we acknowledge as our apostle and high priest. (Heb 3:1)

McLaren seems to be strangely silent about this matter of confessing Christ as Lord, except to contend that when this kind of confession was made by the earliest followers of Jesus, its main meaning was political and not "primarily a theological confession of Jesus' divinity, as many today assume."[87] Despite this debatable assertion (which seems to par-

---

[85]See Clark H. Pinnock, "An Inclusivist View," in *Four Views of Salvation in a Pluralistic World*, ed. Stanley Gundry, Dennis L. Olkhom and Timothy R. Phillips (Grand Rapids: Zondervan, 1996), p. 100.

[86]For more on how evangelicals open to an "orthodox inclusivism" might respond to these questions, see Ross Hastings, *Missional God, Missional Church: Hope for Re-evangelizing the West* (Downers Grove, IL: IVP Academic, 2012), pp. 91-93.

[87]McLaren, *Everything Must Change*, p. 98.

allel Borg's)[88] and fully recognizing that the verbal confession "Lord, Lord" does not in itself guarantee salvation (see Mt 7:21), it still seems odd that nowhere in *A Generous Orthodoxy* (to my knowledge) does McLaren refer to the act, much less the importance, of making the "good confession" that Paul referred to when he wrote to Timothy: "Fight the good fight of the faith. Take hold of the eternal life to which you were called when you made your good confession in the presence of many witnesses" (1 Tim 6:12). Since in my understanding one of the four christological commitments at the heart of the Christian faith is that *Jesus is lord of all*, I must raise a concern about a Christology that does treat not this issue with the seriousness it deserves. This is what a missional orthodoxy that seeks to be faithful to the text as well as the task requires us to do—not in order to decide who's in and who's out, but to articulate a vision of the Christian faith that can lead nonbelievers into an authentic, holistic experience of God's reign in their lives!

THE EMERGING VISION OF CHRIST: HOW JUSTIFIED? HOW NECESSARY?

Though there are some differences between the christologies proffered by my two dialogue partners, there are enough similarities to allow for a composite portrait of the emerging paradigm's conception of Christ. First, with regard to Jesus' *ontology*, Jesus may or may not be the Son of God in a literal sense. Second, with regard to Jesus' *vocation*, Jesus saw himself primarily as a social prophet, self-consciously taking on the domination systems of his day and organizing a band of followers who would do likewise. Third, with regard to Jesus' *death,* his was a tragic end—certainly not the foreordained will of God, something he came into the world to accomplish. Neither was this untimely demise an act that made it literally (or primarily) possible for God to forgive the sins of the world. Instead, Jesus' death should be viewed through a sociopolitical lens as a tragic turn of events resulting directly from his ferocious prophetic activity over against the powers of his day. Jesus' death on the cross is therefore at once a dramatic, poignant unmasking of the presence

---

[88]Borg, HC 135-36.

of systemic, institutionalized evil in our world and the defeat of that evil insofar as it inspires his followers likewise to devote their lives to the liberation of the oppressed. Fourth, with regard to Jesus' *exclusivity,* Jesus should be seen simply as *our* Savior—the one who models *for us* the path of "dying" to self and "rising" to a lifetime of service to others and our planet.

Two key questions come to my mind when pondering this new, "better" Christology put forward by proponents of the emerging paradigm.

Is a reconfigured Christ justified? To be sure, as N. T. Wright reminds us, the question of the historical Jesus does possess missional significance if for no other reason than because so many post-Christians have heard of the work of the Jesus Seminar (to which Borg belongs)[89] or seen televised documentaries questioning the traditional understanding of Jesus of Nazareth.[90] However, this does not necessarily mean that the emerging paradigm's reformulated doctrine of Christ possesses historical validity.

Precisely because of the importance of this issue and the fact that the revisionist christological conclusions of the Jesus Seminar and emerging paradigm are considered by evangelical scholars to be so highly questionable, a spate of books on the historical reliability of the New Testament's portrait of Jesus have been published in the past few years. Although a thorough summary of the evangelical response to the emerging paradigm's reconfigured Christ is beyond the scope of this work, I will briefly summarize significant evangelical responses to two fundamental christological assertions made by my dialogue partners.

The first assertion is that the biblical documents do not provide us with any sort of reliable record of what the historical (pre-Easter) Jesus said and did. A number of recent scholarly works have addressed this line of thought. Richard Bauckham, for instance, argues against the form critical notion that "whatever the form in which the eyewitnesses of the history of Jesus first told their stories or repeated Jesus' teachings, a long

---

[89]The Jesus Seminar is a group of critical biblical scholars who meet periodically to discuss and make pronouncements concerning what the historical Jesus actually said and did.

[90]N. T. Wright, *The Challenge of Jesus: Rediscovering Who Jesus Was and Is* (Downers Grove, IL: InterVarsity Press, 1999), p. 18.

process of anonymous transmission in the communities intervened between their testimony and the writing of the Gospels."[91] Instead, Bauckham marshals much evidence in support of his conclusion that

> the Gospel texts are much closer to the form in which the eyewitnesses told their stories or passed on their traditions than is commonly envisaged in current scholarship. This is what gives the Gospels their character as testimony. They embody the testimony of the eyewitnesses, not of course without editing and interpretation, but in a way that is substantially faithful to how the eyewitnesses themselves told it, since the Evangelists were in more or less direct contact with eyewitnesses, not removed from them by a long process of anonymous transmission of the traditions.[92]

In response to the assertion that the Bible's accounts of the life, death and resurrection of Jesus need not be viewed as historically factual to be meaningful, Craig Blomberg writes:

> At the very least the main outline of the events of Jesus' life, death and resurrection must be historical or the claims of Christianity become incomprehensible. The very distinctiveness of the Judeo-Christian tradition over against its pagan counterparts lay in its belief in one omnipotent God acting in observable events in history, and the distinctiveness of Christianity over against Judaism centered on the belief that such divine action came to a decisive climax with the person and work of Jesus. Sceptics down through the ages argued that those beliefs were not true, but seldom did they maintain that those beliefs were not what Scripture was claiming. That the latter notion has proliferated in recent times may be due to the uneasy conscience of modern scholars who have broken with their traditional Christian heritage but who hope to salvage something of it that scholars from other backgrounds might accept. However well intentioned, it seems likely that such "mediation" is doomed to failure though lack of sufficient evidence and logic.[93]

Specifically taking on the Jesus Seminar in his book *Fabricating Jesus,* Craig Evans asserts that "claims that the Gospels are unreliable, full of

---

[91]Richard Bauckham, *Jesus and the Eyewitnesses: The Gospels as Eyewitness Testimony* (Grand Rapids: Eerdmans, 2008), p. 6.

[92]Ibid.

[93]Craig L. Blomberg, *The Historical Reliability of the Gospels,* 2nd ed. (Downers Grove, IL: IVP Academic, 2007), p. 98.

myth and legend, and so biased that knowledge of what Jesus really said and did cannot be recovered are excessive and unwarranted."[94]

He goes on to explain:

> It is true that the Gospels may tell us much about the concerns of their respective authors (which is the task of redaction criticism) and may even tell us something about early Christians who handed down the tradition (which is the task of form criticism), but the authors' principal concern was to publish the teachings and deeds of Jesus. His words and example were considered normative. Indeed, there is evidence early on that the words of Jesus were considered on par with Scripture, which in a Jewish context is remarkable.
>
> Given such a high regard for Jesus' words, it is not likely that early Christians would have freely invented sayings and then attributed them to Jesus. In fact, the oft-heard assertion that many of the sayings were generated by questions and issues that the early church faced is called into doubt by the observation that many of these questions and issues (as seen in the New Testament letters) are nowhere addressed by the sayings of Jesus. . . . This shows that the Gospel writers were not in the habit of making things up. There is every reason to conclude (again, without invoking theological dogmas) that the Gospels have fairly and accurately reported the essential elements of Jesus' teaching, life, death and resurrection.[95]

Along the same lines, J. Ed Komoszewski, M. James Sawyer and Daniel B. Wallace conclude that

> the ancient Jewish culture, the relation of the disciples to Jesus as their rabbi, the multiple witnesses, and the repetition of the stories about Jesus from the very beginning all point to a strong oral tradition behind the written Gospels. Although this oral culture does not suggest that the Evangelists always wrote down verbatim what Jesus said, they certainly got the essence right. (And this is in line with ancient historical reporting.)[96]

---

[94]Craig A. Evans, *Fabricating Jesus: How Modern Scholarship Distorts the Gospels* (Downers Grove, IL: IVP Books, 2006), p. 234.
[95]Ibid.
[96]J. Ed Komoszewski, M. James Sawyer and Daniel B. Wallace, *Reinventing Jesus: How Contemporary Skeptics Miss the Real Jesus and Mislead Popular Culture* (Grand Rapids: Kregel, 2006), p. 38.

They go on to cite James Dunn's conclusion about the reliability of this oral tradition: "What we today are confronted with in the Gospels is not the top layer (last edition) of a series of increasingly impenetrable layers, but the living tradition of Christian celebration which takes us with surprising immediacy to the heart of the first memories of Jesus."[97]

All of this excellent work in defense of the historical reliability of the Gospels points toward N. T. Wright's eloquent conclusion:

> I simply record it as my conviction that the four canonical gospels, broadly speaking, present a portrait of Jesus of Nazareth which is firmly grounded in real history. . . . The portrait of Jesus we find in the canonical gospels makes sense with the world of Palestine in the 20s and 30s of the first century. Above all, it makes coherent sense in itself. The Jesus who emerges is thoroughly believable as a figure of history, even though the more we look at him, the more we feel once more that we may be staring into the sun.[98]

A perusal of any of the scholarly works cited here will reveal that when contemporary scholars approach the biblical text with anti-supernaturalistic assumptions in place, they will arrive at anti-supernaturalistic conclusions.[99] Such conclusions will, of course, augur against the classic, catholic view of Christ the church has embraced for over two thousand years. But such a reconfiguration of Jesus, while possible, is not at all required by critical scholarship of the New Testament texts and early Christian history.[100] The emerging doctrine of Christ is a preference rather than a scholastically mandated given.

The second fundamental assertion made by my dialogue partners in an attempt to justify the emerging paradigm's reconfiguration of Christ is that Jesus never actually made the claims to divinity that we find in the canonical Gospels. Commenting critically on C. S. Lewis's classic argument in *Mere Christianity* that the self-claims made by Jesus and re-

---

[97]James D. G. Dunn, *Jesus Remembered* (Grand Rapids: Eerdmans, 2003), p. 254, as cited in Komoszewski, Sawyer and Wallace, *Reinventing Jesus*, p. 50.

[98]N. T. Wright, *Simply Christian: Why Christianity Makes Sense* (San Francisco: HarperSanFrancisco, 2006), p. 99.

[99]See Ladd, *Theology of the New Testament*, p. 150.

[100]For example, see Blomberg, *Historical Reliability*, p. 97; Bauckham, *Jesus and the Eyewitnesses*, p. 6; Evans, *Fabricating Jesus*, pp. 19-21, 34.

corded in the Gospels require that his hearers consider him either a liar, lunatic or Lord,[101] Borg avers that

> Lewis's comment depends upon the claim that the christological language of the gospels originates with Jesus himself.
>
> But it almost certainly does not . . . this language is post-Easter. A strong majority of mainline scholars think it unlikely that Jesus said these things about himself; he probably did not speak of himself as the Messiah, the Son of God, the Light of the world, and so forth. Rather, this is the voice of the community in the years and decades after Easter. It is not the language of self-proclamation, but the community's testimony to Jesus' significance in their lives.[102]

In response to this crucial assumption that the historical (pre-Easter) Jesus never claimed to be the Son of God in a literal, ontological sense, I offer the following arguments in support of the assertion that Christ's claims to divinity in the Gospels make perfect sense narratively, historically and theologically.

- While Jesus' most explicit claims to divinity are presented in John's Gospel (as the list of self-claims presented above indicates), the other Gospels also show Jesus claiming to be divine, albeit in a more implicit manner. For example, some reputable biblical scholars believe that, keeping Daniel 7:13 in mind, every occasion in the synoptic Gospels where we find Jesus referring to himself as the "Son of Man" can be interpreted as an implicit claim to be divine.[103]

- The fact that Jesus did think of himself as God's Son and that his destiny was to die a substitutionary death on the cross best explains why he did not attempt to function as the kind of military messiah that even his followers expected and wanted him to be. This being the case, wouldn't some bold claims to divinity on his part be expected?[104]

- The reason that the Sanhedrin condemned Jesus to death (see Mk 14:60-64) was not simply that he claimed to be the Messiah, but be-

---

[101]C. S. Lewis, *Mere Christianity* (San Francisco: HarperSanFrancisco, 2001), p. 52.
[102]Borg, HC 86-87. See also Borg, MJA 9-11; and Borg and Wright, MJ 148-53.
[103]Ladd, *Theology of the New Testament*, pp. 143-57. See also Evans, *Fabricating Jesus*, pp. 226, 228-29.
[104]Ibid., p. 139. See also Wright, *Simply Christian*, pp. 106-11.

cause he "claimed the prerogative of final judgment, a function that belonged to God alone."[105] It was "because of this claim to future exaltation and to the exercise of the prerogatives of God himself that he was condemned to death on the ground of blasphemy."[106]

- The fact that Jesus made bold claims to be divine best explains why the apostolic authors, writing within decades of the Christ-event and with the oral tradition still in force, refer to him as God's Son.[107]

- Jesus' bold claims to be divine best explain why the subapostolic leaders of the church—also still in touch with and accountable to the oral tradition—routinely refer to him as the Son of God in their writings.[108]

- A reliable oral tradition that held that Jesus himself died claiming to be the Son of God and Savior of the world best explains why the earliest believers were willing to die for their new faith. Would any other message have inspired such a radical devotion in the face of such fierce persecution? Would not such a tradition have had to be considered very trustworthy to merit such a faithful response?[109]

- The message of the Bible as a whole requires that Jesus be the Son of God rather than merely a wise human teacher or prophet. For instance, the biblical narrative tells the story of creation, fall, redemption and restoration. At the heart of the fall there seems to be the human creature's rejection of a disciple-teacher relationship with their Creator (see Gen 3:5). One understanding of this biblical narrative is that Jesus reversed the effect of the fall by coming into the world and making disciples on behalf of his Father. According to this perspective, one reason why becoming a disciple of Jesus is salvific is precisely because of the ontological connection that exists between

---

[105]Ladd, *Theology of the New Testament,* p. 168.

[106]Ibid. See also Wright, *Challenge of Jesus,* pp. 119-21.

[107]See Komoszewski, Sawyer and Wallace, *Reinventing Jesus,* pp. 169-90, and Evans, *Fabricating Jesus,* pp. 225, 228. Some specific New Testament texts include: Rom 1:4; 8:9; 9:5; 15:6; 1 Cor 3:23; 2 Cor 1:19; 4:4, 6; 5:18-19; 13:14; Eph 1:3; 4:13; 5:5; Col 1:3, 13-20; Tit 2:13; Heb 1:1-2; 1 Pet 1:3; 1 Jn 5:20.

[108]See Komoszewski, Sawyer and Wallace, *Reinventing Jesus,* pp. 200-205. A specific reference of this type can be found in Ignatius's *Letter to the Ephesians* 18.2.

[109]See Wright, *Simply Christian,* pp. 112-18.

Jesus and the Creator—that is, to become a disciple of Jesus is to also become a disciple of his Father, the Creator of the world. Supporting this view are many New Testament passages that demonstrate a vital connection between the disciple, Jesus and the Father.[110] If the redemptive story of Bible as a whole does not make sense apart from Jesus' divinity, why would we expect him not to have made this claim during the course of his ministry?[111]

- The doctrines of Christ's *homoousion* (i.e., Christ is of the same substance with the Father), hypostatic union (i.e., in Christ humanity and divinity are joined without diminishment to either) and vicarious humanity (i.e., Christ lived his life representatively in both a God-humanward and human-Godward manner) are essential not only to the theological realism so prominently presented in the New Testament but more specifically to the dynamics of revelation and reconciliation. In other words, these christological understandings that emphasize Jesus' ontological divinity are crucial to the inner logic of the Christian faith as a whole![112]

- Jesus' own claims to divinity best account for the fact that from the very beginning of Christian history, he was worshiped, prayed to and counted on to forgive sins and bring to final resolution God's original purposes for Israel and all creation.[113]

New Testament scholar Scot McKnight offers support for some of these arguments when, having surveyed various portraits of Jesus put forward most recently by those eager to wrap their minds around the

[110]For example, see Mt 7:21; 10:32-33; 11:27; 12:50; 16:17; 18:10, 19; 20:23; Lk 10:22; 22:29; 24:49; Jn 5:17; 6:32; 8:19; 10:29; 12:26; 14:7, 20, 21, 23; 15:1-17; 16:23, 25-30; 20:17; Acts 1:4; Rev 3:5, 21.

[111]For an in-depth discussion of how the story of Jesus was viewed by the earliest Christians as the "climax" of the story of Israel and the world, see N. T. Wright, *The New Testament and the People of God* (Minneapolis: Fortress, 1992), pp. 371-417. See also Wright, *Challenge of Jesus,* pp. 37-53, and N. T. Wright, *The Last Word: Beyond the Bible Wars to New Understanding of the Authority of Scripture* (San Francisco: HarperSanFrancisco, 2005), pp. 42-46.

[112]See T. F. Torrance, *Reality & Evangelical Theology* (Downers Grove, IL: InterVarsity Press, 1999), p. 23. See also Ray S. Anderson, *Historical Transcendence and the Reality of God: A Christological Critique* (London: Geoffrey Chapman, 1975), p. 151.

[113]See Wright, *Simply Christian,* pp. 116-19. See also Wright, *The New Testament and the People of God,* 444-52; Wright, *Challenge of Jesus,* pp. 106-77, 111-20; and Komoszewski, Sawyer and Wallace, *Reinventing Jesus,* pp. 181-93.

pre-Easter Jesus (Jesus the sage, genius, social revolutionary), he comes
to the conclusion:

> While it is perhaps inappropriate to offer sweeping criticisms of scholars
> whose work I respect and from whom I have learned a great deal, I must
> say that the above treatments of Jesus are unfair in that each presen-
> tation limits the evidence of the Gospels to a handful of sayings or events
> and builds an entire picture of Jesus primarily from one strand of the
> Gospel tradition. Yes, Jesus was a wise sage and a deeply religious man,
> and his teachings were undoubtedly more socially revolutionary than
> many evangelicals imagine; each of these portraits says something
> truthful about Jesus. At the bare minimum, they need to be combined
> for a fuller presentation.
>
> My fundamental disagreement with each of them is that *such a Jesus*
> *would never have been crucified, would never have drawn the fire that he*
> *did, would never have commanded the following that he did, would never*
> *have created a movement that still shakes the world.* A Jesus who went
> around saying wise and witty things would not have been threatening
> enough to have been crucified during Passover when he was surrounded
> by hundreds who liked him. A Jesus who was a religious genius who
> helped people in their relationship with God and was kind, compas-
> sionate, and gentle would not have been crucified either. A social revolu-
> tionary would have been crucified (and this partly explains Jesus' death,
> in my view), but it is doubtful that such a revolutionary would have given
> birth to a church that was hardly a movement of social revolution. And if
> in the process of surviving, this movement had to shave off the socially
> revolutionary bits of Jesus, it is amazing that they decided to connect
> themselves, even root themselves, into a person who was a social revolu-
> tionary at heart. No, these pictures of Jesus will not do.[114]

On the basis of such reasoning I contend that Christians throughout
the ages have been justified in believing that the historical Jesus did
indeed claim to be divine. C. S. Lewis was right: we really do need to
decide whether Jesus is a liar, a lunatic or the Lord! The emerging paradigm's portrayal of Jesus as *simply* a social prophet of this or that stripe

---

[114]Scot McKnight, "Who Is Jesus? An Introduction to Jesus Studies," in *Jesus Under Fire: Modern*
Scholarship Reinvents the Historical Jesus, ed. Michael J. Wilkins and J. P. Moreland (Grand
Rapids: Zondervan, 1995), pp. 61-62.

is not justified precisely because it is not faithful to the story told in the biblical text, the inner logic of a biblically informed understanding of the revelation and reconciliation effected by Jesus,[115] and the facts of church history.

Is a rehabilitated Christ really necessary? My impression, especially when taking their later works into consideration also, is that both of my dialogue partners believe that a fairly radically rehabilitated doctrine of Christ is necessary if we want our post-Christian peers to be able to take Jesus seriously. The problem is that the Christology that results seems to be at odds with the four christological commitments that constitute the heart of the Christian faith. Once again, my contention is that we simply cannot afford to be imprecise here. Indeed, any fuzziness in our thinking regarding any of the four christological verities will not only serve to separate traditional, missional and emerging evangelicals, but can also result in an accommodation rather than recontextualization of the gospel for our post-Christian ministry context.

In an article titled "Examining the Unchurched," Thom Rainer presents the results of a two-year research project involving personal interviews with numerous unchurched Americans. On the one hand, this research suggests that though many unchurched individuals "have little patience for Christians today and the established church . . . they have tremendous respect for Jesus."[116] However, Rainer goes on to state that according to this study, "the possibility for open dialogue [with the unchurched] is high unless the Christian decides to talk about one key

---

[115]On this score, I am grateful for the following words of encouragement with respect to this chapter offered by one of this book's editors, Dr. Gary Deddo: "Any human being could substitute for Jesus if there is nothing ontologically unique about him—i.e., if he is simply an exemplary creature. If Jesus' origin is not from the divine side of the God/creation distinction, then God is not our Savior; he sent a creature to do the job for him. This would also mean that there is no self-revelation of God; only a creature speaking for God—a creature espousing what would be, at best, an outsider and second-hand knowledge of God, similar to what any human might have had. Finally, if Jesus is not divine, there is no communion with God himself and, as we will soon see, salvation itself must be reconfigured with no possibility of it involving a sharing in Christ's eternal sonship. To the degree the emerging paradigm insists on a rehabilitated Christ, it constitutes a complete departure from classic, catholic Christianity and amounts to the invention of a new and utterly different 'religion.'"

[116]Thom S. Rainer, "Examining the Unchurched," August 17, 2010, www.buildingchurchleaders .com/articles/2005/052505.html. As his book title suggests, this point is also made by Dan Kimball in *They Like Jesus but Not the Church*.

issue regarding Christ: the truth that he is the only way of salvation."[117] Referring to the unchurched subjects of his study as U4s (unchurched folk fairly hardened against traditional approaches to Christian ministry), Rainer states:

> No single issue makes the blood of a U4 boil more than that of exclusivity. . . . Our researchers rarely mentioned this foundational truth of the Christian faith, because the U4s were likely to raise the issue themselves. . . . Exclusivity was seen as intolerant, narrow-minded, and bigoted by many U4s. . . . More often than not, we did not merely hear mild objections to exclusivity; we heard emotional tirades from the U4s. . . . Words do not do justice to the outbursts we often heard. The reader cannot see the red faces and looks of indignation.[118]

I am not unaware of the emergent movement's missional concern as it relates to the classical view of Christ's exclusivity. Indeed, even though not all the unchurched living around us qualify as "U4s," it is understandable why many proponents of the emerging paradigm consider the traditional take on Jesus to be a nonstarter and believe that a new, rehabilitated doctrine of Christ is required if the gospel is to have a chance of gaining a hearing among many of our post-Christian peers. However, just because we understand this emergent ministry presumption does not mean that we have to support it. Over against the argument that a reconfigured, *nonexclusive* Christ is necessary for the purpose of evangelism among post-Christians in the West, I will offer two ministry observations of my own.

First, I have found in my own preaching, teaching and ministry conversations with postmoderns that *the manner in which we present the gospel matters greatly.* As I indicated in chapter one, I am convinced that it is possible for evangelical Christians to engage in the proclamation of biblical truth (including the idea of Christ's exclusivity) in a way that does not seem epistemologically arrogant, morally judgmental or relationally coercive. Perhaps we should imitate the ministry pragmatism of the apostle Paul, whose commitment to become all things to all people

---

[117]Rainer, "Examining the Unchurched."
[118]Ibid.

for the sake of the gospel (1 Cor 9:20-23) might have caused him in our day to boldly contextualize his ministry approach to contemporary post-Christians along postmodern lines. Such an approach might have us arguing with a straight face that in a pluralistic, truly tolerant social environment, we evangelical Christians, as one interpretive community among many, are entitled to hold as our truth the tenets of a classical Christology and to proclaim this truth to others without being considered hateful or imperialistic as long as this sharing occurs in a dialogic rather than demagogic manner.[119] But it should also be clearly stated that because we consider *our* truth concerning Christ to be *the* Truth, we feel compelled to share the gospel message with a universal intent.[120] What this means is that, through dialogue and other forms of experiential interaction (worship, fellowship, service, study, etc.), we cannot help but hope to see others become enabled by the Holy Spirit to recognize in the face of Christ the glory of God himself (see 2 Cor 4:6). At the same time, we are committed to a display of tolerance as traditionally understood: our dialogue partners have the right to refuse our message— and to do so without fear of reprisal or even personal rejection.

Can such an approach function fruitfully in a post-Christian context? I have seen it happen . . . at the local Starbucks, in the university classroom and in my office. *By leaning into, rather than away from, the postmodern passion for conversation, we can invite the Spirit of mission to use our sane, sensible, biblically faithful but relationally sensitive sharing of the gospel as part of his convincing, convicting work in the lives of pre- and post-Christians living around us.*

Then again, this is not to say that all of our post-Christian peers will be convinced. Indeed, some will become incensed instead, no matter

---

[119]Craig Van Gelder and Dwight Zscheile seem to lend support for this proposal when, citing George Hunsberger, they write: "Christians must accept and affirm *particularity in discourse*. They must own the personal character of Christian knowledge; 'to uphold the posture of those who speak from the place where our own commitments and visions have been formed around this good news of God is to be both more honest and more able to invite others to exhibit similar honesty.'" See George R. Hunsberger, "The Missional Voice and Posture of Public Theologizing," *Missiology* 34, no. 1 (2006): 24, as cited in Craig Van Gelder and Dwight J. Zscheile, *The Missional Church in Perspective: Mapping Trends and Shaping the Conversation* (Grand Rapids: Baker, 2011), p. 143.

[120]See Lesslie Newbigin, *The Gospel in a Pluralist Society* (Grand Rapids: Eerdmans, 1989), pp. 35, 50, 77, 92, 126.

how careful the manner of our presentation. Therefore, a second obser-vation is in order: *there has always been a scandal attached to the procla-mation of the gospel concerning Christ.* Because the same gospel message can harden as well as soften hearts, the New Testament presents us with many indications that a missionally faithful lifestyle will likely involve some form of persecution.[121] If Jesus was willing to ask his disciples to be persecuted for him and his message (Mt 5:11, 44; Lk 11:49; 12:12; Jn 15:20), and if those making up the apostolic community not only ac-cepted this responsibility themselves but then proceeded to pass it on to those who followed them in the faith (Phil 1:27-30; 2 Tim 2:1-13; 4:1-8; Heb 12:1-12; 1 Pet 1:3-9; 3:13-16; 4:1-5, 12-19; Rev 12:8-11), should we in our day consider it appropriate out of some supposed sense of ministry ne-cessity to rehabilitate the biblical doctrine of Christ so as to remove the scandal of the cross from our proclamation?[122] I am not saying that this is the only possible motive for the felt need to rehabilitate Jesus and the gospel, but it might in fact be a motive. To the degree we feel the need to back away from our embrace of the four christological verities be-cause of their unpopularity in our current ministry context, our ap-proach becomes essentially *unfaithful* to both the biblical text and the missional task.[123]

THE POSSIBILITY OF A NUANCED CHRISTOLOGY

Having argued that we can and should share the scandalous message of the Christian gospel with both humility and boldness at the same time

---

[121]For example, see Mt 5:10-12; 10:17-39; 13:21; 24:9; Mk 10:29-30; Lk 21:12; Jn 15:20; Acts 11:19; Rom 8:35; 12:14; 1 Cor 4:11-13; 2 Cor 4:7-11; 12:10; Gal 5:11; 6:12; 2 Thess 1:4; 2 Tim 3:12-13; Heb 10:32-39; 1 Pet 1:3-9; 2:19-23; 3:13-17; 4:1-5; Rev 1:9; 2:10; 6:9; 11:7; 12:11, 17; 17:6; 20:4.

[122]David Bosch refers to the need for Christians "take a stand, even it is unpopular—or even dangerous. Tolerance is not an unambiguous virtue, especially the 'I'm ok, you're ok' kind which leaves no room for challenging one another." David J. Bosch, *Transforming Mission: Paradigm Shifts in Theology of Mission* (Maryknoll, NY: Orbis, 2011), pp. 368-69.

[123]Philip Harrold, citing the work of T. F. Torrance, writes: "Catechesis is always confrontational, even offensive, until we yield to its life-saving message in the crucified, resurrected and as-cended Lord Jesus. My take away from this is that if the catechetical process is liable to be of-fensive, how much more so will be the initial proclamation that 'there is only way, truth, and life.'" See Philip Harrold, "Getting to Know Him: Catechesis at Its Very Best Is a Very Personal 'School of Faith,'" *Christianity Today*, September 27, 2012, www.christianitytoday.com/ct/2012/september/getting-to-know-him.html.

(no small task!), I now suggest that an *evangelical* view of Christ should make room for the following contextually sensitive convictions: (1) Jesus' earthly ministry did possess a social action component; (2) Jesus clearly did care about more than just seeing individual souls get to heaven; (3) Jesus' work on the cross can be understood as accomplishing more than a substitutionary death on our behalf; and (4) the experience of Christian salvation possesses existential (temporal) as well as eschatological (eternal) implications. I will have more to say about the latter two soteriology-related themes in chapter eight of this book, but for now I offer the following missional suggestion: Before we lurch toward an uncritical embrace of the emerging paradigm's insistence that the real Jesus has been "dumbed down" and "domesticated" by an evangelical misunderstanding,[124] and before we overcorrect and embrace a radically reconfigured, rehabilitated Christology as a result, let's make sure that a merely nuanced Christology will not do instead!

Though missional faithfulness does require a humble offering of a gospel message that has at its heart a commitment to the doctrines of Christ's divinity, atoning death, bodily resurrection and universal lordship, *there is no need to reject all of the ideas that emerging authors such as Borg and McLaren are putting forward.* Earlier in this chapter I mentioned some biblical passages which undergird my conviction that all Christ-followers should be seriously engaged in the pursuit of social justice. Thus, I want to encourage my traditional evangelical colleagues to join their missional and emerging allies in presenting to our post-Christian peers a Jesus who, precisely because he is concerned about the poor and oppressed, died for the sins of the world. Jesus did this because he is concerned about human beings experiencing abundant life in the here and now *and* eternal life in the age to come. His death can and should be understood as a political and spiritual triumph over the powers, an inspiring evidence of God's love (see 2 Cor 5:14-15) *and* a propitiation for our sins (see Rom 3:25; 1 Jn 2:2; 4:10). The experience of Christian salvation can and should produce within Christ's followers an *existential* commitment to pursue social justice, promote peace and care

---

[124]McLaren, *Secret Message of Jesus,* p. 85.

for the planet here and now that is fueled rather than frustrated by the knowledge that Christ's sacrificial death has *also* made possible for us an *eschatological* rescue from divine judgment. *The Jesus presented to us in sacred Scripture is both a lion (Rev 5:4-5) and a slain but risen lamb (Rev 5:6-14).* How could it be appropriate to proclaim him to others in a monotone? How could it be possible to serve such a Savior in anything other than a multi-varied manner?

What all of this means is that the emerging Christology put forward by my two dialogue partners is neither justified nor necessary. We do not, out of a concern for a social justice agenda, have to choose between a divine Jesus and one who is merely human. A nuanced understanding of the classic conception of Christ will do just fine, providing some much needed common ground between traditional, missional and emerging evangelicals in the process!

It is my hope that this chapter, though not providing a comprehensive Christology, has succeeded in underscoring the fact that Christianity really does stand or fall with Christ. N. T. Wright has made the point that "Christianity is about something that *happened*. Something that happened to *Jesus of Nazareth*. Something that happened *through* Jesus of Nazareth."[125] There really is a difference between *churchianity* and Christianity. It is crucial that we do our best to get Jesus and the good news concerning him right (see 1 Cor 15:1-5; Gal 1:6-9).

And yet, while it is true that Christianity stands or falls on the person of Christ, the New Testament also has much to say about the role of the Holy Spirit in the Christian life. It is no secret that pneumatology is a topic that has been much neglected in the history of the church, even among evangelicals. How interesting that, while a renewed focus on this theological locus is currently occurring among those who hold to the so-called earlier paradigm, those promoting the *emerging* vision seem to be moving in the opposite direction! In the next chapter I will elaborate on this provocative, missionally significant assertion.

---

[125]Wright, *Simply Christian*, p. 91.

6

EVANGELISM, EDIFICATION AND EQUIPPING

Toward a Missionally Orthodox Doctrine of the Holy Spirit

Pneumatology is neglected at both ends of the pendulum's swing. On the one hand, an acquisitions editor for a major publishing company with a primarily mainline readership once warned me that because of a "silence about the Spirit" among liberal Protestants, any book encouraging the experience of a more robust life in the Spirit would need to be written with a whisper rather than a shout. On the other hand, the short-shrift given to the doctrine of the Holy Spirit among conservative Protestant theologians has also been acknowledged. For instance, Timothy Tennent, president of Asbury Theological Seminary has written:

> The reformation's emphasis on the authority of Scripture, ecclesiology, and Christology, as crucial as it was, meant that there was a further delay in a full theological development of the doctrine of the Holy Spirit, and several vital aspects of his work were neglected in Post-reformation Protestant theology, which focused on solidifying and organizing the theological developments of the Reformers. Over time, Western theological traditions that developed greatly limited the active role of the Holy Spirit in the life of the church. The result was a pneumatological deficit that is only now becoming painfully apparent. A typical example can be found in Louis Berkhof's *Systematic Theology,* a classic text in Reformed the-

ology that is still in use today. Berkhof discusses the work of the Holy Spirit but limits it to applying the work of Christ into our lives (e.g., re-generation) and in personal holiness (e.g., sanctification). In his development of ecclesiology, Berkhof is silent about the role of the Holy Spirit in empowering the church for witness and mission or in enabling the church as a whole to live out in the present the eschatological realities of the New Creation. It is not unusual to find Western systematic theologies that do not even develop the person and work of the Holy Spirit as a separate category of study but develop their theology of the Holy Spirit as subsets under the doctrine of God and the doctrine of soteriology.[1]

Having boldly acknowledged the pneumatological deficit in much post-Reformation Protestant theology, Tennent goes on to point out a recent trend in the opposite direction:

> The twentieth century has simultaneously ushered in a renewed emphasis on the work of the Holy Spirit as well as a major renaissance in Trinitarian theology. The emergence of global Pentecostalism has stimulated an unprecedented emphasis on the *work* of the Holy Spirit. Likewise, such influential theologians as Karl Barth, Karl Rahner and Jürgen Moltmann have all made the doctrine of the Trinity the centerpiece of their theological work. The result of both of these developments has served to mature our understanding of the Holy Spirit and thereby to understand better the role of the Holy Spirit to the *missio dei*.[2]

Tennent speaks here of the importance to the mission of God of better understanding the role of the Holy Spirit. Given the emerging paradigm's emphasis on the importance of the missional task, it is somewhat surprising then to find a pneumatological deficit in both *The Heart of Christianity* and *A Generous Orthodoxy*. In my view, both of these theological works lack a serious discussion of the role of the Spirit in the missional endeavor.[3]

---

[1] Timothy C. Tennent, *Invitation to World Missions: A Trinitarian Missiology for the Twenty-first Century* (Grand Rapids: Kregel Academic, 2010), p. 94, emphasis original.

[2] Ibid.

[3] Actually, in their analysis of the seminal work *Missional Church*, Van Gelder and Zscheile offer the critique that due to the multiple authors' failure to adequately "integrate the *sending* work of God in relation to the work of the Son and the work of the Spirit," the book could connote "a *functional modalism* where the works of the three persons of God become separated from one another." They also point out that this tendency "also surfaces regularly among many authors

Thus far in this book I have begun each chapter with a fairly substantial analysis of how each of my dialogue partners, out of a professed
concern for a contemporary missional viability, is calling for a new approach to a traditional theological locus. However, since both Marcus
Borg and Brian McLaren have relatively little to say about the role of the
Holy Spirit in mission, my approach to this chapter will be a bit different. After providing a necessarily brief analysis of how Borg and
McLaren do treat the doctrine of the Spirit in their works *The Heart of
Christianity* and *A Generous Orthodoxy* respectively, I will then offer an
argument for why the curious lacunae mentioned above are indicative
of the emerging paradigm's inadequacy as a vision of the Christian faith
that is faithful to both the biblical text and missional task.

THE "HOLY SPIRIT" IN *THE HEART OF CHRISTIANITY*

We have already taken note of the fact that Marcus Borg disavows the
classic Christian doctrine of the Trinity, presenting instead the view
that God is "the encompassing Spirit in which everything is."[4] This
has huge implications for his doctrine of the Spirit and probably explains why there is no discrete chapter devoted to pneumatology
within this work. If all there is of God is Spirit, and if you have a
chapter on God already (as Borg does), what need is there for a separate chapter on the Spirit?[5]

Borg's conflation of Spirit and God—and his concomitant commitment to religious relativism—is nowhere more apparent than when

---

who have acquired missional language, whose theological starting point is Christology, and who
also stress the example of Jesus as the model to be emulated," but who fail to articulate clearly
the role of the Spirit in the process of representing the reign of God to the world. See Craig Van
Gelder and Dwight J. Zscheile, *The Missional Church in Perspective: Mapping Trends and Shaping
the Conversation* (Grand Rapids: Baker, 2011), pp. 53-54.

[4]Borg, HC 66, 70; Borg, SC 212-15; Borg, GWNK 12, 35-36, 72. Furthermore, the way Borg
speaks of "the Spirit" or simply "Spirit" (without the definite article) in *The Heart of Christianity*
makes it clear that for him there is no Trinity; Spirit is all there is of God (see also Borg, SC 65;
Borg, GWNK 1, 11, 71-72).

[5]Borg does devote a chapter to "Pentecost" in *Speaking Christian*. However, this brief essay which
focuses on the coming of the Holy Spirit to continue Christ's presence and launch the movement
he had begun hardly qualifies as a serious discussion of the role of the Spirit in the missional
endeavor, much less a pneumatology proper (see Borg, SC 183-88). Furthermore, in *The Meaning of Jesus,* Borg includes a discussion of "life in the Spirit" that, while interesting, is remarkably
void of any reference to Scripture (see Borg and Wright, MJ 242-46).

he equates the "More" with "God, Spirit, the sacred, Yahweh, the Tao, Allah, Brahman, Atman, and so forth."[6]

Borg's conflation of God and Spirit, along with his embrace of a theological pluralism and relativism, may explain why Borg never seems to address the role of the Spirit in the missional task. Rather, when Borg himself refers to the Spirit (as opposed to his citations of what Calvin, the Bible, the liturgy or other Christian authors have to say about the Spirit),[7] he usually does so with the idea of life transformation (i.e., salvation/sanctification) in mind. Somewhat startling, really, is the fact that while a good number of Borg's personal references to "the Spirit" occur in a chapter titled "Born Again: A New Heart" (where he treats soteriology and sanctification),[8] there are no references at all to the work of the Spirit in the very next chapter, titled "The Kingdom of God: The Heart of Justice." Borg's failure to refer to the Spirit of mission in a chapter which essentially lays out the Christian mission strikes me as a curious omission. While an oblique association between the Spirit and the practice of compassion and justice can be found near the end of Borg's discussion of Christian practice,[9] Borg is otherwise consistent in his association of the Spirit with the process of life transformation which he refers to synonymously as being "born again" and learning to live "in the Spirit."

The disconnect between the work of the Spirit and the missional task is further evidenced by the way Borg insists that this experience of being born again or learning to live in the Spirit is not unique to the Christian faith, but is something all the world's religions practice in one way or another.[10] What need is there for cross-cultural mission in the traditional sense if the Spirit is already at work salvifically in all the enduring religions?

Anticipating later discussions of soteriology and ecclesiology, I suggest at this point that a historical unwillingness on the part of most evangelicals (and many missional and emerging Christians) to dissociate disciple making from the missional task is going to make it very difficult for them to embrace Borg's emerging vision of the Christian

---

[6]Borg, HC 63; see also pp. 217-18; Borg, MJA 33.
[7]Borg, HC 42, 125, 162, 199.
[8]Ibid., pp. 106-7, 110, 112-13, 117, 118-19, 121-22.
[9]Ibid., pp. 187, 204.
[10]Ibid., p. 119.

faith with its somewhat egregious neglect of a biblically informed, theo-
logically coherent, missionally impactful pneumatology. Not only does
Borg neglect to speak of how the Holy Spirit empowers Christians for
witness (see Acts 1:8), he even fails to connect the promptings of the
Spirit with an inspired engagement in social action. All that Borg has to
offer in this regard is the reminder that for Paul, the primary gift of the
Spirit is love, and that, "for Jesus, the primary quality of a life centered in
God is compassion."[11] While these reminders are valid and important,
they are by themselves an insufficient foundation for a biblically informed missional pneumatology.

THE HOLY SPIRIT IN *A GENEROUS ORTHODOXY*

There are some substantial differences in the emerging "pneumatologies" (if we can call them that) presented by Borg and McLaren. The
way McLaren refers to the Holy Spirit serves to assure the reader of his
commitment to a trinitarian view of God (despite the somewhat ambiguous way McLaren seems to understand Jesus as the "Son of God").[12]
Also, if we view his chapter titled "Why I Am Charismatic/Contem-
plative" as a rudimentary pneumatology, then we can say that by devoting a discrete chapter to the subject of the Spirit, McLaren does a
better job than Borg of demonstrating the importance of the Holy Spirit
to Christian experience.

But there are also some significant similarities between Borg and
McLaren on this subject. For instance, much like Borg, McLaren primarily associates the work of the Spirit in the life of the Christian with
fostering a contemplative spirituality that centers on an ongoing experience of God's presence.[13] Thus, both Borg and McLaren seem to rep-
licate the tendency of many post-Reformation Protestant theologians to
primarily associate the work of the Spirit to salvation and sanctification.

Having personally written about the importance of the practice of the
presence of God to Christian spirituality,[14] I appreciate McLaren's em-

---

[11]Ibid., p. 122. See also pp. 162-63, 204, 217.
[12]McLaren, GO 69 [77], 74 [82], 76 [84], 195 [218].
[13]Ibid., pp. 176-78 [196-99].
[14]See Gary Tyra, *Christ's Empowering Presence: The Pursuit of God Through the Ages* (Downers
Grove, IL: InterVarsity Press, 2011).

phasis on it. However, this appreciation does not preclude me—as an evangelical with a Pentecostal-charismatic heritage—from registering my disappointment with his larger discussion of what it means to be Pentecostal-charismatic, which strikes me as a bit condescending and simplistic in that it fails to include a sufficiently vigorous, substantive examination of the role of the Holy Spirit in empowering the church for witness and mission.

Furthermore, in his chapter titled "Why I Am Missional," McLaren makes no reference at all to the Holy Spirit! (This is another Borg-like move.) The closest McLaren comes to connecting the Spirit and the missional task is when he (1) refers to the Spirit's activity in continually reforming Christians and the church;[15] (2) affirms the Spirit's ability to help Christians live life to the full;[16] (3) identifies the Spirit as the source of evangelicalism's passion for mission;[17] and (4) encourages those engaged in missional activism to avoid burnout by undergirding "their activism with contemplation, with quiet resting, with finding God in the center of normalcy—including the normalcy of struggle and hard work."[18] While these are valuable pneumatological insights, they hardly constitute what Timothy Tennent had in mind when he wrote of the need for new pneumatologies that serve "to mature our understanding of the Holy Spirit and thereby to understand better the role of the Holy Spirit to the *missio dei*."

Finally, McLaren seems to follow Borg in holding that the Holy Spirit is at work in all religions not just to prepare their adherents to hear the gospel of Christ but to actually enable them, as adherents of other religions, to live lives that are pleasing to God and productive for his kingdom.[19] If anything, this pneumatological perspective serves to reinforce the suspicion that for McLaren a ministry of disciple making involving water baptism and Christian catechism (which implies a participation in a local church; see Mt 28:18-20) is simply not integral to the missional task.

---

[15]McLaren, GO 30 [34], 193 [215], 228 [256], 274 [310].
[16]Ibid., p. 97 [106].
[17]Ibid., p. 120 [132].
[18]Ibid., p. 176 [197].
[19]Ibid., pp. 263 [296-97], 266 [299].

TOWARD A MORE BIBLICALLY AND MISSIONALLY FAITHFUL PNEUMATOLOGY

I am suggesting here that the Spirit of mission wants to produce among God's people a missional faithfulness while also providing them with a gospel message that promises more than a conceptual understanding of God. My commitment to this premise derives from both a careful study of Scripture and my personal ministry experience in an increasingly post-Christian world. As a result of both, I have become convinced that because God is a missionary God,[20] the Holy Spirit is a missionary Spirit[21] who has a penchant for using God's people to achieve God's purposes in the world. But for this to happen, a new pneumatology is required: a *missional pneumatology* that succeeds in promoting among evangelicals of all stripes a *pneumatological realism*—an ecclesial environment in which church members expect to interact with the Holy Spirit in ways that are real and phenomenal rather than merely conceptual.

The rough contours of a missional pneumatology. The missional pneumatology I am proposing is grounded in the awareness that at the heart of the missional dynamic overall is a pneumatological question: *What is the Spirit of mission up to in this particular ministry context and how can we cooperate with him?* A missional pneumatology also acknowledges that according to the Bible, the Holy Spirit's method of choice for involving God's people in accomplishing God's purposes in the world is empowering them to engage in some form of prophetic speech or action.[22] A connection between the coming of the Spirit into someone's life and the phenomenon of inspired speech or action is discernible in a plethora biblical passages from both Old and New Testaments.[23]

---

[20]See the chapter titled "Our God Is a Missionary God," in John Stott, *The Contemporary Christian* (Downers Grove, IL: InterVarsity Press, 1992), pp. 321-26, as cited in Christopher J. H. Wright, *The Mission of God: Unlocking the Bible's Grand Narrative* (Downers Grove, IL: InterVarsity Press, 2006), p. 24n2. See Van Gelder and Zscheile, *Missional Church*, pp. 27, 32-33, 52.

[21]See Roland Allen, *The Ministry of the Spirit* (Grand Rapids: Eerdmans, 1960), p. 17.

[22]For more on this, see Gary Tyra, *The Holy Spirit in Mission: Prophetic Speech and Action in Christian Witness* (Downers Grove, IL: IVP Academic, 2011).

[23]For example, see Num 11:25-30; 24:1-3; Judg 3:10; 6:34; 11:29; 14:6, 19; 15:14; 1 Sam 10:5-7, 9-11; 11:6-7; 19:18-24; 2 Sam 23:1-2; 1 Chron 12:18; 2 Chron 15:1-2; 20:13-15; 24:17-20; Is

Scripture also connects the prophetic activity inspired by the Spirit (speech and action, words and works, proclamation and demonstration) and the manifestation of a missional faithfulness. Darrell Guder and the other contributors to the influential *Missional Church* volume[24] emphasize the missional importance of a pneumatological realism that produces Spirit-inspired speech and action in this way:

> While the Spirit is "the unseen Lord," the movement of the Holy Spirit has real and visible effects. The experience of the Spirit brings "the touch of God's presence, the power of God's healing, the liberating experience of forgiveness, the reality of fraternal community, the joy of celebration, the boldness in witness, the blossoming of hope, and the fruitfulness in mission."[25]

Indeed, the book of Acts portrays all these effects of the Spirit taking place in the lives of the earliest followers of Jesus. Acts also highlights the prominence of prophetic activity (Spirit-inspired speech and action) in the early church. Biblical scholar Robert Menzies has observed that "out of 59 references to the Spirit of God in Acts, 36 are unequivocally linked to prophetic activity."[26] My own observation is that no less than twenty-one of the twenty-eight chapters of Acts portray some sort of prophetic activity taking place. Disciples speak to God in a Spirit-inspired manner, hear from God, and speak and act prophetically on behalf of God with the result that lives are changed and even more disciples are made.[27] Given the many incidents of prophetic activity portrayed in the book of Acts, at the very least we must acknowledge the huge role the Holy Spirit played in the birth and subsequent expansion of the Christian movement.

32:14-18; 42:1-4; Ezek 11:4-5; Joel 2:28-29; Mic 3:8; Lk 1:41-45, 67; 2:25-35; Acts 2:1-4, 14-18; 10:44-46; 19:6; Rom 8:15-16, 26-27; 1 Cor 12:3, 8; Gal 4:6; Eph 5:18-20.

[24]For an excellent discussion of the seminal role played by this book to the missional discussion see the chapter "Revisiting the Seminal Work *Missional Church*," in Van Gelder and Zscheile, pp. 41-65.

[25]Darrell Guder, ed., *Missional Church: A Vision for the Sending of the Church in North America* (Grand Rapids: Eerdmans, 1998), p. 146. Quote is from Mortimer Arias, *Announcing the Reign of God: Evangelization and the Subversive Memory of Jesus* (Philadelphia: Fortress Press, 1984), p. 61.

[26]Robert Menzies, *Empowered for Witness* (Sheffield: Sheffield Academic Press, 1994), p. 258.

[27]For a chapter-by-chapter survey indicating the numerous references to prophetic activity in the Book of Acts, see Tyra, *Holy Spirit in Mission*, pp. 65-67.

More precisely, Acts depicts the dynamic connection between prophetic activity and the missional faithfulness (and fruitfulness) among the earliest Christians. A close examination of the ministry practices of the earliest Christians will reveal how important it is that at least some of our own attempts at evangelism, edification and equipping be conducted in a prophetic manner, unmistakably empowered by the Holy Spirit. I will use the term *prophetic evangelism* to refer to sermons (verbal presentations of the gospel) and acts of compassion (physical demonstrations of the gospel) that tend to be delivered in an extemporaneous and spontaneous manner as a result of a sense that the disciple is being prompted by the Holy Spirit to do so. *Prophetic edification* occurs when a Christian disciple, obeying a prompting from the Holy Spirit, offers in an extemporaneous manner words or works that encourage, comfort and strengthen a fellow disciple or group of disciples. *Prophetic equipping* takes place when a disciple equips other disciples for life and ministry through speech and actions prompted by the Holy Spirit that are carried out in an impromptu, ad hoc manner, or that result in a commitment to resourcing that plays out over a long period of time.[28] According to the book of Acts, it is possible for Christ's followers to engage in the ministries of evangelism, edification and equipping in prophetic, Spirit-inspired ways. When this happens, the risen Christ is represented to hurting people in a missionally compelling manner.

Furthermore, given the prolific growth of Spirit-empowered ministries around the world in our own era, there is good reason to believe that this connection between prophetic activity and missional faithfulness (and fruitfulness) is still at work. Over the years many explanations for the explosive growth of the Pentecostal-charismatic segment of the church in the Majority World have been put forward. One explanation focuses on the ease with which Pentecostalism's message and flexible ministry style is contextualized in non-Western cultures. Other explanations center on the physical, spiritual, psychological and

---

[28]There is a sense in which the ministry of Christian disciples in simply helping people (both inside and outside the community of faith) to survive can also take the form of prophetic equipping (see Gal 6:10). However, since these acts of compassion can serve as means by which the gospel is proclaimed and people brought to faith in Christ, they can also take the form of prophetic evangelism.

sociological benefits which are produced when a holistic version of the Christian gospel is contextualized for hurting people living in the developing nations of the world. However, neither the contextualization thesis nor the various benefit-centered explanations can by themselves account for the remarkable ability of Pentecostal-charismatic churches to mobilize huge numbers of laity into an energetic and fruitful engagement in missional ministry in the form of a prophetic speaking and acting into the lives of the hurting people populating their ministry contexts. Without discounting these other explanations, my own research points to one that is more theological in nature and more in keeping with what the Bible as a whole has to say about the Holy Spirit's penchant for using God's people to accomplish God's purposes in the world. I believe that a grace-empowered, Spirit-enabled embrace of a theological realism—the conviction that God, acting through the Spirit, is graciously and faithfully at work in everyday life—compels rank-and-file members of Pentecostal-charismatic churches in the Majority World to speak and act prophetically toward their unchurched friends, neighbors, co-workers and family members in a missionally faithful manner.

Finally, what is desperately needed in our own ministry context— indeed, what will take our attempts at missional ministry to a whole new level—is a widespread openness among evangelical church members here in the West (traditional, missional and emerging) to the idea that the Holy Spirit can and will enable those who are truly surrendered to his leadership to hear his voice, receive ministry assignments, and faithfully speak and act into the lives of others in a Christ-honoring, Christ-evidencing manner. The Holy Spirit helped the earliest Christians experience a missional faithfulness and fruitfulness in their day. He is helping Pentecostal-charismatic Christians ministering in the Majority World to do likewise today. I am convinced that this same kind of missional faithfulness and fruitfulness can be exhibited by Western evangelicals in our post-Christian ministry context as well.

Reasons for hope in the West. The first reason why I believe we evangelicals here in the West can manifest a remarkable missional faithfulness in our own ministry context has to do with the nature of missional ministry itself. According to many missional works, the ultimate goal of a properly contextualized missional ministry is a faithful *representation* of the kingdom of God to a particular ministry neighborhood.[29] Following the lead of Lesslie Newbigin, who is widely recognized as the doyen of the missional church movement,[30] the authors of *Missional Church* have issued a call for churches in the post-Christian West to strive to represent the reign of God to their ministry contexts by means of their *community, service* and *proclamation*.[31] Similarly, Dan Devadatta has asserted the need for contemporary churches to renew three basic commitments: (1) preaching and teaching the truth of the Word of God; (2) communal discipleship, and (3) equipping people for ministry.[32] The three ministry dynamics mentioned in both of these works not only parallel each other but also correspond to the *edification, equipping* and *evangelism* the book of Acts associates with the earliest Christians. A willingness to be empowered by the Spirit to engage in prophetic speech and action will enable evangelical churches in the West (traditional, missional and emerging) to represent the reign of God to their communities in these three principal ways at a whole new level of missional faithfulness.

This kind of evangelical move toward a more experiential, phenomenal, theologically real version of the Christian faith is timely. The second reason why I believe a wonderful degree of missional faithfulness is achievable is that, though it may be increasingly post-Christian, our culture is also increasingly post-secular, filled with spiritually hungry people. *The time is ripe for a bold shift among evangelicals in the West away from an exclusively philosophical version of the Christian faith to one that pulsates with a pneumatological realism.* Indeed, such a realism is crucial to the development of a missional orthodoxy and orthopraxy.

The great need for a pneumatological realism. Several years ago I was working in my second-floor office of the church I was pastoring at

---

[29]See Van Gelder and Zscheile, *Missional Church*, p. 129.

[30]See ibid., pp. 36-38.

[31]Guder, *Missional Church*, p. 102n29.

[32]Dan Devadatta, "Strangers but Not Strange: A New Mission Situation for the Church (1 Peter 1:1-2 and 17-25)," in *Confident Witness—Changing World: Rediscovering the Gospel in North America,* ed. Craig Van Gelder (Grand Rapids: Eerdmans, 1999), pp. 121-24.

the time when my secretary alerted me via intercom that there was a woman downstairs hoping to see me, though she did not have an appointment. I instructed my secretary to send the woman up.

Greeting this visitor at the top of the stairs, I ushered her into my office and offered her a seat in front of my desk. After introducing herself, this mature woman with a kind smile and intelligent eyes came straight to the point. Leaning forward in her chair she said, "Pastor, I've been to a lot of churches that could tell me about God. I'm wondering if this is the kind of church that can help me experience him." In response to this very honest, straightforward query, I simply smiled and said, "I'd like to think so." Thus began a year-long mentoring relationship that resulted in the baptism and discipleship of this retired community college professor who, though part of a post-Christian culture, was because of some personal trials in her life at the same time very hungry for an authentic, personal, real relationship with God.

In this book's preface, I alluded to a *Newsweek* article titled "In Search of the Spiritual," which speaks of "a world of 'hungry people, looking for a deeper relationship with God'" and makes the point that within contemporary society "'spirituality,' the impulse to seek communion with the Divine, is thriving." The woman I just described could serve as the poster child for this world of spiritually hungry people. Indeed, her journey is instructive.

The first stop in her quest for a real relationship with God was on the liberal side of the proverbial pendulum. As she described her spiritual trek during that first meeting she rather off-handedly referred to God as her "ground of being." When I asked her if she had, perchance, been reading Paul Tillich, she cheerfully indicated that she had actually sat in a seminar under his tutelage at a nearby graduate school of theology. But, she went on to tell me, she had not found in classic liberal theology the kind of palpable and existentially meaningful (life-defining) experience of God she was looking for.

She went on to relate that her spiritual quest had caused her also to explore some conservative versions of Christianity at the opposite end of the pendulum's swing. What she had found among the good people she interacted with in these churches was a lot of biblical teaching about God, including information about what the Holy Spirit wanted to do in her life in terms of salvation and sanctification. But when she asked whether and how she could really know God in a phenomenal manner, all she received were blank stares and some encouragement to walk by faith.[33]

Eventually, she found herself wandering into the pastor's office of a nearby Assemblies of God church hoping to find someone who could help her experience God in a way that was more than conceptual. Though by this time she was more than a little desperate, she was also a bit wary as she began this new leg in her spiritual journey, concerned that the rumors might prove true and that all she would encounter in such a church was an emotion-driven, anti-intellectual approach to the Christian faith.

Later, when recounting that first conversation in my office, she would say that she was especially struck by a comment I had made to the effect that "one did not have to assassinate one's brains in order to experience an existentially impactful relationship with God." Though the phrase "false antithesis" was not used by either of us at the time, apparently what she sensed in our initial dialogue was the possibility of an alternative to the two extremes—Christianity of the "heart" and Christianity of the "head"—she had experienced thus far. Furthermore, to put the matter in pneumatological terms, what she had also taken away (rightly or wrongly) from her previous forays into both liberal and conservative versions of Christianity was that she had to choose between thinking of God as an impersonal universal spirit in which everything exists and God as a triune being whose Holy Spirit merely functioned as the means by which he accomplishes his salvation and sanctification purposes among human beings. What led her to a year-long relationship with me as a mentor, pastor and friend (before she moved away to be closer to her adult children), was the hope of an alternative

---

[33]To be fair, the late Stanley Grenz endeavored to make a case for the idea that there is a stream within evangelicalism that has always emphasized the importance of spiritual experience as well as correct doctrine. See Stanley J. Grenz, *Revisioning Evangelical Theology: A Fresh Agenda for the 21st Century* (Downers Grove, IL: InterVarsity Press, 1993), pp. 21-59. Indeed, Grenz writes: "Hence, to be truly evangelical, right doctrine, as important as it is, is not enough. The truth of the Christian faith must become personally experienced truth" (p. 57).

to both of these false antitheses. She could embrace a Christianity that involved *both* her head and her heart and could have her own biblically informed experience of God's Spirit that would prove to be not just conceptual but truly transformational (i.e., spiritually, morally and missionally formational) instead.

This story underscores the fact that despite the post-Christian nature of our current ministry context, the Spirit of mission does seem to be working in people's lives, readying those who are spiritually hungry for an encounter with the risen Christ! The industrialized but increasingly post-secular societies of the West are filled with spiritually hungry pre- and post-Christians who are looking for churches that can help them do more than know about God. They are eager to experience God for themselves! The big question is: How will evangelical churches respond to this huge ministry opportunity?

Once again, I am thoroughly convinced that the kind of missional faithfulness (and fruitfulness) that was experienced by the earliest Christians and is currently experienced by Pentecostal-charismatic believers around the world can also be experienced here in the West. But what is needed is a missional pneumatology that encourages all evangelical believers (whether or not they self-identify as Pentecostal-charismatic) to open themselves to the experience of being used by the Spirit of mission to speak and act in a prophetic manner to the pre-and post-Christians among whom they live and work. Basic to this ministry development is the prior embrace of a pneumatological realism—the conviction that the third person of the Trinity is neither the "sea of being" in which we all exist, nor simply the economical means by which God accomplishes his soteriological work in people's lives. Rather, he is the Spirit of Jesus Christ with whom we should expect to interact in a real, phenomenal manner. He is the Spirit of mission who delights in using God's people to accomplish God's purposes in the world. This is the kind of pneumatology that can take the missional conversation to a whole new level precisely because it is faithful to both the biblical text and the missional task.

So, how is it that those who promote the emerging paradigm can come up with pneumatologies that seem to neglect the role of the Spirit in the missional task, especially when it comes to disciple making? The next chapter will explore the crucial effect that an anthropology informed nearly exclusively by the social sciences, rather than Scriptures, has on the emerging vision of the Christian life. In the process, I will attempt to articulate a doctrine of human beings that once again strives to be faithful to *both* the Bible and the mission.

7

THE NEED FOR A NEW HUMANITY

Toward a Missionally Orthodox
Doctrine of Human Beings

The term *worldview* has become common parlance among academics and non-academics alike to refer to the way people see the world around them and understand how best to navigate their way in and through it. Many Christian scholars suggest that a comprehensive worldview will include a conviction regarding the human condition. For instance, Brian J. Walsh and J. Richard Middleton suggest that the faith commitment that determines a person's worldview will answer the following four questions: (1) *Who am I?* Or, what is the nature, task and purpose of human beings? (2) *Where am I?* Or, what is the nature of the world and universe I live in? (3) *What's wrong?* Or, what is the basic problem or obstacle that keeps me from attaining fulfillment? In other words, how do I understand evil? (4) *What is the remedy?* Or, how is it possible to overcome this hindrance to my fulfillment? In other words, how do I find salvation?[1] This set of questions suggests how important a biblically informed doctrine of human beings is to a Christian worldview. Two of the four questions focus precisely on the human condition: who we human beings are and what has gone wrong with us.

---

[1]Brian J. Walsh and J. Richard Middleton, *The Transforming Vision: Shaping a Christian World View* (Downers Grove, IL: InterVarsity Press, 1984), p. 35. A similar set of questions is suggested by Michael Wittmer in *Heaven Is a Place on Earth: Why Everything You Do Matters to God* (Grand Rapids: Zondervan, 2004), pp. 24, 33; and by the late Chuck Colson in *How Now Shall We Live?* (Carol Stream, IL: Tyndale House, 1999), pp. xi, xii, 268, 294.

What is true of a Christian worldview is also true of Christian theology.

Previously, we noted that the emerging paradigm's theology proper (doctrine of God) has some significant implications for the way the Christian life is conceived.[2] The same might be said for the doctrine of human beings. The theological anthropologies of Marcus Borg and Brian McLaren seem to greatly impact their understandings of soteriology, ecclesiology and eschatology. Therefore, in order to fully appreciate the emerging vision of the Christian faith, we must spend some time trying to understand how these promoters of the emerging paradigm interpret the human condition. By conversing with them, of course, our ultimate goal here is to develop a doctrine of human beings that is faithful to both the biblical text and missional task.

THE EMERGING PARADIGM'S PERSPECTIVE ON THE HUMAN CONDITION

We need to keep in mind that neither *The Heart of Christianity* nor *A Generous Orthodoxy* has a discrete chapter devoted to a comprehensive discussion of theological anthropology. Still, some sense of how each of my dialogue partners responds to the worldview questions regarding who we human beings are and what has gone wrong with us is discernible.

Borg on the human condition. Borg addresses this topic several places in *The Heart of Christianity*, but one in particular is important to consider at this point.[3] In a chapter titled, "Thin Places: Opening the Heart," Borg makes the point that in the Bible the heart is presented as a metaphor for the inner self as a whole.[4] Having acknowledged that "the Bible has many pairs of metaphors for the human condition and our need," Borg chooses to stress the Bible's depiction of "closed" and

---

[2]For example, Borg's insistence that whether we view God as being about requirements and rewards or about love and justice will determine whether we live our lives as Christians preoccupied with the issue of sin management and our own eternal destiny, or whether we experience a spiritual transformation toward becoming more compassionate human beings here and now (Borg, HC 75-76).

[3]Other related discussions occur in chapters titled "Born Again: A New Heart" and "Sin and Salvation: Transforming the Heart." However, because these chapters focus specifically on the doctrine of salvation, I will deal with them more fully in chapter eight.

[4]Borg, HC 151.

"open" hearts.[5] "The condition of the heart matters," says Borg.[6] "The heart, the self at its deepest level, can be turned toward God or away from God, open to God or closed to God. But its typical condition is that it is turned away from God and 'closed.'"[7] Borg proceeds to present what I regard as a very thoughtful list of the qualities of a closed heart: "blindness and limited vision" in general; self-deception in the form of "self-interested self-justification"; selfishness (i.e., "bondage to the desiring of our own hearts"); lack of gratitude; insensitivity to wonder and awe; a tendency to forget God (i.e., to lose track of "the Mystery always around us"); self-imposed spiritual exile (i.e., self-preoccupation that cuts us off from a larger reality); lack of compassion; and insensitivity to injustice.[8]

Borg then explains why people *develop* closed hearts. He indicates that some closed hearts are "a result of chaotic childhood marked by abuse or radical instability. The self builds up layers of protection to defend itself against an unreliable and hurtful world."[9] Of course, not everyone has experienced such trauma in their childhood, so Borg goes on to argue that the condition of a closed heart is ultimately "a natural result of the process of growing up. The birth and development of self-awareness involves an increasing sense of being a separated self."[10]

While affirming that Borg has put his finger on some sociological and psychological realities, what we find in this discussion is a reconfiguration of the doctrines of original sin and human depravity. For Borg, a tendency toward what we might refer to as "self-sins" (e.g., self-centeredness, self-promotion, self-righteousness)[11] is not something we come into the world with—much less a tendency due to the sin of a progenitor whose actions somehow affected all humanity (Rom 5:12-14; 1 Cor 15:21-22). It is simply the natural, "utterly necessary" result of a maturation process that we all must experience: the psychosocial de-

---

[5]Ibid. See also Borg, GWNK 113-15.
[6]Borg, HC 151.
[7]Ibid.
[8]Ibid., pp. 152-53.
[9]Ibid., p. 153; see also pp. 115-16.
[10]Ibid., p. 153; see also pp. 113-14.
[11]For example, see A. W. Tozer, *The Pursuit of God* (Radford, VA: Wilder Publications, 2009), pp. 32-33.

velopment of an individual self.[12] To the degree we learn to be individual selves, we inevitably develop hearts that are closed toward God and others.

However, while Borg acknowledges the seriousness of the evil humans can individually and collectively engage in,[13] he nowhere explains the reason why, in a world that exists within God, we all must experience "the fall"—this *utterly necessary* maturation process that produces people with hearts that are closed toward God and others.[14] This is simply a given for Borg—an inexplicable assumption that is made even more strange when he, without any scriptural support whatsoever, suggests the possibility that we humans may be born into the world with a pristine knowledge of God that we gradually lose over time. Borg indicates an openness to the idea that perhaps

> we come from God, and that when we are very young, we still remember this, still know this. But the process of growing up, of learning about *this* world, is a process of increasingly forgetting the one from whom we came and in whom we live. The birth and intensification of self-consciousness, of self-awareness, involves a separation from God.[15]

According to Borg, the heart condition responsible for human evil is not due at all to any sort of human *depravity,* at least not as classically construed,[16] but solely to a ubiquitous experience of *deprivation.*

---

[12]Borg, HC 114; see also pp. 168-69; and Borg, GWNK 112.

[13]Borg, HC 117.

[14]Ibid., p. 114.

[15]Ibid. Anyone familiar with the basic contours of Gnostic thought will recognize some eerie similarities here. This will be explored further in chapter eight. For a thoughtful and often cited discussion of Borg's promotion of a "new Gnosticism," see Thomas G. Long, *Preaching from Memory to Hope* (Louisville, KY: Westminster John Knox, 2009), pp. 79-110.

[16]For an excellent discussion of the rough "Christian consensus" regarding the human condition as it is portrayed in the Bible, see Roger Olson, *The Mosaic of Christian Belief: Twenty Centuries of Unity and Diversity* (Downers Grove, IL: IVP Academic, 2002), pp. 200-211. Interestingly, Olson indicates that this rough consensus is a tripartite response to three anthropological antitheses that had to be worked through by means of a close look at sacred Scripture: "According to Christianity, and in contrast with most other views of humanity, human beings are *both* animals (natural, biological beings who are mortal) *and* transcendent to nature (spiritual, possessing a supranatural quality, immortal). According to Christianity, humans are *both* essentially good *and* existentially estranged. According to Christianity, humans are *both* sinners because they sin *and* always already sinners." With respect to the last anthropological proposition, Olson elaborates: "*Humans are born 'damaged goods' in the sense of inheriting a spiritual corruption that pervades every aspect of their being and leads inevitably to personal acts of disobedience to*

Human beings are born into the world possessing a pristine knowledge of God but are deprived of this life-giving knowledge through an *utterly necessary* psychosocial maturation process. As a result, they *develop* hearts that are closed toward God and others. Despite the real value of Borg's observations regarding the psychological state of those to whom traditional, missional and emerging evangelicals desire to present the gospel in a compelling manner, this eccentric, essentially naturalistic understanding of the human condition also greatly impacts his understanding of the importance of the notion of sin and what it means to experience salvation.

McLaren on the human condition. Though McLaren offers his readers even less of a formal theological anthropology than Borg, when discussing the phenomenon of salvation he does refer to human evil, specifically speaking of self-delusion, self-deception and denial.[17] Though these characteristics might suggest that at the heart of human evil is an absence or failure of knowledge, it would be wrong to assume that McLaren's understanding of the human condition is a perfect replica of Borg's. Ultimately, McLaren seems more willing than Borg to conceive of human beings as culprits rather than mere victims—agents of evil not simply because of deprivation but because of some form of human deformity that we need to be saved from.

This does not mean, however, that McLaren's understanding of the human condition is beyond critique from a biblically informed perspective. McLaren speaks of the deforming impact on the human species of selfishness, greed, lust, injustice, fear, prejudice, arrogance, apathy, chauvinism and *ignorance*.[18] The reference to "ignorance" here is especially significant. Though it would be assuming too much to conclude that McLaren places "ignorance" last on this list of deformative dynamics because he wishes it to function in a summative manner, its mere presence on such a list suggests to me that, like Borg, McLaren may view human evil as something that may be addressed via *education*

God (that is, they are all sinners even before they commit 'sins'). This third belief is known in Christian theology as 'original sin' and 'inherited depravity'" (p. 201, emphasis original).

[17]McLaren, GO 95 [103].

[18]Ibid., p. 98 [107].

rather than objective *atonement*.[19] Indeed, McLaren's anthropology is evocative of Borg's in several ways: (1) The two times in *A Generous Orthodoxy* where McLaren refers to "total depravity," he does so in a disapproving manner.[20] (2) McLaren offers rather forthright critiques of "an exaggerated understanding of the doctrine of 'original sin'" and "a runaway, exaggerated understanding of 'the fall.'"[21] (3) McLaren speaks of the need to "not take sin more seriously than one should."[22] When considered in the context of his larger discussion of salvation and the Fall, the subtle but significant implication of all this is that while McLaren does not see human beings as mere victims of a psychosocial maturation process, he can give the impression that the biggest problem with human beings is that we are "often ignorantly wrong and stupid."[23] Thus, human evil is subtly portrayed as something that, once brought to light (exposed) by means of Jesus' work on the cross, may then be *educated* out of those who are willing to learn from Jesus the master-teacher how to "live more wisely in the future."[24]

DEPRAVITY, DEPRIVATION OR BOTH?

When formulating a missionally faithful anthropology, must we feel the need to choose between the notions of deprivation and depravity? Or is there another option involving a "both-and" rather than an "either-or" understanding of the human condition that will prove to be even more faithful to the biblical text and missional task?

One of the anthropological presuppositions undergirding my theological work as a whole is that we human beings tend to abhor ambiguity. As psychologist Rollo May has famously observed: "It is an old and ironic habit of human beings to run faster when we have lost our way."[25] In his book *The Myth of Certainty*, Daniel Taylor argues that human beings abhor ambiguity and crave certainty in order to achieve a

---

[19]Once again, we will deal with McLaren's view of salvation more fully in chapter eight.

[20]Ibid., pp. 177 [197], 195 [217].

[21]Ibid., p. 235 [265-66].

[22]Ibid.

[23]Ibid., p. 97 [105].

[24]Ibid., p. 96 [105]. McLaren speaks also in this vein of the need to learn from the Holy Spirit how to "live life to the full" (p. 97 [106]).

[25]Rollo May, *Love and Will* (New York: W. W. Norton, 1969), p. 15.

sense of psychological security.[26] He refers to human beings as "explanation generators" who much prefer the known over the unknown, the
sure thing over speculation, the tried and true over the unproven, certainty over mystery. In other words, most human beings struggle with
paradox, preferring the "either-or" answer to life's most significant questions over the "both-and." This is why the promotion of a false-antithesis
is so often successful![27]

I observe this abhorrence of ambiguity and preference for the "either-
or" every semester when I ask my students to reflect on the worldview
question: *What's gone wrong with the world?* Most students arrive at the
discussion believing with all their being that most of the major ills
present in society are due to *either* the reality of *depravity* (i.e., that all
human beings are born into the world possessing an inherent tendency
to behave in ways that are ultimately hurtful to themselves and others)
or the dynamic of *deprivation* (the absence of resources such as money,
education, employment, status, etc.).Whether a student comes to the
course thoroughly convinced of the sufficiency of either the depravity or
deprivation argument usually depends on where and how their understanding of human nature has been shaped—by what they have heard in
church or elsewhere. This is to say that, in an increasingly post-Christian
society, we should expect to encounter more and more people who are
resistant to the idea that human beings are depraved creatures in the
sense that, while still bearing the *imago Dei,* they also possess an inherent inclination to behave in selfish, greedy, unloving, ultimately self-
destructive ways. The much preferred anthropological perspective these
days, especially in those cultures heavily influenced by the social sciences, is that human beings will sometimes do bad things because they
have been deprived of something they feel they desperately need or are
acting out of ignorance (the lack of requisite knowledge).

I wonder if this contemporary Western sentiment is not fueling the
emerging paradigm's subtle but significant move away from any sort of

---

[26]Daniel Taylor, *The Myth of Certainty* (Waco, TX: Word Books, 1986), p. 93.
[27]In my book *Defeating Pharisaism*, I suggest that a craving for certitude and the psychological
safety it evokes is at the heart of the pharisaical impulse. See Gary Tyra, *Defeating Pharisaism:
Recovering Jesus' Disciple-Making Method* (Downers Grove, IL: InterVarsity Press, 2009), pp. 70-
73.

biblically informed notion of human depravity. If so, I get it. I have interacted with enough post-Christians (both modern and postmodern) to know that the view that human beings are born into the world "bad to the bone" is not going to play well. Most of our post-Christian peers simply do not want to believe that human beings are thoroughly evil creatures completely void of any potential for goodness.

But this "bad to the bone" understanding of human nature is actually based on a *misunderstanding* of the teaching of the Scripture and much of the church's historical reflection on the subject. According to Roger Olson, in a "both-and" rather than "either-or" manner, the "classic Christian consensus" regarding human nature actually underscores the essential goodness of human beings[28] even while it emphasizes the fact that due to humanity's estrangement from God, we are all born into this world possessing an inherent, unavoidable tendency toward pride, selfishness and spiritual rebellion.[29]

Where does this leave us? One option is to *accommodate* what sacred Scripture clearly teaches about the human condition—that we are all sinners[30] in need of an atoning sacrifice for our acts of rebellion against God, ourselves and others[31]—to a more politically correct anthropological perspective that replaces the notion of culpable sin with either spiritual ignorance or psychosocial pathology. But is this anthropological accommodation really necessary from a missional standpoint? Is there not a way to *recontextualize* the Bible's teaching on the nature of humanity in a way that does justice to both the biblical text and the missional task?

What I have found remarkable is how easy it is for the vast majority of my students, once they have been exposed in a thoughtful way to the reality of depravity *and* the dynamic of deprivation, to acknowledge the validity of *both*. At this point I suggest to them that *perhaps both depravity and deprivation are at work in our world*, creating so many of the problems that bedevil humankind and prompt us to wonder about the

---

[28]Olson, *Mosaic of Christian Belief,* pp. 205-7.
[29]Ibid., pp. 207-11. See also Darrell L. Guder, *The Continuing Conversion of the Church* (Grand Rapids: Eerdmans, 2000), pp. 37-38.
[30]See Prov 20:9; Eccles 7:20; Rom 3:23; Eph 2:1-3; 4:17-19; Col 3:5-10; Gal 5:19-21.
[31]See Rom 3:25; Heb 2:17; 1 Jn 2:2; 4:10.

whereabouts of God. Then I introduce two crucial concepts: the primacy of depravity and the exacerbating effect of deprivation.

The primacy of depravity. According to the Bible, people do bad things, not simply because of their external circumstances, but because they possess an innate, unavoidable tendency to behave in selfish, greedy, unloving yet ultimately self-destructive ways toward God and other human beings. Furthermore, according to the Scriptures, this "primal self-concern"[32] is not something that, as Borg suggests, we develop as a result of natural and inevitable life-processes. Neither is it the result of a spiritual ignorance that itself results solely from our being estranged from or deprived of God's presence.[33] On the contrary, the Bible seems to go out of its way to teach that human beings are guilty—personally culpable for—a willful ignorance, a self-imposed, self-perpetuated, self-sabotaging spiritual blindness. *According to the Scriptures, our estrangement from God, while in one sense a result of spiritual ignorance, is also caused by a willful hardening of our own hearts before God* (Rom 1:18-32; Eph 4:17-19).

In his *Confessions,* Augustine wrote: "The blindness of humanity is so great that people are actually proud of their blindness."[34] Augustine seems to be suggesting that behind some people's blindness (epistemological, moral or spiritual) is a stubborn, prideful embrace of the darkness. When I read this I think immediately of several passages in the Gospel of John, where Jesus is referred to as the "light of all mankind" (Jn 1:4) and as the "true light that gives light to everyone" (Jn 1:9), but then we read:

> This is the verdict: Light has come into the world, but people loved darkness instead of light because their deeds were evil. Everyone who does evil hates the light, and will not come into the light for fear that their deeds will be exposed. But whoever lives by the truth comes into the light, so that it may be seen plainly that what they have done has been done in the sight of God. (Jn 3:19-21)

It seems to be a clear teaching in John's Gospel that (1) there is such a

---

[32]Borg, HC 166.
[33]Ibid., p. 167.
[34]Augustine, *Confessions* (New York: Oxford University Press, 1998), p. 38.

thing as willful blindness to the spiritual light that emanates in and through Jesus Christ and that (2) such a love for the darkness rather than the light, rooted in the desire to excuse or maintain one's sinful behaviors, makes a person culpable before God for rejecting the very means by which the Creator is reaching out to reconcile an estranged world to himself (see Jn 3:16-18). This is why the idea of *self-condemnation* is raised here as elsewhere in the Bible.[35]

Once again, according to this biblically informed anthropological perspective, the problem with human beings is not primarily external but internal—a matter of the heart. This explains why some people will behave ignobly even though they have many external resources at their disposal, and why others will behave nobly no matter how many of these resources they lack. My university students understand this; even those who are not religion majors. I cannot remember ever conversing with a person, young or old, who claimed no familiarity at all with the experience of self-sabotaging behavior. Indeed, when I explain to post-Christians the biblical teaching regarding the great need for human beings to experience not just the opening of a closed heart, but *a new heart altogether,*[36] they not only fail to flinch, they actually lean forward as if to say, "Tell me more." This is true even when I go on to make clear that, according to the Scriptures, this new heart requires not just education but repentance (e.g., see Ezek 18:30-32). My experience has been that most post-Christians living in this post-secular era are actually eager to hear that by means of the reception of a new heart and the work of God's Holy Spirit in their lives, they might experience a supernatural empowerment to act in loving rather than hurtful ways toward the hurting people who exist all around them.[37] This one of many areas in which the missional value of a theological realism is abundantly evident!

The exacerbating effect of deprivation. However, having emphasized

---

[35]See Prov 28:14; Rom 1:18-31; and Tit 3:10-11 (cf. Eph 4:17-19).

[36]For example, see Ezek 11:19-20; 36:26; Jer 31:33; Heb 8:7-12; 10:16.

[37]See Jn 14:15; 15:12; Mt 5:13-16, 43-44; 25:31-46; Gal 6:9-10; Tit 3:8; Jas 2:14-17; 1 Jn 3:17-18; 4:7-8. Furthermore, tacit support for this assertion can be found in the opening paragraphs of Richard Mouw, "Getting to the Crux of Calvary: Why Christus Victor Is Not Enough," *Christianity Today,* April 26, 2012, www.christianitytoday.com/ct/2012/may/getting-to-the-crux-of-calvary.html?start=1.

the primacy of depravity, who can deny that one's external circumstances, especially a lack of resources such as money, education, employment, status, and hope itself, will intensify an inherited tendency toward pride, selfishness and rebellion, making it supremely difficult for human beings to refrain from fear-based behaviors that the Bible refers to collectively as unrighteousness and sin? With this in mind, I ask my students to consider the possibility that while it is the reality of depravity that initially stimulates unloving, inhumane behaviors, the dynamic of deprivation can serve to *exacerbate* this natural (fallen) human condition, leading to *habituated* acts of unrighteousness.

Just to be clear, according to this "both-and" explanation for human evil, the primary reason why people do hurtful things to themselves and others is not because of their external circumstances only, but because their hearts are infected with a propensity toward pride, selfishness and rebellion (Rom 7:14-25). At the same time, it is also true that living in a set of adverse circumstances (poverty, hunger, abuse, lack of education and opportunities, etc.) can increase the likelihood that people will act out in sinful ways that end up hurting themselves and others. Fallen, fear-filled rather than faith-filled, people will feel justified in doing what they are convinced they have to do in order to see their needs met (Prov 6:30-31; 30:7-9).

This both-and anthropological perspective explains several things. First, it explains why different people living in the same set of adverse circumstances will react differently to them. Borg is right: the heart matters. However, as we have seen, what is needed is a new heart, not just one that is enlightened.

Second, this more comprehensive view of the human condition explains why the Bible contains so many passages which call for God's people to be concerned about justice (fairness) so as to mitigate the presence of deprivation in our world.[38] While the Bible never relieves human beings of the responsibility to do the right thing regardless of their circumstances (e.g., Prov 30:8-9), it does call for God's people to be concerned that all human beings be treated with dignity and be

---

[38]For example, see Ex 23:6; Lev 19:15; Ps 140:12; Prov 29:7; Ezek 22:29; Amos 5:12; Mt 12:18; 23:23.

provided with opportunities to experience shalom rather than misery in this life!

Third, this view explains why Christians on both sides of the conservative-liberal divide can be so committed to the idea that the cure for humanity's problems requires that the church address both depravity and deprivation instead of just one or the other. This is a common-sense conviction that not very many people, not even those who are post-Christian, will feel the need to repudiate. Thus, whatever the motive for the emerging paradigm's promotion of a reconfigured theological anthropology that downplays the notion of human depravity, my contention is that it, too, fails the faithfulness test. When presented properly, the both-and perspective presented here not only enjoys biblical support, it also has what it takes to "play" well in an increasingly post-Christian context.

THE SPECIAL MISSIONAL IMPORT OF THE "NEW HUMANITY" IN CHRIST

Yet another feature of a theological realism that has huge anthropological (and missional) significance is the biblical teaching that, through his incarnation, atoning death, resurrection and bestowal of his Spirit,[39] Jesus Christ not only models for us what it means to be truly human, but actually heals our humanity and creates within himself a "new humanity" altogether.[40] This christological and anthropological conviction possesses existential and ethical implications badly needed and often well received by many of the post-Christians I have interacted with over the past few years.

The "new humanity" in a nutshell. In the introduction to T. F. Torrance's *Atonement,* Robert Walker writes:

> The bodily resurrection of Jesus is literally the beginning of a new creation headed by Jesus. He is the new man, the head of the new race, the firstborn of the dead, the firstfruits of the new creation, the new Adam

---

[39]See Acts 16:7; Rom 8:9; Phil 1:19 for references to the Holy Spirit as "Christ's Spirit" or the "Spirit of Jesus."

[40]See Ross Hastings, *Missional God, Missional Church: Hope for Re-evangelizing the West* (Downers Grove, IL: IVP Academic, 2012), pp. 91-92, 168-71.

who breathes life into others and who, as such is said to be "a life-giving spirit." . . . What has happened to Jesus will happen to the whole human race and indeed to the whole of creation. He is the pioneer, the one who is in his person the secret and life-giving renewal of the whole universe. That as Torrance emphasizes is the cosmic significance for the New Testament of the incarnation, atonement and resurrection of the Son of God in our humanity.[41]

The idea that the incarnation and vicarious life, death and resurrection of Jesus Christ possess cosmic significance—that by virtue of these things Christ has inaugurated within himself a new, true way of being human—finds ample support in the New Testament. Evidence for this teaching is present in the way these scriptures refer to the possibility of Christ's followers experiencing the phenomena of new hearts and minds (Rom 2:29; Heb 8:10; 10:16), making it possible for them to put on a "new self" (Eph 4:24; Col 3:10), to live a "new life" (Acts 5:20; Rom 6:4), to become a "new creation" (2 Cor 5:17; Gal 6:15) and to form "one new humanity" (Eph 2:11-16 ISV)—what some Christian scholars have referred to as a "third race" of human beings.[42] The idea of a new humanity in Christ also finds support in the way the New Testament refers to all human beings existing either "in Adam" or "in Christ" (Rom 5:12-19; 1 Cor 15:20-23, 42-49), and the manner in which the New Testament authors (especially Paul) speak of the significance of being "in Christ."[43]

What all of this suggests is that Jesus has done much more than simply provide humanity with an example to follow. In the vicarious life, death and resurrection of Jesus the God-human, there is an actual healing of our humanity (1 Pet 2:24), making it possible for us to begin living now in anticipation of what life will be like in the new Eden (Rev 21:1-4; 22:1-5).

---

[41]Thomas F. Torrance, *Atonement: The Person and Work of Christ,* ed. Robert T. Walker (Downers Grove, IL: IVP Academic, 2009), pp. xlix-l.

[42]For example, see F. F. Bruce, *The Epistles to the Colossians, to Philemon, and to the Ephesians* (Grand Rapids: Eerdmans, 1984), pp. 296, 319-20; Charles H. Talbert, *Ephesians and Colossians* (Grand Rapids: Baker, 2007), pp. 81-82; R. Kent Hughes, *Ephesians: The Mystery of the Body of Christ* (Wheaton: Crossway, 1990), pp. 92-93, 97-102, 105, 262.

[43]For example, see Rom 6:11; 8:1; 12:5; 1 Cor 1:2, 4, 30; 3:1; 4:17; 15:18, 19, 22; 2 Cor 1:20, 21; 2:14; 3:14; 5:17-19; Gal 2:4; 3:28; 5:6; Eph 1:3-14; 2:4-13; 3:6-12; 4:32; Phil 3:14; 4:7, 19; Col 1:28; 2:6-12; 1 Thess 4:16; 5:18; 1 Tim 1:14; 2 Tim 1:9; 2:1, 10; 3:12; Philem 1:6; Heb 3:14; 1 Pet 5:10.

242 A Missional Orthodoxy

Following the lead of the Nicene theologians, T. F. Torrance speaks of the importance of several christological concepts that are absolutely critical to the inner logic of the Christian faith:

- *homoousion*—the reality that Jesus is of the same substance as the Father (i.e., ontologically divine)

- *incarnation*—that when Jesus was born of the Virgin Mary, this was not God becoming *like* a human, but the Son of God *actually* becoming human so as to function on humanity's behalf

- *hypostatic union*—the fact that in Christ there was a joining of the divine and human without diminishment to either

- *healing*—indeed, because of the hypostatic union, there occurred a healing of fallen humanity without this constituting a divinization of it

These four key concepts (along with the importance of the outpouring of Christ's Spirit upon those who are "in him") explain why Torrance indicates that the atonement provided by the incarnate Christ had the "cleansing," "healing" and "restoring" of humanity as its objective.[44]

Obviously, the theologically real conviction that because he is both true God and true human, Jesus Christ has not only assumed our fallen, estranged humanity, but has actually effected a healing of it, making it possible for us to live a categorically new kind of life "in him," has tremendous implications for a missionally relevant doctrine of human beings.

The existential and ethical implications of the "new humanity" teaching. One of the main claims in the book *Truth Is Stranger Than It Used to Be* is that the advent of postmodernity, with its emphasis on the cultural and social determination of the self and the rejection of grounding metanarratives, has created for its adherents an identity crisis of critical importance.[45] To be more precise, the embrace of cultural linguistic constructivism has implications for our view of reality (the *where are we?* worldview question) and our view of the human self (the *who are we?* question). Middleton and Walsh explain how postmodernism has presented us with a withering critique of the "humanist under-

---

[44]T. F. Torrance, *The Trinitarian Faith* (Edinburgh: T & T Clark, 1993), pp. 163-64.
[45]J. Richard Middleton and Brian J. Walsh, *Truth Is Stranger Than It Used to Be: Biblical Faith in a Postmodern Age* (Downers Grove, IL: InterVarsity Press, 1995), p. 51.

standing of the self-constructed and self-centered ego."[46] *In the place of an autonomous, self-determining, self-reliant individual, postmodernism has installed the view that the human self is just as socially constructed as anything else.*[47] Furthermore, they assert that while the dismantling of the autonomous self is in some ways a welcome development, it also has a downside: "When we come to realize that the autonomous self is a fiction which can no longer be believed, we are thrown into apocalyptic doubt about all previous beliefs about humanness and all courses of action that such beliefs sustained."[48] In other words, the loss of the modern self that is produced by the postmodern turn has huge existential and ethical consequences. Because of the critical nature of these anthropological consequences, and their importance to the missional endeavor, they need to be explored a bit further.

First, Middleton and Walsh explain that because people lack a grand narrative and are inundated with "a multitude of clamoring voices proffering alternative identities . . . between which it is impossible to choose,"[49] the postmodern decentering of the self has created an identity crisis of huge proportions, producing within many members of the emerging generations a state of "mulitiphrenia" in which the individual is split "into a multiplicity of self-investments."[50] Citing the work of Kenneth Gergen, Middleton and Walsh provide the following clarification:

> A multiphrenic person is populated by a plethora of selves. "In place of an enduring core of deep and indelible character, there is a chorus of invitations." What Gergen describes as postmodern "multiphrenia" is strikingly similar to a pathological condition which is increasingly coming to light in the twentieth century. We are referring to "multiple personality disorder."[51]

---

[46]Ibid., p. 50.

[47]Ibid.

[48]Middleton and Walsh, *Truth Is Stranger*, p. 51. Citation from Steven Best and Douglas Kellner, *Postmodern Theory: Critical Interrogations* (New York: Guilford, 1991), p. 284.

[49]Middleton and Walsh, *Truth Is Stranger*, p. 52. See also Craig Van Gelder and Dwight J. Zscheile, *The Missional Church in Perspective: Mapping Trends and Shaping the Conversation* (Grand Rapids: Baker, 2011), pp. 127-28.

[50]Ibid., p. 55. Citation from Kenneth J. Gergen, *The Saturated Self: Dilemmas of Identity in Contemporary Life* (New York: Basic Books, 1991), p. 5.

[51]Middleton and Walsh, *Truth Is Stranger*, pp. 55-56.

They proceed to make the bold suggestion that the condition of the demon-possessed man in Mark 5 is in some ways analogous to multi-phrenia. Just as the demoniac, tormented by a multitude of false identities, was homeless and in need of healing, so is "the contemporary postmodern psyche."[52]

> Rather than valorizing the emerging postmodern worldview, we ought to recognize the tragic character of the answers to the first two worldview questions provided by contemporary culture:
>
> > *Where are we?* In a pluralistic world of our own construction.
> > *Who are we?* We are legion.[53]

Middleton and Walsh then spell out the existential implications of the postmodern worldview:

> This is a crucial point. If we are in a world of our constructions (the implicit postmodern answer to the first worldview question), and there is no accessible world beyond those constructions, then *where* we are depends on *who* we are. The tragedy of postmodernity, however, is that we are Legion. Therefore, the undecidability that has come to characterize our answer to the first worldview question is only heightened in the second worldview question. We know neither where we are nor who we are.[54]

Second, the authors proceed in their treatment of the decentered self to discuss the moral and relational paralysis that the postmodern condition produces. The same kind of "undecidability" that characterizes the identity of postmoderns—who they are—also affects their ethics as well—how they are to live.

> Well then, what are we to do? The second worldview question, Who are we? inquires about both the nature and task of being human. How we are to live is deeply implicated in the vision we have of ourselves. This is the question of normativity, of ethics. But will we be able to offer any satisfying answer to this question if we have been caught in the quagmires of undecidability? How can we know what we should do if we can have no

---

[52]Ibid., p. 56.
[53]Ibid.
[54]Ibid.

clear idea of ourselves or the world? This is precisely the root of the moral paralysis that characterizes the postmodern age.[55]

Going further still, Middleton and Walsh also suggest that this "undecidability" about who we are also impacts our ability to truly commit ourselves to others:

> By definition, a saturated, multiphrenic self will find it problematic to enter into a relationship of commitment and intimacy. Such relationships necessarily assume that there is a real self (a real "me") that is being known and loved. How could a postmodern self ever make such a commitment? Who would be the *I* in the *I do?* Is this why we see an incredible difficulty with commitment in our culture? Perhaps the problem is that we find ourselves unable to answer the Who am I? question, and thus we are without enough self-knowledge to be able to enter into a relationship of committed intimacy with another.[56]

As someone who routinely engages with young adult university students in classroom discussions and personal counseling sessions, I am painfully familiar with this kind of existential confusion and ethical paralysis. This past week I had lunch with a student who, prior to his arrival at the university, had lived his entire life within a particular ethnic enclave. Veritably wringing his hands, this student agonized out loud over the deep sense of identity confusion he is experiencing. Even before he left the enclave, his embrace of some nontraditional practices had created some tension between him and other, older, members of his community. Now that he is away from the enclave and living in Southern California—a hotbed of postmodern diversity—he is even more confused about who he is and how he is to live. The reason for our meeting was that this identity-related ambiguity is creating within him a tremendous sense of existential and relational angst. Participating in a course that is challenging him to think deeply and biblically about what it means to embrace a Christian worldview has been sweet-torture for him. On the one hand he has no clue how to answer the worldview questions the course is posing. On the other hand, he is genuinely eager,

---

[55]Ibid., p. 57.
[56]Ibid.

desperate even, to arrive at some answers to these crucial questions rather than adopt the "whatever" attitude so often associated with his emerging generation peers.

While this student's discomfort with ambiguity can, to some degree perhaps, be attributed to his cultural background, my sense is that a desire to arrive at some existentially relevant convictions regarding questions such as *where am I? who am I?* and *how should I live my life?* goes beyond any one culture. Though we all differ in the degree to which we are comfortable with the presence of ambiguity in our lives, all of us need at least a modicum of confidence about a few basic issues simply to survive. This is why there are so very few, if any, thoroughgoing nihilists in our world. Most of us end up making existential choices of one kind or another in order to press a sense of meaning, purpose and hope into our lives.[57] Sensing deep in his heart that there is something wrong with the idea that just any choice will do, the ultimate question my young student friend was asking me at lunch was this: "Please, can you help me experience some divine direction in my life?"

With respect to the question of ethics in particular, I have found that while it is not uncommon for students who are convinced of the argument for a cultural linguistic constructivism to embrace the entailment of cultural relativism, it is very difficult for them to actually live with a full-blown moral relativism. Many of my students are like the young woman who recently raised her hand in class, offering with a confused, conflicted look on her face that while she feels compelled to accept the notion of cultural relativism, she cannot, except in theory, bring herself to embrace the moral relativism such a view would seem to require. Her comment was accented in such a way as to form an implicit question—really, a plea. She was asking me, her professor, for help in sorting all this out. Her sense of intellectual and moral confusion, and the head and heart pain this cognitive dissonance is producing in her life, was palpable.[58]

---

[57]Support for this assertion can be found in David J. Bosch, *Transforming Mission: Paradigm Shifts in Theology of Mission* (Maryknoll, NY: Orbis, 2011), p. 363.

[58]For a cogent critique of the notion of cultural relativism offered by an anthropological insider, see Robert B. Edgerton, *Sick Societies: Challenging the Myth of Primitive Harmony* (New York: The Free Press, 1992).

Present in the life of each of these students is a significant degree of the "anomie" and resulting existential confusion and ethical paralysis of which Middleton and Walsh warn.[59] But it does not have to be this way. We human beings do not have to wander aimlessly, homeless and in need of healing, tormented by a cacophony of voices, each proffering a different identity possibility. Jesus Christ has made it possible for all of us to find a new home, receive a new heart, and live a new life that is oriented toward true North. There is "in Christ," the one true human being, a sufficiently definitive answer to the *Where are we? Who are we?* and *How shall we live?* worldview questions.

The compelling quality of theologically "real" Christian discipleship. We have already observed how Thom Rainer's research makes the point that though many unchurched individuals "have little patience for Christians today and the established church . . . they have tremendous respect for Jesus."[60] Likewise, we have noted Dan Kimball's book which makes the similar observation that while many members of the emerging generations may not like the church, they do like Jesus.[61] The evidence does seem to indicate that many post-Christians possess a basic respect for who Jesus is and what he was and is about. Therefore, properly presented, the message that "in him" there can be found living "light" (Jn 8:12), living "bread" (Jn 6:35), living "water" (Jn 7:37-38) and "life" itself (Jn 14:6)—the answers to all the most basic, existentially meaningful worldview questions—does indeed have a chance of being taken seriously.

And just how is this message to be presented *properly* to our post-Christian peers? I will not merely repeat at this point my previously stated conviction that our manner matters; what I have in mind here actually refers to the content of the message itself. Rather than simply encouraging post-Christians to view Jesus as a great moral example— perhaps even the wisest, most mature, most spiritually enlightened human being who ever lived—a biblically faithful Christology and the theological anthropology that derives from it mandate that we go

---

[59]Middleton and Walsh, *Truth Is Stranger,* pp. 25, 36, 57, 78, 130, 161-62, 187, 201.
[60]Thom S. Rainer, "Examining the Unchurched," August 17, 2010, www.buildingchurchleaders .com/articles/2005/052505.html.
[61]Dan Kimball, *They Like Jesus but Not the Church: Insights from Emerging Generations* (Grand Rapids: Zondervan, 2007), pp. 7, 20.

further. Jesus does not simply invite us to *imitate in principle* his "dying and rising."[62] His call to a life of discipleship is an invitation for us to *actually become* born-again members of a new humanity he has come into the world to create. His promise is that in and through him we can, in a theologically *real* manner, become new selves with new hearts. Because we already possess eternal life (see Jn 5:24), and because it is possible to be filled with and to follow the lead of his Spirit (see Rom 8:1-14), we can be empowered to live a new kind of life here and now (see Rom 6:1-4). This new kind of life is one that, because it is informed by the values of the already and coming kingdom of God,[63] does not involve our becoming either imperial, "I want it all" tyrants or impotent, "I'm paralyzed by it all" victims.[64] *Through a Spirit-empowered life of Christian discipleship we can become ethically responsible actors on the stage of human history.*[65] I do not know very many post-Christians, especially those who belong to the emerging generations, who do not crave such a hopeful sense of identity and life purpose. If the post-Christian university students I interact with everyday are any indication, this recontextualized doctrine of human beings will prove to be quite compelling to those who make up our current ministry context!

In the chapters that follow we will explore further the implications of this biblically informed Christology and anthropology for understanding salvation, the church and the kingdom of God. I trust that it will become increasingly clear that a theological anthropology that dismisses or even downplays the biblically-supported notion of the reality of depravity, while focusing solely or even primarily on the dynamic of deprivation, possesses neither biblical nor missional warrant. For the sake of the many pre- and post-Christians living around us, we can and must do better.

---

[62]Borg, HC 107-13.

[63]See Darrell Guder, ed., *Missional Church: A Vision for the Sending of the Church in North America* (Grand Rapids: Eerdmans, 1998), p. 108. See also Guder, *Continuing Conversion,* p. 36.

[64]For a thorough discussion of the "empowered self" that can be experienced in Christ, see Middleton and Walsh, *Truth Is Stranger,* pp. 108-42.

[65]This is one of the reasons why I place so much emphasis on the dynamic of discipleship in the next chapter's discussion of soteriology.

8

ESCAPE AND EXAMPLE

Toward A Missionally Orthodox Doctrine of Salvation

The Christian doctrine of salvation has taken a beating in recent years. The very word *salvation* puts some people on edge, evoking the image of a street preacher confronting passersby with the abrupt query: "Brother (or sister), are you saved?"

But while the style and message of the street preacher might for a variety of reasons get under our skin, we have to admit that from a biblical perspective his concern is legitimate. Given that the New Testament authors felt the need to provide numerous metaphors for the meaning of Christian salvation (justification, reconciliation, redemption, adoption, spiritual healing, deliverance, enabled victory, divinely effected triumph, liberation, etc.), while we might write off the style of the street preacher as being a bit obnoxious and the nature of his ministry incomplete, we really cannot consider his emphasis on salvation to be completely irrelevant.[1]

Indeed, I have suggested that it is this very theological locus—the doctrine of salvation—that constitutes the criterion for differentiating between *doctrines* and *dogma*. The New Testament does not teach that an embrace of every biblical doctrine, not even every christological doctrine, is crucial to the experience of salvation. But it is precisely because of their soteriological significance that four christological doctrines in

---

[1]For an excellent discussion of the need for evangelicals to be familiar with all the atonement metaphors present in the New Testament, see Richard Mouw, "Getting to the Crux of Calvary: Why Christus Victor Is Not Enough," *Christianity Today,* April 26, 2012, www.christianitytoday.com/ct/2012/may/getting-to-the-crux-of-calvary.html?start=1.

particular should be considered Christian dogma and at the heart of Christian orthodoxy. These four soteriologically-crucial doctrines call for us to embrace (in the sense of *both* mental assent and existential trust) that (1) Jesus is both God and human; (2) Jesus' death had an atoning significance;[2] (3) Jesus rose bodily from the grave; and (4) Jesus is now Lord of all.[3]

This chapter will specifically focus on the second of these four crucial christological doctrines. As we endeavor to sketch the rough contours of a doctrine of salvation that is faithful to both the biblical text and the missional task, and as we look at the soteriological views on both sides of the proverbial pendulum, there are several questions we need to ask: (1) What is it about the street preacher's question: "Brother (or sister), are you saved?" that gets under our skin? (2) In what sense are the doctrines of salvation put forward by Marcus Borg and Brian McLaren overcorrections to the street preacher's ministry message? (3) Where on the wide swing of the pendulum is the soteriological view that Jesus did not die simply to make it possible for us to go to heaven someday, nor simply to present us with a good example to follow here and now, but that his death possessed an *atoning* aspect designed to radically impact us human beings both objectively and subjectively, for both time and eternity?

WHY "BROTHER (OR SISTER), ARE YOU SAVED?" GETS UNDER OUR SKIN

There are at least two reasons—in addition to the abrupt, intrusive way the street preacher's question is posed—why many people find his query obnoxious.

Pride. First of all, the street preacher's question implies that something is true of us that many simply do not want to acknowledge: that we

---

[2]For a discussion of why the doctrine of Christ's atoning death should be considered dogma despite the fact that it is not a formal article in the Nicene Creed, see Mark DeVine, "Can the Church Emerge Without or with Only the Nicene Creed," in *Evangelicals and Nicene Faith*, ed. Timothy George (Grand Rapids: Baker, 2011), pp. 190-95.

[3] On (1) see Jn 20:31; 1 Jn 5:5, 11-12; 2 Jn 1:7-9; on (2) see 1 Cor 15:1-3; 1 Jn 2:2; 4:10; on (3) see Rom 10:9-10; 1 Cor 15:1-5; and on (4) see Rom 10:9-10; 14:9-12; 1 Cor 12:3; Phil 2:9-11; Heb 3:1, 15.

need to be *saved*—that is, that there is something wrong with us that we cannot fix ourselves.

To some degree this cause for offense cannot be avoided since the most basic, common-sense meaning of the idea of *salvation* or *being saved* would seem to involve a *rescue from some sort of trouble or peril.* Indeed, perhaps the simplest explanation for why the New Testament presents us with various metaphors for Christian salvation is because there are a variety of ways for human beings to fall into trouble and therefore various ways to picture the peril into which our distrust in, disobedience to, disrespect for and resulting estrangement from the God who created the world places us. So, because we human beings are familiar with what it means to encounter legal, relational, economic, political and health-related kinds of trouble, the New Testament authors, endeavoring to be "seeker-sensitive" in the best sense of the term, use the language of *justification, reconciliation, redemption, deliverance and spiritual healing* to explain what it means to be saved in and through Jesus Christ.

The problem is that when we share the "good news" with people whose pride will not allow them to view themselves as existing in any state of trouble or peril from which they need to be saved (or that they cannot handle themselves), the "good news," no matter how sensitively shared, can not only be heard as "not-so-good news," but can actually strike some folks as an irritating announcement of "bad news" that they consider to be thoroughly bogus and offensive in nature.

Confusion. However, to be fair, pride is not the only reason for the feelings of antipathy the street preacher's ministry often evokes. Since his rhetoric invariably goes on to speak of the cross of Christ and the need to be saved "by his blood," another cause for frustration is a genuine sense of *confusion.* Why all this talk about "sacrifice" and "substitution" and "atonement"? What kind of God requires such a thing? Timothy Keller, an evangelical pastor who is currently modeling for other evangelicals what a missionally faithful and fruitful ministry among post-Christians might look like, describes our current ministry dilemma this way:

> The primary symbol of Christianity has always been the cross. The death of Jesus for our sins is at the heart of the gospel, the good news. Increas-

ingly, however, what the Christian church has considered good news is considered by the rest of our culture to be bad news.

In the Christian account, Jesus dies so that God can forgive sins. For many, that seems ludicrous or even sinister. "Why would Jesus *have* to die?" is a question that I have heard from people in New York far more often than "Does God exist?" "Why couldn't God just forgive us?" they ask. "The Christian God sounds like the vengeful gods of primitive times who needed to be appeased by human sacrifice." Why can't God just accept everyone or at least those who are sorry for their wrongdoings? While the Christian doctrine of the cross confuses some people, it alarms others. Some liberal Protestant theologians reject the doctrine of the cross altogether because it looks to them like "divine child abuse."[4]

Keller goes on to pose some crucial questions: "Why then, don't we just leave the Cross out? Why not focus on the life of Jesus and his teachings rather than on his death? Why did Jesus have to die?"[5] These queries set us up nicely for a discussion of how my two dialogue partners present an emerging understanding of the doctrine of salvation.

THE EMERGING PARADIGM'S OVERCORRECTION TO THE STREET PREACHER'S MESSAGE

Judging by the number of times both Marcus Borg and Brian McLaren refer to the concept of salvation, both are fully aware of how important one's soteriological perspective is to Christian orthodoxy.[6] The problem is not that those promoting the emerging paradigm ignore the doctrine of salvation, but that they feel the need to rehabilitate it, making it more palatable to the soteriological sensitivities that Keller mentioned. What follows is a fairly thorough analysis of how my two dialogue partners, Borg in particular, goes about this task of rehabilitation.

Borg's doctrines of sin and salvation. We have already seen that— despite the many passages in the New Testament that specifically speak of

---

[4]Timothy Keller, *The Reason for God: Belief in an Age of Skepticism* (New York: Dutton, 2008), pp. 186-87.
[5]Ibid., p. 187.
[6]The word *salvation* occurs forty-two times in *The Heart of Christianity* and twenty times in *A Generous Orthodoxy*.

Christian salvation as involving the "forgiveness of sins,"[7] or that explicitly refer to Jesus dying for "our sins,"[8] or that connect salvation with the spilling of Christ's "blood,"[9]—Borg steadfastly insists that what occurred on the cross was not actually or really atoning. Jesus' death was in one sense a tragic accident, the result of the prophetic challenges he had brought to the temple cultus—the domination system of his day.[10] In another sense, says Borg, Jesus' death functions as an inspiring demonstration of "God's love for us."[11] In yet another sense, the death of Jesus serves as an example for his followers to imitate—a "revelation of the 'way' or 'path' of transformation."[12]

Those familiar with the history of Christian theology will recognize that Borg is simply taking a side here in the classic debate between those who argue that the death of Christ on the cross had an *objective* aspect to it—that Jesus was literally atoning for actual, objective guilt that human beings have before a holy God[13]—and those who insist that the effect of Jesus' demise on those who meditate on it is merely *subjective* in nature—that it has the power to inspire us to live, not for ourselves, but for God and the kingdom cause.[14]

In Borg's case, the reason for his dismissal of the idea that Jesus literally died for our sins seems to extend beyond his rejection of the divinity of Christ. Informing Borg's radical *reinterpretation* of Christian salvation is the manner in which he *redefines* the fall as something that happens to each of us when we lose an innate knowledge of God as a result of psychosocial maturation processes, and his rather significant *reconceptualization* of the nature and importance of sin (and hence the need for forgiveness).

---

[7]See Mt 26:28; Mk 1:4; Lk 1:77; 3:3; 24:47; Acts 2:38; 5:31; 10:43; 13:38; 26:18; Eph 1:7; Col 1:14; Heb 9:22.
[8]See Rom 4:25; 1 Cor 15:3; Gal 1:4; Col 2:13; 1 Pet 2:24; 3:18; 1 Jn 1:9; 2:2; 3:5; 4:10; Rev 1:4-6.
[9]See Mt 26:28; Mk 14:24; Lk 22:20; Acts 20:28; Rom 3:25; 5:9; 1 Cor 10:16; 11:25; Eph 1:7; 2:13; Col 1:20; Heb 9:12, 14, 22; 10:29; 12:24; 13:12, 20; 1 Pet 1:2, 19; 1 Jn 1:7; 5:6; Rev 1:5; 5:9; 7:14; 12:11.
[10]Borg, HC 94-96. See also Borg, SC 13-14, 97-100.
[11]Borg, HC 96.
[12]Ibid.
[13]See Rom 3:25; Heb 2:17; 1 Jn 2:2; 4:10.
[14]For a discussion of the effect of modernity on the Christian notion of salvation, see David J. Bosch, *Transforming Mission: Paradigm Shifts in Theology of Mission* (Maryknoll, NY: Orbis, 2011), pp. 404-7.

It is not that Borg lacks an answer to the worldview question "What's gone wrong with the world?" Citing the work of author Frederick Buechner, Borg affirms the idea that the central plot of the biblical story is that "God creates the world; *the world gets lost;* God seeks to restore the world to the glory for which God created it."[15] However, he argues that the fact that "for centuries, Christians have seen the central issue separating us from God as 'sin,'"[16] has been a colossal mistake.[17]

According to Borg, the biggest reason why this focus on sin in soteriology has been errant is that the root meaning of "sin" has, until the modern era, been misunderstood as being about "disobeying God's laws," "breaking the rules" and "being bad," when its real meaning has to do with "estrangement" or *"being separated from that to which we belong."*[18] Essentially turning the historically held notion of sin on its head, Borg asserts that sin is not the cause of the fall but the result of it. He explains, "Our lives are estranged from God. We live in exile, east of Eden. And our sense of separation leads to centering in the self or the world (or both) rather than in God and the more specific behaviors we commonly call sins."[19] While Borg can affirm that pride, disobedience, and spiritual infidelity are real problems, ultimately he sees them as the fruits of our fallen condition rather than the root cause of it (cf. Prov 21:4). By grounding the problem of the human condition in a *theological deprivation*—our being separated from God—Borg conflates the concepts of depravity and deprivation as usually understood and thereby essentially empties depravity of meaning. Ultimately, while "sins" are ways fallen human beings can behave, the root problem is "sin," *over which none of us has any control.* The logical implication of Borg's argument is that we are all the *victims* of sin—the condition of being estranged from (deprived of) God due to necessary psychosocial maturation processes.

---

[15]Frederick Buechner, "The Good Book as a Good Book," in *The Clown in the Belfry: Writings on Faith and Fiction* (San Francisco: HarperSanFrancisco, 1992), p. 44, as cited in Borg, HC 165, emphasis original.

[16]Borg, HC 165.

[17]See Borg, SC 12, 143-52; Borg, GWNK 161.

[18]Borg, HC 166, emphasis original.

[19]Ibid., p. 167. See also Borg, GWNK 112.

This is what makes the traditional Christian focus on the forgiveness of sins so problematic for Borg.[20] According to his emerging paradigm, sin, properly understood, is not something we humans do, but something that happens to us. Or, at least, it is a condition we find ourselves in due to inevitable maturation processes by which we become separate, individuated selves. Thus, for Borg, a more accurate image depicting the problem which any message of Christian salvation needs to address is that of a closed heart (toward God and others): "If we have closed hearts, we don't need forgiveness as much as we need to have our hearts opened."[21]

And what do we do with those biblical passages which indicate that we human beings bear some responsibility for the condition of our own hearts?[22] Borg is willing to grant that "our blindness can be the result of our own doing; it can become willful, a refusal to see."[23] But he is not willing to concede the primacy of depravity over deprivation. No, contrary to what I suggested in my discussion of the human condition,[24] Borg insists that theological deprivation is primary and the resulting depravity becomes the exacerbating dynamic:

> Estrangement, the birth of the separated self, is the natural result of growing up; it cannot be avoided. For the same reason we develop closed hearts, a shell around the self. There is a sense in which we are blinded by the imprinting of culture on our psyches and our perception. In a sense, we fall into bondage through no fault of our own. It's the inevitable result of growing up.[25]

This theological anthropology leads Borg to say that he favors "letting go of sin as the umbrella description for the human problem."[26] The idea of forgiveness just does not address humanity's root problem, which is a spiritual blindness, bondage and exile that has occurred through no fault of our own.[27] Indeed, says Borg, this focus on forgiveness is mis-

---

[20]See Borg, SC 12-13, 153-54.
[21]Borg, HC 168.
[22]For example, see Ex 8:15, 32; 9:34; 1 Sam 6:6; 2 Chron 36:13; Ps 95:8; Prov 28:14; Dan 5:20; Zech 7:12; Mt 13:15; 19:8; Acts 28:27; Eph 4:17-19; Heb 3:8, 12-15; 4:7; cf. Lk 11:35.
[23]Borg, HC 168.
[24]See chapter seven above.
[25]Ibid., pp. 168-69.
[26]Ibid., p. 169.
[27]Ibid., pp. 168-69.

sionally inappropriate since "for many, the central existential issue is not a sense of sin," and because for others, "the issue is not their own sin, but their victimization by others."[28]

Borg proceeds to explicate how his redefinition of the human problem affects his soteriology. In the process he treats the *when, what, who,* and *how* of Christian salvation.

As he deals with the "when" issue, Borg presents an antithesis between a salvation that is focused on eternity and one that is focused on the here and now. According to Borg, the trouble with the question "Are you saved?" is that it nearly always connotes the idea that "salvation is about the next world."[29] We have already noted how, according to Borg, "the earlier way of being a Christian . . . sees the Christian life as centered in believing now for the sake of salvation later."[30] Having made the bold assertion that one of "Christianity's ten worst contributions to religion" is "popular Christianity's emphasis on the afterlife,"[31] Borg states rather unequivocally his view that "the biblical understandings of salvation are focused on this world, not the next."[32] Then, despite the many references in the Gospels to the "end of the age,"[33] the "age to come,"[34] the "last day,"[35] "the resurrection"[36] and "eternal life,"[37] Borg famously insists that

> Jesus himself seems to have believed in an afterlife, but he doesn't talk about it very much. Most often in the gospels, the topic is brought up by somebody else. And when Jesus does talk about it, it's not clear whether we should understand him as providing "information" about the afterlife, or whether we should hear him primarily as subverting overly confident notions of what it will be like. In any case, it's clear that his message was not really about how to get to heaven. It was about a way of transfor-

[28]Ibid., p. 170. By "existential," Borg has in mind those issues that are most basic to our existence, our way of being in the world.
[29]Ibid., p. 171.
[30]Ibid., p. xii.
[31]Ibid., pp. 171-72.
[32]Ibid., p. 172. See also Borg, GWNK 157.
[33]See Mt 12:32; 13:38-42, 47-50; 24:3-14; 28:19-20.
[34]For example, see Mk 10:29-30; Lk 18:28-30; 20:34-36.
[35]See Jn 6:39, 40, 44, 54; 11:24; 12:48.
[36]For example, Mt 22:28, 30; Mk 12:23; Lk 14:14; 20:33, 35-36; Jn 11:24-25.
[37]See Mt 19:16, 29; 25:46; Mk 10:17, 30; Lk 10:25; 18:18, 30; Jn 3:15, 16, 36; 4:14, 36; 5:24, 39; 6:27, 40, 54, 68; 10:28; 12:25, 50; 17:2-3.

mation in this world and the Kingdom of God on earth. If he also believed in heaven, it would not be remarkable. But Jesus wasn't very much concerned with life beyond death, either his own or that of others.[38]

As for the way other New Testament authors also make a distinction between this age and the one to come,[39] express a real interest in the notion of eternal life,[40] and steadfastly affirm a future resurrection of both the righteous and wicked dead,[41] Borg steadfastly contends that "even though the affirmation of an afterlife is found in the New Testament, it does not seem to have been the primary message of early Christianity."[42] Borg's justification for this bold assertion is that while Paul did have much to say about the *existential* and *temporal* aspects of new life "in Christ," we search in vain for passages in which Paul counsels his readers: "Here's what you must do to get to heaven."[43] In defense of his virtual dismissal of the *eschatological* and *eternal* aspects of Christian salvation in favor of a nearly exclusive focus on the *existential* and *temporal* benefits of the same, Borg offers a couple of word studies in which he endeavors to prove that "eternal" or "everlasting" life does not refer to an afterlife experience after all, but to life in an "age to come" that has already come.[44] What is at work in Borg's emerging paradigm is an over-realized eschatology that seems void of any apocalyptic aspect whatsoever. According to Borg, "salvation in the Bible is primarily a this-worldly phenomenon. It happens here."[45]

---

[38]Borg, HC 173. Not all New Testament scholars would concur with the idea that Jesus was not much concerned with the issue of life beyond death. For example, see George E. Ladd, *A Theology of the New Testament* (Grand Rapids: Eerdmans, 1993), pp. 181, 194, 205.

[39]For example, see Gal 1:3-5; Eph 1:18-21; 1 Tim 6:17-19; Tit 2:11-14; Heb 6:4-6.

[40]See Acts 13:46, 48; Rom 2:7; 5:21; 6:22, 23; Gal 6:8; 1 Tim 1:16; 6:12; Tit 1:2; 3:7; 1 Jn 1:2; 2:25; 3:15; 5:11, 13, 20; Jude 1:21.

[41]See Acts 4:1-2; 17:16-18, 32; 23:6-8; 24:10-16, 21; 1 Cor 15:12-58; Phil 3:7-11; 2 Tim 2:17-18; Heb 6:1-2; 11:35; 1 Pet 1:3-4; Rev 20:4-6.

[42]Borg, HC 174.

[43]Ibid.

[44]Ibid., pp. 174-75. Passages such as John 6:40, 51, 54, 58; 10:28; 12:25 and 1 Jn 2:17 provide evidence that, though John the Evangelist can speak of eternal life as a present experience, his understanding of this phenomenon does possess an eschatological aspect as well.

[45]Ibid., p. 175. It is interesting that a nearly contrary position is taken by New Testament scholar George Ladd who, while observing that in the Gospels, "the words 'to save' and 'salvation' refer both to an eschatological and a present blessing," goes on to make the assertion: "Salvation is primarily an eschatological gift" (Ladd, *Theology of the New Testament*, p. 71).

Concomitant with this temporal (rather than eternal) understanding of salvation is an essentially exclusive focus on its existential (rather than eschatological) impact. To some degree we have already seen that Borg's method of dealing with the "what" issue of Christian salvation is to insist that the earlier paradigm is guilty of having focused too much on the issue of forgiveness, and not enough on how salvation is about transformation—becoming whole in this life.[46] Frankly, this is a concern that many evangelicals (traditional, missional and emerging) likewise share. Thus, the problem is not that Borg's emerging paradigm's focus on life transformation constitutes a soteriological error, but that, ironically, its overreaction and overcorrection to a legitimate concern runs the risk of leading unwary readers away from a balanced, holistic, fully adequate understanding of Christian salvation.

Borg contributes to this problem when, in treating the "what" issue, he focuses on the morphology of the English word "salvation" rather than the way the Greek terms $s\bar{o}z\bar{o}$ ("save") or $s\bar{o}t\bar{e}ria$ ("salvation") are used in the New Testament. Making much of the fact that the English word "salve" is associated with the term "salvation," Borg concludes that "in its broadest sense, salvation . . . means becoming whole and being healed."[47] While he will also state that "salvation means to be saved from our predicament," the overall impression one gains from the way Borg describes the human predicament and endeavors to connect the "macro-stories" of the Hebrew Bible—exodus, exile and temple—with the story of Jesus—as liberator, "the way," and sacrifice,[48] is that salvation is *primarily* subjective and existential in its impact, rather than objective and eschatological. In other words, though Borg never completely denies that Christian salvation is about being rescued from the "present evil age" (Gal 1:4) or the "dominion of darkness" (Col 1:13) or the "coming wrath" (1 Thess 1:10), this more eschatologically oriented understanding of Christian salvation is essentially dismissed. This should come as no surprise given Borg's reticence to think of God as a

---

[46]See Borg, SC 53.

[47]Borg, HC 175. Though it should be noted that Borg never explicitly associates this idea of salvation as spiritual healing with the New Testament's teaching regarding the healing of our humanity "in Christ."

[48]Ibid., pp. 175-77. See also Borg, MJA 128-33.

lawgiver and judge[49] and his stated ambivalence toward the notion of an afterlife.[50] Thus, in terms of the "what" issue, Borg pictures Christian salvation *primarily* as a temporal, existentially related dynamic.

Furthermore, the existential (over the eschatological) impact of salvation is underscored by the way Borg proceeds to deal with the "who" issue. In this case, the antithesis that he sets up is between salvation as a personal versus communal experience. Granting that salvation is personal, Borg's burden is to emphasize that it is also social. In the process, he makes some statements that seem less comprehensive than they need to be—statements that insinuate a nearly completely existential soteriological position: "Salvation is about life together. Salvation is about peace and justice with community and beyond community. It is about *shalom*, a word connoting not simply a peace as the absence of war, but peace as the wholeness of a community living together in peace and justice."[51]

Now, many evangelicals (even those of the traditional camp) share with Borg and other promoters of the emerging paradigm a deep concern over the individualistic consumerism that seems to mark many traditional evangelical churches.[52] However, given Borg's emphasis on the temporal and existential nature of salvation, his rather stark statements (like those quoted above) can appear to constitute more than a call for Christians to become meaningfully engaged in Christian community for the sake of their own spiritual formation and a more fruitful missional witness to their respective ministry contexts. Borg's emphasis on the social nature of salvation suggests a view of the kingdom of God as a primarily temporal reality brought about by human social action. In anticipation of the criticism that I am reading too much into these statements, I will counter in advance that such a concern is legitimized when Borg states in such a stark manner that "the Bible is not about the saving of individuals for

---

[49]Borg, HC 75-76.

[50]Ibid., pp. 181-84. See also Borg, SC 11-12, 197-202; Borg, GWNK 171-75.

[51]Borg, HC 178.

[52]See Darrell Guder's prophetic challenge of an "evangelistic reductionism" which separates the benefits of the gospel from the mission of the gospel so that rank-and-file evangelical church members are turned into mere consumers of church programs rather than witnesses to and for Christ in the world. See Darrell L. Guder, *The Continuing Conversion of the Church* (Grand Rapids: Eerdmans, 2000), pp. 118-41.

heaven, but about a new social and personal reality in the midst of this life."[53] Even though I am personally sympathetic to some of the soteriological concerns raised by the emerging paradigm, when critiques are presented in such an overstated manner, they strike me as reactionary—more suggestive of an overcorrection than a Spirit-led reform.

This brings us to the "how" issue and Borg's discussion of the role of repentance in the emerging view of salvation. For Borg, just as the earlier paradigm tends to trivialize sin and salvation, it has likewise trivialized the idea of repentance. Borg complains that too many Christians associate repentance with "introspective guilt," with "feeling really sorry" for what they "have done or left undone," and with "feeling really bad about the horrible person" they have become.[54] On the contrary, Borg asserts that "the biblical meaning of 'repent' is not primarily contrition, but resolve."[55] Failing to cite any of the numerous New Testament passages which indicate that repentance, though it can connote simply a change of mind,[56] also involves remorse and contrition,[57] Borg instead focuses on the Old Testament story of the exile. Having made the somewhat arbitrary assertion that the "metaphorical home" of the idea of repentance "is the exile," Borg goes on to redefine this soteriologically significant action in the following narrow manner: "To repent means to return from exile, to reconnect with God, to walk the way in the wilderness that leads from Babylon to God."[58]

While this can be an apt image, in the same way that Borg conflates depravity and deprivation, he also seems to conflate repentance and restoration. Thus he can describe repentance as the "way *of* Jesus" rather than as the way *to* Jesus.[59] This is seen in Borg's insistence that the real meaning of *metanoia* is not, as traditionally understood, "a change of mind or heart," but instead means to "go beyond the mind that you

---

[53]Ibid., p. 179.
[54]Ibid., p. 180.
[55]Ibid. See also Borg, SC 157-59.
[56]See Ladd, *Theology of the New Testament*, p. 36.
[57]See 2 Kings 20:5; 2 Chron 7:13-14; Ps 51:17; Is 57:15; 66:2; Jer 50:4; Lam 2:18; Lk 7:37-48; Heb 12:17.
[58]Borg, HC 180.
[59]Ibid., emphasis added.

have."[60] Repentance is not the prelude to the experience of salvation[61] but the process by which the Christian pursues salvation, understood as life transformation without any need for the forgiveness of sins. In a nutshell, for Borg, repentance has nothing to do with forgiveness; it is simply the resolve that is necessary to "go beyond the mind that you have been given and acquired. Go beyond the mind shaped by the culture to the mind that you have 'in Christ.'"[62] Indeed, earlier in *The Heart of Christianity*, Borg lays the groundwork for his later rejection of the idea of repentance functioning as a prelude or prerequisite to Christian salvation when he states that "the Christian life is not about believing or doing what we need to believe or do so that we can be saved. Rather, it's about seeing what is already true—that God loves us already—and then beginning to live in this relationship. It is about becoming conscious of and intentional about a deepening relationship with God."[63]

Keeping in mind Borg's rejection of the traditional understanding of depravity—that human beings possess an innate tendency toward behaviors that are self-destructive, dismissive of God, and hurtful to others—and his downplaying of the importance of the forgiveness of sins, it is understandable why he would feel the need to redefine repentance away from the notion of being sorry for sin toward a resolve to acquire that innate knowledge of God that has been lost due to necessary psychosocial maturation processes. Instead of being the path *to* such things as being born again and a transformational discipleship relationship with the risen Christ, repentance is, for Borg, the path *of* these things.[64] All things considered, I fail to see in Borg's soteriology any real reference to the need to be remorseful, to be sorry for our sin as a prelude to entering into the life of Christian discipleship. Instead, what we find is an encouragement to rise up and leave Babylon, to resolve to escape exile, to stay engaged in the process of regaining the knowledge of God

---

[60]Ibid.
[61]See Mt 3:2, 8, 11; 4:17; 11:20; 21:32; Mk 1:4, 15; 6:12; Lk 3:3, 8; 5:32; 13:3, 5; 15:7; 16:30; 17:4; 24:47; Acts 2:38; 3:19; 5:31; 8:22; 11:18; 13:24; 17:30; 19:4; 20:21; 26:20; Rom 2:4; 2 Cor 7:9-10; 2 Tim 2:25; Heb 6:1, 6; 2 Pet 3:9; Rev 2:5, 16, 21, 22; 3:3, 19; 9:20, 21; 16:9, 11.
[62]Borg, HC 180.
[63]Ibid., p. 77.
[64]Ibid.

that has been lost to us due to the fall. Ironically, the attitude behind such repentance might be just the opposite of remorse. It might just as well take the form of a righteous indignation at our having been victimized by others and life itself for far too long!

I wholeheartedly affirm that the experience of Christian salvation involves more than a mere management of our sins and that, if genuine, it will express itself in a commitment to enter into a lifetime of Christian discipleship from which we "learn" from the risen Christ how to love God supremely and our neighbors as ourselves. However, Borg's excising from this soteriological experience the atoning death of Jesus toward the forgiveness of sins can lead to the idea that Jesus is *a* way to the experience of salvation rather than *the* way (Jn 14:6; Acts 4:12; 1 Tim 2:5). Indeed, a final component of Borg's soteriological proposal concerns his commitment to religious relativism—the idea that all of the world's religions, as "communities of transformation" that are equally in touch with "the absolute," can adequately enable the opening of the closed hearts of human beings to God and one another.[65] While later chapters will offer a more thorough discussion of Borg's religious relativism, it seems appropriate to at least acknowledge it at this point as an important aspect of his emerging doctrine of salvation.

McLaren's perspective on how Jesus saves. In a chapter titled "Jesus: Savior of What?" Brian McLaren begins his soteriological discussion by suggesting that traditional Christianity has promoted a doctrine of salvation that is too "inward turned," "individual-salvation-oriented" and "unadapted" (i.e., not contextualized).[66] Offering that the traditional view constitutes a "colossal and tragic misunderstanding" of Christian salvation, McLaren encourages his readers to give the matter some "fresh attention."[67]

To his credit, McLaren, unlike Borg, allows for a greater sense of human culpability in the evil that afflicts the planet. Thus, in a much more traditional manner, McLaren speaks of repentance as being "truly sorry" for our actions and possessing a "change of heart."[68] At

---

[65]Ibid., p. 215. See also Borg, SC 174.
[66]McLaren, GO 93 [101].
[67]Ibid.
[68]Ibid., p. 95 [103].

the same time, McLaren is somewhat dismissive whenever he refers to classical Christianity's doctrines of the fall, depravity, original sin[69] and penal substitution.[70]

So, while McLaren correctly observes that "in the Bible, *save* means 'rescue' or 'heal,'"[71] his disdain for the street preacher's salvation message is apparent in the way he often complains of the tendency among Christians to assume that the language of "rescue" that permeates Scripture has to do with being saved from hell or going to heaven after we die.[72] This explains why, as he presents his version of an emerging soteriology, McLaren is careful to point out that the Bible contains stories of people being rescued or saved from many things: "sickness, war, political intrigue, oppression, poverty, imprisonment"—all kinds of "danger or evil."[73] Not taking into consideration the possible difference that might exist between discrete accounts in the Old Testament of people being saved from various kinds of physical, temporal peril, and how the New Testament authors were led by the Spirit to describe the phenomenon of Christian salvation in a fuller, more spiritual, eternal sense, McLaren proceeds to assert that God saves people "in three primary ways." He saves them by *judging* or confronting the evil that is being perpetrated upon his people;[74] by *forgiving* any evil, self-created, self-inflicted, self-sabotaging behaviors his people have been guilty of due to their own spiritual ignorance (i.e., their "self-delusion," self-deception, and "denial");[75] and by *teaching* us how "to live more wisely in the future."[76] Then, in a move reminiscent of Borg's interpretation of Jesus through the grid of the Hebrew Bible's macro-stories, McLaren takes an essentially Old Testament perspective on salvation and, applying it to Jesus, explains:

---

[69]Ibid., pp. 234-35 [264-65]. See also McLaren, NKC 34, 37, 139.

[70]McLaren, GO 48 [54]n18, 197 [220].

[71]Ibid. p. 93 [101]. Though it should be noted that, like Borg, McLaren never explicitly associates the idea of salvation as spiritual healing with the New Testament's teaching on the healing of our humanity "in Christ."

[72]Ibid. See also pp. 85-86 [94-95], 100 [108-9], 107 [117-18], 112 [122], 160 [178], 237-39 [267-68].

[73]Ibid., 93 [101].

[74]Ibid., pp. 93-95 [101-3].

[75]Ibid., pp. 95-96 [103-4].

[76]Ibid., pp. 96-97 [104-6].

> Jesus comes then not to condemn (to bring the consequences we deserve) but to save by shining the light on our evil, by naming our evil as evil so we can repent and escape the chain of bad actions and bad consequences through forgiveness, and so we can learn from Jesus the master-teacher to live more wisely in the future.[77]

As far as it goes (and besides the fact that it seems not to be informed by the entirety of what the New Testament has to say about the experience of salvation), there is nothing really wrong with this soteriological statement. However, McLaren then proceeds to take this less than thorough understanding of salvation and apply it in a way that is evocative of Borg's insistence that the death of Jesus was all about the unmasking and overthrow of the domination system of his day. McLaren writes:

> This is a window into the meaning of the cross. Absorbing the worst that human beings can offer—crooked religiosity, petty political systems, individual betrayal, physical torture with whip and thorn and nail and hammer and spear—Jesus enters into the center of the thunderstorm of human evil and takes its full shock on the cross. Our evil is brutally, unmistakably exposed, drawn into broad daylight, and judged—named and shown for what it is. Then, having felt its agony and evil firsthand, in person, Jesus pronounces forgiveness and demonstrates that the grace of God is more powerful and expansive than the evil of humanity. Justice and mercy kiss; judgment and forgiveness embrace. From their marriage a new future is conceived.[78]

This is an eloquent description of what Jesus was doing on the cross that focuses on the idea that his death ultimately had the effect of *exposing* human evil for what it is and *demonstrating* that God's grace is more powerful and expansive. As a matter of fact, this description is not only eloquent but inspirational as well. My only concern is that missing from it is any reference to Jesus' death on the cross functioning in any sort of *sacrificial* manner.[79] Instead of providing any reference whatsoever to an atoning aspect of Christ's passion, McLaren goes on to

---

[77]Ibid., p. 96 [104-5].
[78]Ibid., p. 97 [105].
[79]Cf. Rom 3:25; 1 Cor 5:7; Eph 5:1-2; Heb 7:27; 9:23-28; 10:1-14; 1 Jn 2:1-2; 4:10.

argue that, having exposed humanity's capacity for evil behavior, Jesus continues to confront the spiritual ignorance and stupidity that lies at the heart of the human condition by offering us his "saving teaching" which seeks to enable us, like him, to love God supremely and our neighbors as ourselves.[80]

I appreciate that, like Borg, McLaren emphasizes the idea that Christian salvation should involve more than a "management" of our sins. There are, unfortunately, too many Christian church-goers who, having prayed the "sinner's prayer" tend to view the entire Christian experience as a sort of "fire insurance policy." This is a truncated, myopic understanding of Christian soteriology that deserves to be critiqued.[81] However, keeping in mind McLaren's disdain for the doctrines of the fall, human depravity and penal substitution—and the way in which he criticizes conservative Protestants for an overemphasis on the cross-work of Christ to the neglect of his teaching ministry[82]—at the end of the day I wonder if ultimately, despite his rhetoric regarding human culpability for evil behavior and the need for a repentance that involves remorse as well as resolve, McLaren does not end up promoting something very similar to the neo-gnostic "salvation by illumination" that has been attributed to Borg.[83] As we have seen, McLaren does not seem to have any real room in his soteriology for the idea that Jesus' death on the cross served to atone for any objective guilt that exists between sinful human beings and a holy God. Moreover, later in *A Generous Orthodoxy,* he will, like Borg, indicate his embrace of the idea that it is unnecessary for a person to become a distinct disciple of Jesus in order to experience the kind of life transformation that he and Borg understand as the ultimate goal of salvation.[84]

---

[80]Ibid. [105-6].

[81]For an extended critique of the concept of "cheap grace," see Dietrich Bonhoeffer, *The Cost of Discipleship* (New York: Touchstone, 1995), pp. 43-56. However, see also the editorial "The Evangelical Jesus Prayer: It's Not Perfect, but the Sinner's Prayer Is a Work of Genius," *Christianity Today,* September 10, 2012, www.christianitytoday.com/ct/2012/september/the-evangelical-jesus-prayer.html, which argues that the sinner's prayer, for all its imperfections, can play an important role in the process of Christian discipleship.

[82]McLaren, GO 62-63 [69-70].

[83]See Thomas G. Long, *Preaching from Memory to Hope* (Louisville, KY: Westminster John Knox, 2009), p. 64.

[84]McLaren, GO 263-64 [295-97].

Thus, it does indeed appear that McLaren's version of the emerging soteriology, like Borg's, tends to focus rather exclusively on the existential aspects of salvation to the neglect of the eschatological. This conclusion is supported by the fact that, while failing to acknowledge the Bible's many passages which clearly refer to a postmortem experience of "judgment" or reckoning,[85] the rest of McLaren's soteriological discussion focuses mainly on his conviction that Jesus' concern is to save "planet Earth and all life on it" (rather than individual human souls) and to do so here and now rather than in an age to come.[86] Toward this end McLaren argues that the idea of Jesus as a "personal savior," inevitably leads to a "self-centered" and "hell-centered" understanding of salvation that, because it is so focused on heaven, ignores the needs of a hurting world all around us.[87]

As I have already noted, it is not that McLaren's critique of a too-introspective, too-individualized and unadapted soteriology is completely unfounded. Indeed, many of his concerns (despite some hyperbole) are valid and should therefore not only be heard but acted on. Likewise, much of what Borg has to say about the tragic effects of the psychosocial maturation process all of us must endure en route to becoming individuated selves rings true. His observation that our hearts can be relatively closed or open to God and others is spot on. Furthermore, I eagerly affirm the idea promoted by both of my dialogue partners that the experience of Christian salvation should involve life transformation rather than simply management of our sins.

Nevertheless, my concern is that the emerging understanding of salvation is missing any endorsement of the second christological commitment that I have argued is at the heart of the Christian message—that is, that Jesus' death was atoning in that it constituted a sacrificial offering to God that made the forgiveness of sins and the healing of our

---

[85]For example, see Mt 12:36; Acts 10:39-43; 17:29-31; Rom 2:5-16; 14:10; 1 Cor 4:4-5; 2 Tim 4:1, 8; Jas 2:12-13; 3:1; 5:9; 1 Pet 1:17; 4:5; 2 Pet 3:7; 1 Jn 4:15-17; Jude 1:14-15; Rev 6:10; 20:12-13.
[86]McLaren, GO 97 [106]. Later McLaren will elaborate on this contention that Jesus died for the sake of all living things rather than just for a world of sinful human beings (pp. 238-39 [269]). Since this understanding of the scope of salvation is informed by McLaren's emerging eschatology and, in turn, impacts his perspective on the *missio Dei,* we will pick up this theme again in later chapters on ecclesiology and eschatology.
[87]Ibid., pp. 99-100 [108-9]. See also p. 109 [120]n48.

humanity possible (1 Pet 2:24). This is a theological theme that, as we have seen, possesses too much scriptural support to be ignored if we want our doctrine of salvation (and our gospel) to be faithful to the biblical text. Thus, the soteriologies of my dialogue partners constitute *unbalanced overcorrections* to the earlier paradigm's doctrine of salvation. Overreacting to a soteriology that often is too *eschatologically* focused, they are guilty of proffering one that is too *existentially* fixated. In the place of a doctrine of salvation that focuses too narrowly on the *objective* nature of the cross-work of Jesus, they are promoting one that fixates too intently on its *subjective* impact.[88]

Though this overreaction is to some degree understandable, it is still unacceptable in terms of both the primary and secondary goals of this book. Whether or not it has anything to do with the street preacher's salvation harangue or the psychological sensibilities of our post-Christian peers, such an accommodation of the gospel, involving as it does a rehabilitation rather than recontextualization of the doctrine of salvation, is simply not permissible if we want to do justice to Jude 3 as well as 1 Corinthians 9:20-22. Neither is it helpful in terms of a doctrine of salvation that can unite rather than separate traditional, missional and emerging evangelicals.

WHITHER A BIBLICALLY AND MISSIONALLY FAITHFUL SOTERIOLOGY?

Built into my analysis of the soteriologies of my two dialogue partners have been some lengthy lists of biblical passages which serve to belie some of their principal arguments. For example, one litany of references indicated places where Scripture teaches that we human beings bear some responsibility for the condition of our own hearts and are not mere victims of a theological deprivation unavoidably experienced in the process of growing up. Another list referred to the many biblical passages that speak of the crucial importance of a repentance that in-

---

[88]Unfortunately even their existential understanding of salvation does not take seriously the need for our fallen human nature to be transformed, regenerated, renewed with the glorified humanity of Christ. We, in ourselves, do not need to be changed, in the view of Borg and McLaren, just our actions and ideas.

volves remorse as well as resolve. Several other lists combine to provide numerous references from different angles to the New Testament's teaching that, rather than simply serving as a good example, Jesus' sacrificial death on the cross actually atoned for "our sins" in anticipation of a postmortem experience of reckoning before a loving but holy God.[89]

It is incredibly important to do more than nod at the impressive number of biblical passages in these lists. All of this biblical material, carefully exegeted and prayerfully reflected on, seems to indicate that Jesus' death on the cross did in fact possess an atoning aspect to it that is objective and eschatological as well as subjective and existential in its impact.[90] Thus, if our doctrine of salvation is to be faithful to the biblical text, we must do more than conceive of Christ's work on the cross as an unmasking of human evil and as an inspirational example of what it means to live with a heart wide open toward God and others (though, as 2 Cor 5:14-15 indicates, it does do this).[91] We must also acknowledge

---

[89]In support of this assertion, Scot McKnight has written: "One of the central elements of the gospel, according to the apostle Paul's statement in 1 Corinthians 15:3, is that 'Christ died *for our sins*.'" See Scot McKnight, *The King Jesus Gospel: The Original Good News Revisited* (Grand Rapids: Zondervan, 2011), p. 87 (as part of his fuller discussion of Jesus' death "for our sins" on pp. 87-89). Also, see Ladd, *Theology of the New Testament,* for an even more in-depth treatment of the apostle Paul's understanding of Jesus' death as sacrificial, vicarious, substitutionary, propitiatory, redemptive and triumphant (pp. 466-77); a brief description of the ransom and penal substitutionary understandings of atonement in 1 Peter (pp. 645-46); and a brief description of the emphasis on propitiation in 1 John (p. 658).

[90]For an interesting argument in support of the use of "proof texts" as a method of citation rather than a hermeneutical method, see R. Michael Allen and Scott R. Swain, "In Defense of Proof-Texting," *Journal of the Evangelical Theological Society* 54, no. 3 (September 2011), pp. 589-606. Though I have not had space to provide here the lengthy "exegetical excurses" ideal for this use of Scripture, I trust I have sufficiently encouraged my readers to engage in a careful and prayerful study of these passages on their own. In addition, I offer here my conviction that there is a distinction between the practice of encouraging readers to consider the import of certain biblical passages for a certain theological position and the "proof-texting" that occurs when an argument is founded on a single or small group of texts in complete disregard for their immediate and canonical contexts, and then offered as all that the Bible has to say on the matter. While always being careful to encourage an adequate, humble exegesis of biblical texts, we should also be on guard against adopting a cynical disdain for the practice of encouraging readers to explore the Scriptures on their own or of failing to cite biblical material that might provide support for a theological position for fear of being labeled a biblicist. For more on this, see Justin Taylor, "In Defense of Proof-Texting" (October 12, 2011), thegospelcoalition.org/blogs/justin taylor/2011/10/12/in-defense-of-proof-texting.

[91]Richard Mouw offers support for this important assertion in, "Getting to the Crux of Calvary: Why Christus Victor Is Not Enough," *Christianity Today,* April 26, 2012, www.christianitytoday .com/ct/2012/may/getting-to-the-crux-of-calvary.html?start=1.

that salvation is about much more than receiving new "saving teaching" that enables us to escape the chain of bad actions and consequences that have plagued us thus far and learn to live more wisely in future.

Furthermore, a biblically faithful doctrine of salvation must also intentionally proffer an eschatological hope that goes beyond this life to the age to come.[92] Indeed, given the fact that there is an eschatological element present in the contexts in which most New Testament references to "hope" (Greek *elpis*) occur, and that, in addition to its forty-two references to "eternal life" (various forms of the Greek *zōē aiōnios*) the New International Version of the New Testament refers to such concepts as "eternal redemption" (Heb 9:12; Greek *aiōnian lytrōsin*), an "eternal inheritance" (Heb 9:15; Greek *aiōniou klēronomias*),[93] the experience of "eternal glory" (2 Cor 4:17; 2 Tim 2:10; 1 Pet 5:10; Greek *aionion baros doxēs, doxēs aiōniou* and *aiōnion autou doxan*, respectively), an "eternal kingdom" (2 Pet 1:11; Greek *aiōnion basileian*) and the prospect of being with Christ "forever" (2 Jn 1:1-3; Greek *eis ton aiōna*), it seems that a biblically faithful message of salvation cannot help but also include what is considered by some emerging Christians to be the unthinkable—a significant (though not sole) focus on the afterlife![94] Moreover, for such a focus on the afterlife to be truly biblically faithful, it needs to offer a thoughtful and careful treatment of those biblical passages that indicate that the salvation Jesus effected in this world rescues sinful human beings from an experience of divine wrath (Greek *orgē*),[95] as well as some negative consequences for persistent human rebellion the apostolic authors described as "eternal fire" (Mt 18:8; 25:41; Greek *pyr to aiōnion;* Jude 1:7; Greek *pyros aiōniou*),

---

[92]See Acts 23:6; 24:15; 26:6-8; Rom 5:1-10; 8:18-25; 12:12; 1 Cor 15:19; Eph 1:3-14, 18; Col 1:3-5, 21-23, 27; 1 Thess 1:2-10; 2:19; 4:13-18; 5:1-11; 2 Thess 2:1-16; 1 Tim 4:6-10; 6:11-19; Tit 1:1-2; 2:11-14; 3:3-7; Heb 6:9-11; 10:19-25; 1 Pet 1:3-5, 13, 17-21; 1 Jn 3:1-3.

[93]Other New Testament passages that refer to an "inheritance" in an eschatological sense include: Mt 25:34; Acts 20:32; Eph 1:3-14, 18; 5:5; Col 1:10-14; 3:23-24; Heb 9:15; and 1 Pet 1:3-5.

[94]Of course, eternal life can be thought of as a present experience, but according to New Testament scholar George Ladd, the teaching of Jesus seems to have been that "inheriting eternal life and entering into the Kingdom of God are synonymous with entering into the Age to Come," something Jesus associated with "the final and total destruction of the devil and his angels." Ladd, *Theology of the New Testament*, p. 62.

[95]For example, see Jn 3:36; Rom 2:5-8; 5:9-10; Eph 2:1-7; 5:1-14; Col 3:1-11; 1 Thess 1:4-10; 2:13-16; 5:1-11.

"eternal punishment" (Mt 25:46; Greek *kolasin aiōnion*), "eternal de-struction" (2 Thess 1:9; Greek *olethron aiōnion*) and "eternal judgment" (Heb 6:1-2; Greek *krimatos aiōniou*).

In pointing out the presence of biblical passages such as these it is not my intention to wade into the hell debate,[96] nor to argue for or against the notion of the annihilation of the wicked,[97] but simply to draw attention to the fact that, according to the Bible, sin is a much more serious matter than the emerging soteriology seems willing to concede; Jesus' death is atoning as well as inspiring; and the intended effect of Christian salvation has to do with our eternal destiny as well as our current existential experience. For sure, the Bible does not limit Christian salvation to penal substitution.[98] Still, the task before us is to forge a message of Christian salvation that is faithful to these three biblically supported themes while also remaining mindful of the lack of appreciation among our contemporaries for the street preacher's ministry method.[99]

---

[96]I am referring of course to the controversy created by the publication of Rob Bell's *Love Wins: A Book About Heaven, Hell and the Fate of Every Person Who Ever Lived* (New York: Harper-Collins, 2011). See also the responses to this work offered by Mark Galli, *God Wins: Heaven, Hell, and Why the Good News Is Better Than Love Wins* (Carol Stream, IL: Tyndale House Books, 2012) and Francis Chan and Preston Sprinkle, *Erasing Hell: What God Said About Eternity, and the Things We Made Up* (Colorado Springs: David C. Cook, 2011).

[97]Indeed, I am quite aware that even a traditional evangelical such as John Stott was led by his analysis of these biblical passages to embrace the annihilationist perspective. See David L. Edwards and John R. W. Stott, *Evangelical Essentials: A Liberal Evangelical Dialogue* (Downers Grove: IL: InterVarsity Press, 1989), pp. 312-20.

[98]For example, the New Testament speaks also of reconciliation (2 Cor 5), renewal (being given new natures, renewed, regenerated spirits toward the experience of transformation; Rom 12), even of being sanctified (with Christ's sanctification; Jn 17).

[99]While I end up agreeing with David Bosch's advocacy of a "comprehensive" view of salvation, my concern is that his discussions in *Transforming Mission* titled "Traditional Interpretations of Salvation" (pp. 402-4) and "Toward a Comprehensive Salvation" (pp. 408-10) do not do adequate justice to what the New Testament authors say on this important topic. Historical theological inquiry regarding this doctrine can be instructive, but only after the many New Testament passages that I have listed in this chapter have been worked through in a careful, prayerful manner. Doing so will serve to refute the idea that such a diversity existed among the New Testament authors that it is not possible to find among them a shared, essentially unified, if not uniform, understanding of Christian salvation. My own exegetical and pastoral interaction with these texts leads me to agree with Bruce Nicholls who, speaking more broadly, opines: "The Bible's theological pluralism is a pluralism of complementarity within a single divinely controlled whole." Bruce J. Nicholls, *Contextualization: A Theology of Gospel and Culture* (Vancouver: Regent College Publishing, 1979), p. 44. It is then instructive to discover how the early church fathers seemed to resonate with this shared understanding in a way that eventually took shape in the earliest creeds of the church.

Sin and forgiveness: The surprising center of a biblically faithful soteriology. While Borg is willing to concede that "the language of sin (and forgiveness) dominates the Christian imagination,"[100] he presses on to question "whether 'sin' is the best way to name what is wrong and why we are lost."[101] Likewise, even though early on in *A Generous Orthodoxy* McLaren indicates that the conservative Protestant understanding of Jesus dying to atone for people's sins is a view he can still celebrate,[102] McLaren's apparent disdain for this idea is later evidenced when he asserts that "Protestants will someday see their . . . 'pop-atonement theology' . . . with embarrassment."[103]

What neither Borg nor McLaren seem willing to acknowledge is that the language of sin and forgiveness does not just dominate the Christian imagination, but the Scriptures as well.

We have already seen that forgiveness of sins is a major theme of the New Testament, as is Jesus' atoning and sacrificial death for our sins. While I, along with Borg and McLaren, appreciate Dallas Willard's critique of a gospel that focuses entirely on "sin management" (to the neglect of Christian discipleship),[104] given the place the Bible affords the forgiveness of sins, I do not know how a biblically faithful soteriology can do otherwise than take this theme (as a prelude to a genuine discipleship) seriously. Whatever we think of the street preacher's method, a careful reading of the New Testament seems to mandate that we proclaim the atoning and sacrificial death of Christ as key to our experience of justification, reconciliation, adoption, redemption, spiritual healing, liberation and so on. Just because this focus on sin and forgiveness is currently not a fashionable tenet of faith does not make it untrue or unimportant.

But what is it about sin that makes it so serious—serious enough to require such a monumental sacrifice in order to achieve forgiveness? And how might the seriousness of sin be communicated to a post-Christian society? Questions such as these are at the heart of a missional orthodoxy.

---

[100]Borg, HC 165.
[101]Ibid., p. 166.
[102]McLaren, GO 45-66 [51-74].
[103]Ibid., p. 126 [138-39].
[104]Willard, *Divine Conspiracy,* pp. 41-58.

Earlier in this chapter we noted how Borg scorns the idea that the root meaning of sin is "disobedience."[105] For Borg and others, the notion that at the heart of the peril we humans face is a simple failure on our part to obey some divine laws is reflective of a flawed understanding of God and serves to overemphasize a forensic (legal) understanding of the cause of our being "lost."[106] We need to remember that, according to Borg, we must choose between viewing God as an "ancient king," a "law-giver and judge who has requirements that must be met," or as a "God of love and justice" (i.e., justice in the sense that he is committed to caring for the poor and oppressed).[107] The view of God as a lawgiver and judge, Borg suggests, is responsible for the earlier paradigm's mistaken understanding of Jesus' death "as the sacrifice that makes forgiveness and salvation possible."[108]

However, there are many passages in the Bible that refer to "disobedience" as a critical factor in the rupture between God and humanity.[109] Furthermore, there are also many passages which suggest that the reason why God takes human disobedience so seriously, so personally, is because at its heart it is not simply a disregard for his *laws,* but a basic disrespect for and distrust of his *person*—who he is, his good purposes for his creation, the very nature of love, his commitment to overcome evil and put things right, and so on.[110] According to Darrell Guder, "To be a sinner meant to be lost before God, for human sin is rebellion against the will of God, which results from human intention and leads to disobedient actions."[111] This explains why forty-five of the fifty times the English word "unfaithful" appears in the New International Version of the Bible (translating such Hebrew words as *māʿal,* connoting the idea of trespass; *bāgad,* connoting the idea of treachery; and *zānâ,* connoting the idea of marital infidelity), it refers to someone's unfaithfulness

---

[105]See Borg, HC 166.
[106]Ibid.
[107]Ibid.
[108]Ibid., p. 75.
[109]For example, see Neh 9:26; Lk 1:17; Rom 5:19; 10:21; 11:30-32; Eph 2:1-2; 5:6, 12; Tit 1:16; 3:3; Heb 2:2; 4:6, 11; 11:31.
[110]For example, see Lev 26:40; 1 Sam 2:12, 17, 30; 2 Sam 12:9-10; Job 21:13-15; Ps 10:2-13; 28:3-5; 36:1-2; 68:21; 73:3-11; 75:4-5; 94:1-7; 119:21; Prov 14:2; Eccles 8:12-13; Jer 9:3; Hos 5:4; Zeph 1:12.
[111]See Guder, *Continuing Conversion,* p. 42.

toward God. Another way to get at this is to point out that the word "law" (Greek *nomos*) occurs in the Pauline corpus of the New Testament no less than ninety-eight times. In Paul's use of the term, "the law" actually represents the moral character, the heart as well as the will, of God. This is why Paul can at times speak of "the law" in a positive, respectful manner (e.g., Rom 3:31; 7:7, 12, 14-25), and why, according to the apostle, to break "the law" is to "dishonor God" himself: "You who brag about the law, do you *dishonor God by breaking the law?*" (Rom 2:23, emphasis added). Thus, for Paul, sin is serious because it is personal. Sin is not simply a matter of breaking *a law*, but of breaking *the Law* and, in so doing, breaking God's heart—that is, disrespecting God by distrusting his very character, heart, mind and intentions.[112]

Timothy Keller is the pastor of a Manhattan church committed to the task of *contextualizing* a biblically informed version of the Christian message for some fairly cynical post-Christian New Yorkers. In his book *The Reason for God,* Keller provides an example of how a soteriology that *takes sin seriously* can prove compelling to a post-Christian audience. Because Keller seems to offer his readers a recontextualization rather than a rehabilitation of the doctrine of sin and salvation (i.e., he maintains the essential message of the street corner preacher while revisioning it for a contemporary audience), I want to present his soteriology as a possible model for other evangelicals—traditional, missional and emerging.

Keller begins a chapter boldly titled "The Problem of Sin" by saying: "It is hard to avoid the conclusion that there is something fundamentally wrong with the world. According to Christianity, our biggest problem is sin. Yet the concept of 'sin' is offensive or ludicrous to many. This is often because we don't understand what Christians mean by the term."[113] Keller then proceeds to ground his understanding of the primary meaning of sin *not* in the notion of "breaking divine rules" but in Søren Kierkegaard's suggestion that sin is "the despairing [and, hence, disrespectful] refusal to find your deepest identity in your relationship and

---

[112]For an excellent (if brief) treatment of Paul's understanding sin, see Ladd, *Theology of the New Testament,* pp. 444-45.
[113]Keller, *Reason for God,* p. 159.

service to God. Sin is seeking to become oneself, to get an identity, apart from him."[114] Elaborating on this idea, Keller says that "according to the Bible, the primary way to define sin is not just the doing of bad things, but the making of good things into *ultimate* things. It is seeking to establish a sense of self by making something else more central to your significance, purpose, and happiness than your relationship with God."[115] This is, at heart, an act of idolatry—an extreme unfaithfulness toward the God who created us and whose image we bear whether we are inclined to acknowledge it or not.

Keller goes on to explain that this identity-building dynamic is universal: "Every person must find *some* way to 'justify their existence,' and to stave off the universal fear that they're 'a bum.'"[116] He also makes the following comparison: "In more traditional cultures, the sense of worth and identity comes from fulfilling duties to family and giving service to society. In our contemporary individualistic culture, we tend to look to our achievements, our social status, our talents, or our love relationships."[117] The point is that apart from God "there are an infinite variety of identity-bases. Some get their sense of 'self' from gaining and wielding power, others from human approval, others from self-discipline and control. But everyone is building their identity on something."[118]

Keller's cultural sensitivity (and an incarnational approach to gospel recontextualization) is apparent here. Given the current identity crisis produced by the postmodern critique of life-shaping metanarratives,[119] Keller's use of an existential understanding of sin which, while doing justice to the biblical notion of sin as disrespect, focuses on the contemporary tendency toward flawed, idolatrous approaches to identity formation, is a compassionate, contextually sensitive strategy that avoids the charge of accommodation precisely because it ends up affirming the biblical teaching concerning the seriousness of sin.

Keller goes on to treat the personal, social and cosmic consequences of

---

[114]Ibid., 162.
[115]Ibid., emphasis original.
[116]Ibid., p. 164.
[117]Ibid.
[118]Ibid.
[119]See chapter seven above.

sin. At the personal level, he observes that since the attempt to forge an identity apart from our relationship with God is "inherently unstable," by doing so we are setting ourselves up to experience huge amounts of neurotic fear, self-loathing, or bitter resentment toward anyone or anything who hinders our being, doing or obtaining that to which we ascribe "ultimate value."[120] At the social level, Keller argues that the loss of the doctrine of original sin and the near ubiquitous attempt to circumvent God in the identity-formation process combine to produce the kind of pride and selfishness that lead to such social ills as the demonization of the other in general, and racism, classism and sexism in particular.[121]

It is when he describes the cosmic consequences of sin that Keller subtly reintroduces the idea that a biblical understanding of sin cannot help but include the dynamic of human disobedience—a disregard for God's instruction and person that leads to estrangement (rather than vice versa).[122] Having pointed out that, according to Genesis 1–2, the pre-fall world was filled with *shalom,* which not only means "peace" but also "absolute wholeness—full, harmonious, joyful, flourishing life,"[123] Keller goes on to explain how and why the disobedience of human beings impacted all of creation:

> The devastating loss of *shalom* through sin is described in Genesis 3. We are told that as soon as we determined to serve ourselves instead of God—as soon as we abandoned living for and enjoying God as our highest good—the created world became broken. Human beings are so integral to the fabric of things that when human beings turned from God the entire warp and woof of the world unraveled. Disease, genetic disorders, famine, natural disasters, aging, and death itself are as much a result of sin as oppression, war, crime, and violence. We have lost God's *shalom*—physically, spiritually, socially, psychologically, culturally. Things now fall apart. In Romans 8, Paul says that the entire world is now "in bondage to decay" and "subject to futility" and will not be put right until we are put right.[124]

---

[120]Ibid., pp. 164-67.
[121]Ibid., pp. 167-69.
[122]Ibid., pp. 169-70.
[123]Ibid., p. 170.
[124]Ibid., emphasis original.

In other words, according to Keller, the practice of sin is an inherently self-sabotaging course of action that, in both an objective and subjective manner, adversely affects our relationships with God, ourselves, our neighbors and the cosmos itself. Thus sin is indeed at the heart of the human problem!

Jesus' death: A "substitutional sacrifice." Keller also explains what it is that God the Creator and Lord of the universe has done to put us, and creation itself, in the right again with him. In a chapter titled "The (True) Story of the Cross" Keller addresses a central soteriological issue: "Why did Jesus have to die? Couldn't God just forgive us?"[125] The answer to these two crucial questions, according to Keller, is that Jesus had to die because *real forgiveness* and *real love* require a costly suffering on the part of the one doing the forgiving and the loving.

Put in socioeconomic terms, the logic of *forgiveness* says that any serious offense between two people necessarily creates a moral debt that someone has to bear if reconciliation is ever to take place. Keller points out that it is impossible for this moral debt to simply be ignored. When such a debt is incurred there are only two real options (a true antithesis!). On the one hand, we can "seek ways to make the perpetrators suffer for what they have done." On the other hand, we can forgive, which means "refusing to make [the perpetrator] pay for what they did." But this is easier said than done, Keller asserts, because

> to refrain from lashing out at someone when you want to do so with all your being is *agony.* It is a form of suffering. You not only suffer the original loss of happiness, reputation, and opportunity, but now you forgo the consolation of inflicting the same on them. You are absorbing the debt, taking the cost of it completely on yourself instead of taking it out of the other person. It hurts terribly. Many people say it feels like a kind of death.[126]

This, says Keller, is what God in Christ was doing on the cross—bearing the cost of our sins while at the same time honoring moral justice. It is not that God, having unmasked human evil, simply winked

---

[125]Ibid., p. 192.
[126]Ibid., pp. 188-89.

at it, as if to say, "Let's just pretend that the fall in general, or your sin in particular, never happened. Be inspired by this act of forbearance on my part to try to do better in the future." No, there was a real, objective, moral debt that stood between God and sinful human beings. God was in Christ bearing the cost of that debt himself so that, while maintaining his own commitment to moral justice, he could also justify and reconcile to himself obviously sinful human beings (see Rom 3:21-26).

Keller goes on to explain the logic of *love* as involving a similar suffering for the sake of the other. Keller explains that "in the real world of relationships it is impossible to love people with a problem or a need without in some sense sharing or even changing places with them."[127] Whether we are talking about helping a hurting friend, nurturing our children, or providing a warm bed for a homeless person, a certain sacrifice on our part is involved. Indeed, says Keller, "All life-changing love toward people with serious needs is a substitutional sacrifice. If you become personally involved with them, in some way, their weaknesses flow toward you as your strengths flow toward them."[128]

Having made this observation that loving others always involves a *substitutional sacrifice,* Keller then explains the connection between Jesus' sacrificial death for the forgiveness of sins and the unmasking of evil that also occurred during his passion. He inquires, "How can God be a God of love if he does not become personally involved in suffering the same violence, oppression, grief, weakness, and pain that we experience?"[129] Fully aware of the postmodern, postcolonial concern for the marginalized, poor and oppressed, Keller recontextualizes a balanced, biblically informed understanding of the gospel for his post-Christian readers:

> Therefore the Cross, when properly understood, cannot possibly be used to encourage the oppressed to simply accept violence. When Jesus suffered for us, he was honoring justice. But when Jesus suffered with us he was identifying with the oppressed of the world, not with their oppressors. All life-changing love entails an exchange, a reversal of places,

---

[127]Ibid., p. 193.
[128]Ibid., p. 194.
[129]Ibid., p. 195.

but here is the Great Reversal. God, in the place of ultimate power, re-verses places with the marginalized, the poor, and the oppressed.[130]

The pattern of the Cross means that the world's glorification of power, might, and status is exposed and defeated. On the Cross Christ wins through losing, triumphs through defeat, achieves power through weakness and service, comes to wealth via giving all away.[131]

To understand why Jesus had to die it is important to remember both the result of the Cross (costly forgiveness of sins) and the pattern of the Cross (reversal of the world's values). On the cross neither justice nor mercy loses out—both are fulfilled at once. Jesus's death was necessary if God was going to take justice seriously and still love us.[132]

Keller seems to be proffering a pendulum-taming, biblically and mis-sionally faithful soteriology that does not focus *solely* on either God's justice or his mercy. Neither, according to Keller, must we embrace an interpretation of the cross that allows for *only* an objective or subjective impact. The death of Jesus produced both a *result*—the forgiveness of our sins that had produced a genuine moral debt before God—and a *pattern*—a stunning reversal of the world's values and defeat of its ability to press us into its mold.

Christian salvation: From here to eternity. After providing a Christian understanding of "where we came from, what's wrong with us, and how it can be fixed,"[133] Keller goes on to, in so many words, address the most famous of all existential queries: Why? What is this life all about? In the process, he provides an alternative response to the false antithesis between a doctrine of salvation that mainly emphasizes a tem-poral impact and one that myopically focuses only on getting people to heaven. Keller ends up promoting a recontextualized soteriology that heartily affirms God's intention to spend eternity with people created in his image but also challenges the idea that the hope of this future expe-rience should lead in the here and now to an escapist mentality and failure to engage in social action and creation care.

Keller begins the chapter titled "The Dance of God" by offering a

---

[130]Ibid., pp. 195-96.
[131]Ibid., p. 196.
[132]Ibid., p. 197.
[133]Ibid., p. 213.

cogent argument for the idea that God, as a triune being, is "essentially, eternally interpersonal love."[134] His own version of a theological realism has as its beginning point the following conviction: Ultimate reality "is a community of persons who know and love one another. That is what the universe, God, history, and life is all about."[135] Citing the work of American theologian Jonathan Edwards, Keller affirms the theological presupposition that "within God is a community of persons pouring glorifying, joyful love into one another. . . . That is why God is infinitely happy, because there is an 'other-orientation' at the heart of his being, because he does not seek his own glory but the glory of others."[136]

This theological presupposition is significant in one regard because it suggests a reason why Scripture takes sin so seriously. An innate, inherited tendency toward self-centered behaviors that end up being dismissive of God and destructive to ourselves and others is antithetical to the very purpose of human existence. As Keller puts it, "We [Christians] believe the world was made by a God who is a community of persons who have loved each other for all eternity. You were made for mutually self-giving, other-directed love. Self-centeredness destroys the fabric of what God has made."[137]

Another reason why Keller's theological realism is significant is that it hints at an answer to that preeminent existential question: "Why are we here?" Implied in Keller's understanding of ultimate reality as a divine community of three persons—Father, Son and Holy Spirit—eternally engaged in knowing, loving and joyfully serving one another is that this life is all about those who bear the *imago Dei* likewise becoming enabled to know, love and joyfully serve the *other* (Mt 22:34-40). The metaphor Keller uses for this idea is that of a "divine dance" that has been, is now, and forever will be engaged in by the members of the Trinity. Everything about the biblical story, says Keller, can be related to this divine dance. It is the reason why humanity was created, redeemed

---

[134]Ibid., p. 216.

[135]Ibid.

[136]Ibid., pp. 217-218. See the discussion of the "social Trinity" back in chapter four (pp. 173-75).

[137]Ibid., p. 217. I wish to note in passing how connotative of the idea of a spiritual malignancy is Keller's understanding of human sin. I will return to this type of conceptualization later in this chapter.

and, along with the cosmos itself, will someday be restored.[138] We have been invited to the dance—the divine dance of love and interpersonal caring and service that will go on forever! Keller also ties the cross work of Christ to this divine dance:

> We lost the dance. The dance of joyful, mutually self-giving relationships is impossible in a world in which everyone is stationary, trying to get everything else to orbit around them.
>
> However, God does not leave us there. The Son of God was born into the world to begin a new humanity, a new community of people who could lose their self-centeredness, begin a God-centered life, and, as a result, slowly but surely have all other relationships put right as well. Paul calls Jesus "the last Adam." As the first Adam was tested in the Garden of Eden, the last Adam (Jesus) was tested in the Garden of Gethsemane. The first Adam knew that he would live if he obeyed God about the tree. But he didn't. The last Adam was also tested by what Paul called a "tree," the Cross. Jesus knew that he would be crushed if he obeyed his Father. And he still did.
>
> Why did Jesus die for us? What was Jesus getting out of it? Remember, he already had a community of joy, glory, and love. He didn't need us. So what benefit did he derive from this? Not a thing. And that means that when he came into the world and died on the cross to deal with our sins, he was circling and serving *us*. "I have given them the glory that you gave me" (John 17). He began to do with us what he had been doing with the Father and the Spirit from all eternity. He centers upon us, loving us without benefit to himself.[139]

It is true that as Keller proceeds to discuss the "future of the dance," he describes the age to come only in positive terms. However, we should note that earlier in the book Keller included a frank and earnest discussion of the topic of hell. Though Borg and McLaren might consider it a missionally futile move to proffer in our contemporary time and place a doctrine of salvation which says that one of the reasons Jesus died was to rescue people from a self-imposed experience of an everlasting, conscious, painful separation from a life-giving God, Keller is

---

[138]Ibid., pp. 217-23.
[139]Ibid., pp. 220-21.

doing it—and with no little degree of missional fruitfulness![140]

Given the kinds of courses I teach, I will from time to time receive emails requesting advice regarding spirituality and ministry matters. One such email arrived in my inbox just this week. Its content serves to support my claim that a doctrine of salvation that is faithful to both the biblical text and the missional task will need to possess both an objective and subjective impact. To be more specific, such a soteriology will need to focus on the seriousness of sin, the sacrificial death of Jesus by which our fallen humanity finds healing (as well as enlightenment), and the hope of both eschatological and existential rescue.

This email from one of my students described a friend whom the student was concerned about. The student—not a religion major, but someone interested in being missionally faithful—described this non-Christian friend as very "skeptical," "intelligent" and "careful" about "what he chooses to believe or not to believe." The issue they had been discussing was "life after death." When my student asked him if he believed in an afterlife, this non-Christian friend replied that he did not believe in hell and was not certain of a heaven or any sort of afterlife. He went on to explain that while the idea that this life may be all there is to human existence used to frighten him, it no longer does. Why? He has come to believe that all that matters is doing good here and now, experiencing in the process all the "heaven" he will ever need.

A moment's reflection will reveal that this young man is articulating a position not only regarding the afterlife, but the meaning of this life. It was because my student found herself not knowing what to say in response to a friend so satisfied with his own moral goodness, so certain of the fact that no postmortem judgment is forthcoming, and so comfortable with the thought that it is in this life that "heaven" is to be experienced, that she sent me the email asking for help.

So, what do we say to someone who holds that an afterlife is simply not important to them because they are essentially experiencing as much heaven as they will ever need in and through their "doing what's right" here and now? While a downplaying (or outright rejection) of the

---

[140]Ibid., pp. 68-83.

notions of "righteousness, self-control and the judgment to come" (see Acts 24:25) would certainly seem to play well with the young man in question, in what sense does this ministry approach offer any sort of *rescue* to someone who is already convinced that he, as a nonparticipant in any faith tradition, is already "saved" in the sense that he is doing "what's right" and experiencing "heaven" in the process? If salvation is *ultimately* (despite any rhetoric to the contrary) conceived of as becoming the kind of person who is making the world a better place right now, then it would seem that the emerging paradigm's soteriology would have nothing to offer my student's friend except perhaps a "Well done, you!" and some encouragement to keep up the good work.

Of course, it's possible, tempting even, to embrace a soteriological inclusivism which would hold that this young man serves as an example of an "anonymous Christian" who is saved by the atoning death of Christ even though he does not know it.[141] While a theological humility requires that we cannot rule this possibility out,[142] and as much as we might like for a soteriological inclusivism or even pluralism to prove true, the biblical arguments for these perspectives have not been strong enough to produce within a majority of evangelicals a wholehearted confidence. This lack of confidence may be significant missionally. For sure, it's up to God, not us, who is ultimately saved. And, once again, I personally am pretty sure that some folks have been, and are being saved though they have not explicitly called on Christ (e.g., "Old Testament saints, infants who die young, and the severely mentally challenged").[143] But with so much at stake, is it appropriate to feel a freedom when interacting with nonbelievers such as the young man described in my stu-

---

[141]The concept of an "anonymous Christian," first introduced by Roman Catholic theologian Karl Rahner, suggests that people who live by their conscience and who love in a self-sacrificing manner someone or something bigger and other than themselves will be eternally saved whether they have explicit faith in Christ or not. See Karl Rahner, Paul Imhof and Hubert Biallowons, *Karl Rahner in Dialogue: Conversations and Interviews 1965-1982* (New York: Crossroad, 1986), p. 135; see also Karl Rahner, *Theological Investigations*, vol. 14, trans. David Bourke (London: Darton, Longman & Todd, 1976), p. 283; and David Bosch's summary and critique of Rahner's concept in *Transforming Mission*, pp. 492, 494-95.

[142]See Daniel Clendenin, "The Only Way: Answering the Argument That All Religions Are More or Less True," *Christianity Today*, January 12, 1998, www.christianitytoday.com/ct/1998/january 12/8t1034.html.

[143]Ibid.

dent's email to refrain from doing our best to contextualize the apostle's kerygmatic call: "Repent and be baptized, every one of you, in the name of Jesus Christ for the forgiveness of your sins. And you will receive the gift of the Holy Spirit" (Acts 2:38)? Even many missional and emerging evangelicals share the conviction that any soteriological perspective that doesn't mandate a ministry approach which lovingly points people toward the experience of repentance, baptism and discipleship toward a lifetime of Spirit-empowered service to Christ as Lord is not going to be fully faithful to the biblical text or the missional task.

The email I received from my student serves as a sobering illustration of the reality that because we live in a world where many of our peers are absolutely convinced that any sense of "fall" they might have experienced growing up has been sufficiently overcome by the dint of their own efforts at self-improvement, it is vitally necessary that the street preacher's message not be completely abandoned. Though unwilling to endorse the street preacher's confrontational method, I am willing to wonder: How can the Spirit of mission "prove the world to be in the wrong about sin and righteousness and judgment" (Jn 16:8) if the salvation message proclaimed by the people he indwells and empowers for witness never refers to these things? For sure, it is not *our* job to convict people of sin or to convince them of their need for righteousness in the face of a judgment to come. But that does not mean that the Holy Spirit might not want to use us as ministry agents who, within the context of an ongoing, loving, caring relationship, pose to our self-righteous peers such questions as:

- What if there is such a thing as sin, and it is more serious than we suspect?

- What if the essence of sin is not disobedience but *disrespect*—the product of a spiritual pride that, because it causes people to dismiss God's person and disobey God's will (see Gen 3:4-5) also causes them to behave in ways that are ultimately self-destructive and hurtful to others?

- What if sin (i.e., spiritual pride), is like a deadly virus that can be present in someone's life without their being aware of it?

- What if it's possible that unless our humanity is healed (rather than

A MISSIONAL ORTHODOXY

simply enlightened), the spiritual disease that is sin *will* eventually manifest itself, wreaking havoc in our lives spiritually, physically, psychologically, socially, culturally, ecologically, and so on (Gen 3–11)?

- What if human pride is like a spiritual malignancy that, because it "destroys the fabric of what God has made," is not something he can simply slap a Band-Aid on, but must quarantine for eternity for the sake of moral justice and the welfare of the cosmos?

- What if this is what hell really is: a place of eternal quarantine which, because it is completely void of a loving God's life-giving presence and, therefore, any sense of human flourishing, can also be described as a place of eternal torment (Lk 16:19-31)?[144]

- What if God never intended human beings to experience hell (see Mt 25:41) and is doing everything possible to keep anyone and everyone from choosing this awful fate (2 Pet 3:8-9; Jn 3:16-17)?

- What if the cure for this spiritual disease—the essence of which is pride—is to humble ourselves (Mt 18:3) and gratefully embrace the healing of our humanity available to us through an existential surrender to the loving lordship of God's Son, Jesus Christ (Rom 10:5-10)?

---

[144]Again, it is not my intention to suggest that a cardinal component of a missional orthodoxy is a particular view of the eternal state. My commitment to an orthodoxy that is modest rather than overreaching in scope fairly mandates that I not provide in this work detailed arguments for or against the notions of soteriological universalism versus the eternal, conscious suffering of the impenitent wicked versus their ultimate annihilation. It is because I suspect that many of my evangelical readers, whether traditional, merging or emergent, are not convinced of the universalist position that I offer here the metaphor of an eternal quarantine as a *possible* way of speaking about hell which, because of the way it accords with our understanding of the nature of physical malignancies, and the manner in which it deemphasizes the idea that hell is about retribution—i.e., a vengeful God ultimately having his way with impertinent creatures who owe their very existence to him—might make sense to many of our post-Christian contemporaries, their postcolonial, anti-imperialistic sensibilities notwithstanding. The challenge for those who hold such a view, however, is to *reconcile* (no pun intended) the quarantine or exile model of hell with those biblical passages that speak of the cosmic and universal reconciliation and consummation of all things in the eschaton (e.g., 1 Cor 15:28; Col 1:20; Phil 2:9-11). For more on the need for any view of hell to deal with the passages just cited, see Shawn Bawulski, "Reconciliationism, A Better View of Hell: Reconcilationsim and Eternal Punishment," in *Journal of the Evangelical Theological Society*, 56, no. 1 (2013): 123-38. For those interested in learning more about the quarantine/exile model, a good place to start is the very accessible online article titled "Deconstructing the Traditional Hell" (October 2012), http://matthew2262.wordpress.com/2012/10/14/deconstructing-the-traditional-hell/ and a paper this article references: Eleonore Stump, "Dante's Hell, Aquinas' Moral Theory, and the Love of God," *Canadian Journal of Philosophy*, 16, no. 2 (1986): 181-98.

- What if there is, in truth, a joy to be experienced in an eternal kingdom of God that renders any attempt on our part at present to presume on the nature of "heaven," ludicrous in the extreme?

Furthermore, because I believe that my student's friend, as described in the email, fairly accurately represents the mindset of many members of the emerging generations, I might go on to lovingly yet boldly make the following three inquiries:

First, how is it that you can be so uncertain about an afterlife in general, but so very certain about hell in particular? Can you see how the uncertain-yet-certain position you espouse can seem a bit arbitrary?

Second, it sounds as though you see yourself as someone who doesn't need God because you're good without him. But what happens when, in all truth, you're not so good? What happens when you find yourself doing (or not doing) to someone else, something that you wouldn't (or would) want that person to do to you? What happens when you become aware that you live in a world where there are others who are much better at doing good than you? Speaking existentially, don't these kinds of experiences have the potential to make you question your worth, whether you are the person you should be? If not, why not? In other words, haven't you built your sense of self, your identity, on an inherently unstable foundation? What if there were a better foundation, one that could provide you with an even greater degree of existential peace, joy, hope, meaning, purpose and empowerment in this life, while also preparing you for whatever cosmic justice-ensuring reckoning that might await us in an afterlife after all?

Third, since you readily acknowledge some genuine ambivalence with regard to the possibility of an afterlife, and given the possibility that there might be an even better foundation on which to ground your sense of self, what would it hurt for you to "taste and see" for yourself whether Jesus is risen and real or not?[145] Wouldn't such an existential "taste test" be the "scientific," intellectually honest, humble and smart thing to do? *What could it hurt to hang out with me and my faith community for a while, prayerfully giving Jesus a chance to reveal himself to you? If he*

---

[145]See Ps 34:8; Jn 1:37-39, 44-46; 4:42.

doesn't, what will you have lost? If he does, how do you put a value on what you will have gained?

Once again, I wish to reiterate that these kinds of questions need not, should not, be posed to our post-Christian peers in a confrontational, "drive-by" manner. In fact, we should not only make sure that such questions are part of a respectful, conversational, relationship-affirming dialogue, we should also steep the whole process in prayer, inviting the guidance and anointing of the Spirit of mission, and in this way make ourselves available to be used by the Spirit in a prophetic, missionally faithful manner.

Granted, this is not exactly the street preacher's message and definitely not his manner. Then again, the purpose of this chapter was not to apologize for the street preacher, but to suggest that there is a third, biblically and missionally faithful alternative to the false antithesis which holds that we must either affirm the street preacher's doctrine of salvation or embrace the one promoted by the emerging paradigm. We need not, must not, make this ministry mistake! I find great support for a commitment to avoid a rehabilitation of the Christian message of salvation in a passage written by missional ministry expert Darrell Guder. It almost seems as though he has one or both of my dialogue partners in mind here:

> "In fulfillment of his mission, Jesus died the death of atonement on the cross for his friends and his enemies." At this point, the good news begins to be a problem for many modern people. A gospel of a loving, compassionate God is possibly still welcomed news. A gospel that speaks of new beginnings and envisions a radically different kind of world may gain a hearing, even if it uses the somewhat arcane language of "the kingdom of God." A gospel that is candid about the struggles, injustices, and cruelty of human existence will possibly be respected. But a gospel that unswervingly focuses on the New Testament's central emphasis, Jesus' death upon the cross, will encounter resistance. Paul spoke about the continuing experience of the church when he described the proclamation of Christ crucified as "a stumbling block to Jews and foolishness to Gentiles" (1 Cor. 1:22).[146]

---

[146]Guder, *Continuing Conversion*, p. 40. The citation is from Peter Stuhlmacher, "Die Mitte der

Guder seems to suggest that the correct missional response to any resistance we might face from our post-Christian peers to the biblical message of Jesus' atoning death on the cross is to follow Paul's lead and preach it anyway (1 Cor 2:1-2; Rom 1:16)! Indeed, he goes on to affirm, "The starting point of our proclamation is Christ and Christ crucified."[147] I am convinced that the Spirit of mission can, even in our day, use such a ministry message to bring people into a holistic experience of the kingdom of God. Such a ministry message is required if we are to see greater numbers of traditional, missional and emerging evangelicals functioning as colleagues rather than competitors in the ministry contextualization endeavor.

In the next chapter we will delve even more deeply into the questions of ministry focus, approach and style. In the process we will shift our attention ever so subtly from issues related to orthodoxy to those concerning orthopraxy. I trust the reader is ready to wrestle with several more false antitheses!

Schrift—biblisch-theologisch betrachtet," in *Wissenschaft und Kirche: Festschrift für Eduard Lohse*, ed. Kurt Aland and Siegfried Meurer (Bielefeld: Luther Verlag, 1989), p. 46.
[147]Guder, *Continuing Conversion*, p. 41. The citation is from World Council of Churches, *Mission and Evangelism: An Ecumenical Affirmation* (Geneva, 1982), paragraph 7.

9

NICE AND NECESSARY

Toward a Missionally Orthodox
Doctrine of the Church

Theologian Roger Olson reminds us that "the Nicene Creed, formulated finally at the First Council of Constantinople in 381 and
widely accepted as the unifying creed of Christendom, says that the
church is *one, holy, catholic and apostolic.* It also confesses belief in
one baptism for the remission of sins."[1] I want to suggest that this article of the creed intends to emphasize both the *nature* of the church
and its *necessity.* With regard to the church's nature, Olson acknowledges that though "Christians agree that the church of Jesus Christ is
one, holy, catholic (universal) and apostolic,"[2] the "diversity of
Christian belief about these matters is extensive and the *disagreements* very profound."[3] These disagreements have been especially
sharp between Protestants and Roman Catholics, dating back five
hundred years to the Protestant Reformation.[4]

However, with respect to the church's necessity, Olson indicates that
historically there has been significant *agreement* between Christians of
all communions:

For much of Christian history, the Great Tradition of Christian thought

---

[1]Roger Olson, *The Mosaic of Christian Belief: Twenty Centuries of Unity and Diversity* (Downers
  Grove, IL: IVP Academic, 2002), p. 289.
[2]Ibid., p. 294.
[3]Ibid., p. 295, emphasis added.
[4]Ibid., pp. 295-97.

held the church, the "body of Christ," in high regard, and even after the undivided visible church split and then fragmented, most Christian leaders and theologians considered the church an important aspect of Christian belief and witness. The very idea of authentic, vital Christianity apart from the church was virtually unheard of before the twentieth century.[5]

Indeed, Olson goes on to state that "the Great Tradition of Christianity, at least up until recently, has included belief in the unity of the church and even the necessity of the church for authentic Christian living if not for salvation itself," and "nowhere in the Great Tradition of Christianity before the twentieth century can one find the uniquely modern phenomenon of 'churchless Christians.'"[6]

Ironically, there is at present even among evangelical Christians a growing acceptance of a religious relativism,[7] which in turn tends to result in an embrace of a "religious universalism" the conviction that, as Bruce Nicholls describes it, "all human beings, not just Christians, are 'part of God's activity in the world and share a common future.'"[8] While many, if not most, evangelicals (traditional, missional and emerging) would affirm the fact that God's concern extends past the Christian community to all humankind, an ecumenical or generalized understanding of the *missio Dei* that leans toward the embrace of a religious universalism will tend to minimize the importance of the church in what God is up to in his creation. According to this understanding of what it means to be missional, "the center of God's activity is 'the human community.' There is nothing particular about the Christian community,

---

[5]Ibid., p. 287.
[6]Ibid., p. 292.
[7]According to a 2007 survey conducted by the Pew Forum on Religion and Public Life, 70 percent of Americans who affiliate themselves with a particular religious tradition nevertheless believe that many religions can lead to eternal life. Astoundingly, it also indicated that more than half (57 percent) of evangelical Protestant church members said they agreed with idea that many religions can lead to eternal life. See "U.S. Religious Landscape Survey" (March 7, 2009), http://religions.pewforum.org/reports#. Furthermore, the research conducted by Ed Stetzer, Richie Stanley and Jason Hayes and reported in *Lost and Found: The Younger Unchurched and the Churches That Reach Them* (Nashville: Broadman & Holman, 2009), p. 51, indicates that 58 percent of American adults between the ages of 20-29, and 67 percent of American adults 30 years or older believe that the God of the Bible is no different from the gods or spiritual beings depicted by world religions such as Islam, Hinduism, Buddhism, etc.
[8]Bruce J. Nicholls, *Contextualization: A Theology of Gospel and Culture* (Vancouver: Regent College Publishing, 1979), p. 28.

whose self-realization does not 'exclude God's purposeful activity in and through other faiths.'"[9] This view insists that "salvation history is the history of the whole of humankind and that 'human history is the arena of God's saving purpose.' At best the Christian community is the 'provisional, the sign of community.'"[10] In other words, there is an understanding of what it means to be missional which tends toward the conviction that, since the cosmic reconciliation God is concerned about allows for all religious faiths to be paths to "salvation," belonging to the Christian church is nice but not necessary.

For sure, the purpose of this chapter is not to defend the Niceno-Constantinopolitan position with respect to the church. That said, it is not only because of what I believe Scripture itself has to say about this theological topic, but the fact that my own faith and ministry journey owes so much to the church in its local expression, that I am more than a little chagrined at the way those promoting the emerging paradigm have, in my opinion, drastically downplayed the historical commitment to the necessity of the Christian church. Even though both Marcus Borg and Brian McLaren refer often to the church, and nowhere explicitly endorse the idea of a "churchless Christian," it is interesting, perhaps even telling, that neither *The Heart of Christianity* nor *A Generous Orthodoxy* contains a discrete, dedicated, detailed discussion of the church's necessity. More than that, for reasons that will become clear, I am concerned that the emerging version of the Christian faith, with its trajectory toward a religious relativism, fails to do justice to the biblical teachings concerning the importance of the Christian church and the connection between water baptism and the forgiveness of sins (i.e., the experience of salvation). Of course, exceptions can occur (e.g., the thief on the cross to whom Jesus promised paradise even though he lacked both water baptism and ecclesial involvement) and I fully recognize that

[9]Ibid.

[10]Ibid. While critical of this missional tack as "an overreaction to Western theology," Nicholls suggests that it is "understandable" in light of the colonial imperialism and insensitivity to cultural values historically associated with Western missionaries. As I have suggested in earlier sections of this work, the challenge for biblically informed Christians in mission is to embrace the idea that there is such a thing as Christian dogma without doing so in a dogmatic and ethnocentric manner.

my own personal faith and ministry journey should not be made normative. Still, a doctrine of the church that is going to be faithful to both the biblical text and the missional task, while avoiding a hypersacramentalist understanding of water baptism (i.e., baptismal regeneration) and the idea that only one denomination is the true church (i.e., hypersectarianism), will nevertheless hold that an eager, genuine participation in the life of a Christian faith community is not just nice but necessary in terms of a complete experience of incorporation into the people of God, the new humanity that exists "in Christ."[11]

Thus, with all this in mind, along with the book's goal of forging an orthodoxy that is faithful to both the biblical text and the missional task, the principal ecclesiological question for this chapter is: *Just how important is it for us evangelicals (traditional, missional and emerging), our post-Christian ministry context notwithstanding, to continue to obey Christ's command for his church to make disciples for him by preaching the gospel and baptizing new believers into a new life devoted to a distinctly Christian discipleship (see Mt 28:18-20; cf. Mk 16:15-16)?* Is there a biblically and missionally faithful doctrine of the church that all evangelicals, despite our sectarian tendencies, can get behind to the glory of God (see Jn 17:20-23)?[12]

THE BIBLICAL CASE FOR THE NECESSITY OF THE CHURCH

It is not uncommon for theologians to argue for the cardinal importance of the church to God's plan for the planet by focusing on his desire to create among human beings a "community of oneness" that can image to the rest of creation the joy-producing "other-orientation" at the heart of the triune Godhead.[13] According to this understanding of the bib-

---

[11]For more on "the biblical notion that without the church there is no salvation," see Ross Hastings, *Missional God, Missional Church: Hope for Re-evangelizing the West* (Downers Grove, IL: IVP Academic, 2012), pp. 70, 131-35.

[12]I should point out that, if this discussion of ecclesiology and the discussion of eschatology in the next chapter, seem weighted toward a discussion of the church's mission, it is because, as indicated in chapter one, it is my conviction that the purpose of all theology is precisely to help the local church fulfill its disciple-making mission to the world it inhabits. This is what a missional orthodoxy is all about!

[13]Gilbert Bilezikian, *Community 101: Reclaiming the Local Church as Community of Oneness* (Grand Rapids: Zondervan, 1997) and Gilbert Bilezikian, *Christianity 101* (Grand Rapids: Zondervan, 1993), pp. 175-226.

lical narrative, the church of Jesus Christ constitutes what God has been up to from before the foundation of the world and is the only thing that will endure from this present age into eternity![14]

Biblical support for the idea that the church Jesus himself founded (see Mt 16:18) is of vital importance to him and the salvation he came into the world to effect is discernible at various places in the New Testament. For example, the dominical reference in Matthew 18 is well known in discussions of the role of the church in the reconciliation of estranged disciples to one another and ultimately to God himself (see Mt 18:15-19). Subsequent contributions to a New Testament ecclesiology that emphasizes the crucial importance of the church include the apostle Paul's reference to Jewish and Gentile church members becoming "one new humanity," "one body," "fellow citizens," "God's people," "members of God's household," a "holy temple in the Lord" and a "dwelling in which God lives by his Spirit" (Eph 2:14-22). See also Paul's highly intimate allusion to the Corinthian congregation as a "pure virgin" betrothed to Jesus (2 Cor 11:1-3), the reference in the letter to the Hebrews to "the church of the firstborn, whose names are written in heaven" (Heb 12:23), and Peter's reference to Christian believers functioning in a collective manner as a "spiritual house" and "holy priesthood, offering spiritual sacrifices acceptable to God through Jesus Christ" (1 Pet 2:5).

Of special significance to a discussion of the importance of the Christian community are Paul's references to the church as Christ's body.[15] Commenting on this Pauline association, Roger Olson writes:

Paul's identification of the church with Christ—which should not be

---

[14]Bilezikian, *Christianity 101*, p. 177. For his part, George Ladd argues for the idea that Jesus intended to create a church and, therefore, for the importance of the church to the cosmic plan of God: "If Jesus' mission was, as we contend, that of inaugurating a time of fulfillment in advance of an eschatological consummation, and if in a real sense the Kingdom of God in his mission invaded history even though in an utterly unexpected form, then it follows that those who receive the proclamation of the Kingdom were viewed not only as the people who would inherit the eschatological Kingdom, but as the people of the Kingdom in the present, and therefore, in some sense of the word, a church." George E. Ladd, *A Theology of the New Testament* (Grand Rapids: Eerdmans, 1993), p. 104. See also p. 117, where Ladd boldly states that even though they must never be completely identified with each other, "there can be no Kingdom without a church—those who have acknowledged God's rule—and there can be no church without God's Kingdom."
[15]For example, 1 Cor 12:12-27; Eph 5:23, 29; Col 1:18, 24.

taken to mean that the church is literally Jesus Christ but should be taken to mean that it is mystically one with him and represents him in a special way—is very revealing. For him and for the early church after the apostles, the corporate community of God's people, united by "one Lord," "one Spirit," "one faith," "one baptism," is the locus of union with Christ. There is no hint of Lone Ranger Christianity in the New Testament; there is no suggestion that a person can be vitally united with Christ and growing spiritually apart from the church. The assumption throughout is that the church is the indispensable vehicle of Christian spiritual life, the locus of Christ's special presence and the Spirit's power.[16]

Finally, we should consider also the remarkable way in which Paul in his first letter to Timothy refers to the church not only as "God's household" but as the "pillar and foundation of the truth" (1 Tim 3:15). Because of Paul's rather consistent habit of speaking of *truth* in a manner rich with soteriological significance,[17] it is my contention that when Paul refers to the church as the "pillar and foundation of the truth," he is doing nothing less than linking the church with the experience of Christian salvation. It is hard to imagine a more superlative expression of the church's importance to human existence and God's plan for the cosmos.

THE BIBLICAL CASE FOR THE IMPORTANCE OF WATER BAPTISM

Not only does the Bible seem to connect the church with Christ and the experience of salvation (in the sense of being included in "God's household" and "God's people"), it also strongly affirms the role which water baptism plays in the conversion and incorporation process.[18] Jesus, in addition to honoring the significance of water baptism by being baptized himself (Mt 3:13-15), commanded his followers to make disciples for him by baptizing new believers into him: "Therefore go and make disciples of all nations, baptizing them in the name of the Father

---

[16]Olson, *Mosaic of Christian Belief,* pp. 289-90.

[17]For example, see Rom 1:18-32; 2:7-11; 15:7-12; 2 Cor 4:1-6; Gal 2:1-5, 11-21; 5:1-7; Eph 1:13-14; 4:14-15, 17-24; 5:6-10; 6:13-14; Col 1:3-6; 2 Thess 2:9-13; 1 Tim 2:3-6; 4:1-3; 6:3-5; 2 Tim 2:15-18, 24-26; 3:1-8; 4:1-4; Tit 1:1-3, 10-16.

[18]For a helpful discussion of the meaning of baptism and its orientation toward a participation in Christian community, see Stanley J. Grenz, *Theology for the Community of God* (Grand Rapids: Eerdmans, 1994), pp. 521-24.

and of the Son and of the Holy Spirit" (Mt 28:19). "Go into all the world and preach the gospel to all creation. Whoever believes and is baptized will be saved, but whoever does not believe will be condemned" (Mk 16:15-16).

The challenge before me here is to indicate how important water baptism is not only to the task of making disciples but also to the experience of salvation itself without at the same time communicating the idea that it is the ritual itself that saves us (a view which an oversimplified reading of such passages as 1 Pet 3:21-22 might understandably produce).[19] In order to accomplish this I want to preface this discussion with the following three observations: First, water baptism is rather consistently portrayed in the book of Acts as the normative manner in which new believers are initiated into the Christian life.[20] In other words, *the practice of immediately baptizing new believers into the Christian life and community of faith does not seem to be viewed as optional in the missional practice of Christians in the apostolic era.*

Second, the importance of water baptism is also evident in the apostle Paul's references to this practice as the sacramental means whereby new believers are initiated into Christ in a mystical, soteriologically significant manner.[21] According to these passages, the believer's baptism points to the reality of Christ's baptism and what it accomplishes for us with Jesus functioning as our high priest. We are not just baptized, but are baptized into him and so into his baptism. While baptism is a sign of the believer's faith, which explains why the book of Acts routinely refers to the presence of explicit faith in the lives of those being baptized,[22] it is not simply faith in the power of faith, but *faith in Christ* and what he has accomplished for us. Thus, the act of being baptized is an act of faithfulness on our part, expressing an existential reliance on the reality of his baptism for us and in our place and in the Holy Spirit's ability to make real and applicable to us the efficacy of Christ's baptism.

Third, at the same time, the fact that water baptism was not "di-

---

[19]For a helpful discussion of whether baptism should be thought of as a divine act, human act or divine-human act, see ibid., pp. 524-27.
[20]See Acts 2:36-41; 8:12, 35-38; 9:17-18; 10:44-48; 16:13-15, 25-34; 18:7-8; 19:1-7; 22:12-16.
[21]For example, see Rom 6:1-4; 1 Cor 10:1-12; Gal 3:26-29.
[22]For example, see Acts 2:41; 8:12-13, 36-38; 16:15, 29-34; 18:7.

vinized," "hyper-ritualized," "overly sacramentalized," or invested with saving power in an *ex opere operato* (i.e., essentially automatic) manner[23] by the apostolic community can be seen in the way the book of Acts indicates that at times the ritual did not result in an immediate bestowal of the Holy Spirit (e.g., Acts 8:14-16; 19:1-7) or was performed after the Spirit had already been received (Acts 10:44-48). This can also be discerned in the way Paul refused to put a *personal* performance of this ritual at the very top of his ministry agenda (see 1 Cor 1:14-17).

On the basis of these three observations, it should be perfectly clear that the baptism of new believers into Christ and the community of faith, while not salvific in and of itself, should nevertheless be seen as much too important to the missional task to be neglected or dismissed out of hand, regardless of the sensibilities at work in any ministry context. Indeed, Roger Olson goes so far as to suggest that a "rejection of the two ordinances of baptism and the Lord's Supper" not only contradicts the Great Tradition of Christian belief,[24] but constitutes a "heresy of neglect."[25]

With all this in mind, my question is: Where in *The Heart of Christianity* or *A Generous Orthodoxy* is a serious discussion of the crucial importance of belonging to the church (the "community of oneness") that Christ came into the world to create and the need to make disciples for Jesus by baptizing new believers into a life devoted to a distinctly Christian discipleship?[26]

THE FALSE ANTITHESIS THAT CURRENTLY CONFRONTS US

One of the main messages of this book has been that overcorrections happen. The story of the Christian church is filled with accounts of radical swings of the proverbial pendulum, with the result that church members are led to believe that when it comes to some important issues

---

[23]See Grenz, *Theology for the Community of God*, pp. 525-26, for a brief historical treatment of the notion of baptismal regeneration.

[24]Olson, *Mosaic of Christian Belief*, p. 292.

[25]Ibid., p. 294.

[26]In *A New Kind of Christianity*, McLaren includes a chapter titled "What Do We Do About the Church?" Though the theme of this chapter is the proper purpose of the church, it contains no reference at all to water baptism as a prelude to discipleship or as the prescribed rite of incorporation into Christ's church. See McLaren, NKC 161-72.

related to orthodoxy (right belief), they must choose between one of two extreme alternatives—the *traditional* view (usually thought of as the biblically informed position regarding the doctrine in question) and the *progressive* perspective (often thought of as the position required for the doctrine in question to possess missional impact in the contemporary ministry context). The same is true when it comes to orthopraxy (right practice) and the doctrine of the church itself.

However, even our brief exploration of the biblical case for a connection between the church, water baptism and Christian salvation above should be sufficient to indicate how false is the antithesis which says that we must *either* believe that everyone has to belong to our particular ecclesial sect in order to be saved[27] *or* that people can be saved without being baptized into a life of Christian discipleship at all.

To my knowledge, in neither *The Heart of Christianity* nor *A Generous Orthodoxy* do we find encouragement to go into all the world and make disciples per Matthew 28:19 or Mark 16:15-16—that is, with a view toward converting people from their prior non-Christian religious commitments to the type of exclusive loyalty to Christ which the apostle Paul apparently looked for in the lives of those to whom he ministered the gospel. For example, in the opening of his first letter to the Thessalonians, the apostle wrote:

> For we know, brothers and sisters loved by God, that he has chosen you, because our gospel came to you not simply with words but also with power, with the Holy Spirit and deep conviction. You know how we lived among you for your sake. You became imitators of us and of the Lord, for you welcomed the message in the midst of severe suffering with the joy given by the Holy Spirit. And so you became a model to all the believers in Macedonia and Achaia. The Lord's message rang out from you not only in Macedonia and Achaia—your faith in God has become known everywhere. Therefore we do not need to say anything about it, for they themselves report what kind of reception you gave us. They tell how *you turned to God from idols to serve the living and true God, and to wait for his Son from heaven, whom he raised from the dead—Jesus, who rescues us from the coming wrath.* (1 Thess 1:4-10, emphasis added)

---

[27]See the story of the young seminarian in chapter one above (pp. 30-32).

Neither is there in either work any sort of indication that water baptism does more than function, along with the Eucharist and a spate of other practices, as means by which Christians self-identify as Christians and increase a sense of the sacred in our lives.

Borg on baptism, spirituality, practice and religious pluralism. Though Borg can speak of baptism as symbolizing "the internal transformation of dying to an old way of being and birth into a new way of being," his meager depiction of its actual practice in the life of the church is embedded in a discussion of Christian spirituality in general and "thin place" experiences in particular.[28] Thus, even though we have in previous chapters already noted his emphasis on thin places, because he identifies the rite of baptism as a thin-place experience, we need to delve a bit more deeply into this subject.

For Borg, the test of religious experience is the degree to which it helps our hearts open up toward reality (i.e., God, others and the world around us). It is with this idea in mind that he expounds on the crucial importance of "thin places" in a Christian spirituality. Borg suggests that our hearts become open when we become aware that God is all around us and that we exist in him. The key is to experience a thin place where we are allowed to connect with the divine reality which is all around us. According to Borg, "'Thin places' are places where these two levels of reality meet or intersect. They are places where the boundary between the two levels becomes very soft, porous, permeable. Thin places are places where the veil momentarily lifts, and we behold God, experience the one in whom we live, all around us and within us."[29] According to Borg "thin places can literally be geographical places" such as the island of Iona off the west coast of Scotland, Jerusalem, Rome, Canterbury, Mecca, Medina, or various mountains and high places.[30] Furthermore, thin places can be "secular" in that they are not explicitly religious. For example, nature as a whole can function as a thin place, as can music, poetry, literature, the visual arts, dance and so on. Even times of serious illness, suffering and grief can become thin places. A thin place can be

---

[28]Borg, HC 158.
[29]Ibid., pp. 155-56.
[30]Ibid., p. 156.

any place or thing where "the boundary between one's self and the world momentarily disappears."[31] Indeed, Borg goes on to insist that people can become thin places. In a somewhat relativizing manner he suggests that Jesus "must have been a remarkable thin place," and "the saints, known and unknown, Christian and non-Christian, were (and are) thin places."[32] Finally, in a section titled "Thin Places and Christian Practices," Borg (again in a somewhat relativizing manner) identifies the sacraments of baptism and the Eucharist as thin-place experiences, along with hymn singing, listening to sermons, reading the Bible, saying the liturgy, reciting the creeds and so on.[33]

In another section of *The Heart of Christianity,* Borg elaborates on the theme of Christian practice and presents his version of Christian discipleship in terms of a cultural-linguistic socialization of people into the Christian faith tradition. The influence of postmodernity is evident as Borg explains how engaging in Christian practice will serve to form the *identity* and the *character* of church members.

With regard to identity formation, Borg's focus is on the need for self-esteem. We have grown up being wounded by the sense that we have not been enough, that we have not measured up. We might recall how Borg insists that a "requirements-and-rewards" version of the Christian message is part of the problem here. What is needed is for people to hear the message of God's unconditional love and acceptance and then to truly internalize this message. This internalization happens as we are socialized, enculturated into the Christian community and learn the language and behaviors that reinforce the message of God's love.[34] Toward this end, Borg encourages his readers to become involved in a church that will both nourish and stretch them. He then describes

---

[31]Ibid.

[32]Ibid.

[33]As an aside, I cannot help but be somewhat amused by the way Borg has to qualify the value of the liturgical practice of reciting the Christian creeds together in worship. Borg's commitment to both modernism and postmodernism is evident as he encourages his readers not to think that they are affirming the creedal statements to be literally true propositions. Instead, the recitation functions sacramentally, almost magically, as we "join ourselves in the sound of the community saying these words together" (Borg, HC 159). I wonder how the church fathers who forged and affirmed the great creeds of the church would have viewed Borg's qualifications of their usefulness in contemporary churches.

[34]Ibid., pp. 190-91.

various collective and individual practices that can serve to nourish church members. Chief among these practices are prayer, a daily discipline (quiet time), friendship and education.[35]

With regard to the importance of character formation, Borg insists that a necessary result of a changed identity is a changed character. His argument is that because we become what we do, we can help shape our own character by deliberately engaging in deeds of compassion. The result will be a growing "counteridentity" that is an alternative to the one formed by the surrounding culture. With this mind, Borg encourages his readers to become involved in the practice of compassion and justice.[36]

Overall, I agree with Borg that we Christians should actually practice our faith rather than just talk and sing about it. I can also affirm the importance of engaging in each of the practices he refers to in this treatment of Christian discipleship. My only concern is that these otherwise helpful discussions of baptism, spirituality and practice evoke the feeling that actually participating in a local church, as important as the pursuit of the sacred is to Borg's emerging paradigm, is simply nice rather than necessary. This is because, set against his unashamed embrace of religious pluralism, such a pursuit is only arbitrarily rather than necessarily Christian. According to Borg, all of the enduring religions are efficient paths to a salvation defined as existential transformation effected by our contact with "the sacred." He explains:

> To use the metaphor of paths going up a mountainside, the enduring religions are all paths up the same mountain. Envision a mountain, broad at the bottom, narrow at the top, the peak finally disappearing into air, space, emptiness. At the bottom, the paths are farthest apart (the external forms). But as the paths lead higher, they become closer together until they con-

---

[35]Ibid., pp. 193-200. Apparently the idea of a church-based education presents a special hazard. Borg takes pains to caution his readers to avoid churches that promote the earlier paradigm where the Bible is interpreted in a literal manner: "It is difficult to give one's heart to something that one's head rejects" (p. 195).

[36]Ibid., p. 192. While a call to become involved in ministry to the poor and hurting is supported by Scripture and should certainly be heeded rather than ignored, I cannot help but be concerned when authors such as Borg feel the need to argue that this kind of ministry is an alternative to the preaching of the gospel rather than a means of doing so (p. 200). More will be said about this unnecessary antithesis between gospel proclamation and demonstration later in this chapter and in chapter ten.

verge on the mountaintop. And then, of course, they disappear. And the place to which they lead, the mountaintop, is not "heaven," but "the sacred." The religions are not primarily about the next life, not about paths to an afterlife, but to life centered in the sacred in the here and now.[37]

Thus, in the concluding paragraphs of the final chapter of *The Heart of Christianity*, Borg acknowledges that the biggest reason why he is a Christian rather than a Buddhist, Hindu, Muslim, Jew, or anything else, is that, since he was socialized as a Christian from childhood onward, this path is simply the most comfortable for him. For a variety reasons, it works for him.[38]

As much as I appreciate the honesty and sincerity with which Borg expresses his fondness for what his Christian heritage has provided him, given his embrace of religious relativism, I simply cannot escape the conclusion that for him and the emerging paradigm he is promoting, belonging to the church Jesus founded is simply nice rather than necessary. Furthermore, Borg's essential disavowal of the Great Commission as historically understood is also apparent:

> When a Christian seeker asked the Dalai Lama whether she should become a Buddhist, his response, which I paraphrase, was: "No, become more deeply Christian; live more deeply into your own tradition." . . . A Christian is one who does this within the framework of the Christian tradition. Just as a Jew is one who does this within the framework of the Jewish tradition, a Muslim, within the framework of the Muslim tradition, and so forth. And I cannot believe that God cares which of these we are. All are paths of relationship and transformation.[39]

Once again, given Borg's commitment to religious relativism, how can anything he says about the church, baptism and Christian discipleship be viewed as anything other than merely arbitrary—simply nice rather than actually necessary?

McLaren on disciple making and Christianity as a "religion." As for McLaren's contribution to this particular false antithesis, my concerns roughly echo those expressed by Scot McKnight in his *Christianity*

---

[37]Ibid., p. 218.
[38]Ibid., p. 223.
[39]Ibid.

Today article titled "McLaren Emerging." After acknowledging McLaren's prominence among emergent thinkers, and having affirmed McLaren's desire to see Christians live out the gospel they say they believe, Mc-Knight goes on to express concern over McLaren's truncated treatment of the atonement, as well as his tendency to emphasize the kingdom while essentially *understating the importance of the church.*[40] My suggestion is that all of these moves, fairly common among emergent thinkers, are at odds with the biblical text and have the effect of relativizing the Christian faith, making it more palatable to post-Christians enamored with the concept of religious relativism. Indeed, in another article, McKnight offers an explanation for why many emergents seem to be comfortable with "a commitment to Jesus Christ alongside a more pluralistic view of world religions, or a broadening of what it means to be Christian."[41]

The reason why McLaren's work in particular is included in a discussion of religious relativism is due, at least in part, to his discussion of interfaith dialogue in chapter seventeen of *A Generous Orthodoxy.* To many observers, McLaren goes beyond merely suggesting that Christians should be more respectful of other religions and their adherents. He also goes beyond advocating that, toward the goal of making the world a better place, Christians can and should make common cause with the adherents of other religions and even learn a thing or two from these other faith traditions. No, the problem centers in McLaren's failure within this discussion to do justice to the historical understanding of the Great Commission (Mt 28:18-20; Mk 16:15-16). Though McLaren refers in this treatment of interfaith dialogue to the possibility of a type of "evangelism" and "disciple making," what he seems to have in mind is something other than a biblically informed understanding of these missional endeavors. Having already implied that a Christian engaging in interfaith dialogue for the sake of converting his dialogue partner to the Christian religion is comparable to an "Internet pedophile who pretends to be a teenager so he can enter their trust," or a "network marketer who

---

[40]Scot McKnight, "McLaren Emerging," *Christianity Today* 52 (September 2008): 59-66.
[41]Scot McKnight, "The Ironic Faith of Emergents," *Christianity Today* 52 (September 2008): 62-63.

pretends to be your friend so he can add you to his down-line,"[42] McLaren proceeds to clarify his understanding of what it means to make a disciple in a manner that is quite reminiscent of Borg.[43] His rather infamous disclaimer goes like this:

> I must add, though, that I don't believe making disciples must equal making adherents to the Christian religion. It may be advisable in many (not all!) circumstances to help people become followers of Jesus *and* remain within their Buddhist, Hindu, or Jewish contexts. This will be hard, you say, and I agree. But frankly, it's not at all easy to be a follower of Jesus in many "Christian" religious contexts, either.[44]

As I pointed out in chapter five of this work, many missionally minded evangelicals would have no problem with the idea of sending baptized believers back into their cultural contexts in order to represent Christ and his gospel there.[45] But is this what McLaren has in mind?

---

[42]McLaren, *GO* 251 [283]. McLaren, *Why Did Jesus*, p. 223.

[43]Actually, the influence of David Bosch's discussion of "Mission as Witness to People of Other Living Faiths" in *Transforming Mission: Paradigm Shifts in Theology of Mission* (Maryknoll, NY: Orbis, 2011), pp. 485-501, on McLaren's treatment of this topic is fairly apparent. What is ironic, from my perspective, is that McLaren ultimately adopts a perspective more in line with Borg than Bosch—i.e., a perspective I believe Bosch would have, himself, critiqued. See Bosch's discussion in that same work of "Dialogue and Mission" (pp. 494-501). For example, Bosch writes: "If Knitter says that the goal of mission has been achieved when announcing the gospel has made the Christian a better Christian and the Buddhist a better Buddhist, he may be describing one of the goals of *dialogue,* but certainly not *mission.* . . . The Christian faith cannot surrender the conviction that God, in sending Jesus Christ into our midst, has taken a definitive and eschatological course of action and is extending to human beings forgiveness, justification, and a new life of joy and servanthood, which, in turn, calls for a human response in the form of conversion. These inalienable elements of mission became abundantly clear in our chapters on the missionary character of the early church" (p. 499).

[44]McLaren, GO 260 [293].

[45]John J. Travis reminds us of the fact that in some cases, Muslims who have come to faith in Christ must live out their Christian discipleship in a quite clandestine manner due to the threat of serious persecution. Referring to this as a "C6" type of community (a noncommunity, really), Travis acknowledges that this form of Christian experience "is not ideal; God desires his people to witness and have regular fellowship (Heb 10:25)." See John J. Travis, "The C-Spectrum: A Practical Tool for Defining Six Types of 'Christ-Centered Communities' Found in Muslim Contexts," in *Perspectives on the World Christian Movement: A Reader,* ed. Ralph D. Winter and Steven C. Hawthorne, 4th ed. (Pasadena, CA: William Carey Library, 2009), p. 665. Still, Travis goes on to assert: "Nonetheless C6 believers are part of our family in Christ. Though God may call some to a life of suffering, imprisonment or martyrdom, He may be pleased to have some worship Him in secret, at least for a time." Though I am sympathetic to this assertion, given what McLaren has to say about the "missional challenge" in his later work *Why Did Jesus, Moses, the Buddha, and Mohammed Cross the Road?* I am not all confident that it is this "C6" type of ministry situation that McLaren has in mind when he argues that it is advisable for

Absent any reference to baptism or participation in a Christian community, McLaren's commitment to helping people become followers of Christ can be interpreted in a Borg-like manner to mean simply that our goal should be to enable people, whatever their religious affiliation, to follow the path of dying and rising (i.e., to live their lives the way Jesus did—for the sake of God and others rather than themselves). I hope I am wrong about what McLaren is suggesting here.[46] If I am not, then the crucial question all traditional, missional and emerging evangelicals must wrestle with is: How soteriologically significant is it, for McLaren and other promoters of the "emerging" vision, that people experience Christian baptism, confessing in the process that Jesus Christ is the Lord of their lives?[47]

In other words, we must ask ourselves once again: Is there anything particular and personal about Jesus and what he accomplished? Is he a unique source of the presence and activity of God, in person? Does Jesus offer us *himself* and a share in *his own* fellowship and communion with the Father in the Spirit, or is he merely a creature who offers us an example and teachings that anyone else might have given us? Is he the object of our worship or not?

If it is decided that Jesus is the object of our worship, then it seems to me that a case can be made for the idea that there is something about his body—the church—that should not, must not be relativized. Though Jesus, of course, as head of the church, cannot be reduced to his body, especially not to any historically or culturally conditioned expression of it, would it not be an overcorrecting, essentially *docetic* move to assume that the body of Christ has not taken on a flesh and blood, time and space, embodiment?[48] Have we not adopted an essentially dualistic/

---

members of other faith traditions to become followers of Jesus *and* remain within their Buddhist, Hindu or Jewish contexts. See McLaren, *WDJ* 233-73.

[46]Based on what I see in McLaren's later works, I fear I am not wrong.

[47]See Acts 19:1-7; Rom 10:9-10; 1 Cor 12:2-3; Phil 2:9-11; 1 Tim 6:12; 2 Tim 2:19; Heb 3:1.

[48]*Docetism* (Greek *dokēsis,* "appearance") is the view held by gnostic Christians that Jesus only *appeared* to possess a body of flesh and blood. The apostle John seems to have been arguing against such teaching when he wrote: "This is how you can recognize the Spirit of God: Every spirit that acknowledges that Jesus Christ has come in the flesh is from God, but every spirit that does not acknowledge Jesus is not from God. This is the spirit of the antichrist, which you have heard is coming and even now is already in the world" (1 Jn 4:2-3). See also 2 Jn 1:7.

gnostic/docetic notion of the church when we, failing to sufficiently acknowledge its historical and embodied particularity, call for no particular historical and embodied participation in and commitment to it?
It is my bold suggestion that we run the risk of missing Jesus the head
and Lord of the church when we abandon the particularity of the
worship and lordship of Jesus that defines the church.

Based on what I see in *A Generous Orthodoxy* and some of his later
works, I am concerned that the way McLaren might respond to this argument could prove disappointing to those who take the exhortation
found in Jude 3 seriously. Indeed, McLaren goes on to suggest that we
Christians have throughout the ages simply misunderstood the real
meaning of the gospel. To use McLaren's words: "We must continually
be aware that the 'old, old story' may not be the 'true, true story.'"[49] The
context of this antithetical response to Jude's concern that Christians
"contend for the faith that was once for all entrusted to the saints" (Jude 3)
makes it fairly clear that McLaren's intent is to suggest (along with Borg)
that because the good news is not *primarily* about the saving of individual souls toward an eternity in heaven (cf. 1 Pet 1:3-9) but saving the
world as a whole here and now,[50] perhaps there is a sense in which those
adherents of other religions who are reality-centered and working to
make the world a better place are essentially followers of Jesus already
and, therefore, fine right where they are. This interpretation finds support
in another infamous passage from McLaren's pen which, while affirming
his own commitment to the Christian path, also manages to relativize it:

> Ultimately, I believe "they" and "we" can all experience this transfor-
> mation *best* by becoming humble followers of Jesus, whom I believe (as I
> said in the earliest chapters of this book) to be the Son of God, the Lord
> of all, the Savior of the world.
>
> In this light, although I don't hope all Buddhists will become (cul-
> tural) Christians, I do hope all who feel so called will become Buddhist
> followers of Jesus; I believe they should be given that opportunity and
> invitation. I don't hope all Jews or Hindus will become members of the

---

[49]McLaren, GO 261 [294].
[50]See ibid., pp. 93 [101], 99-100 [108-109]; cf. Borg, HC 200. See also McLaren, *Everything Must Change*, 21.

Christian religion. But I do hope all who feel so called will become Jewish or Hindu followers of Jesus.

Ultimately, I hope that Jesus will save Buddhism, Islam, and every other religion, including the Christian religion, which often seems to need saving as much as any other religion.[51]

Note that here McLaren suggests that while the kind of existential transformation he and Borg associate so closely with salvation occurs "best" via Christian discipleship, apparently this need not be the path followed. Note also how McLaren avoids any reference here to the "church" or the "body of Christ," choosing instead to speak of the "Christian religion." That this omission was intentional is indicated by the fact that McLaren goes on to say:

I am more and more convinced that Jesus didn't come merely to start another religion to compete in the marketplace of other religions. If anything, I believe he came to end standard competitive religion (which Paul called "the law") by fulfilling it; I believe he came to open up something beyond religion—a new possibility, a realm, a domain, a territory of the spirit that welcomes everyone but requires everyone (now including members of the Christian religion) to think again and become like little children. It is not, like too many religions, a place of fear and exclusion but a place *beyond* fear and exclusion. It is a place where everyone can find a home in the embrace of God.[52]

I am certainly not averse to some of the sentiments expressed in this critique of religion. However, I must go on to pose the crucial question: Where in this discussion of "disciple making" is any reference to water

[51]McLaren, GO 264 [297], emphasis added. McLaren's later work, *Why Did Jesus, Moses, the Buddha and Mohammed Cross the Road?* seems to be an extended book-length elaboration on this essential viewpoint.

[52]Ibid., p. 266 [299], emphasis original. It should be noted that in *A New Kind of Christianity* McLaren seems to address his earlier failure to refer specifically to the role that the church is to play in disciple making. In what strikes me as a grudging, condescending manner, McLaren asserts: "This kind of evangelism would celebrate the good in the Christian religion and lament the bad, just as it would in every other religion, calling people to a way of life in a kingdom (or beautiful whole) that transcends and includes all religions. Yes, it would welcome people into communities of faith in which they would experience formation in the way of Jesus, and yes, you could call these communities Christian churches if you'd like, although you could call them other things too. But whatever you call these communities, they would be interested in breaking out of the cocoons of Christianity" (McLaren, NKC 216).

baptism as an introduction to a life of devotion to Christ and participation in the community of faith, which according to Scripture, constitutes "God's household" and the "pillar and foundation of the truth"?
The late Stanley Grenz, a theologian whom McLaren refers to as a
"friend and mentor from a distance"[53] has written concerning the significance of water baptism:

> Bound up with our confession of faith is a transfer of loyalties—the re-
> placement of former allegiances by a new allegiance to Christ as Lord.
> This transformation of loyalty places us in a new fellowship, the com-
> munity of those who confess the Lord Jesus. Hence, our union with
> Christ includes presence within his body, the church (1 Cor 12:13). At
> baptism we enter the community of believers concretized in the local
> congregation. As baptized persons we are members of the community of
> faith, which means we share the one story of the people of God.[54]

Again, though I certainly do not want to endorse a hyper-sectarianism
or confessionalism which insists that everyone must belong to my particular denomination in order to be saved, it is difficult for me to reconcile the understanding of the identity-marking and loyalty-shifting
significance of water baptism described by Grenz with McLaren's
statement: "I don't hope all Jews or Hindus will become members of the
Christian religion." I have great respect for much of what McLaren has
to say about the local church here and elsewhere, especially in his earlier
work *The Church on the Other Side*.[55] However, because his later work on
the church, though expressing a concern for "missional vitality,"[56]
actually lacks a strong commitment to the Great Commission as biblically informed and historically understood, I cannot help but find his
emerging ecclesiology to be deficient with respect to biblical faithfulness.
Furthermore, such a deficiency will function as a serious nonstarter as
it relates to the goal of uniting significant numbers of believers belonging
to the traditional evangelical, missional and emerging church movements in the ministry contextualization task. In the end, I see McLaren's

---

[53]McLaren, GO 23 [28].
[54]Grenz, *Theology for the Community*, p. 522.
[55]Brian McLaren, *The Church on the Other Side* (Grand Rapids: Zondervan, 2003).
[56]McLaren, GO 261 [293].

doctrine of the church, along with the one put forward by Borg, contributing to the false antithesis that is this chapter's focus—that is, that the church is either nice or necessary but not both at the same time.

This is not to say, however, that I am affirming a business-as-usual approach to the doing of ministry. No, I am very serious when I state that many of the ecclesial observations and critiques put forward by the emerging paradigm need to be heeded. For this reason, I will go on here to discuss what an ecclesiology that attempts to be faithful to both the biblical text and missional task might look like.

THE GREAT CO-MISSIONAL CHURCH: A MEDIATING MINISTRY MODEL

It just so happens that for many contemporary church leaders the false antithesis du jour has less to do with the necessity of the church and more with how to be the church in an increasingly post-Christian context. To be more specific, there are actually several false antitheses related to orthopraxy that currently confront church leaders eager to render to the Spirit of mission a corporate missional faithfulness. Though there may be many more, the three false antitheses I have in mind refer to *ministry focus*—that church leaders must choose between an emphasis on disciple making *or* social action; *ministry approach*—that church leaders must choose between adopting an approach to ministry that is *either* attractional and institutional *or* incarnational and missional in orientation;[57] and *ministry ethos*—that church leaders must choose between embracing a classical Pentecostal-charismatic *or* non-Pentecostal-charismatic ecclesial identity.

A doctrine of the church that is faithful to both the biblical text and the missional task will strive to provide biblically informed and contextually sensitive "answers" to these ministry-related antitheses. Toward this end I offer an alternative ecclesial model—*the great co-missional church*. It is my hope that the necessarily brief philosophy of ministry

---

[57]See J. Todd Billings, "The Problem with Incarnational Ministry," *Christianity Today,* July 16, 2012, www.christianitytoday.com/ct/2012/july-august/the-problem-with-incarnational-ministry.html, for an important critique of a problematic understanding of and approach to incarnational ministry engaged in by some proponents of missional ministry, both mainline and evangelical.

making up the remainder of this chapter[58] will prove to be a compelling alternative to a traditional, business-as-usual approach to doing church on the one hand, and the ecclesiastical overcorrection that the emerging paradigm is recommending on the other.

A foundational ministry assumption. Before we begin our look at these three ministry-related antitheses, it is important to remember a foundational ministry assumption that has been operative throughout this work and will greatly inform the great co-missional church model: *One of the most basic meanings of "missio Dei" is that all ministry is God's ministry!*[59]

Throughout this book, a commitment to a *missional* approach to ministry has been presumed. The famous Swiss theologian Emil Brunner is well known for this succinct statement concerning the nature and purpose of the church: "The Church exists by mission as fire exists by burning."[60] Citing the work of J. Andrew Kirk, Christopher Wright observes that "it is not so much the case that God has a mission for his church in the world but that God has a church for his mission in the world."[61] Missiologist Charles Van Engen speaks of the local church as "God's missionary people in a local context."[62] David Bosch argues that the church is "missionary by its very nature," and, citing Karl Barth, writes: "Here the church is not the sender but the one sent. Its mission (its 'being sent') is not secondary to its meaning; the church exists in being sent and in building up itself for the sake of its mission."[63] The multiple authors of the book *Missional Church* define the church as "God's sent people" and argue that the great challenge today is for con-

---

[58]I will have more to say about the great co-missional church model in chapter ten where I discuss the "already" and "not yet" connection between the church and the kingdom of God.

[59]This is because the mission of the church is God's mission. David Bosch writes: "Mission is, primarily and ultimately, the work of the Triune God, Creator, Redeemer, and Sanctifier, for the sake of the world, a ministry in which the church is privileged to participate. Mission has its origin in the heart of God" (Bosch, *Transforming Mission*, p. 402).

[60]Charles Van Engen, *God's Missionary People: Rethinking the Purpose of the Local Church* (Grand Rapids: Baker Book House, 1991), p. 27.

[61]Christopher J. H. Wright, *The Mission of God: Unlocking the Bible's Grand Narrative* (Downers Grove, IL: InterVarsity Press, 2006), p. 62, citing, "God's Mission and the Church's Response," in J. Andrew Kirk, *What Is Mission? Theological Explorations* (London: Darton, Longman & Todd; Minneapolis: Fortress Press, 1999), pp. 23-37.

[62]Ibid., p. 27.

[63]See Bosch, *Transforming Mission*, p. 381.

gregations to move from being churches with a mission to being missional churches.[64]

The fact is, however, that we live in a culture chiefly characterized by the attitudes of individualism and consumerism. Together these attitudes cause many traditional evangelical church-goers to approach the local church with a "What's in it for me?" attitude. It is this prevailing cultural perspective that makes it so difficult for many congregation members to wrap their minds around the idea that the purpose of the local church is to be "God's sent people"—"God's missionary people in a local context."[65]

It should come as no surprise that the solution to the dilemma just posed is theological in nature. That is, from the outset we need to acknowledge that, properly understood, *all Christian ministry is ultimately God's ministry.*[66] The concept of missional ministry takes this idea seriously and argues on this basis that it is wrongheaded to engage in ministry in God's name and then hope that God approves of and blesses our

[64]Darrell Guder, ed., *Missional Church: A Vision for the Sending of the Church in North America* (Grand Rapids, MI: Eerdmans, 1998), p. 6.

[65]Dallas Willard, *The Divine Conspiracy* (San Francisco: HarperSanFrancisco, 1998), p. 342. See also Stanley J. Grenz, *Revisioning Evangelical Theology: A Fresh Agenda for the 21st Century* (Downers Grove, IL: InterVarsity Press, 1993), pp. 15-17; and Alan J. Roxburgh and M. Scott Boren, *Introducing the Missional Church: Why It Matters, How to Become One* (Grand Rapids: Baker, 2009), p. 45. See also Darrell L. Guder, *The Continuing Conversion of the Church* (Grand Rapids: Eerdmans, 2000), pp. 120-41.

[66]Ray Anderson, *The Soul of Ministry: Forming Leaders for God's People* (Louisville, KY: Westminster John Knox Press, 1997), p. 5. Furthermore, according to the analysis provided by Craig Van Gelder and Dwight Zscheile in *The Missional Church in Perspective: Mapping Trends and Shaping the Conversation* (Grand Rapids: Baker, 2011), chapter four of *Missional Church* endeavored to make the crucial point that the understanding of the gospel as the announcement of the already and not yet reign of God "calls for the church to reorient itself away from an overreliance on its own agency for carrying out its mission in the world. Relying on its own agency has resulted in the church functioning primarily as a vendor of religious goods and services within a consumer society. The grammar of the kingdom invites the missional church to understand how the agency of the Triune God is at work in shaping our true identity. This Triune God is a missionary God who sends the church as a community into the world to represent the reign of God to a watching world. The identity of the missional church in this understanding stands in sharp contrast to the increasingly marginalized church of late modernity and of the emerging postmodern culture, a church that has lost its favored-status arrangement" (p. 50). See also Darrell Guder's perceptive survey of the gospel reductionisms that have taken place in the history of the church leading to the current "evangelistic reductionism" of our day which separates the benefits of the gospel from the mission of the gospel so that rank-and-file evangelical church members are turned into mere consumers of church programs rather than witnesses to and for Christ in the world (Guder, *Continuing Conversion*, pp. 97-141).

efforts. Rather, a missional approach to ministry calls for church leaders and members to strive to be as certain as possible that we are engaging in the ministry to which God through the Spirit of mission has called us, and that we are doing so in a way that is pleasing to him.[67] Because the goal of ministry is to be faithful, leaving the issue of effectiveness to the Holy Spirit, a foundational principle for ministry is that all attempts at ministry in God's name should be informed by God's ministry purposes (i.e., the *missio Dei*).[68]

But just what does the *missio Dei* involve? This crucial and oft-debated question leads to a consideration of the first of the three ministry-related antitheses.

Disciple making versus social action. As I have indicated elsewhere, over the years the term *missio Dei* has come to mean different things to different people.[69] It seems to have developed initially as a justification for Christian missionary activity (over against the postcolonial criticisms that had been leveled against it in the early and mid-twentieth century) by rooting such activity in the nature of God himself rather than the church (or, rather, in the foreign policy of missionary-sending nations).[70] However, over time, this "elastic concept," which is "capable of accommodating an ever-expanding range of meanings,"[71] took on two distinctly different understandings: a *specialized* understanding of *missio Dei* that focuses on "God's work of redemption" and sees "the church as the primary way in which God works in the world"; and a

---

[67]John G. Flett, *The Witness of God: The Trinity, "Missio Dei," Karl Barth, and the Nature of Christian Community* (Grand Rapids: Eerdmans, 2010), p. 37.

[68]Christopher Wright gets at the heart of the matter: "Mission, then, in biblical terms, while it inescapably involves us in planning and action, is not *primarily* a matter of our activity or our initiative. Mission, from the point of view of our human endeavor, means the committed *participation* of God's people in the purposes of God for the redemption of the whole creation. The mission is God's. The marvel is that God invites us to join in" (Wright, *Mission of God*, p. 67). See also Flett, *Witness of God*, p. 5; Bosch, *Transforming Mission*, p. 400.

[69]Gary Tyra, *The Holy Spirit in Mission: Prophetic Speech and Action in Christian Witness* (Downers Grove, IL: IVP Academic, 2011), pp. 24-26. See also Wright, *Mission of God*, pp. 62-64. Perhaps the most thorough treatment of the history of the *missio Dei* concept is provided by Bosch in *Transforming Mission*, pp. 398-402. A more succinct but equally helpful treatment can be found in Van Gelder and Zscheile, *Missional Church*, pp. 29-30, 42. See also the incisive historical analysis in Flett, *Witness of God*, pp. 4-17, 35.

[70]Flett, *Witness of God*, pp. 4-7.

[71]Ibid., p. 5; see also pp. 76-77.

generalized understanding of *missio Dei* that focuses on the "broader agency of God in relation to all creation and God's continuing care of that creation."[72] According to missiologists Craig Van Gelder and Dwight Zscheile, this generalized understanding "became a secular version of the *missio Dei*" which "came to be identified with a process of historical transformation whereby humankind would gradually achieve the goals of the messianic kingdom through the processes of secular history."[73] In this secular version of the *missio Dei*, both Christology and ecclesiology—the *sent* Christ and his *sent* church—"take a hit," so to speak, experiencing a certain degree of marginalization with respect to their importance to the outworking of God's purposes in the world.[74]

In the same way that *missio Dei* is an elastic term allowing for a variety of understandings, so is the concept of missional.[75] Van Gelder and Zscheile's linguistic archaeological study of the word *missional* seems to indicate that the earliest usage of the word (in the late-nineteenth and early- to mid-twentieth centuries) was as an adjective referring to some mission-related entity, whether it be a title, an activity, an objective, a structure or so on.[76] When the word *missional* was first used in a "more substantive, theologically informed" manner, it was tied to the "mission of a *sending* God." The argument ran something like this: Mission is not one of many possible ecclesial activities; mission is what the church is all about precisely because mission is what God is all about. Since God is a sending God, "what is needed is not so much a theology of mission but a missional theology. In other words, mission does not so much need to be justified theologically as theology needs to be understood missionally."[77]

Eventually, however, the word *missional* began to take on the more

---

[72]Van Gelder and Zscheile, *Missional Church*, p. 30. See also Flett, *Witness of God*, p. 41. Flett later labels the two divergent forms of *missio Dei* slightly differently as the "classical" and "ecumenical" forms respectively, and then provides a helpful comparison of them (pp. 54-55).

[73]Van Gelder and Zscheile, *Missional Church*, p. 31.

[74]Over against this dynamic, one should take note of the passionate manner in which missional church expert Darrell Guder argues for the centrality of the church to God's missional purposes. For example, see Darrell Guder, *Be My Witnesses: The Church's Mission, Message and Messengers* (Grand Rapids: Eerdmans, 1985), pp. 15-17.

[75]Ibid., pp. 3, 42.

[76]Van Gelder and Zscheile, *Missional Church*, pp. 42-44.

[77]Ibid., p. 44.

restricted meaning of "the multiple ways that a church intersects with its local context," as opposed to the idea that missionary activity should be restricted to the winning of souls.[78] Evangelism and disciple making were downplayed as the pursuit of peace and social justice was emphasized.

Then came the publication in 1998 of the hugely influential work, *Missional Church: A Vision for the Sending of the Church in North America.* Since then, the missional conversation has tended to revolve around four major themes: (1) God is a missionary God who sends the church into the world, (2) God's mission in the world is related to the reign (kingdom) of God. (3) The missional church is an incarnational (versus an attractional) ministry sent to engage a postmodern, post-Christendom, globalized context. (4) The internal life of the missional church focuses on every believer living as a disciple engaging in mission.[79] One of the many contributions this book has made to the missional conversation is its articulation of a missiology that seeks to do justice to the concept of the *missio Dei* while maintaining a strong christological and ecclesiological focus. That said, it is also true that, even though Craig Van Gelder was a member of the writing team responsible for *Missional Church,* he and Dwight Zscheile are not reluctant to critique this seminal work, identifying certain weaknesses and encouraging further theological reflection toward the goal of an even greater integration between the specialized (redemption focused) and generalized/secular (creation focused) understandings of the mission of God referred to above.

I am a biblical and practical theologian who approaches the theme of missional ministry from a perspective that tends to be more evangelical (specialized, focusing on redemption) than ecumenical (generalized/secularized, focusing on creation).[80] Still I am appreciative of the desire for a synthesis between the two approaches precisely because I am able to discern biblical and, therefore, theological support for both. The problem is that not every missional author seems to be interested in a genuine synthesis. It appears that some advocates for missional ministry

---

[78]Ibid., p. 45.
[79]Ibid., p. 4.
[80]See ibid., p. 25.

are not shy about downplaying the importance of disciple making to missional ministry. Indeed, for some, "missional ministry" is a synonym for Christian social action *over against an emphasis on the making of disciples.* As part of his noteworthy attempt to forge a missional hermeneutic, New Testament scholar Michael Barram makes the observation that *missional* has come into usage among many missiologists for the express purpose of countering the historical tendency, even among scholars, to use the term *mission* to refer almost exclusively to evangelism.[81] Barram states that *it is in reaction to this very specific, narrow understanding of mission* that "many have begun to experiment with alternative adjectives, such as the term 'missional.'"[82] Though Barram clearly indicates that this alternative adjective *missional,* while conveying a "broader, more appropriately holistic sense of mission as purpose or vocation," is nevertheless still "inclusive of the church's evangelistic outreach,"[83] the fact is that, in some circles, the mission of God is held to be all about such things as justice and peacemaking and actually excludes any evangelistic activity on the part of the church.[84] Once again, overcorrections happen!

It was in response to this equally truncated perspective that the well-known missiologist Lesslie Newbigin offered the following caveat with respect to the meaning of *missio Dei:*

> The concept of *missio Dei* has sometimes been interpreted so as to suggest that action for justice and peace as the possibilities are discerned within a given historical situation *is* the fulfillment of God's mission, and that the questions of baptism and church membership are marginal or irrelevant. That way leads very quickly to disillusion and often to cynical despair.[85]

I am not alone in lamenting the fact that Newbigin's admonition re-

---

[81]For an insightful discussion of the history of the early usage of the term *missional*, see Van Gelder and Zscheile, *Missional Church,* pp. 42-46. In this survey, the authors note that though the term was initially used in various works to "make the point that a congregation is responsible for engaging its larger context," it later came to be used in a more "substantive, theologically informed" way to connote the idea that the church, rather than functioning as the agent of mission, is an instrument of the "mission of a sending God" (pp. 44-45).

[82]Ibid., p. 47.

[83]Ibid.

[84]Wright, *Mission of God,* p. 63.

[85]Lesslie Newbigin, *The Gospel in a Pluralist Society* (Grand Rapids: Eerdmans, 1989), p. 138.

garding the meaning of *missio Dei* (and, hence, *missional*) has not been
heeded by all the contributors to the missional conversation. Ed Stetzer
and David Putnam likewise speak to this issue, commenting on how
inappropriate and unnecessary it is for some missional advocates to feel
the need to speak in a completely disparaging manner of the church
growth and church health movements.[86]

Darrell Guder also offers a powerful word of clarification regarding
the meaning of *missio Dei* which affirms God as the primary ministry
agent whose concern extends to the whole world, while also associating
God's mission with both Christ and his church. In the end, Guder emphasizes that evangelism is indeed at the heart of God's mission and that
the church is central to God's ongoing purposes in the world for which
Christ died:

> The *missio Dei* has always been the gospel, good news about God's
> goodness in God's Word through Israel's experience, leading up to its
> climax and culmination in Jesus Christ. Throughout the biblical witness,
> God acts, initiates, and sends. God's compassion leads to his salvific
> action in human history. The Father sends the Son. This exclusive focus
> upon God as the subject of his mission is essential to the gospel, for it
> makes clear that humans, in their lostness, find hope in what God has
> done for them, not in what they might imagine they can do for them-
> selves. Now, however, on the cross and at Easter, the salvation of the
> world was accomplished. God's mission now broadens to embrace the
> whole world for which Christ died. The gospel of God's love fulfilled in
> Christ is now to be made known to everyone. Because of the evangel, the
> call to evangelize is now heard. God's mission continues as that call takes
> shape in the apostolic community, the church.[87]

So, I stand by my commitment to the idea that making Christian
disciples by baptizing them into an identification with Christ and his
community of disciples and then teaching them to observe all that he
taught his first followers during his earthly ministry (Mt 28:18-20)

---

[86]See Ed Stetzer and David Putnam, *Breaking the Missional Code: Your Church Can Become a Missionary in Your Community* (Nashville: Broadman & Holman, 2006), pp. 49-50.
[87]Guder, *Continuing Conversion,* pp. 46-47. See also p. 132, where Guder clearly says "evangelism
is the heart of ministry."

should be thought of as absolutely integral to the *missio Dei*.[88] There is no good reason to draw a line between an explicit command of Christ—the Great Commission—and a trinitarian-based understanding of the *missio Dei* that focuses more on the "great commandment." I offer instead that *the aim of the local church should be to make Christian disciples* through *gospel proclamation* and *demonstration* for the sake of *gospel proclamation* and *demonstration*.[89] Doing so will allow us to participate in God's mission as it relates to *both* redemption (disciple making) and creation (social and environmental activism).[90]

At the same time, I have a confession to make: I have not always viewed the mission of the church as requiring the kind of balanced participation in both proclamation and demonstration that this mantra calls for. While I am appreciative of the spiritual and ministry formation accorded me by the evangelistically vital church in which I became a Christ-follower, there was a glaring defect. I cannot remember hearing many sermons, if any, that emphasized the importance of Christians engaging in social action. It was not until my seminary days (a full seven years into my life as a ministry professional) that my awareness was raised regarding the many biblical passages which indicate God's concern for social justice and the responsibility of his people to become engaged in its passionate promotion.[91] Furthermore, having worked for a number years now with many university students possessing a similar

---

[88]The issue of what constitutes missional ministry is yet another ecclesial theme that will be treated in chapter ten below.

[89]Though the disciple making referred to in this section principally has the evangelism rather than edification and equipping dynamics in mind, I want to direct the reader to a helpful discussion of the "missional practices of discipleship" provided by Van Gelder and Zscheile. Their concern is that spiritual formation and ministry formation should go together and ideally result in an ability on the part of the disciple to follow Christ "into participation in God's mission in the world in the power of the Spirit" (*Missional Church*, pp. 148-55).

[90]Bruce Nicholls reminds us that the covenant derived from International Congress on World Evangelization, 1974, Lausanne, contains the following affirmation: "Although reconciliation with man is not reconciliation with God, nor is social action evangelism, nor is political liberation salvation, nevertheless we affirm that evangelism and socio-political involvement are both part of our Christian duty" (Nicholls, *Contextualization*, p. 23; see also pp. 52, 68 for Nicholls' own affirmation of a contextualized theology that involves both disciple making and social action).

[91]For example, see Deut 16:20; Ps 11:7; 106:3; Prov 28:5; 29:7; Is 56:1; Jer 21:12; Amos 5:15, 21-24; Zech 7:9-10; Mt 23:23; Lk 11:42.

conservative evangelical background, it is my sense that this lack of emphasis on social action was not unique to my faith and ministry journey. Thus, I really do understand the emerging paradigm's embrace of the radical swing of the pendulum away from an emphasis on disciple making toward social action. However, just because it is possible to understand this overreaction does not keep it from being one. As an overreaction and overcorrection, the emerging paradigm's nearly sole focus on social action and creation care over disciple making must be resisted. If the goal truly is a missional orthopraxy that is faithful to both the text and task, all of the extreme pendulum swings must be resisted.[92]

Because of its pendulum-taming potential, I affirm the understanding of *missio Dei* inherent in Scot McKnight's summary of the Christian gospel as "the work of God to restore humans to union with God and communion with others, in the context of a community, for the good of others and the world."[93] As a tacit articulation of the *missio Dei,* this statement of the essence of the gospel succeeds at the important task of holding disciple making, social action and creation care in a healthy tension, all the while reminding the church that she exists to serve God and others rather than herself.[94]

---

[92]According to Van Gelder and Zscheile, this is what the missional conversation should be about. They describe two alternative missiologies—ecumenical and evangelical—and their relationship to the missional conversation: "The ecumenical approach seeks to attend primarily to a larger theological understanding of mission, especially the mission of the Triune God, leaving many evangelicals concerned that evangelism is being diluted or lost. The evangelical approach seeks to attend primarily to obeying the Great Commission and thereby focuses especially on Christology and human obedience, leaving many ecumenical concerned that a holistic gospel is being compromised. The introduction of the missional church conversation, along with earlier initiatives, helped to provide for some bridging to reconceive mission in light of the mission of the Triune God" (Van Gelder and Zscheile, *Missional Church,* p. 25). This suggests that, at its best, the concept of missional seeks to bridge rather than bifurcate these two ways of thinking about the Christian mission (see also p. 148).

[93]Scot McKnight, *Embracing Grace: A Gospel for All of Us* (Brewster, MA: Paraclete Press, 2005), p. xiii.

[94]Many of the contributors to the missional conversation seem to have room in their understanding of "missionality" for a commitment to disciple making that includes gospel proclamation and demonstration. See Newbigin, *Gospel in a Pluralist Society,* pp. 119, 123, 128-40; Roxburgh and Boren, *Introducing the Missional Church,* pp. 54, 87; Stetzer and Putnam, *Breaking the Missional Code,* pp. 30-42, 79-81, 83-84; and Guder, *Missional Church,* pp. 12, 238, 247. See also Michael Frost and Alan Hirsch, *The Shaping of Things to Come: Innovation and Mission for the 21st-Century Church* (Peabody, MA: Hendrickson Publishers, 2003), p. 11; Dan Devadatta, "Strangers but Not Strange: A New Mission Situation for the Church (1 Peter 1:1-2 and 17-25)" in *Confident Witness—Changing World: Rediscovering the Gospel in North America,* ed. Craig Van

What all this means is that *it is thoroughly unnecessary to have to choose between disciple making and social action/creation care.*[95] Instead, we can and should see *both* of these ministry endeavors working together to make disciples for Jesus—through gospel proclamation *and* demonstration, for gospel proclamation *and* demonstration. Or, to put it differently, the goal should be disciples who, having been baptized into Christ's school of life and ministry, will be empowered by the Word, Spirit and people of God to learn how to love God supremely and their neighbors as themselves.[96] The great co-missional church will see itself as a disciple-making community of believers that is committed to a faithful fulfilling of the Great Commission (Mt 28:18-20; Mk 16:15-16), while at the same time being careful to obey the great commandment (Mt 22:33-34)[97] and engaging in creation care.[98]

Attractional and institutional versus incarnational and missional.

Gelder (Grand Rapids: Eerdmans, 1999), pp. 111-12, 121-24; James Davison Hunter, *To Change the World: The Irony, Tragedy, and Possibility of Christianity in the Late Modern World* (New York: Oxford University Press, 2010), p. 226. See also "The Missional Manifesto," April 28, 2011, www.missionalmanifesto.net.

[95]Support for this assertion can be found in Hastings, *Missional God,* pp. 99, 149-63.

[96]Two excellent works that promote a holistic embrace of both disciple making and social action are Ronald J. Sider *Good News and Good Works: A Theology for the Whole Gospel* (Grand Rapids: Baker, 1993); and Ronald J. Sider, Philip N. Olson, and Heidi Rolland Unruh, *Churches That Make a Difference: Reaching Your Community with Good News and Good Works* (Grand Rapids: Baker Books, 2002). For a thoughtful argument which insists that it is impossible to successfully communicate the gospel in a completely nonverbal manner, see Duane Litfin, "Works and Words: Why You Can't Preach the Gospel with Deeds (And Why It's Important to Say So)," *Christianity Today,* April 26, 2012, www.christianitytoday.com/ct/2012/may/litfin-gospel-deeds .html.

[97]For a thoughtful discussion of the "authority" of both the Great Commission and the Great Commandment, and how behind them both is the Great Communication—"the revelation of the identity of God, of God's action in the world and Gods' saving purpose for all creation"— see Wright, *Mission of God,* pp. 59-60.

[98]In sum, I believe that a careful reading of Scripture does support the idea that God's redemptive concern extends beyond individual human beings to creation as a whole. Genesis 1:26-30 can be interpreted to indicate that God expects human beings to develop the creation, to carry on his work of creating a world that reflects his original plans and intentions for the planet. Furthermore, Romans 8:21 indicates that a future liberation awaits not only human beings but creation itself. Likewise, Colossians 1:15-20 specifies that God's plan is for "all things" (all creation) to be eventually reconciled in Christ. And, finally, Revelation 21:5 boldly declares that God will someday make "everything" new. Taken together, these passages can be interpreted to at least imply that God's redemptive concern ultimately extends beyond the salvation of individual souls, to human cultures, to the welfare of the planet itself. Finally, as I will also indicate in chapter ten, I find value in the McLaren's argument that to care for the planet is a way for us to love our neighbors who are "downstream from us in time" (McLaren, GO 242 [273]).

Of the three false antitheses, the one that is currently commanding the most attention is the debate between two ministry models: the *attractional and institutional* versus *incarnational and missional* approaches to local church ministry. A first step toward finding an "answer" to this antithesis is to carefully define and delineate its principal terms.

The word *attractional* refers to an approach to ministry that has an "if you build it they will come" presumption behind it. The idea is that the church conducts worship and teaching services to which unbelievers are invited. Ministry happens inside the church building and is performed by professional and lay ministers who have special training for this task. Often associated with the attractional ministry approach is an *institutional* understanding of the nature of the church. This perspective sees the church as the sole and authoritative purveyor of the means by which saving grace is communicated to people. Again, the presumption here is that most if not all ministry will occur within the church building and at the hands of trained professionals.

As we have seen, a *missional* understanding of the church insists that mission or outreach is not simply one of many programs in which a church might engage. Instead, each local church should understand itself as a missionary outpost, adopting a missionary (rather than chaplaincy) posture toward its surrounding community, endeavoring to cooperate with what the Holy Spirit is up to not only within the church building but in the surrounding neighborhoods as well. The way a missional church conceives of its ministry approach is *incarnational*. This means that just as Jesus left heaven to "pitch his tent" among sinful, hurting humanity in order to *communicate* God's saving grace to them (Jn 1:14, 16-18), so should the members of his body.[99] In other words, the emphasis here is on encouraging church members to become involved in gospel proclamation and demonstration outside the church building in their respective neighborhoods and places of employment. Indeed, church members might form missional communities—groups of church members who move into a targeted community in order to discern what the Spirit of mission is up to there so that they, through

---

[99]See Roxburgh and Boren, *Introducing the Missional Church*, p. 32.

their gospel proclamation and demonstration, might cooperate with his missional purposes.[100]

So, are these two basic ministry approaches mutually exclusive? It is my contention that that they are not, despite the fact that some missional authors give the impression that if a church spends any significant amount of effort conducting worship or teaching gatherings to which the unchurched are invited (in the hope that they might experience the convicting, regenerating work of the Holy Spirit), this is an indication that the church is de facto still rooted in an "attractional" versus "missional" ministry paradigm. In other words, they give the impression that one must choose between either being missional or conducting worship and teaching events which the unchurched are invited to attend. But this is a false antithesis.

Much to their credit, Michael Frost and Alan Hirsch will sometimes contrast missional with *institutional* instead of attractional. This slight change in nomenclature rightly portrays the reality that a church can conduct an "attractional" event to which the unchurched are invited without at the same time defining itself in institutional terms—that is, "as an institution to which outsiders must come in order to receive a certain product, namely, the gospel and all its associated benefits" or as a sanctified space "into which unbelievers must come to encounter the gospel."[101]

Likewise, Ed Stetzer and David Putnam also caution against an overreaction in this regard, allowing room in their missional paradigm for a church to conduct attractional events while still seeking to impact its community in an incarnational manner. As a matter of fact, they not only presume attractional worship gatherings but suggest that inviting the unchurched to experience them is key to evangelism and disciple

---

[100]When speaking in this way about the need to impact our neighborhoods, we should ever keep in mind the call of Van Gelder and Zscheile (*Missional Church,* pp. 129-31) to recognize and adapt to the "nongeographical character of community life today." They elaborate: "The question, who is my neighbor? is now much more complex. It is not enough to merely focus on an immediate geographic neighborhood. If one does, one will likely discover that the neighbors' tightest relational networks may span hundreds of thousands of miles. Building relationships with neighbors and participating in their lives and livings spaces must engage virtual, as well as physical, forms of community."

[101]See Frost and Hirsch, *Shaping of Things,* pp. xi, 12.

making.[102] In other words, a church can endeavor to be attractional without buying in hook, line and sinker to an institutional ecclesiology and can conduct some "attractional" gatherings while still functioning in an essentially missional manner within its community.

Ross Hastings speaks of the need for local churches to be attractional in the right sense—that is, attractive.[103] He warns that an exclusive focus on going out to be with people by itself constitutes a one-sided approach to incarnational ministry and reflects an ecclesiology/missiology that is less than fully christological.[104] He explains:

> Christ not only came down to become human, he became one in order to form a new community of humanity in particular located places, in which he still dwells. Christ and his church are together, as Bonhoeffer famously said, the collective Christ. . . . To be at Starbucks and wherever else folk meet in our culture is crucial. However, if we are to be truly missional, the same folks we encounter need to be brought into the gathered community, which, after all, if it really is the community of Christ, will be irresistibly attractive. . . . Stereotypes about churches are overcome when people discover churches of resurrection celebration and the intimate presence of Jesus. If "they want Jesus but not the church," let's give them Jesus in the church. It's not that we have an option—we are to be in union with him.[105]

A careful reading of the New Testament will reveal that the earliest Christians had no problem with the idea that ministry might happen as people visited the worship and teaching gatherings conducted by the church (e.g., Acts 2:46-47; 1 Cor 14:23-25). Thus some theological support for an attractional approach to ministry can perhaps be found in the notion of the local church functioning in a sacramental way in the lives of people living all around it.

My theological mentor in graduate school, the late Ray Anderson, conceived of a sacrament as a tangible expression of the grace of God, a point of connection between a holy God and sinful, imperfect human

[102]See Stetzer and Putnam, *Breaking the Missional Code*, pp. 65, 102-7, 145-52.
[103]Hastings, *Missional God*, pp. 129-30.
[104]Ibid., p. 130.
[105]Ibid.

beings. Accordingly, Anderson (following Karl Barth and T. F. Torrance) describes Jesus as the "primary sacrament," the primary point of connection between God and humanity.[106] Anderson goes on to speak of the church as the continuing sacramental presence of Jesus Christ. He writes, "The church as the body of Christ now lives between the cross and the return of Christ *(parousia).* The original sacramental relation of God to humanity through Jesus Christ is now represented through the enactment of the life of the church itself."[107]

In the most basic sense, then, the local church, as a tangible expression or "body" of the resurrected and ascended Christ, is intended by God to function as a point of connection (sacrament) between hurting people and Jesus Christ, who in turn functions as the primary point of connection (sacrament) between them and God. The local church gathered can and should be a place where hurting people can find and touch the hem of Jesus' garment, so to speak, in order to experience the grace of God through him. This is good news: there are places where people can go to meet with, and be encountered by, the resurrected and ascended Jesus! To use the language of Marcus Borg, there is a sense in which the local church gathered can and should, in the power of the Spirit, function as a "thin place" within its neighborhood.

So there is some theological justification for an attractional ministry dynamic. However, because the default for many evangelical churches has tended to be the attractional ministry model (exclusively), it seems wise to provide a theological rationale for an eager engagement in a more incarnational approach as well. In the process I wish also to encourage a consideration of some of the important stylistic ministry implications of such an approach.

A careful look at the Bible as a whole will indicate that God's ultimate ministry is one of self-revelation. Everything we know about God, all theology, is only possible because of God's ministry of self-revelation. Ray Anderson summarizes the essence of ministry this way: "Ministry is God's way of reaffirming and expounding the truth of who God is and

[106]Anderson, *Soul of Ministry*, pp. 167-69.
[107]Ibid., pp. 169-70. See also Bosch, *Transforming Mission*, pp. 383-85.

what God wishes to reveal through what he has said and done."[108] Among other things, this observation that God's self-revelation is the ground of all Christian ministry means that the outreach efforts of the local church should mimic the manner of God's self-revelation. Obviously, this argues for an incarnational approach to ministry. Just as Jesus the Word of God (Jn 1:1) became flesh and dwelt among the people he sought to save (Jn 1:14), so should his disciples routinely spill out of their church buildings in order to address, in his name, whatever pain, suffering and confusion is present in the lives of people living and working in the surrounding neighborhoods.[109] Some of Jesus' final words to his apostles were these: "As the Father has sent me, I am sending you" (John 20:21).

Furthermore, this very basic awareness that our attempts at ministry find their foundation in God's own ministry of self-revelation should say something to us about not only the content of our message, but the attitude that is appropriate in its communication. For one thing, we should approach the ministry endeavor with the same kind of *humility* and "other-orientation" that marks the members of the Trinity. This is important because when we dare to minister to others in God's name, every act of ministry will purport to reveal something of the heart of God to people who need him and matter to him greatly. Therefore, before we engage in any act of ministry, it is incumbent on us to *humbly* ask ourselves: *What will this act of ministry say to people about the nature and purpose of God?* Is there a solid biblical, theological foundation for this ministry message? Am I genuinely pursuing God's purposes through this ministry activity or my own? Will the recipients sense the compassion of Christ in my ministry manner?

At the same time, since all genuine ministry is ultimately God's ministry, effected through us by the Spirit of mission, we must continually remember that we are never "on our own" when engaging in it. This awareness can and should produce within us an attitude of *confidence*. It is ennobling (confidence inspiring) to realize that our sometimes feeble, always flawed attempts at ministry in God's name, when performed at

---

[108]Anderson, *Soul of Ministry*, p. 7.
[109]See Roxburgh and Boren, p. 94. See also Guder, *Missional Church,* pp. 13-14; and Frost and Hirsch, *Shaping of Things,* pp. 35-41.

the behest of the Spirit, are underwritten by God himself![110]

As well, an attitude I refer to as *careful boldness* is required for a properly contextualized ministry endeavor. On the one hand, an attitude of *carefulness* can help us avoid becoming tradition-bound, big-picture-missing Pharisees in our ministry engagement. Simply being busy speaking and acting on God's behalf does not guarantee that we are doing so in a manner that is pleasing to him. In fact, Jesus' scathing denunciation of the missionary activity of the Pharisees provides us with a sobering indication that even a person's missional endeavors can be displeasing to the God he or she claims to serve: "Woe to you, teachers of the law and Pharisees, you hypocrites! You travel over land and sea to win a single convert, and when you have succeeded, you make them twice as much a child of hell as you are" (Mt 23:15).

Overall, Jesus' various interactions with the Pharisees as portrayed in all the Gospels evince the fact that we displease God when we reduce ministry to a set of inviolable rules, rituals and human-made traditions, missing the big picture and heart of God in the process. The negative example provided by the Pharisees should serve to remind us that God is love and that his desire is to bless rather than punish people. Whenever we find ourselves, like the Pharisees, hurting rather than helping those to whom we are called to minister, pushing them further away from a personal connection with God rather than drawing them near to him, we need to stop what we are doing and prayerfully strive to improve our understanding of what the Holy Spirit is really up to in their lives and ours (cf. Jn 7:21-24).[111]

On the other hand, a properly contextualized ministry endeavor also calls for an attitude of *boldness*. Missional ministry requires not only the skill of theological discernment—the ability to discern what God is up

---

[110]See 1 Cor 12:4-6; 15:58; Gal 2:8; Eph 3:7; Phil 1:4-6; 2:12-13; Col 1:10-12; Heb 13:20-21.

[111]This ministry principle is especially relevant today in terms of the interaction between local evangelical churches and the gay, lesbian and transgendered people living nearby. Overall, we evangelicals must strive to do a better job of genuinely, thoughtfully, missionally demonstrating God's love for members of these communities while at the same time remaining faithful to the moral instructions of God's Word. Since space will not allow for a full discussion of this topic here, it must suffice for me to advise that with regard to this, as well as any ministry issue, we must be on guard against falling prey to a false antithesis and the either-or ministry approach it mandates!

to in this or that ministry context—but also a willingness to engage in the kind of theological and methodological innovation discussed in chapter two.[112] Recall that I presented Peter's preaching the gospel to and then baptizing the household of Cornelius as a prime example of a theological innovation that led to a ministry innovation—what Ray Anderson refers to as "theological praxis."[113] No church leader had ever baptized a Gentile before this time! But Peter, accurately discerning that God's Spirit was at work in the situation, *courageously created a new ministry structure so as to cooperate with what God was doing in that ministry moment.* Theological discernment led to theological innovation which in turn led to a *bold* theological praxis![114]

In all likelihood Peter knew his actions would be challenged by those members of the headquarter church in Jerusalem who possessed a Pharisaical heritage and apparently maintained a fondness for it (see Acts 15:5). He may also have had in mind the way Jesus himself had been forced to defend his own ministry innovations in the face of some fierce Pharisaical criticism (Mt 12:1-14; cf. Lk 13:10-17). That Peter was well aware (and concerned) that he would have to provide some sort of rationale for this bold ministry move is indicated by the significance he attached to the spontaneous outpouring of the Holy Spirit on this group of new believers (Acts 10:44-48)! But, sensing that God was up to something in this ministry moment, Peter acted boldly and did what was necessary to cooperate with him. In the process, the apostle provided the church of all ages with a vivid portrait of what a carefully bold missional faithfulness looks like.

It is vital for all evangelicals in our place and day to come to terms with the need for such a careful boldness. I know from my personal experience as a missional church pastor that the creation of new wineskins necessary to carry the new wine of the Spirit is likely to ruffle the feathers

---

[112]See Anderson, *Soul of Ministry*, pp. 10, 17-32.
[113]Ibid., pp. 25-32.
[114]Missiologist David Bosch reminds us that "a paradigm shift always means both continuity and change, both faithfulness to the past and boldness to engage the future, both constancy and contingency, both tradition and transformation" (Bosch, *Transforming Mission*, p. 375). I think of this quote when I consider the radical, carefully bold missional move taken by Peter in this ministry interaction.

of those around us who are less willing to push past traditional ministry practices in order to do justice to what God is up to (the ministry *telos*) in a particular ministry context. Following Jesus' lead, Peter's example and the guidance of the Holy Spirit, we need to be bold—*carefully bold*—anyway.[115]

Classical Pentecostal-charismatic versus non-Pentecostal-charismatic. Speaking of the need to follow the guidance of the Spirit of mission, the New Testament is clear that the dual ministry of Christ (revelation and reconciliation) was empowered by the third person of the Trinity, the Holy Spirit.[116] The New Testament is also clear that the purpose of the divine activity that took place on the day of Pentecost in Acts 2 was to unleash on the world a Spirit-empowered body of believers that would continue the revealing and reconciling work of Jesus. Ray Anderson writes:

> It is important that we have a theology of Pentecost as an experience of the Spirit which empowers.
>
> With the resurrection of Jesus and the coming of the Spirit on the early believers at Pentecost, the earthly life of Jesus took on new significance. The *content* of the Spirit's work was understood to be a continuation of the ministry of the same Jesus who performed the works of God from his baptism to his death on the cross.
>
> Pentecost is the pivotal point from which we can look back to the incarnation of God in Jesus of Nazareth and look forward into our contemporary life and witness to Jesus Christ in the world. Pentecost is more than a historical and instrumental link between a theology of the incarnation and a theology of the institutional church. Pentecost is more than the birth of the church; it is the empowerment of the church; it is the in-

---

[115] Again, as I pointed out in chapter two, this openness to theological innovation and praxis does not mean that just anything goes as long as the proposed ministry goal seems to be a loving one. No, before we break with long established theological and ministry tradition, *we should be able to discern not only the sovereign activity of the Spirit in people's lives but also a theological antecedent present in sacred Scripture.* As we examine God's Word, we must look past specific ministry structures and zero in on the big picture: the *telos*, the ultimate purpose, of what God is really up to in people's lives. If, in a missional context, a new, innovative, ministry structure will help us achieve God's ultimate purposes in the lives of the people we are ministering to, then we have not only the freedom but also the responsibility to engage in this theological (ministry) praxis.

[116] Anderson, *Soul of Ministry*, pp. 73-74.

dwelling of the Spirit as the source of the church's life and ministry.

The nature of the church as the continuing mission of God through Jesus Christ is determined by its relation to Pentecost, not only to the Great Commission, given by Jesus after his crucifixion and resurrection. The Great Commission gives the church its instructions; Pentecost provides its initiation and power. The command, "Go and make disciples of all nations" (Matt. 28:19), anticipates the promise, "you will receive power when the Holy Spirit has come upon you; and you will be my witnesses . . ." (Acts 1:8).[117]

In other words, the empowerment of the Spirit is crucial to a church's ability to continue the ministry works of Christ. Only a Spirit-empowered church is able to function effectively as Christ's body, the re-presentation of him to the world.[118]

In chapter six I provided a rough outline of the missional pneumatology I believe is crucial to a missional faithfulness. By way of review, a missional pneumatology is one that acknowledges the way the Bible connects (1) the coming of the Spirit and the phenomenon of prophetic activity (Spirit-inspired speech and action), and (2) the phenomenon of prophetic activity and a missional faithfulness as exemplified in the book of Acts. In a nutshell, the argument for a missional pneumatology holds that the Spirit of God has a penchant for using the people of God to achieve the purposes of God in the world. In addition, his missional method of choice seems to be to inspire rank-and-file believers to speak and act prophetically (on God's behalf) into the lives of hurting people in evangelizing, edifying and equipping ways. Like Ananias of Damascus, Spirit-filled followers of Christ are able to hear God's voice, receive ministry assignments from him, speak and act prophetically into the lives of others, making a difference in the world and building up Christ's church in the process (Acts 9:10-20). This kind of Spirit-inspired

---

[117]Ibid., p. 111. See also Roger Stronstad, *The Charismatic Theology of St. Luke* (Peabody, MA: Hendrickson Publishers, 1984), pp. 34-35; Roger Stronstad, *The Prophethood of All Believers* (Cleveland, TN: CPT Press, 2010), pp. 69-70; Clark Pinnock, *Flame of Love: A Theology of the Holy Spirit* (Downers Grove, IL: InterVarsity Press, 1996), p. 118; Christopher J. H. Wright, *The Mission of God's People: A Biblical Theology of the Church's Mission* (Grand Rapids: Zondervan, 2010), p. 43.

[118]Anderson, *Soul of Ministry*, pp. 169-70.

missional faithfulness is apparent on nearly every page of the book of Acts and in the phenomenal growth currently occurring among Pentecostal-charismatics worldwide. I am convinced that once we evangelicals in the West (traditional, missional and emerging) recognize the crucial role which prophetic speech and action play in the achievement of the missional purposes of God, and once we open ourselves to this empowering work of the Spirit in our lives, we can, like Ananias, be used of God in wonderful, missionally fruitful ways—our post-Christian ministry context notwithstanding!

In his excellent work *Worship and the Reality of God,* John Jefferson Davis issues a strong call for evangelical churches in post-Christian North America to adopt a theological realism that is rooted in an ontology of *trinitarian supernaturalism.* This philosophical understanding of reality argues that the eternal triune God is that which is most real—that to which all physical and virtual realities in our universe owe their existence. Furthermore, because this view embraces the concept of the supernatural, it insists that the universe is an open system in which miracles are possible. Among other things, this means that Christians are justified in taking seriously the possibility of interacting with a *real presence* of God during their times of corporate worship. According to Davis, such an ontology, in contradistinction to the ones offered by modernity *(scientific materialism)* and postmodernity *(digital virtualism),* is required if the worship occurring in evangelical churches is going to be renewed[119] and these churches better equipped to present the "absolute truth of the Bible and the Christian faith" in a compelling manner to people living in an increasing post-Christian, religiously pluralistic ministry context.[120] Toward this end, Davis boldly calls for the evangelical church in the West to unsaddle itself from theological views "that can handcuff the Holy Spirit in the life of the church and blind it to where the Spirit may be working dramatically in the world today."[121]

Indeed, given the importance of the Holy Spirit to the spiritual and

---

[119]See John Jefferson Davis, *Worship and the Reality of God* (Downers Grove, IL: IVP Academic, 2010), pp. 21-25, 197-98.

[120]Ibid., pp. 19-20.

[121]Ibid., p. 30. Dan Kimball makes essentially the same point in *The Emerging Church: Vintage Christianity for New Generations* (Grand Rapids: Zondervan, 2003), p. 115-16.

ministry formation of individual believers and entire communities of faith,[122] we simply cannot continue to fight the Spirit-wars of yesteryear—debating back and forth about boundary marking and boundary-reinforcing pneumatological doctrines. I continue to believe that all true evangelicals, regardless of their pneumatological heritage (Pentecostal-charismatic or non-Pentecostal-charismatic), are committed to the mission and to the Book. I would also like to believe that this missional pneumatology, precisely because it focuses on the issue of mission and derives from a serious study of the entirety of Scripture, has the power to unite rather than divide evangelicals of all stripes (traditional, missional and emerging). There is another option besides embracing and cultivating *either* a classical Pentecostal-charismatic *or* a non-Pentecostal-charismatic ecclesial ethos. We can and must have the best of both worlds! A pneumatology that is missional in orientation and biblical in derivation can create an ecclesial ethos that is open to spiritual experience (prophetic speech and action) while also committed to an intelligent surrender to the authority of Scripture (see 1 Cor 14:39-40).[123]

Much more could be said about how the great co-missional church provides a compelling answer to the false antitheses currently confronting the traditional evangelical, missional and emerging church communities. Though space will not allow for a more thorough treatment here, I will pick up this theme again in the chapter that follows.

In sum, the great co-missional church—an ecclesial model that attempts to faithfully recontextualize (rather than accommodate) the gospel message in an attractional *and* incarnational manner, through both gospel proclamation *and* social action, via the cultivation of an empowering ecclesial ethos that is sensitive to both the Word *and* the Spirit—has what it takes to achieve God's missional purposes while at the same time resisting the wide swings of the pendulum. All of this is possible because the great co-missional church model reflects an

---

[122]Van Gelder and Zscheile assert that recognizing and seeking the leadership of the Spirit in the church's communal life and practice is nothing less than the key to the missional church (*Missional Church*, p. 149).

[123]Ed Stetzer and David Putnam speak of the need for missional churches to be both Spirit-empowered and biblically informed (see *Breaking the Missional Code*, pp. 39-42, 53-58, 190).

ecclesial orthopraxy that is faithful to both the biblical text and missional task.

Writing this chapter has occasioned for me an opportunity to engage in a nostalgic reflection of my faith and ministry journey. Even more importantly, it has encouraged me to reconsider how important the church is to Christ and his revelation and reconciliation ministries and to recommit myself here and now to an eager participation in what Paul referred to as "God's household" and the "pillar and foundation of the truth." I hope that reading this chapter has served to inspire others to do likewise.

In the final chapter of this book our focus will be on eschatology—what the Bible has to say about the final things. Is it true that because some Christians and churches seem to be so heavenly minded that they are of little or no earthly good that all evangelicals should essentially call for a moratorium on speech about the next life? Or could it be that an eschatological orientation that takes life in the age to come seriously is actually crucial to the ability of individual Christians and local churches to engage in a missional faithfulness here and now? The essentially dismissive posture of my two dialogue partners toward certain aspects of this last theological locus is either quite right or horribly wrong.

10

NOW AND NOT YET

Toward a Missionally Orthodox
Doctrine of the Final Things

As it happens, I am scheduled to present a lecture today on the theme
of eschatology—what the Bible has to say about the final or last
things—to a classroom full of freshmen university students. If previous
experience is any indication, while there will be a few students who will
go away from today's class session *nonplussed*—wondering what all the
fuss is about—many others will leave the lecture hall significantly impacted. These "impacted" students will fall into three categories: (1)
some will be *disturbed* that I did not rehearse and affirm the end-times
portrait of Christ's *parousia* (advent or coming) that is portrayed in
many popular books and preached often in their home churches; (2)
some will be *sobered* by the reminder that the Bible really is serious
about the need for Christ's followers of every era to remain "ready" for
his return by refusing to compromise with the spirit of the age; and, I am
happy to say, (3) a good number of my students will go to their next class
intensely intrigued by the way the lecture they just heard explained why
eschatology matters not just for the next life, but for the one we are living
right now.

It probably goes without saying that traditional evangelicals tend to
take the issue of eschatology very seriously. Is this interest misguided?
In my opinion the best answer to this query is: "It all depends." Depending on the way we approach this theological locus, the seriousness

which we evangelicals attach to it can prove to be either a blessing or a bane to our ability to manifest a missional faithfulness. On the positive side, it cannot be denied that a sense of urgency produced by a belief in a literal return of Christ and ensuing experience of divine judgment has motivated many sincere Christ-followers to share their faith with others in ways that have produced many new disciples.[1] On the negative side, we must also acknowledge that, regardless of one's position with respect to a cultural mandate,[2] historically some evangelicals have tended to focus so much on an attempt to pin down the precise timing of Christ's *parousia* that they have failed to engage in the kind of gospel demonstration (i.e., social action) necessary for many lost and hurting people in our world to be able to really "hear" the good news of God's love being proclaimed to them. So, the need for nearly all evangelicals to engage in more careful thinking about what the Bible actually says about the final things, and why it says it, is *not* something I will dispute.

At the same time, however, I cannot help but register a concern when I see yet another false antithesis put into play by those advocating the emerging vision of the Christian faith. The emerging paradigm is overreacting to the acknowledged tendency of some evangelicals to myopically obsess over getting ready to go to heaven when it in turn insists that life in an age to come is not something Jesus really had much interest in,[3] and that the kingdom of God he proclaimed and demonstrated is primarily political and here and now.[4] In an attempt to provide a missionally orthodox answer to this false antithesis, I will argue here that while the emerging paradigm gets a lot of things right in terms of the kingdom of God, it has put forward an essentially unbalanced eschatology that tends to produce an unbalanced missiology as well. To be even more specific, the central focus here will be on how a properly

---

[1]See Gary Tyra, *The Holy Spirit in Mission: Prophetic Speech and Action in Christian Witness* (Downers Grove, IL: IVP Academic, 2011), p. 116, for a brief discussion of how such a sense of eschatological urgency is thought to be at least one of the reasons behind an aggressive engagement in evangelism that has resulted in the prolific growth of Pentecostalism around the world.
[2]For example, see Ross Hastings, *Missional God, Missional Church: Hope for Re-evangelizing the West* (Downers Grove, IL: IVP Academic, 2012), pp. 12, 31, 33, 42, 46, 106, 108, 155-57, 159, 166, 183-84, 189, 209, 215.
[3]See Borg, HC 173.
[4]See ibid., p. 172. See also McLaren, GO 93 [101], 99-100 [108-9].

balanced understanding of the kingdom of God as both "already" and "not yet" is crucial to a ministry engagement that possesses the necessary balance between the individual and communal, and between disciple making and social action.

THE IMPORTANCE OF A BIBLICALLY INFORMED ESCHATOLOGY

In previous chapters we have seen how that the emerging paradigm tends to downplay, if not dismiss, the significance of what the Bible has to say about the final things. I have suggested that this essential neglect of a biblically informed eschatology has resulted in emerging reformulations and rehabilitations of the doctrines of salvation and the church that fail to pass the biblical-faithfulness test. With this thought in mind and at the risk of redundancy, I want to return to some of the eschatological material we find in the New Testament.

In the four Gospels we find many references to the "end of the age,"[5] the "age to come,"[6] the "last day,"[7] an event referred to as "the resurrection,"[8] and the experience of "eternal life."[9] In the rest of the New Testament we find the apostolic authors making a clear distinction between this age and the one to come,[10] expressing a real interest in the notion of eternal life,[11] and steadfastly affirming a future resurrection of both the righteous and wicked dead.[12] Furthermore, the New Testament as a whole seems to take pains to teach its readers that the salvation Jesus came into this world to effect provides sinful human beings with a *rescue* from an eschatological rather than merely existential experience of divine wrath[13] and some postmortem experiences/conditions of divine judgment (however they are

---

[5]See Mt 12:32; 13:38-42, 47-50; 24:3-14; 28:19-20.

[6]For example, see Mk 10:29-30; Lk 18:28-30; 20:34-36.

[7]See Jn 6:39, 40, 44, 54; 11:24; 12:48.

[8]For example, see Mt 22:28, 30; Mk 12:23; Lk 14:14; 20:33, 35-36; Jn 11:24-25.

[9]See Mt 19:16, 29; 25:46; Mk 10:17, 30; Lk 10:25; 18:18, 30; Jn 3:15, 16, 36; 4:14, 36; 5:24, 39; 6:27, 40, 54, 68; 10:28; 12:25, 50; 17:2, 3.

[10]For example, see Gal 1:3-5; Eph 1:18-21; 1 Tim 6:17-19; Tit 2:11-14; Heb 6:4-6.

[11]See Acts 13:46, 48; Rom 2:7; 5:21; 6:22, 23; Gal 6:8; 1 Tim 1:16; 6:12; Tit 1:2; 3:7; 1 Jn 1:2; 2:25; 3:15; 5:11, 13, 20; Jude 1:21.

[12]See Acts 4:1-2; 17:16-18, 32; 23:6-8; 24:10-16, 21; 1 Cor 15:12-58; Phil 3:7-11; 2 Tim 2:17-18; Heb 6:1-2; 11:35; 1 Pet 1:3-4; Rev 20:4-6.

[13]For example, see Jn 3:36; Rom 2:5-8; 5:9-10; Eph 2:1-7; 5:1-14; Col 3:1-11; 1 Thess 1:4-10; 2:13-16; 5:1-11.

interpreted) that the New Testament authors depict as being "eternal" in nature.[14] It refers to such concepts as "eternal redemption,"[15] an "eternal inheritance,"[16] the experience of "eternal glory,"[17] an "eternal kingdom,"[18] and the prospect of being with Christ "forever."[19] Finally, the New Testament also underscores the crucial importance to the Christian life of an eschatological *hope* that goes beyond this life to the age to come.[20]

As I have argued in previous chapters, I do not see how any soteriology or ecclesiology that does not take the eschatological content of Scripture seriously can possibly prove faithful to both the biblical text and the missional task. I will go on in this chapter to point out how it is not simply the emerging paradigm's doctrines of salvation and the church that are impacted by its essential dismissal of eschatology,[21] but its understanding of what it means to be missional as well.

THE KINGDOM CONNECTION BETWEEN ESCHATOLOGY AND MISSIOLOGY

Since the primary purpose of this work is to forge the rough contours of a *missional* theology, it is important that we explore the crucial connection that exists between our eschatology and how we engage in mission. After all, Jesus himself demonstrates this connection for us.

It is well known that the fourth Gospel possesses a special interest in

---

[14]See Mt 18:8; 25:41, 46; Jn 3:36; 2 Thess 1:9; Heb 6:1-2; Jude 1:5-7, 12-13; Rev 14:9-12.

[15]See Heb 9:12.

[16]See Heb 9:15. Furthermore, other New Testament passages that refer to an "inheritance" in an eschatological sense include: Mt 25:34; Acts 20:32; Eph 1:3-14, 18; 5:5; Col 1:10-14, 3:23-24; Heb 9:15; and 1 Pet 1:3-5.

[17]See 2 Cor 4:17; 2 Tim 2:10; 1 Pet 5:10.

[18]2 Pet 1:11.

[19]See 1 Thess 4:17; 2 Jn 1:1-3.

[20]See Rom 5:1-10; 8:18-25; 12:11-13; 1 Cor 15:19; Eph 1:3-14, 18; Col 1:3-5, 21-23, 27; 1 Thess 1:2-10; 2:19; 4:13-18; 5:1-11; 2 Thess 2:1-16; 1 Tim 4:6-10; 6:11-19; Tit 1:1-2; 2:11-14; 3:3-7; Heb 6:9-11; Heb 10:19-25; 1 Pet 1:3-5, 13, 17-21; 1 Jn 3:1-3.

[21]Not that this fact alone is determinative, but *The Heart of Christianity* contains no explicit references to "eschatology," while the three times it shows up in *A Generous Orthodoxy,* the term is used in a derisive manner. See McLaren, GO 237-38 [267-68]. Furthermore, while Borg seems not to take seriously the idea of a literal second coming of Jesus to the earth (see Borg, HC 75, 104, 181; Borg, SC 195; and Borg and Wright, MJ 195), and despite his overall agnosticism regarding what may or may not occur after this life is over (see Borg, HC 181-84; and Borg, SC 198-201), he does indicate an openness to the possibility that just as we "live in God," "move in God," and "have our being in God," we will "die into God" instead of an abject nothingness (Borg, HC 182).

the concept of eternal life. As noted in chapter eight, Marcus Borg contends that the many references to "eternal" or "everlasting" life should not be interpreted eschatologically, but existentially instead. However, passages such as John 6:40, 51, 54, 58; 10:28; 12:25 and 1 John 2:17 indicate that though John could speak of eternal life as a present experience, his understanding was that eternal life possessed an eschatological, futuristic, final-things dimension as well. Furthermore, a careful reading of John 12:44-50, which refers to a coming "judgment," the "last day" and "eternal life," certainly seems to suggest that Jesus grounded his preaching ministry in a concern produced by eschatological realities:

> Then Jesus cried out, "Whoever believes in me does not believe in me only, but in the one who sent me. The one who looks at me is seeing the one who sent me. I have come into the world as a light, so that no one who believes in me should stay in darkness.
>
> "If anyone hears my words but does not keep them, I do not judge that person. For I did not come to judge the world, but to save the world. There is a judge for the one who rejects me and does not accept my words; the very words I have spoken will condemn them at the last day. For I did not speak on my own, but the Father who sent me commanded me to say all that I have spoken. I know that his command leads to eternal life. So whatever I say is just what the Father has told me to say."

In other words, according to the Fourth Gospel, Jesus' *ministry motive* was, to some degree at least, informed by his understanding of the final things.

Furthermore, in the synoptic Gospels (Matthew, Mark and Luke) Jesus speaks often of the "kingdom of God." Indeed, passages such as Mark 1:15 and Luke 4:43 indicate that the good news regarding the availability of the kingdom was at the heart of Jesus' *ministry message*,[22] while Matthew 4:23-24; 9:35; 12:28 and Luke 11:20 demonstrate that the kingdom also informed Jesus' *ministry method*. Moreover, passages such as Matthew 10:1; Mark 16:17-18; Luke 9:1-2 and the book of Acts as a whole suggest that the nature of God's kingdom (or rule) also informed the ministry method that was prescribed for and actually engaged in by

---

[22]See Darrell L. Guder, *The Continuing Conversion of the Church* (Grand Rapids: Eerdmans, 2000), p. 36.

Jesus' first followers. The question, then, is this: Is the kingdom of God an eschatological concept? I am convinced it is.

To begin with, even though Matthew's Gospel sometimes refers to the "kingdom of God" as such (see Mt 12:28; 19:24; 21:31, 43), the author of the first Gospel much preferred the phrase "kingdom of heaven," most likely out of sensitivity to his intended Jewish audience's reticence to refer to God in such a direct manner.[23] One possible reason why Matthew could so easily substitute "kingdom of heaven" for "kingdom of God" suggests that Jesus' first followers understood the kingdom of God to be something that possesses a future-oriented, "not yet" aspect to it.

However, the apparently synonymous manner in which Matthew referred to the kingdom of God and the kingdom of heaven is not the only reason to hold that the kingdom of God is an eschatological concept. Even though the New Testament authors will at times refer to the kingdom of God as a present reality that can and should be experienced here and now, they also refer to it as something that is yet future.[24] It is this dual manner in which the kingdom of God is referred to in the New Testament that has given rise to the notion that God's kingdom should be thought of as both "already" and "not yet" rather than one or the other. To the degree that the kingdom possesses a "not yet" aspect, it can and should be considered an eschatological concept.[25]

Now, if we grant that the kingdom of God is an eschatological concept and that the kingdom-oriented ministry motive, message and method of Jesus should inform the ministry motive, message and method of his followers (of every age), it stands to reason that a crucial *kingdom* connection can and should exist between eschatology and missiology—

---

[23]See Mt 3:2; 4:17; 5:3, 10, 19-20; 7:21; 8:11; 10:7; 11:11-12; 13:11, 24, 31, 33, 44-45, 47, 52; 16:19; 18:1, 3, 4, 23; 19:12, 14, 23; 20:1; 22:2, 23:13; 25:1.

[24]For example, see Mt 5:19-20; 7:21-22; 8:11-12; 13:36-43, 47-50; 16:26-28; 25:1-46; 26:26-29; Mk 9:42-48; Lk 12:32-34; 13:22-30; 17:20-37; 18:29; 19:11-27; 21:25-36; 22:14-17, 29-30; 23:42-43; Jn 18:36; 1 Cor 6:9-10; 15:24, 50; Gal 5:21; Eph 5:5; 1 Thess 2:12; 2 Thess 1:5; 2 Tim 4:1.

[25]Throughout this chapter I will make reference to the "already, not yet" paradigm that has garnered wide acceptance among biblical scholars ever since it was popularized by evangelical biblical theologian George E. Ladd in *A Theology of the New Testament* (Grand Rapids: Eerdmans, 1993), pp. 368, 638, 651-52.

between what we believe the Bible teaches about the final things and how we engage in missional ministry.

Darrell Guder speaks to the importance for our mission of maintaining the tension between the already and not yet aspects of Christ's kingdom:

> Jesus proclaims that the kingdom is present and is also coming. . . . The tension between the kingdom come and coming has always been difficult for the Christian tradition . . . the temptation has always been very strong to resolve this tension in favor of one its poles, either the kingdom's present or future. It is, however, crucial to the mission of Jesus and his followers that the tension be maintained: "It is precisely in this creative tension that the reality of God's reign has significance for our contemporary mission."[26]

THE EMERGING PARADIGM'S UNBALANCED ESCHATOLOGY AND MISSIOLOGY

To their credit, both Marcus Borg and Brian McLaren rightly focus attention on the kingdom of God in their respective works, *The Heart of Christianity* and *A Generous Orthodoxy*. The problem is, however, that because of their essential dismissal of eschatology, their treatments of the kingdom largely empty the concept of any significant eschatological meaning. As a result, regardless of the fact that they can in one or two places speak of the Bible's references to an afterlife, overall they end up promoting an understanding of the kingdom of God that is *primarily* political and temporal and a concomitant approach to missional ministry that is *primarily* (and ironically) individualistic in nature. While there is nothing wrong with encouraging individual Christ followers to become involved in activist causes—political, social and environmental—the danger arises when this is not balanced by an accompanying encouragement to engage in missional ministry that is *ecclesial* (i.e., communal) and *evangelical* (i.e., related to the proclamation of the evangel or gospel) as well.

Borg on the "what," "when" and "wherefore" of the kingdom. Early on in *The Heart of Christianity*, in a chapter titled "The Kingdom of God:

---

[26]See Guder, *Continuing Conversion*, p. 36. The citation is from Bosch, *Transforming Mission*, p. 32.

The Heart of Justice," Borg associates the kingdom with "social and political transformation."[27] After providing what is actually an excellent reminder of God's passion for justice, Borg goes on to discuss in this context the concept of the kingdom of God. Rightly pointing out that the kingdom was central to Jesus' ministry message,[28] Borg allows for the fact that for Jesus the kingdom of God had more than one meaning.[29] Well and good. The problem is that despite this passing acknowledgement, Borg chooses to focus his attention exclusively on the kingdom of God as a "religious-political" or "theo-political" metaphor, formally expressing its political meaning as "what life would be like on earth if God were king and the rulers of this world were not. The Kingdom of God is about God's justice in contrast to the systemic injustice of the kingdoms and dominations systems of this world."[30]

The way Borg explains the "what" of the kingdom of God has obvious implications for his view of the "when." Since the kingdom is primarily political—that is, about "God's justice in contrast to the systemic injustice of the kingdoms and domination systems of this world"—it should come as no surprise to find Borg going on to assert that "significantly, the Kingdom of God for Jesus was something *for the earth*."[31] That this statement has reference to chronology as well as geography is made clear as Borg proceeds to explain why generations of Christians have mistakenly associated the kingdom of God with an afterlife. He argues that because Matthew the Evangelist so often utilized the phrase "kingdom of heaven" rather than "kingdom of God," and "because Matthew was the synoptic gospel most commonly read in the lectionary of the church through the centuries," the "natural assumption was that Jesus was talking about heaven, that is, about an afterlife." "But," Borg insists, "the Kingdom of God is not about heaven; it is for the earth."[32] That these statements argue for a primarily temporal, historical rather than eschatological, eternal understanding of the kingdom

---

[27]Borg, HC 126.
[28]Ibid., p. 131.
[29]Ibid., p. 132.
[30]Ibid., pp. 132-33.
[31]Ibid., p. 133, emphasis original.
[32]Borg, HC 133.

is made even more apparent by the presence of some ancillary kingdom references located here and elsewhere in the book which explicitly assert that the kingdom of God and salvation are for "this world" in the "here and now."[33]

Having essentially defined the kingdom of God as a political and temporal construct, Borg presses on to argue that to take God's passion for justice (i.e., the kingdom) seriously calls for two ministry-related "wherefore" responses. First, there must be a deliberate attempt to raise the consciousness of church members regarding the reality of "unjust social systems" and "the way they shape and affect the lives of people, including our own."[34] Then, after providing some models of what such consciousness raising in churches might look like, Borg goes on to say that taking the kingdom seriously calls for an "advocacy of God's justice" in terms of health care, the environment, economic justice and the use of imperial power.[35]

Again, well and good; there is nothing wrong with raising the awareness of church members regarding these social issues and encouraging advocacy for God's justice in the face of them. The problem arises in that, as Borg discusses these kingdom issues and concerns, he not only fails to reference the importance of *hope* for the Christian life,[36] he also, quite surprisingly, never explicitly refers to an ecclesial (in the sense of communal) response to the very issues he has raised. This leaves the impression that the call is for individual church members to make personal decisions to become engaged in these advocacy causes. Though Borg picks up this theme in a later chapter's discussion of the practice of compassion and justice,[37] where he elaborates even more on the need and nature of consciousness-raising in the church, the ultimate goal of

---

[33]For example, see ibid., pp. 136, 147 (nn. 9, 10), 173, 178-79, 182. A contrary view is put forward by George Ladd who argues that while "the Synoptic Gospels give no hint as to the nature of the Kingdom Jesus expected . . . one thing is clear; he is not concerned to teach a temporal earthly kingdom before the eternal order in the Age to Come" (*Theology of the New Testament,* p. 205).

[34]Borg, HC 139-42.

[35]Ibid., pp. 142-46.

[36]That is, a sanctification- and service-inspiring hope grounded precisely in the promise of the return of Christ, a reckoning event and the advent of an era during which the reign of God will make all things right. See Rom 12:11-13; 2 Cor 5:6-15; 2 Pet 3:10-14; 1 Jn 3:2-3.

[37]Ibid., pp. 200-204.

this awareness-raising activity is to affect the way individual church members *vote* on justice-related issues[38] and *contribute financially* to organizations that will "change the world in the direction of greater justice."[39] Note that the acts of voting and making financial contributions are intensely personal endeavors. Though both activities can have a great impact on society as a whole, we engage in neither of them in a communal manner. Indeed, it would seem from this discussion that the bulk of the real work of justice advocacy is to be performed by those parachurch organizations receiving our financial support. I am not suggesting that Borg's intention is to encourage an overly individualized, nonecclesial understanding of the kingdom, only that his view can end up having that effect, whether intended or not.

In sum, Borg's conception of the kingdom is decidedly non-eschatological. Because of this, his approach to mission lacks any real emphasis on the importance of *Christian hope* to Christian life and service, is missing any serious focus on evangelism, and seems to be overly individualistic in its approach to its nearly exclusive call for social action.

McLaren on the negative impact of eschatology on missional ministry. There are two primary places in *A Generous Orthodoxy* where McLaren treats the meaning of missional ministry—in his chapters titled "Why I Am Missional" and "Why I Am Green." Note that while McLaren broaches the topic of eschatology in both of these ministry-oriented chapters, he does so in a derisive, dismissive manner, as if to suggest (along with Borg) that the earlier paradigm's focus on eschatology is the problem rather than the cure. (Recall that, according to Borg, one of "Christianity's ten worst contributions to religion" is "popular Christianity's emphasis on the afterlife."[40])

The first sense one gets from "Why I am Missional" is that McLaren has little use for a traditional eschatological focus on the return of Christ, a day of judgment and an eternal state. This is seen in his promotion of the idea that "the Christian message is universally good news for Chris-

---

[38]Borg focuses his attention on such issues as: the funding of public schools; the funding of health care for those without insurance; the need for a living wage; tax policy; and international policy, both economic and military.

[39]Borg, HC 203-4.

[40]Ibid., pp. 171-72.

tians and non-Christians alike."[41] Though at first blush it is hard to find fault with such a magnanimous sentiment, a bit of reflection reveals that in the long run this conviction proves true only if the kingdom of God at the heart of the Christian message is understood in some sort of soteriologically universalist manner.[42] However, the fact is that while McLaren flirts with an "everybody's in!" soteriological universalism, which holds that all human beings will experience some sort of heaven when this life is over, he does not end up marrying himself to this concept (at least not in this work).[43] Instead, he explicitly promotes a new type of universalism which maintains that the reason why the kingdom of God is of benefit to *everyone* regardless of religious affiliation—"Christians and non-Christians alike"[44]—is precisely because it is *a historical rather than eschatological phenomenon* that concerns the whole world.[45] In other words, despite a few passing acknowledgments here and there that salvation does ultimately include an eschatological aspect, McLaren's overall treatment of what it means to be missional strongly suggests a view of the kingdom which sees it as a better world *here and now*.[46]

This emphasis can be found not only in McLaren's repeated dismissals of the idea of a heaven- and hell-oriented understanding of salvation,[47] but also in the way he describes the nature and goal of missional ministry in a decidedly non-eschatological manner. McLaren begins this discussion posing the question: "Is it any surprise that it's stinking hard to convince churches that they have a mission to the world when most Christians equate 'personal salvation' of individual 'souls' with the ultimate aim of Jesus?"[48] Near the end of this discussion he writes:

---

[41]McLaren, GO 110 [120].

[42]One should take note of the way McLaren portrays the Kingdom of God in a religiously pluralistic manner in Brian McLaren, *Why Did Jesus, Moses, the Buddha, and Mohammed Cross the Road? Christian Identity in a Multi-Faith World* (New York: Jericho Books, 2012), pp. 252-53.

[43]McLaren, GO 109 [119].

[44]Ibid., p. 110 [120]. See also McLaren, NKC 139; McLaren, *Why Did Jesus*, pp. 254-64.

[45]McLaren, GO 114 [124].

[46]Ibid., pp. 113-14 [123-24].

[47]Ibid., pp. 85-86 [94-95], 93 [101], 100 [107-9], 107 [117], 112 [122], 160 [178], 237-39 [267-68].

[48]Ibid., p. 107 [117].

But what about heaven and hell? You ask. *Is everybody in?*

My reply: Why do you consider me qualified to make this pronouncement? Isn't this God's business? Isn't it clear that I do not believe this is the right question for a missional Christian to ask? Can't we talk for a while about God's will being done on earth as in heaven without jumping to how to escape earth and get to heaven as quickly as possible? Can't we talk for a while about overthrowing and undermining every hellish stronghold in our lives and in our world?[49]

Even many traditional evangelicals, especially younger ones, will find themselves resonating with, rather than reacting defensively to, the rhetorical questions posed above. The problem is that this set of questions functions collectively as a red herring, leading us toward a false antithesis—the idea that Christ's followers must *either* embrace an eschatology that necessarily promotes an escapist mentality and myopic focus on personal evangelism, *or* be missional, focusing our attention on the goal of forging of a better world for everyone here and now. Darrell Guder calls attention to this false antithesis in his attempt to encourage Christians to care about *more* than their own salvation:

The crux, for Barth, is the question of God's reasons for carrying out the work of salvation. In answering this question, we begin to disclose the subtle power of our reductionism. The egocentricity or anthropocentricity of Western reductionisms from the right to the left end of the spectrum emerges as the real issue. In a sense, the world-renouncing pietist and the world-reforming social activist are both displaying their concern for their own salvation. On the one hand, salvation is secured by means of the spiritual experience one testifies to. On the other hand, salvation is secured by means of the concrete changes one is able to project and implement to make the world a better place to live. Christian experience in both cases is understood from the central point of the Christian who relates the effects or impact of salvation to oneself and one's environment.[50]

Guder, following Barth, essentially goes on to make the argument that the purpose of Christian existence is not simply to enjoy the benefits of salvation, but to be witnesses to what God has done through

---

[49]Ibid., p. 112 [122].
[50]Guder, *Continuing Conversion*, pp. 126-27.

Christ for the benefit of the world. Citing Barth, Guder writes:

> Thus, Christian existence can be defined in these words: "With their whole being, action, inaction and conduct, and then by word and deed, they have an announcement to make to other people, a definite declaration to communicate. The essence of their vocation is that God makes them His witnesses."[51]

To be sure, at one place in his chapter on what it means to be missional, McLaren himself argues against a dichotomizing between "evangelism" and "social action."[52] However, because he then proceeds to primarily portray the kingdom as a historical possibility while downplaying the importance of personal evangelism to missional ministry, he ends up sending a mixed message—that evangelism and missional ministry are not integrally related after all.[53]

Fully recognizing the possibility that McLaren is simply trying to push the pendulum in the opposite direction away from what he perceives to be a myopic and misguided focus among evangelicals on gospel proclamation, his treatment of what it means to be missional overcorrects and ends up suggesting that missional ministry is mainly about becoming engaged in social action toward a better world here and now.

This raises the issue of what McLaren means when he refers to the "world." His discussion in the chapter titled "Why I Am Green" makes perfectly clear that he has in mind *this world, here and now*. What is also clearly communicated is McLaren's real concern over the deleterious effect a "pop-evangelical eschatology," also referred to as an "eschatology

---

[51]Ibid., p. 131. The citation is from Barth, *Church Dogmatics*, trans. G. W. Bromiley, 4/3.2 (Edinburgh: T & T Clark, 1962), p. 575.

[52]McLaren, GO 108 [118-19].

[53]Contrast this with the way David Bosch ends up affirming the evangelism endeavor in his excellent and thorough discussion titled "Toward a Constructive Understanding of Evangelism" in *Transforming Mission*, pp. 421-30. Moreover, citing another work by Bosch, Darrell Guder writes: "David Bosch correctly observes that 'evangelism is the *core, heart,* or *center* of mission; it consists in the proclamation of salvation in Christ to nonbelievers, in announcing forgiveness of sins, in calling people to repentance and faith in Christ, inviting them to become living members of Christ's earthly community and to begin a life in the power of the Holy Spirit.'" See David Bosch, "Evangelism: Theological Currents and Cross-Currents Today," *International Bulletin of Missionary Research* 11, no. 3 (July 1987): 100, as cited in Guder, *Continuing Conversion*, pp. 25-26.

of abandonment," has had on the well-being of the planet.[54] Overall, I am in agreement with McLaren's call for more Christians to be concerned for the environment. He makes an important point in an eloquent manner when he connects a concern for the environment and a love for our neighbors "downstream" in space and time.[55] However, at the same time, he makes some assertions that I am uncomfortable with—assertions that, in my mind, seem redolent of a false antithesis. For example, McLaren:

- implies that prevalent among Christians who take the doctrine of an "ontological fall" of creation seriously is a desire to exploit nature for economic profit[56]

- implies that all Christians who take the doctrine of the fall seriously deny the ongoing beauty of creation [57]

- suggests that all evangelical eschatologies are dispensational and escapist (or, at least, he does not acknowledge that there are evangelical eschatologies that are not "pop-evangelical")[58]

- fails to acknowledge those Bible passages that do seem to speak of the demise of this earth with a new one taking its place (e.g., 2 Pet 3:7, 10-13; Rev 21:1)

- tries to link all forms of eschatological dualism to dispensationalism, and dispensationalism to modernism, with the result that all eschatological dualism is linked to modernism (something most postmodern readers will abjure)[59]

- suggests that any eschatology that contains an apocalyptic element is necessarily based on an illegitimate reinterpretation of Old Testament prophetic passages and a marginalization of Jesus' message concerning a kingdom that is temporal and historical in nature[60]

---

[54]McLaren, GO 237-38 [267-68].

[55]Ibid., p. 242 [273].

[56]Ibid., p. 234 [265].

[57]Ibid., p. 235 [265-66].

[58]Ibid., p. 237 [268]. This association of eschatological with dispensational shows up also in McLaren, NKC 191-93.

[59]McLaren, GO 237 [268].

[60]Ibid., p. 238 [268]. McLaren seems to overlook the fact that it was not pop-evangelical theolo-

- keeps insisting that Jesus' message was that the kingdom of God is primarily temporal and historical rather than something that will be fully and even primarily experienced in an age to come[61]

Overall, there is much in these two chapters to laud and applaud. McLaren rightfully draws attention to some aspects of missional ministry that many evangelicals need to take much more seriously than we have in the past. Again, as with other issues related to a missional orthodoxy, the question is not whether McLaren has completely missed the mark, but rather, whether he has overcorrected. Indeed, though his intentions are surely noble, McLaren has tended to overreact to an extreme swing of the pendulum with the result that, alongside of some very needed critiques of an escapist eschatology, he provides some bold prescriptions that push the pendulum too far in the other direction. Rather than strike the needed biblical balance between the "already" and "not yet" aspects of the kingdom of God, McLaren seems to move in a Borg-like trajectory toward an eschatology that emphasizes the "already" at the expense of the "not yet," essentially prescribing a missional ministry that, because it focuses too much on the individual, the po-

---

gians who were the first to reinterpret Old Testament kingdom passages in a spiritualizing manner, but the New Testament authors and the early church fathers! The irony here is that McLaren is actually making the dispensational argument that the Old Testament's "kingdom" passages must be interpreted literally in a temporal, historical manner (rather than applied to the church as the new people of God—the new Israel, as in Rom 9:6; 11:13-27; Gal 6:14-16; Eph 2:11-22; 3:6)! Furthermore, New Testament scholar George Ladd has argued that "Jesus and Paul shared the same worldview that prevailed in Judaism"—a worldview he characterizes as an "apocalyptic view of history" (*Theology of the New Testament,* p. 45). Ladd also asserts that, in the Synoptics, the terms "Age to Come" and "Kingdom of God" are interchangeable/synonymous (pp. 44, 62) and that Jesus' "proclamation of the Kingdom includes the hope, reaching back to the Old Testament prophets, that anticipates a new age in which all the evils of the present age will be purged by the act of God from human and earthly existence" (p. 46).

[61]McLaren, GO 238 [268]. See also Brian McLaren, *Everything Must Change: When the World's Biggest Problems and Jesus' Good News Collide* (Nashville: Thomas Nelson, 2007), p. 21. To be fair, it should be noted that, perhaps due to criticisms like those presented here, McLaren does a much better job in *A New Kind of Christianity* of bringing some needed to balance between the already and not yet to his eschatological teaching (NKC 191-206). That said, the problem I continue to have with McLaren's "new kind of eschatology" of hope, anticipation and participation is the way it fails to take seriously the apocalyptic aspect of the eschatology presented in Scripture and insists on giving short shrift to the concept of eternal life. Furthermore, it seems to me that to pit a deterministic, escapist eschatology against one that is anticipatory and participatory is yet another example of a false antithesis. For Scripture's emphasis on the kingdom's fulfillment in an age to come, see Mt 12:32; 13:38-42; 13:47-50; 24:3-14; 28:19-20; Mk 10:29-30; Lk 18:28-30; 20:34-36; cf. Gal 1:3-5; Eph 1:18-21; 1 Tim 6:17-19; Tit 2:11-14; Heb 6:4-6.

litical and the temporal, fails to pass the biblical-faithfulness test.

But it does not have to be this way. There is an alternative to this false antithesis that is faithful to both the missional task and the biblical text—a Christian eschatology that enables a missional faithfulness on the part of both individual Christians and communities of faith and that seems evocative of the holistic "great co-missional church" model described in chapter nine.

AN ESCHATOLOGICALLY INFORMED MISSIOLOGY

From the outset I wish to express my support for the cause of world missions. I am aware that some missiologists, especially those who have spent time serving the cause of Christ on foreign mission fields, are uncomfortable with the way the missional conversation can seem to give foreign missions short shrift. This concern is well taken: overcorrections happen! It is possible for us to overreact to a historical tendency to relegate the church's "outreach" to the prayer and financial support of foreign missionaries around the world by making the decision now to redirect *all* our time, energy and resources toward ministry in the local context. Though the ensuing discussion will focus on how an understanding of the kingdom as "already" and "not yet" can and should impact the missional ministry of the local church in its neighborhood, it is vital for churches to continue to support the cause of missional ministries around the globe as well.

The local church and the contextualization of the gospel. In the previous chapter we took note of the idea that the local church, as a tangible expression (or "body") of the resurrected and ascended Christ, is intended by God to function as a point of connection (sacrament) between hurting people and Jesus Christ, who in turn functions as the primary point of connection (sacrament) between them and God. Such an ecclesiology, because it focuses on the idea of the church gathered, not only allows for, but in some sense actually calls for, ministry activities that are *attractional* in nature.

However, it was also noted that an emphasis on the church gathered need not preclude an *incarnational* ministry engagement in the neighborhood. We are reminded of how missiologist Charles Van Engen speaks of the local church as "God's missionary people in a local context."[62] Interestingly, he seems to marry the concept of the church gathered to the dynamic of missional ministry when he refers to the local church as "a marvelous, mysterious creation of God that takes concrete shape in the lives of the disciples of Jesus as they gather in local congregations and seek to contextualize the gospel in their time and place."[63] Though Van Engen does not use the term *missional* in either of these quotes, a ministry approach that is missional in its orientation is precisely what he is alluding to since, according to many missional authors, the contextualization of the gospel for a particular "neighborhood" (i.e., "time and place") is what missional ministry is all about. For example, Alan Roxburgh and Scott Boren speak of the importance of gospel contextualization to missional ministry:

> Each of our contexts is unique; each has its own particular intermixing of cultural interactions. The gospel, therefore, must always be understandable in the language and thought patterns of that context. Specific forms of missional church, therefore, will be constructed locally. The primary need is for local strategies of engagement with the people in the neighborhoods, which is why it is so important for churches to become skilled in listening to their own setting. Missional life emerges from the kind of listening that connects us with what God might be up to in a particular context.[64]

The missional ecclesiology put forward by missiologists such as Van Engen, Roxburgh and Boren prompts two crucial questions: (1) What does it mean to contextualize the gospel? (2) What is the *gospel* that must be contextualized? Though I have already dealt with both of the questions at some length in chapter two of this work, I offer here some additional, hopefully summative thoughts for consideration.

As for what it means to contextualize the gospel, according to missional church proponents Michael Frost and Alan Hirsch:

---

[62]Charles Van Engen, *God's Missionary People*, p. 27.
[63]Ibid., p. 17.
[64]Roxburgh and Boren, p. 87. See also Richard Mouw, "The Missionary Location of North American Churches," in *Confident Witness—Changing World: Rediscovering the Gospel in North America,* ed. Craig Van Gelder (Grand Rapids: Eerdmans, 1999), pp. 3-15.

Contextualization, then, can be defined as the dynamic process whereby the constant message of the gospel interacts with specific, relative human situations. It involves an examination of the gospel in light of the respondent's worldview and then adapting the message, encoding it in such a way that it can become meaningful to the respondent. Contextualization attempts to communicate the gospel in word and deed and to establish churches in ways that make sense to people within their local cultural context. It is primarily concerned with presenting Christianity in such a way that it meets peoples' deepest needs and penetrates their worldviews, thus allowing them to follow Christ and remain in their own cultures.[65]

I want to suggest that this understanding of what it means to contextualize the Christian faith resonates with the "recontextualization" model I advocated in chapter two.

This brings us, then, to the question: What is the "gospel" the local congregation is supposed to contextualize for its neighborhood (in its time and place)? What follows is an extended discussion of Christianity's main message designed to highlight its essentially eschatological character and the implications of this for an ecclesial (communal) missional ministry.

The gospel of the "kingdom." Once again, according to the Bible, the good news that Jesus went about proclaiming and demonstrating in the power of the Spirit concerned the nearness or availability of God's kingdom: "From that time on Jesus began to preach, 'Repent, for the kingdom of heaven has come near'" (Mt 4:17). "After John was put in prison, Jesus went into Galilee, proclaiming the good news of God. 'The time has come,' he said. 'The kingdom of God has come near. Repent and believe the good news!'" (Mk 1:14-15).

Because both Borg and McLaren interpret Jesus' main message as being primarily temporal and essentially political in nature, they end up prescribing a missional ministry that is likewise temporal and political in orientation. But, of course, this is not the only way to interpret the meaning of Jesus' kingdom message, nor what it means to be missional.

It is true that there are Old Testament passages that might be construed as referring to God's kingdom as a literal geopolitical realm to be

---

[65]Frost and Hirsch, *Shaping of Things to Come*, p. 83.

realized with God's help at some point in the future. For instance, the prophet Isaiah announced:

> In the last days
>> the mountain of the LORD's temple will be established
>>> as the highest of the mountains;
>> it will be exalted above the hills,
>>> and all nations will stream to it.
> Many peoples will come and say,
>> "Come, let us go up to the mountain of the LORD,
>>> to the temple of the God of Jacob.
>> He will teach us his ways,
>>> so that we may walk in his paths."
> The law will go out from Zion,
>> the word of the LORD from Jerusalem. (Is 2:2-3)

However, according to many scholars, though Zionist language is often utilized, the prophetic vision of God's kingdom in the Old Testament is better interpreted figuratively and universally as a future world order characterized by peace, justice and celebration under God's loving lordship and compassionate rule.[66] Now the question becomes: Is this future world order, sans the Zionist language, still *essentially* political and temporal in nature as the emerging paradigm suggests?

Turning to the New Testament, it has become increasingly clear to many scholars that the phrase "kingdom of God" refers not so much to a spatial, geopolitical *realm* but to the dynamic of God's *reign* in people's lives.[67] To receive or enter the kingdom of God is to surrender one's life to the reign or authority (Greek *basileia*) of God. According to Darrell Guder: "To enter into the kingdom means to experience the forgiveness of sins, the liberation from all the demons which possess us, the gift of new life, and the invitation to a new kind of community."[68] In other words, to receive or enter the kingdom of God is to become a disciple of

---

[66]Darrell Guder, ed., *The Missional Church: A Vision for the Sending of the Church in North America* (Grand Rapids: Eerdmans, 1998), p. 91.
[67]For a thorough discussion of this understanding of God's kingdom, see the chapter titled "The Kingdom: Reign or Realm," in George Eldon Ladd, *The Presence of the Future: The Eschatology of Biblical Realism* (Grand Rapids: Eerdmans, 1996), pp. 122-48.
[68]Guder, *Continuing Conversion*, p. 37.

Jesus, God's Son—a person committed to spending the rest of his or her life learning from Jesus, in communion with others, how to become a trusting and obedient child of the Father. This is what makes the four christological verities emphasized throughout this book so crucial to Christianity. *The good news Jesus came to announce was the availability to others of the same type of intimate, interactive, obedient relationship with God as Abba that he himself enjoyed.* Of course, such an experience, while personal, is anything but private. It will have social, political and environmental ramifications. But this understanding of the gospel also explains why, according to the New Testament, the same kind of belief and repentance that are the initial steps toward discipleship, are also crucial to receiving and entering God's kingdom.[69] In a nutshell, this understanding of the kingdom holds that to enter God's kingdom one must become a fully devoted follower of the king, Jesus Christ.[70] The kingdom of God cannot be so easily portrayed as *simply* a more just, humane, environmentally sustainable world here and now. Surely, the kingdom will lead to such a world, but not, according to the New Testament, in a utopian (i.e., primarily human and historical) manner. Instead, the apostolic witnesses to Christ tell us that coming under the reign of God has implications for life in this age and the age to come.

The relationship between the church and the "reign" of God. This topic is important because many Christians have, over the years, made the mistake of thinking of the church itself as God's kingdom. This has had the effect of turning the church into a place instead of a people, an organization rather than an organism, an institution rather than a community of people committed to living their lives under the rule of God.[71]

The truth is that the church is not the kingdom (or reign) of God, though it is dynamically related to it. The church is made up of people

---

[69]See Mt 4:17-22; Mk 1:14-20, noting the way Jesus' general call to repentance is juxtaposed to accounts of the making of his first disciples.

[70]Once again, note the way McLaren portrays the kingdom of God in a religiously pluralistic manner in McLaren, *Why Did Jesus*, pp. 252-53. I suspect that McLaren would consider this association of the kingdom with Christ the king to be much too imperialistic, as well as particularistic (see pp. 254-64).

[71]Guder, *Missional Church*, p. 84.

who are entering and experiencing the "already" and "not yet" reign of God. The church is also the place where the "children of the reign" corporately manifest the presence and characteristic features of God's already/not yet reign.[72] The bottom line is that *the purpose of the church is to represent the already/not yet reign of God to the world around it.*[73] In other words, each local church functions as an anticipatory sign or foretaste now of what life under the rule of God will someday be like. Once again, the eschatological aspect of this understanding of what it means to be missional should not go unnoticed.

We can be even more specific about what it means for the local church to represent the reign of God to the world around it. As we do so, it is important to keep in mind the already/not yet aspect of the kingdom which the church is endeavoring to represent—and how precisely it encourages a missional ministry that is ecclesial (i.e., communal) rather than merely individual, and involves a commitment to disciple making that includes both gospel proclamation and demonstration (i.e., social action).

Van Engen refers to local congregations as "branch offices of the kingdom, the principal instrument, anticipatory sign, and primary locus of the coming of the kingdom."[74] As such, the primary mission of the local congregation is to "spread throughout the world the knowledge of the rule of the King."[75] As for how this is to be done, Van Engen suggests that the key is for the local church to engage in the same four main ministry activities that marked the life of the New Testament church: *koinōnia* (fellowship), *kerygma* (proclamation), *diakonia* (service) and

---

[72]Ibid., p. 99. Ladd famously used five key statements to describe the relationship between the kingdom Of God and the church: (1) the church is not the kingdom; (2) the kingdom creates the church; (3) the church witnesses to the kingdom; (4) the church is the instrument of the kingdom; and (5) the church is the custodian of the kingdom (*Theology of the New Testament*, pp. 109-17). Among other things, I believe Ladd was rightly concerned about three issues possessing missional significance: (1) that people not project onto God's kingdom the real imperfections of the historical church (i.e., that we help post-Christians distinguish between "churchianity" and biblical Christianity); (2) that the church never promote itself rather than the kingdom (i.e., God's reign) as the answer to people's problems; and (3) that the church never forget its dependence on God and its need for the power of the kingdom.

[73]Guder, *Missional Church*, p. 100.

[74]Van Engen, *God's Missionary People*, p. 101.

[75]Ibid., p. 111.

martyria (witness). Van Engen's thesis is that for the local church to truly function as the missionary congregation God expects it to be, it must become proficient in these four activities.[76]

The writers of *Missional Church* also believe that the ultimate ministry purpose of the church is to represent the reign of God. They suggest that each local church is therefore called to follow the lead of Jesus and to represent the reign of God as its *community, servant* and *messenger*.[77] Because of the prominence of this book in the missional conversation, I will allow this ministry agenda to function as the organizing framework for my discussion of the shape of an eschatologically informed missional ministry.

The church as the "community" of the already/not yet reign of God. Just as Jesus felt it his responsibility to model for others how to live one's life under the authority of the reign of God, so should the community of his apprentices.[78] Thus, each local church should do its best (in the power of the Spirit) to embody before the world the *shalom* that marks the coming reign of God (see Is 2:4; Mic 4:3).[79] The following quote is both helpful and inspiring:

> Like Jesus, the church is to embody the reign of God by living under its authority. We live as the covenant community, a distinctive community spawned by God's reign to show forth its tangible character in human, social form.
>
> Before the church is called to do or say anything, it is called and sent to be the unique community of those who live under the reign of God. . . . It is the harbinger of the new humanity that lives in genuine community, a form of companionship and wholeness that humanity craves.[80]

---

[76]Ibid., p. 89.

[77]Guder, *Missional Church*, p. 102.

[78]As indicated, the idea that the church should strive to model for our contemporaries the characteristics of the life and fellowship of the coming kingdom is a main theme in *Missional Church*. Note that support for this important assertion can also be found in Ladd, *Theology of the New Testament*, p. 113.

[79]James Davison Hunter advocates something he refers to as a "faithful presence" on the part of the local church. Such a faithful presence calls for each local church to function within its community as an agent or enactment of God's *shalom*. See James Davison Hunter, *To Change the World: The Irony, Tragedy, and Possibility of Christianity in the Late Modern World* (New York: Oxford University Press, 2010), pp. 234, 243-48.

[80]Guder, *Missional Church*, p. 103. See also Bosch, *Transforming Mission*, p. 397.

Community is a term often bandied about in Christian circles. But what does it actually involve? I want to suggest that at the heart of genuine Christian community is the experience of a significant degree of both *support* (unconditional acceptance, honest but gracious affirmation) and *accountability* (with respect to a commitment to Christ's kingdom and the leadership of the Spirit in our lives). Too many Christian groups lack both of these dynamics, or emphasize one but not the other. Rare is the ecclesial environment where both support and accountability can be experienced in a healthy, functional, biblically informed, Spirit-directed manner. While the anecdote that follows does not do full justice to what is involved in the experience of the kingdom support and accountability I have in mind, it comes close.

A young couple came to faith in Christ in one of the churches I pastored. One day the husband (I'll call him Rich) called the church office to let me know that he and his wife (I'll refer to her as Miranda) would not be attending the small group meeting that was scheduled to occur at my home that evening. He went on to indicate the reason why. He and Miranda were in the midst of a significant disagreement over a serious matter and did not think it would be a good idea to be around other couples that evening. They both felt that it would seem hypocritical to come to the meeting, pretending that everything was fine in their lives when the reality was otherwise.

When I asked Rich if he wanted to talk about what was going on, he told me the story. In brief, Miranda had recently received news from her OB/GYN confirming a suspicion that she might be pregnant. Immediately, without discussing the matter with Rich, she had scheduled an appointment to have the pregnancy terminated. My wife, Patti, recollects that there was some sort of health concern at work in the situation. All I remember is Rich explaining that Miranda did not want to be pregnant again at that point in her life. Their daughter was just emerging from the "terrible twos" and they had both been looking forward to certain changes in their lifestyle which that development would bring. Rich indicated to me that though he was sympathetic to Miranda's desire not to be pregnant again, he felt that such a huge decision merited a discussion between the two of them and some serious consideration of where God's heart was on the matter. Becoming more and more heated, the disagreement had begun to spiral out of control. According to Rich, they had come to the point where they were not communicating at all.

Though I indicated to Rich that it is often during such tough times that a Christian couple most needs the love and support of a caring community, I put no pressure on him with respect to the small group meeting scheduled that evening. I told him I would be praying for him and Miranda and would, of course, keep the matter we had just discussed to myself.

Later that evening, the small group meeting was about to begin when, to my surprise, Rich and Miranda arrived, filling two empty chairs to my immediate left. Pleased that this young couple, new in the faith, had made the decision to attend the meeting after all, I began the meeting in the usual way by asking the members of the group to "check in," sharing what they sensed the Lord was currently "up to" in their lives based on their experiences the previous week, their study of Scripture, or perhaps what the Spirit of the Lord had spoken to them by means of his still small voice. It seemed wise at the time to begin with the person on my right who happened to be Patti, my wife. As Patti explained briefly what she sensed the Lord might be doing in her life at the moment, I took note of the fact that what she shared had an amazing degree of relevance for Rich and Miranda. Apparently Miranda sensed this as well; she began to dab at tears welling up in her eyes.

The really astounding thing is that this dynamic of the Holy Spirit speaking to Rich and Miranda through the "innocent" sharing of the others in the group repeated itself over and over again as everyone else checked in, commenting on what they felt like God was saying to or doing in them. And what was happening was not lost on this couple, especially Miranda. Before long she was a mess, mascara running down both cheeks!

Eventually, it came to be Rich's turn to weigh in. He simply deferred to Miranda. Everyone in the room sensed that God was, at that moment, effecting some work within her. When she was finally able to speak, she slowly articulated what was going on: that she had discovered that week that she was pregnant; that she had wasted no time in scheduling the procedure that would end the pregnancy. "But," she went on to say, "God has spoken to me through the sharing of each and every one of you tonight. I now know that I can't go through with the procedure. God wants me to have this baby."

I am convinced that the interests of the already and not yet kingdom were well served in the small group meeting that took place that night. Walking around somewhere today is a young woman in her twenties who owes her very existence, at least in part, to the fact that her mom and dad were part of a community of Spirit-filled Christ-followers who were doing their best to obey the ecclesial exhortations of Hebrews 10:23-25:

> Let us hold unswervingly to the hope we profess, for he who promised is faithful. And let us consider how we may spur one another on toward love and good deeds, not giving up meeting together, as some are in the habit of doing, but encouraging one another—and all the more as you see the Day approaching.

Endeavoring to function as an authentic Christian community that is committed to living out the values of Christ's kingdom come and coming is not easy. But when it happens, the results are both breathtaking and inspiring, just what we need to stay at the task.

The church as the "servant" of the already/not yet reign of God. Just as Jesus believed it to be his responsibility to demonstrate the reality and nearness of the already/not yet reign of God by exercising its authority over disease, death and the demonic in the lives of hurting people, so should the community of his apprentices. It is on the basis of Jesus' healing and deliverance ministries that the authors of *Missional Church* argue that *each local church must become radically involved in compassion-based ministries which address human needs.*[81]

As a proponent of theological realism, I further suggest that an imitation of Jesus' kingdom demonstration and the component of missional ministry that corresponds to it, also calls for all evangelical churches, whether they self-identify as Pentecostal-charismatic or not, to avoid the false antithesis discussed in the previous chapter and recognize that

---

[81]Guder, *Missional Church*, p. 106.

there is a *missional* option to both classical Pentecostalism and non-Pentecostalism. This missional Pentecostalism is a pneumatological option that, because it focuses on the biblically supported connection between prophetic activity (Spirit-inspired speech and action) and missional faithfulness, is faithful to both the biblical text and the missional task. The story of how Miranda experienced the Spirit speaking to her in an existentially impactful manner through the members of her community of faith is an apt illustration of this prophetic dynamic.

The fact is that people are hurting in the West just as they are in the Global South. The same Spirit of mission that is healing the sick and delivering people from oppressive demonic forces in other parts of the world desires to do so here as well! This is the type of "new universalism" those genuinely committed to missional ministry should consider adopting: a universalism which allows the Spirit of mission to empower prophetic speech and action into the lives of *everyone, everywhere in the world*—producing missionally effective demonstrations of the present and coming kingdom of God. An openness by more and more rank-and-file evangelical church members (traditional, missional and emerging) to the idea that, like Ananias of Damascus (see Acts 9:10-20), they might be led by the Spirit to speak and act into the lives of hurting people in the name of Christ, could be a game-changer in terms of a missionally fruitful contextualization of the gospel in our current ministry context.

The church as the "messenger" of the already/not yet reign of God. Finally, just as Jesus gave himself to the task of announcing the presence of the reign of God through his preaching and teaching, so should the community of his apprentices. *Therefore, each local church must do more than engage in good deeds; they must add Jesus' signature to these demonstrations of love by boldly proclaiming his birth, life, death, burial, resurrection, ascension and lordship over all.* According to the authors of *Missional Church,* there must be no ambiguity about the local church's service to the poor and hurting; people must know that it is Jesus Christ's love and authority they are experiencing. The plain sense of the New Testament as a whole is that it is only through a willingness of the church to boldly affirm the uniqueness of the risen Christ—that is, the four christological verities—that the reign of God through Jesus Christ is made accessible to the people to whom we minister.[82]

The authors of *Missional Church* seem to suggest that gospel proclamation and demonstration—disciple-making and social action—should go hand in hand. At the same time, however, a balanced approach to these missional activities is not always easy to achieve. For instance, the community of faith my wife and I belong to serves our community with a food distribution center. Literally thousands of clients are served each year by means of this church-based ministry of compassion. The perennial question facing such church-based ministries is: How, at the very least, do we add Jesus' signature to the caring that is demonstrated in such food distribution? At best, how might a contextually sensitive version of the Jesus story that is faithful to the four christological verities be proclaimed? Just what is the proper relationship between preaching and caring in a relief-oriented ministry that seeks to be faithful to both the biblical text and the missional task?

Figure 10.1 can help us gain a sense of perspective regarding our ministry options with respect to these important questions. It represents five different ministry approaches along a continuum that reflects (1) a commitment to gospel proclamation (preaching) and/or demonstration (social action); (2) the kingdom concept that informs the approaches (i.e., not yet vs. already); (3) the position each approach tends to take with respect to the goal of kingdom work (i.e., personal salvation vs. social change); and (4) where each approach might be located on the pendulum's swing between historic fundamentalism on the one hand and classical liberalism on the other.

Notice how, not surprisingly, I associate the "middle way" with missional orthodoxy—an approach to ministry that emphasizes both preaching and social action, but insists that at the end of the day, it is crucial that the risen Jesus rather than the socially active Christian be recognized as the principal incarnation of God's loving concern, and the primary proclaimer and demonstrator of God's kingdom come and coming. Thus, it is always important for our acts of compassion, peace-

---

[82]Ibid., p. 107.

making, creation care and so on to be performed "over Jesus' signature" as it were. In other words, given its commitment to the four christological verities and how they underwrite the good news of the Jesus story, a missional orthodoxy will insist that, when providing the weary with a cup of cold water, we should always strive to do so "in Jesus'

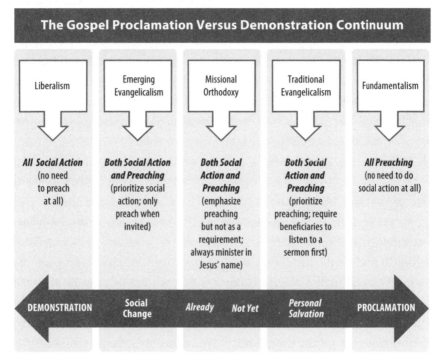

Figure 10.1.

name" rather than our own (see Mk 9:35-41). The fact that each local church is called by the Spirit of mission to serve its particular ministry context as a *messenger* of the kingdom (as well as a *servant*) requires nothing less.

THE KINGDOM MANDATE: A *DISCIPLE-MAKING* COMMUNITY OF BELIEVERS

The authors of *Missional Church,* go on to say that certain ecclesial practices can and should be engaged in if we want to nurture the kind of congregation that can effectively represent to its neighborhood the already/not yet reign of God as its community, servant and messenger. Such practices include baptism; the Lord's Supper; reconciliation; communal discernment of God's will for the church as a whole and individual disciples; hospitality; reading and interpreting Scripture; the development and exercise of leadership; loving care and support of one another; the proclamation of God's Word; active evangelization of all peoples; exploration and learning of the faith; responsible and responsive stewardship of God's abundant gifts; and so on.[83] We should not overlook the fact that most of these practices are themselves, or seem to require a serious engagement in, what have come to be known as spiritual disciplines.[84] Since, as the term suggests, an engagement in the spiritual *disciplines* is key to the process of *discipleship,* we are reminded once again that the great co-missional church will see itself as a disciple-making community of believers that is committed to a faithful fulfilling of the Great Commission (Mt 28:18-20; Mk 16:15-16), while at the same time being careful to obey the Great Commandment (Mt 22:33-34) and engaging in creation care.[85] Even an advocate for social action such as Ronald Sider can speak of the "primacy of evangelism" while at the same time arguing that a proper understanding of the "whole gospel" will never be content with a wholesale neglect of social action.[86] In search of a broader concept under which both evangelism (proclamation) and social action (demonstration) can be subsumed as complimentary rather than competitive endeavors, Sider lands on the term *mission.*[87] While I appreciate this choice, my preference is for the term "disciple making" because, according to the Scriptures, both gospel proclamation (Mk 16:15-16; Mt 28:19) and demonstration are integral to it (Mt 5:13-14).

This commitment to forge churches that function in their neighborhoods as *disciple-making* communities of believers finds further support in the fact that the authors of *Missional Church* press on to advocate

---

[83]Ibid., p. 159.
[84]See ibid., p. 186, where these ecclesial practices are referred to as spiritual disciplines.
[85]See discussion in chapter nine above, pp. 310-17.
[86]Ronald J. Sider *Good News and Good Works: A Theology for the Whole Gospel* (Grand Rapids: Baker, 1993), pp. 165-71.
[87]Ibid., pp. 164-65.

strongly for a very intentional and communal approach to the spiritual and ministry formation components of disciple making. According to these missional experts, one of the main ministry activities of the local church should be the instruction of church members in the way of the Christian life, which is viewed as a participation in a "new culture." Take special note of their citizenship and naturalization language:

> Those who hear the good news and want to become citizens of the reign of God will need teaching. The church as holy nation has a culture, an accepted way of doing things, a specialized vocabulary to talk about life under the reign of God. The church should not expect new people in its midst to know these things automatically. Becoming a citizen of the reign of God does not come naturally. It is different from just being civil or being a good person. It requires a new loyalty to a new ruler. It demands that we acquire the new habits of a new culture. New people need to become "naturalized" citizens of the reign of God, and teaching is part of the naturalization process.[88]

Based on what both Van Engen and the authors of *Missional Church* are saying, becoming a part of a distinctly Christian disciple-making community of believers is, contra Borg and McLaren, crucial to the experience of God's reign (i.e., kingdom). Once again, given its commitment to the four christological commitments at the heart of the kingdom message, a missional orthodoxy will insist that the dynamic of making Christian disciples *through* gospel proclamation and demonstration *for* gospel proclamation and demonstration should be seen as absolutely crucial to any church's attempt to function as a missionally faithful and fruitful representation of the already/not yet kingdom (or reign) of God.

This chapter has suggested that to the degree the kingdom of God is indeed an eschatological concept and is central to what it means to be missional, it is only a missiology that maintains the proper tension between the "already" and "not yet" aspects of the kingdom that will prove faithful to both the biblical text and missional task.[89] Further, an understanding of missional ministry that possesses solid biblical and theo-

---

[88]Guder, *Missional Church*, p. 137.
[89]See Guder, *Continuing Conversion*, p. 36.

logical support will be ecclesial (communal) rather than individual in nature, and will emphasize disciple making as well as social action. Not a few observers have taken note of the lack of disciple making that marks too many emerging and missional churches.[90] Could it be that—perhaps out of deference to the commitment to religious relativism so prevalent in our increasingly postmodern, post-Christian ministry context—the emerging paradigm's downplay of eschatology has ironically exercised a mitigating effect on its missional impact? This is tragic, given the New Testament's repeated calls for Christ's followers to remain "ready" until his return (Mt 24:42-44; 25:1-13; Lk 12:35-40) and the fact that a steadfast commitment to disciple making is part of a what such an eschatological readiness looks like (1 Thess 1:2-10).

Again, it does not have to be this way. As indicated above, John 12:44-50, with its reference to a judgment at the "last day," suggests that Jesus' *ministry motive* was influenced by eschatological realities. Mark 1:15 and Luke 4:43 both state that the coming "kingdom of God" was at the heart of Jesus' *ministry message*. Matthew 4:23-24; 9:35; 12:28 and Luke 11:20 all serve to demonstrate that a kingdom conceived of as "already and not yet" also informed his *ministry method*. If Jesus allowed an eschatological understanding of the kingdom of God to influence his ministry motive, message and method, should not his followers as well (cf. Jn 20:21)? Rather than downplay the eschatological content of Scripture, a missionally orthodox missiology will lean into it, allowing the reality of the coming kingdom, through the Spirit of mission, to enable the founding of missionally faithful communities of believers committed to making disciples through and for both gospel proclamation and demonstration.

As I bring this chapter to a close, I am happy to report that the lecture on eschatology I mentioned earlier did seem to exercise its usual effect. Though a few of the nearly sixty students in attendance may have left the classroom a bit nonplussed, the majority seemed to leave sobered, intrigued and even inspired!

Frankly, I am hopeful that the message of this chapter has had a

---

[90]For example, see Steve Addison, "Missional Fad vs. Missional Movement," January 12, 2010, www.movements.net/2010/01/12/missional-fads-vs-missional-movements.html.

similar effect—that is, that only a few readers will move on to the book's conclusion still wondering what all the fuss is about, and that many more will turn the page having been sobered, intrigued, perhaps even inspired. What a privilege to be a part of Christ's church, the "harbinger of the new humanity" called to represent to an estranged cosmos the reality of Christ's life, death, resurrection and lordship and to serve his already/not yet kingdom as its community, servant and messenger! And what a responsibility as well! But God is faithful, and with the help of the Spirit of mission, we can render to him a missional faithfulness in return.

CONCLUSION

The goal of this work has been to provide the larger evangelical community (traditional, missional and emerging) with a unifying alternative to a fighting fundamentalism, on the one hand, and an orthodoxy that is so generous that it ends up being no orthodoxy at all, on the other. Toward this end I have endeavored to identify and answer the false antitheses that currently confront and tend to divide us with respect to our doctrines of the Bible, theology proper, Christ, the Holy Spirit, human beings, salvation, the church and the final things. Over against the earlier and emerging paradigms' visions of the Christian faith, I have put forward a third option—one I believe possesses a missional viability while at the same time doing justice to the call in Jude 3 to contend for the faith that was once for all entrusted to the saints. My message to fellow evangelicals has been that it is not necessary to choose between a fighting fundamentalism and a new liberalism. Together we can forge a missional orthodoxy that seeks to be faithful to both the biblical text and the missional task, which in turn will produce a missional orthopraxy the Spirit of mission can use to invite post-Christians living in our current ministry context to take another look at the claims of Christ.

CONCLUDING CAVEATS

The missional and ecumenical optimism reflected above notwithstanding, before I bring the book to a close I feel the need to assure my readers that *I really do get it*. I understand the critiques and concerns of those promoting the emerging paradigm. I get the critique leveled against the religious Pharisaism and fundamentalism that, unfortunately, really is present in too many traditional evangelical churches. I also understand the concern that the earlier paradigm's portrayal of Christianity has, due to the influence of both modernity and postmodernity, become actually odious to significant numbers of people living in our day and place. So, if in the previous pages of this work, I have somehow given the impression that I consider the missional orthodoxy proffered here to be a *magic bullet,* some sort of *spiel* that when presented properly cannot fail to reclaim post-Christian hearts and minds for the Christian cause, I want to set the record straight here and now.

I am fully aware that we are living in a post-secular, post-denominational world where, according to that Los Angeles Times article cited in the book's initial chapter, about 75 percent of Americans between the ages of eighteen and twenty-nine now consider themselves "spiritual but not religious." I am likewise fully cognizant of the fact that in the case of many of those claiming this status, the "not religious" designation means that they now consider themselves "over" Christianity and "done" with the church.

I also recognize that many of these post-Christians, rather than adopting a spiritual apathy, have opted for a spiritual eclecticism instead. I am all too aware of just how alluring to the emerging generations is the spiritual eclecticism fueled by the postmodern contention that, since there is no one right way to believe and behave, there is also no one right way to connect with God or cultivate one's spirituality. Sadly, I have seen young adults graduate from a Christian university that is dedicated to producing world-changing disciples of Jesus only to succumb eventually to the idea that when it comes to spirituality, Christianity is no longer the only viable game in town. This trend among young, emerging evangelicals toward an embrace of a religious relativism is a disturbing reality that must be bravely acknowledged rather than ignored.

Furthermore, I understand the need for those of us who are rightly concerned over this current state of affairs to reckon with the fact that, though not impossible, it seems to be very difficult for a person, once they have embraced a spiritual eclecticism, to "come home" again to a biblically informed walk with Christ.

Several years ago my wife Patti engaged in a ministry conversation with a friend and neighbor who had embraced a new-age, highly eclectic approach to spirituality. This neighbor had boldly commented to Patti how sorry she felt for her. "How sad," she said to Patti, "that you are locked into just one way to know and worship God."

Patti suggested to her friend that while her feelings of sympathy were appreciated, they were also unnecessary. As Patti put it, "My walk with Christ is anything but boring!"

Then Patti went on to ask this neighbor, who denied the unique importance of Jesus, to consider the possibility that after this life is over she might discover that he is Lord after all. "If this is true," Patti explained, "I will have been blessed by my devotion to Christ in both in this life and the next." "But," she went on to ask, "where would this discovery leave you?"

With a wry, almost perverse smile on her face this friend and neighbor replied, "I'm just dying to find out!"

This is all to say that I completely understand how "over" Christianity many of the spiritual-but-not-religious members of our society really are, and how difficult it is, once they have embraced a spiritual eclecticism, to see them return to the place where their great desire is to manifest the "sincere and pure devotion to Christ" the New Testament calls for (2 Cor 11:1-4).

Moreover, I am also aware that the spiritual-but-not-religious statistic cited above does not in and of itself sufficiently indicate the fact that an increasing number of people living in the West are not simply *post-Christian* in their sentiment and practice but *anti-Christian* as well. Just this past week I had a conversation with two young adults (one male, one female) who seem to fall into this anti-Christian category. In a manner reminiscent of Nietzsche and the "new atheists," these young adults are convinced that Christianity is one of the worst things that ever happened to humanity. Heavily influenced by both modernity and postmodernity, especially the manner in which the latter delights in drawing attention to the colonizing, marginalizing impact of first-world Christianity, these two university students actually feel the need to try to disabuse Christians of their faith. Ironically, there is a certain fundamentalism at work here. It is not simply that some nonbelievers are absolutely dead certain that the Christian message is bogus and harmful; they also feel the need to convert others to their anti-Christian way of thinking, often manifesting the same kind of obscurantism, dogmatism and pugilism traditionally associated with intellectually and culturally imperialistic Christians!

This was not our first conversation, and I must confess that I care about these two young adults very much. So, while listening to them excoriate everything about Christianity except the person of Jesus himself, I could not help but think of how easy it would be to succumb to the temptation to try to salvage for them some vestige of the Christian faith by offering to them a neo-gnostic version of it that, while appealing to their post-secular openness to spirituality in general,[1] would also be less offensive to their postmodern sensibilities.

While I maintain that most of the post-Christians among whom we evangelicals (traditional, missional and emerging) live, work and play are not as "studied" in their rejection of Christianity as my two young friends, it is true that an increasing number are. When dialoguing in a missional manner with such folks it is not enough to simply acknowledge (perhaps even help them articulate) their frustration with the philosophical foundationalism, religious fundamentalism and political conservatism they associate with traditional Christianity while at the same time emphasizing that crucial distinction between "churchianity" and a more biblically informed understanding of Christianity. Frankly, I have found that in the real world such an approach—its relational sensitivity and intellectual humility notwithstanding—can sometimes seem insufficient for the task. What do we do then?

CONCLUDING COUNSEL

It is vitally important that we allow the content of the missional orthodoxy we have begun to forge in these pages to impact the method in which we minister it to our post-Christian peers, especially those who

---

[1]See Ross Hastings, *Missional God, Missional Church: Hope for Re-evangelizing the West* (Downers Grove, IL: IVP Academic, 2012), p. 57.

seem to be, like my two young-adult friends, especially resistant to the message of historic Christianity. This ministry strategy involves two really important missional moves.

First, we must continue to encourage a theologically real encounter with Christ. The fact that the heart of Christian orthodoxy is so christocentric—four doctrines related to Christ's divinity, atoning death, resurrection and lordship—should suggest to us that our presentation of it to our post-Christian peers should be Christ-centered as well. In other words, I have found that the place to start when talking to any post-Christian, regardless of how well studied they are in their rejection of the Christian faith, is the person of Christ. While discussions regarding the nature of God and the problem of evil can go on and on, something remarkable happens when we focus on what our post-Christian peers think of Jesus. I have heard hard-core modernists and postmodernists say the ugliest things about God. I rarely hear the same epithets and vitriol directed at Jesus of Nazareth. It has been my experience that something truly remarkable occurs when, after having listened patiently and compassionately to the stories of those who have been hurt or disappointed by the church, we eventually ask these wounded and jaded folks to carefully articulate what they think of Jesus. Any reply to this crucial question other than one that actually demonizes him can be followed up with (1) a gentle call for the post-Christian to consider the possibility that, despite what the church has done in his name, Jesus is still Lord, and (2) a sincere invitation for our post-Christian friends to spend some time with us—to "taste and see" for themselves whether Jesus is risen by participating in the worship, nurture, community and service of our faith community. I hear testimonies all the time of people who, precisely because they were invited to belong even before they believed, ended up having their lives changed by a theologically real encounter with the risen Christ.

This leads to a consideration of the second missional move that is mandated by the content of our orthodoxy.

We must learn to lean on (as well as be led by) the Spirit of mission. The theological realism I have referred to so often in this work—the idea that because of the incarnation; vicarious life, death and resurrection of

Christ; and the outpouring of his Spirit, it is possible for human beings to know and interact with God in a real rather than a merely conceptual manner—must not only affect our understanding of right belief (orthodoxy) but of right practice (orthopraxy) as well. According to the New Testament, it is not my job to convince my two anti-Christian young adult friends of their need for an intimate, interactive relationship with the risen Jesus. That is the Holy Spirit's job (see Jn 16:5-11). In other words, I am not called to be missionally effective, just to be missionally faithful, trusting that a missional fruitfulness will follow. More and more I am becoming convinced that the best way to do this is to (1) obey the Holy Spirit's promptings for me to speak and act prophetically into people's lives so as to re-present to them the reality of the risen Christ, and then (2) prayerfully trust the Holy Spirit to do his work of conviction in their lives.

I find support for these two missional moves throughout the New Testament. For instance, the apostle Paul seems to allude to both of them in 1 Corinthians 2:1-5:

> And so it was with me, brothers and sisters. When I came to you, I did not come with eloquence or human wisdom as I proclaimed to you the testimony about God. For I resolved to know nothing while I was with you except Jesus Christ and him crucified. I came to you in weakness with great fear and trembling. My message and my preaching were not with wise and persuasive words, but with a demonstration of the Spirit's power, so that your faith might not rest on human wisdom, but on God's power.

Likewise, I see both moves at work in the Acts 17 account of Paul's speech before the Areopagus (Acts 17:16-34). Note that although Paul began his address with a brief discussion of the nature of God and the implications of this for worship, he ended up talking to this group of Athenian philosophers about the resurrection of Christ and the need for repentance in light of a coming day of judgment that will be overseen by him (see Acts 17:31). It should be obvious to us that though Paul was careful to recontextualize the message of the gospel for this particular ministry setting, he did not accommodate it to his audience's religiously relativistic convictions. Instead of pandering to the sensibilities at work in this ministry context, Paul spoke prophetically of Christ's resurrection and lordship, apparently trusting the Spirit of mission to do his convicting, convincing work in their lives.

And what was the result? Acts 17:32-34 tells us that while some sneered at this message, others were intrigued enough to want to hear more, and a few apparently believed on the spot! As I wrestle with the reality that not every post-Christian I speak with about spiritual matters will immediately accept the invitation to "taste and see" for themselves that Jesus really is risen, I am aware that I am in good company—even the apostle Paul had to live with the fact that his ministry in Athens immediately yielded only a few disciples! However, I take some solace in this: if Paul was willing to make it his goal to simply be missionally *faithful*, leaving the issue of ministry *fruitfulness* to God, perhaps I can and should do likewise.

So, yes, I want to do the best job I can at responding faithfully to the Holy Spirit's promptings for me to speak and act in a prophetically missional manner into the lives of the people among whom I live, work and play. Toward this end I want to familiarize myself with the ins and outs of a missional orthodoxy and orthopraxy. Still, at the end of the day, I have to prayerfully entrust the folks to whom I minister, like my two young adult friends, to the convincing, convicting work of the Holy Spirit. Given the human craving for certainty and control, this business of walking with, being guided by and depending on the Holy Spirit is very difficult.[2] But, then again, where in Scripture is the promise that the life of Christian discipleship will be easy? The bottom line is that I suspect I speak for many missionally minded evangelicals when I assert that our experience has been that the Spirit of mission is faithful. If we do our part, we can and should leave the rest to him. What we must not do is feel the need to rehabilitate the message, downplaying any of the four christological verities in the process, in order to make it more acceptable to our post-Christian peers. Nor should we buy into the idea that the meaning of the gospel has somehow been misunderstood for two thousand years and is only now beginning to be correctly compre-

---

[2]See Darrell Guder's discussion "Sin as Control," especially as it relates to the translation of the gospel, in Guder, *Continuing Conversion*, pp. 74-77, 87, 90, 97.

hended by those promoting an emerging paradigm. No, at some point we need to drive a stake in the ground and reckon with the reality that by virtue of the incarnation; vicarious life, death and resurrection of Christ; and the inspiring, illuminating work of the Spirit past and present, we possess a good enough knowledge of spiritual truth to be able to forge a missional orthodoxy that can enable us to render to God a missional faithfulness in our time and place.

As for my two young adult friends, I am happy to report that the conversation continues, and not without effect! There are some very real indications that, as hardened as their hearts have become toward the Christian faith, they are slowly but surely beginning to take seriously the idea that behind my unconditional love and concern for them may just be the love and concern of a risen Jesus. In the meantime, I continue to pray for them and love them, trusting in the Holy Spirit's ability to work in their hearts, convincing them that perhaps the message of real Christianity (versus "churchianity") deserves another look.

So, the ultimate call of this work is for all evangelicals (traditional, missional and emerging) to continue the process of forging a missional orthodoxy that all of us can rally around as colleagues rather than competitors, united by a common commitment to the task of engaging the non- and post-Christians living around us in a manner that is faithful to both the biblical text and the missional task. We can do this! By encouraging theologically real encounters with Christ the Son (Col 2:6-10), and learning to lean on (as well as be led by) the Holy Spirit (Lk 12:11-12), we can render to God the Father the missional faithfulness he desires and deserves.

Name and Subject Index

and the human condition, 230-33, 237,
  253-56, 271
and the interpretation of Scripture, 142-44
and the kingdom of God, 336-39, 344
and liberalism of, 60n96
and mainline Protestantism, 52
and mental assent vs. existential trust, 141
missional concerns of, 113, 149-50, 166,
  182-83, 259, 265
and the nature of God, 138n37, 156-64,
  166-67, 169-70, 172-73
and pneumatology, 216-19
and recitation of the creeds, 182n9
and a reconfigured Christ, 186-99
and religious pluralism/relativism, 216,
  219, 299-300, 302-5
and repentance, 260-62
and revelation, 138n36, 160, 190-91
and sin and salvation, 252-62, 264-66,
  267n88, 271-72
and spirituality/thin places, 297-98
and two Christianities, 66
and the use of Scripture, 145
See also afterlife; Christology, antitheses
  related to
Bosch, David J., 25n3, 26n5, 43n43, 45, 47n57,
  63n99, 65n1, 70-71n119, 76n36, 77n40, 79n46,
  80n51, 81-82, 85n67, 93, 109n122, 118n143,
  119n148, 211n122, 246n57, 253n14, 270n99,
  282n141, 302n43, 308, 310, 321n107, 324n114,
  336n26, 342n53, 351n80
Braaten, Carl E., 98n101, 99, 102n114, 103
Brownson, James, 37n30, 42n42
Brunner, Emil, 308
Buber, Martin, 140
Buechner, Frederick, 254n15
Calvin, John, 31, 81, 217
Campbell, David, 37
Carnell, E. J., 32n16
Carson, D. A., 28n11, 34n24, 41n41, 90n79,
  112n128
catholic, 181, 203, 208n115, 288. See also
  Roman Catholic
certainty, human craving for, 88n73, 234-35,
  368. See also security, psychological
Christ. See Christology; Jesus Christ
Christianity, as a religion, 300-305

Christianity Today, 29n14, 36, 38n32, 54,
  94n89, 139, 156, 169n61, 176n83, 197n84,
  211n123, 238n37, 249n1, 265n81, 268n91,
  282n142, 301, 307n57, 317n96
Christians
  anonymous, 282
  churchless, 289-90
Christology
  antitheses related to, 184-86, 192n60
  nuanced, 184, 211-13
  and realism, 37n39
  rehabilitated/reconfigured, 183, 208-9, 212
  and support for the incarnation ministry
    response, 95-110
  See also verities, christological
church
  attractional/institutional, 317-25
  body of Christ, 289, 292, 303, 305, 321, 326
    345
  branch offices of the kingdom, 351
  classic view of, 288-89
  and disciple making vs. social action, 310-17
  as a disciple-making community, 357-60
  dualistic/gnostic/docetic notion of, 303-4
  as eschatological community, 351-54
  as eschatological messenger, 351, 355-57
  as eschatological servant, 351, 354-55
  faithful presence of, 351n79
  fathers, 270n99, 298n33, 343-44n60, 81,
    96-97, 101, 106, 119-20n150, 145, 165n47,
    173-4
  God's household. See pillar and
    foundation of the truth
  great co-missional model of, 307-8, 317,
    328, 345, 358
  as the harbinger of the new humanity, 351,
    361
  identification with Christ, 292-93
  incarnational/missional. See church,
    attractional/institutional
  necessity of, 291-93
  New Testament metaphors for, 292
  non-Pentecostal-charismatic. See church,
    Pentecostal-charismatic
  Pentecostal-charismatic, 325-28
  pillar and foundation of the truth, 293,
    306, 329

Oden, Thomas C., 85n65, 87n71, 88n72,
    142n47
Okholm, Dennis L., 198n85
Olson, Philip N., 317n96
Olson, Roger, 28n11, 32n16, 34n24, 39n38, 95,
    97-100, 103, 106, 112n129, 134, 145, 155, 229n1,
    232n16, 236, 288-89, 292-95
ontology
    of Christ, 135, 186-88, 192-94, 199, 204-6,
        208n115
    and the fall, 343
    theistic (trinitarian), 242, 327
    See also supernaturalism, trinitarian
option, third. *See* alternative, third
orthopraxy/orthopraxis, 28n10, 181-82, 224,
    287, 296, 307, 316, 329, 362, 367-68
overcorrection/overreaction
    bibliological, 143
    christological, 196, 197n83
    ecclesiastical (ecclesiological), 290, 308,
        313, 316, 319
    missiological, 345
    missional, 14-16, 62, 109
    soteriological, 196, 197n83, 250, 252-58,
        260, 267
    theological, 28, 101, 175-77, 295
    See also liberal/emergent overcorrection/
        overreaction
Paggitt, Doug, 60-61n96, 139n39
panentheism, 157-59, 167-68, 185
pantheism, 167
paradigm
    already, not yet, 335n25
    earlier, 113, 129-131, 134, 144, 146, 149, 152,
        156-57, 158n13, 163-64, 181, 190-91, 213,
        258, 260, 267, 272, 299n35, 339, 363
    emergent. *See* emergent, paradigm
    emerging. *See* emerging paradigm
    ministry. *See* ministry, paradigm
    missional, 319, 324n114
    theological, 118n143, 164, 335n25
    See also kingdom of God, already and not
        yet
paradox, 98, 138, 169, 175, 179, 235
parousia, 321, 330-31
Paul of Samosata, 99
Paul the apostle, 12, 17, 27, 35, 44, 48-49,

51n69, 69, 71-75, 104, 106, 120, 134, 141,
    143-44, 147-49, 161, 169-70, 178, 183, 199,
    209, 218, 241, 257, 268n89, 273, 275, 280,
    286-87, 292-96, 305, 329, 344n60, 367-68
Penner, Myron, 62n98, 118n146, 128n2
Pentecost, 216n5
    day of, 325-26
    power of, 326
    theology of, 325
Pentecostalism
    classical, 325-28, 355
    global, 68n7, 215, 222, 331n1
    missional, 355
    Pentecostal-charismatic, 106, 171, 219,
        222-23, 227, 307, 354
    See also non-Pentecostalism
perichoresis, 174
persecution, 211, 302n45, 205
Peter, apostle, 44, 75, 78-79, 83, 292, 324-25
Pew Forum on Religion and Public Life, 37,
    289n7
Pharisaism, 32, 38n33, 39, 88n73, 91n81, 104-5,
    142n47, 235n27, 323-24, 363. *See also*
    dogmatism; fundamentalism; hypocrisy;
    judgmentalism; legalism; obscurantism;
    pugilism; separatism
Phillips, Timothy R., 198n85
pilgrim principle, 76n38
Pinnock, Clark H., 198n85, 326n117
Placher, William C., 117n141
planet
    care for, 114, 200, 212-13, 317n98, 343
    God's plan for, 291, 317
    salvation of, 266
    See also creation care; eschatology, new
        earth
plausibility structure, 77, 79, 89
pluralism, theological, 87n71, 217, 270n99,
    282, 299
pneumatology
    missional, 218, 220-23, 227, 326-28
    neglect of, 213-16
    See also Borg, Marcus, and pneuma-
        tology; McLaren, Brian, and pneuma-
        tology
Polanyi, Michael, 44, 119n147
politics, 34, 42, 59, 77-79, 89, 112-13,

Scripture Index